The Challenge of Liberty

The Challenge of Liberty
Classical Liberalism Today

Edited by
Robert Higgs and Carl P. Close

The INDEPENDENT INSTITUTE

Oakland, California

The Independent Institute
100 Swan Way, Oakland, CA 94621-1428
Telephone: 510-632-1366 · Fax: 510-568-6040
Email: info@independent.org
Website: www.independent.org

Library of Congress Cataloging-in-Publication Data

The challenge of liberty : classical liberalism today / edited by Robert Higgs
and Carl P. Close.

p. cm.

ISBN-13: 978-1-59813-002-7 (pbk. : alk. paper)
ISBN-10: 1-59813-002-1 (pbk. : alk. paper)

1. Liberalism. 2. Liberty. I. Higgs, Robert. II. Close, Carl P.
JC574.C47 2006
320.51'2–dc22

2005032584

10 9 8 7 6 5 4 3 2 1   06 07 08 09 10

The INDEPENDENT INSTITUTE

THE INDEPENDENT INSTITUTE is a non-profit, non-partisan, scholarly research and educational organization that sponsors comprehensive studies of the political economy of critical social and economic issues.

The politicization of decision-making in society has too often confined public debate to the narrow reconsideration of existing policies. Given the prevailing influence of partisan interests, little social innovation has occurred. In order to understand both the nature of and possible solutions to major public issues, The Independent Institute's program adheres to the highest standards of independent inquiry and is pursued regardless of political or social biases and conventions. The resulting studies are widely distributed as books and other publications, and are publicly debated through numerous conference and media programs. Through this uncommon independence, depth, and clarity, The Independent Institute expands the frontiers of our knowledge, redefines the debate over public issues, and fosters new and effective directions for government reform.

THE INDEPENDENT INSTITUTE
100 Swan Way, Oakland, California 94621-1428, U.S.A.
Telephone: 510-632-1366 • Facsimile: 510-568-6040
Email: info@independent.org • Website: www.independent.org

Contents

Introduction

Robert Higgs and Carl P. Close

Is liberty advancing or retreating? Are people gaining more political *and* economic freedom? Which policies, institutions, and attitudes support a free society, and how well are these pillars holding up around the globe?

A growing number of scholars and other writers have considered these questions in recent years, but perhaps the most widely noted studies of freedom's progress have been those producing empirically derived indexes that quantify, or rank comparatively, various freedom-related trends. Publications such as Freedom House's annual *Freedom in the World Survey*, the *Wall Street Journal*/Heritage Foundation's *Index of Economic Freedom*, and Reporters Without Borders' worldwide index of freedom of the press provide informative snapshots. They tell us, for example, whether a country has moved recently in the direction of greater political and civil liberties, and some of them generate useful data to help us determine which reforms contribute the most to fostering economic prosperity. For those of us interested in concrete measurements of the existential status of liberty, these indexes are a welcomed addition to the intellectual storehouse.

Still, a snapshot of statistics, however detailed it might be, is insufficient to provide a reliable prognosis for liberty's prospects. One component that such indexes typically neglect is public opinion—an omission that can compromise the predictive power of a freedom index, especially when public opinion runs counter to recent government policies. For example, an opinion survey conducted in Latin America in 2003 found that approximately 70 percent of the poll's more than 18,000 respondents thought the region's privatization of state-owned industries had not benefited their country—results that one scholar explained by the respondents' common belief that the privatizations had unfairly lined the pockets of well-connected political elites (Shirley 2005). It is doubtful that anyone who had considered only the economic freedom indexes for Latin America would have

Hayek's new respectability is also attested by the recent publication of serious biographies (Ebenstein 2001; Caldwell 2003).

What was this great thinker's ideology? Hayek claimed to have racked his brains searching fruitlessly for a satisfactory term to describe his political orientation (1960, 408). He had thought of himself as a liberal, rather than a socialist, ever since he read Ludwig von Mises's powerful critique *Socialism: An Economic and Sociological Analysis* ([1922] 1981). Yet Hayek recognized that in the United States and elsewhere, the term *liberal* had come to mean something far different from the proliberty orientation it had originally denoted. Although Hayek refused to call himself a liberal, because the term had become too misleading, he also refused to consider himself a conservative. In "Why I Am Not a Conservative," the postscript of his book *The Constitution of Liberty* (1960), Hayek explained that when liberalism burst onto the scene in Europe, its main foil was a conservative tradition that had served to rationalize the Continent's absolute monarchies.

Hayek's aversion to calling himself a "conservative" rested, however, on more than historical grounds. It also derived from his fundamental commitment to a social order that allowed for pluralism in values—a condition he considered incompatible with many conservatives' desire to use the state's coercive powers to promote broad moral or religious values (1960, 402). "Libertarian" did not suit Hayek because it carried, he wrote, "too much the flavor of a manufactured term and of a substitute" (408). It is also worth noting that at the time he wrote *The Road to Serfdom* and *The Constitution of Liberty*, Hayek defended policies, such as Social Security, that self-described libertarians would denounce. (By the time he wrote *Law, Legislation and Liberty*, however, Hayek had become somewhat more thoroughgoing in his advocacy of the market and his rejection of government intervention in the economy.)

Thus, by default and by historical affinity, "classical liberal" seems to be the label that best describes Hayek's political orientation throughout his career. Unfortunately, despite the rebirth of classical liberal scholarship and the resurgence of freedom in many parts of the world during the final decades of the "Hayek century," the general public has either forgotten classical liberalism or has become conditioned to accept a caricature that no more resembles the genuine article than Friedrich Hayek resembles the actress Salma Hayek.

CLASSICAL LIBERALISM: THE IDEOLOGY OF LIBERATION

Classical liberalism's greatest advance began in the late eighteenth century and continued into the late nineteenth century, with its energetic attacks on government-sanctioned coercion—it opposed chattel slavery, tariffs that kept the poor on the brink of starvation, and government-sanctioned monopolies that harmed workers and consumers. The founding of the American Republic and to varying degrees the nineteenth-century constitutions of many European states, along with the relative peace, growing international trade, and buoyant spirit of progress and optimism that spread across Europe and beyond before World War I, constituted victories for classical liberalism.

These successes had been long in the making. Perhaps their oldest ingredient is the natural-law tradition, elements of which can be found in the writings of Western antiquity. Greek rhetorician Alkidamas, for example, attacked the idea of natural slavery in his "Messenian Oration": "God left all men free; Nature has made no man a slave." Continuing in this natural-law vein, Cicero in *De Republica* argued that neither Rome's senate nor its people could justify the issuance of a decree that superseded the "one eternal and unchangeable law" that is "valid for all nations and for all times." References to a higher, natural law to which people could appeal to justify their longing for freedom later found their way into the Magna Carta (1215) and the Declaration of Arbroath (1320).

This tradition surely influenced John Locke (1632–1704), who is often credited with founding classical liberalism through his refutation of the doctrine of the divine right of kings and, more important, his positive theory of individual rights, private property, and just government articulated in *Two Treatises of Government*. Critics of Locke who mistakenly describe him as an apologist for the propertied classes fail to grasp the revolutionary nature of his political writings, especially his theory of the right to rebel against unjust political authority and even to commit regicide. Although Locke is considered primarily a thinker, he was also a man of action, and his political entanglements forced him to flee to Holland, where he traveled under assumed names to escape extradition.

Although not as well known, Locke's contemporary Algernon Sidney (1622–83) developed a theory of natural rights in his *Discourses Concerning Government* (1698) that complements and extends the fundamentals that Locke laid down. This work's implications were so clear that it was used at Sidney's trial as evidence of treason against the English crown, resulting in his conviction and execution. To contemporary readers, the revolutionary nature of Sidney's and Locke's writings is most apparent in their influence on Thomas Jefferson (1743–1826) and the Declaration of Independence he penned, and perhaps also in the fiery rhetoric of abolitionists such as William Lloyd Garrison (1805–79).

Along with moralists and philosophers, economists have played an equally prominent role in disseminating classical liberalism's political program. Adam Smith (1723–90), the father of British classical economics, set the stage with the 1776 publication of his monumental treatise *An Inquiry into the Nature and Causes of the Wealth of Nations*. Smith and his intellectual progeny developed a powerful new understanding of economics whose proliberty implications were readily grasped even by those who were not fully conversant in its details. Smith's critique of the economic fallacies of mercantilism, along with David Ricardo's (1772–1823) formulation of the law of comparative advantage, paved the way for reformers Richard Cobden and John Bright, who campaigned in England against tariffs and military adventurism.

As the works of the classical liberal economists were disseminated across the Western world, their enemies took note. Apologists for government-granted privilege, slavery, and the ancien régime, as well as the radicals of a budding egalitarian movement, denounced liberalism. Because classical liberalism was perceived as the political program of the Enlightenment, some of its foes attempted to appropriate its scientific appeal, as Marx and Friedrich Engels did with their "scientific socialism," whereas others, such as Jean-Jacques Rousseau's followers, denounced it as cold and materialistic. Some opponents of classical liberalism damned economic theorizing and even logic itself (Mises [1922] 1981; Hicks 2004).

LIBERTY AND PROPERTY

Readers of this book are probably familiar with the broad themes of classical liberalism—its belief in the worth and dignity of the individual and, on that basis, its belief in the morality of individual rights and the presumption of liberty rather than collective rights and the presumption of servitude to society or the state; the justice of the rule of law rather than rule by arbitrary decree; the political superiority of a constitutionally limited government relative to a government whose functions and powers multiply over time; and the material superiority and social progressiveness of free-market economies compared to mercantilist, welfare-state, and socialist economies. Less understood, perhaps, is the classical liberals' belief in the fundamentality of the principle of private property.

In his book *Liberalism: In the Classical Tradition*, first published in German in 1927, Austrian economist Ludwig von Mises, an early mentor and later colleague of Hayek, does not equivocate on the importance of private property in the classical liberal credo. Classical liberals, he states, contend that private property is a necessary condition for sustained economic progress. With greater government ownership or control of property—especially of the means of production (capital goods, natural resources, and labor)—comes a diminution in the productivity of labor and thus in the amount of wealth produced. Mises writes:

The program of liberalism, therefore, if condensed into a single word, would have to read: *property*, that is, private ownership of the means of production (for in regard to commodities ready for consumption, private ownership is a matter of course and is not disputed even by the socialists and communists). All the other demands of liberalism result from this fundamental demand. ([1927] 1996, 19)

Private property is necessary for economic progress, classical liberals hold, but it is also integral to the achievement of other noble aims—a point its critics overlook or misunderstand. For example, critics typically portray the principle of private-property rights as if it stood in opposition to "human rights." If food, shelter, clothing, education, health care, and retirement income are essential human needs, they claim, then the right to have them—and, by implication, the right to have the government attempt to ensure their provision through public ownership or control of their production and distribution—follows inexorably. In the critics' crudest caricature, the classical liberals' adherence to the principle of private-property rights is portrayed as a dogmatic and perverse "fetish" detrimental to the basic requirements of human life and well-being.

Classical liberals offer both practical and moral objections to such claims. First, as suppliers are more highly remunerated for their efforts, they have a stronger incentive to bring goods and services to the market, whereas they have a strong disincentive to make their wares available to consumers if criminals or government officials are likely to expropriate their wealth. Classical liberals do not claim that monetary gain is everyone's primary motive all the time (a caricature that Steven Horwitz debunks in chapter 4), but they are ever aware that incentives matter greatly and that policy makers often ignore this basic economic truth. Mises himself formulated (and Hayek further elaborated) a brilliant economic defense of private property, arguing that under a purely socialist regime, in which the means of production are publicly owned and therefore do not have market prices, rational economic calculation and planning would be impossible (a point that socialists still have not fully grasped, as Michael Wohlgemuth explains in chapter 21).

Second, classical liberal rights theorists distinguish two opposing notions of rights. "Negative rights" are claims that reduce to the right not to be aggressed against—ultimately the right to one's own life. Under a regime that enforces negative rights, person A and person B are left free to enter into contracts to trade with each other voluntarily, agreements that each party expects will make him better off. The right to life, liberty, property, and the pursuit of happiness are standard examples of basic negative rights in the classical liberal tradition. In wider range of motivations, knowledge, and fallibility than that of the "economic man" depicted in many textbooks.

In chapter 5, "Liberalism, Loose or Strict," political philosopher Anthony de Jasay examines a topic that has puzzled intellectual historians across the spectrum: liberalism's shift from an orientation that favored individual liberty, private-property rights, and the rule of law (classical liberalism) to one that discounted liberty in favor of social welfare, "equal opportunity," and "social justice" (contemporary North American liberalism or European social democracy). De Jasay traces the roots of this development to John Stuart Mill's essay *On Liberty* and other nineteenth-century utilitarian tracts, which introduced into classical liberalism ideas incompatible with its essence. For classical liberalism to resist elements hostile to liberty, de Jasay argues, it must vigorously affirm two basic principles, which he calls "the presumption of freedom" and "the rejection of the rules of submission to political authority."

Freedom and the Moral Society

Classical liberals in general—and the free-market economists among them in particular—are famous for arguing that economic freedom is unrivaled in its ability to foster prosperity. The contributors to Part II, "Freedom and the Moral Society," present a different but complementary argument for liberty. A free society not only fosters material well-being, they argue, but also encourages moral conduct and human flourishing of the noneconomic kind. One way that free societies do so is through their creation and use of networks of private associations of individuals, often collectively called civil society.

The importance of civil society, a topic that received renewed interest in the years immediately following the Soviet bloc's collapse, had been stressed by John Locke and the young John Stuart Mill, who articulated the case for limiting the scope of government. Those who seek a full understanding of how voluntary institutions contribute to human flourishing would do well to review the historical development of the concept of civil society, as Charles K. Rowley does in chapter 6, "On the Nature of Civil Society."

Voluntary institutions also contribute to human flourishing by promoting mutually reinforcing tendencies that foster character development. In chapter 7, "Liberty, Dignity, and Responsibility: The Moral Triad of a Good Society," Daniel B. Klein argues that liberty and individual responsibility preserve and affirm the individual's dignity, whereas coercion and self-indulgence are demeaning. Suri Ratnapala develops a related theme in chapter 8, "Moral Capital and Commercial Society." Commerce coevolves with moral rules and leads not only to prosperity, Ratnapala argues, but also to the accumulation of "moral capital"—the disposition to act morally—as Adam Smith and David Hume observed in the mid-eighteenth century.

Civil society—especially the public's active participation in its network of civic groups—is a cause championed recently by so-called communitarians, thinkers who stress the importance of strong communities and who typically discount the individualism associated with classical liberalism. Linda C. Raeder responds to recent communitarian attacks on modern liberalism in chapter 9, "Liberalism and the Common Good: A Hayekian Perspective on Communitarianism." Because Hayek's classical liberalism scarcely resembles the rationalistic, positive-rights-based claims of modern liberalism—and is sympathetic at least in part to the communitarians' vision of the good society—the Hayekian tradition easily withstands the communitarians' critique of modern liberalism, Raeder argues.

Securing Freedom

Part III, "Securing Freedom," pertains to some of the challenges of establishing—and keeping—a limited, constitutional government. Although every country in the world claims to have a constitution, most of the world's people do not live under *constitutional government*. Only societies that have adopted a particular conception of the rule of law have secured constitutional government and therefore considerable freedoms, a point developed in detail by Suri Ratnapala in chapter 10, "Securing Constitutional Government: The Perpetual Challenge."

In chapter 11, "The Primacy of Property in a Liberal Constitutional Order: Lessons for China," James A. Dorn brings a similar perspective on constitutionalism to his analysis of how to establish a foundation for liberty in China. The key to a successful future for that country, Dorn argues, is the adoption of a constitution that protects persons and property against arbitrary government power and lays a framework for freedom under the rule of law. According to Dorn, just as Adam Smith successfully articulated the principles of liberalism in the West, so the writings of Lao Tzu can play a similar pivotal role in China's transition from market socialism to "market Taoism."

Securing its citizens from the aggression of foreign states is typically cited as the nation-state's fundamental raison d'être. Whether a nation-state can protect its citizens from foreign military domination depends on its ability to mobilize human resources (the population's size, skill, and motivation), natural resources (including geographic features), and capital goods (wealth and technology). An additional variable—ideology—also plays a crucial role in the determination of military outcomes, as historian Jeffrey Rogers Hummel explains in chapter 12, "The Will to Be Free: The Role of Ideology in National Defense." Motivating people with the will to be free may be one of the most effective ways to help restrain government power, Hummel concludes.

Even people who live under (a large measure of) constitutional government and who possess the "will to be free" have found their rights violated egregiously by their government's bureaucracies. In chapter 13, "The Inhumanity of Government Bureaucracies," Hans Sherrer discusses ten factors that contribute to the oppressiveness of government bureaucracies—factors that have led to bureaucratically enforced or encouraged conformity, irresponsibility, moral relativism, ruthless opportunism, and sadism.

Individualism versus "Group Think"

Earlier chapters by Daniel Klein and by Hans Sherrer argue that coercive government institutions have helped to erode moral autonomy and individual responsibility. Closely related to this theme is the classical liberal affinity for freedom of conscience or cognitive independence, as against intellectual conformity, which is examined in Part IV, "Individualism versus 'Group Think.'"

One by-product of the early emphasis on freedom of conscience is the legal separation of church and state, as expressed in the U.S. Constitution's First Amendment. Government support of religion, the Constitution's framers argued, commits three vices: it violates freedom of conscience, it politicizes and trivializes important values, and it violates individual rights. A government-established church is not the only institution guilty of such abuses, however, according to philosopher James R. Otteson. Government schooling is vulnerable to many of the same objections, he argues in chapter 14, "Freedom of Religion and Public Schooling."

Perhaps the most historically significant cause and consequence of "group think" is nationalism. In chapter 15, "Is National Rational?" Anthony de Jasay argues that classical liberals and others have not examined nationalism as closely as the subject merits. "Even if in fact it springs from sentiment fueled by historical accidents, it may be worthwhile to try to see whether nationalism could possibly be the product of rational choice," he writes. De Jasay presents an elementary thought-experiment to help us determine whether nationalism—the archetypical example of an ideology of collective action—can ever be a sound strategy for individuals who seek to maximize their own utility.

Philosopher Laurie Calhoun considers a closely related but broader issue in chapter 16, "A Critique of Group Loyalty." Loyalty to one's group is not necessarily a virtue, as the horrors of Nazi Germany, among many other things, amply demonstrated. On the contrary, a commitment to group loyalty—a standing order to abandon one's principles for the sake of the group—is irrational whether one subscribes to moral absolutism or to moral relativism, Calhoun argues.

Psychiatrist Thomas S. Szasz, who has publicly championed freedom of conscience and opposed psychiatric coercion since the publication of his controversial book *The Myth of Mental Illness* (1961), examines a grave and gathering new threat to cognitive independence and other freedoms in chapter 17, "The Therapeutic State: The Tyranny of Pharmacracy." Joining the traditional rationalizations for state coercion—"God's will," "the consent of the governed," and "social justice"—now comes a fourth: "coercion as treatment." Unlike theocracy, democracy, and socialism, however, pharmacracy has met little opposition, Szasz notes as he proceeds to unmask this growing menace to liberty.

Classical Liberals Respond to Their Critics

Recent objections to classical liberalism are confronted head-on in Part V, "Classical Liberals Respond to Their Critics." In chapter 18, "What Is Living and What Is Dead in Classical Liberalism?" Charles K. Rowley examines the retreat from classical liberalism by two of its former exponents, John Gray and the late Robert Nozick. (Coincidentally, both announced their antipathy to classical liberalism in 1989, the same year that the Berlin Wall fell and took down with it, symbolically at least, classical liberalism's archenemy, Marxist-Leninist ideology.) Nozick's and Gray's retreat, according to Rowley, is explained by their shift from a preoccupation with the goal of preserving liberty to that of preserving order; that is, from a commitment to the philosophy of John Locke to that of Thomas Hobbes.

Because Gray's retreat was more thoroughgoing than Nozick's, his intellectual migration is an anomaly that merits especially close study—a task taken up by Daniel B. Klein in chapter 19, "The Ways of John Gray: A Libertarian Commentary." Although Gray often misrepresents classical liberals' ideas and fails to hold his own ideas to the same standards that he demands of his classical liberal opponents, he may be sounding in effect a useful alarm for his former allies when he complains that the "liberty maxim" they loudly trumpet sounds more like a reflexive mantra than a well-grounded principle, according to Klein.

Perhaps the leading challenge to classical liberalism from a contemporary political philosopher came from John Rawls in his famous treatise *A Theory of Jus-*

tice (1971). That book made Rawls the twentieth century's most influential mainstream political philosopher and the welfare state's leading defender. Yet, despite his reputation, Rawls barely broached the vital topic of property and ownership. Given his neglect of a topic so important in the real world and in the history of political thought, Rawls's theory of "justice as fairness" must be regarded as highly incomplete and thus deeply flawed, argues Quentin P. Taylor in chapter 20, "An Original Omission? Property in Rawls's Political Thought."

To this point, contributors to *The Challenge of Liberty* have said little of substance with regard to the economic case for the free society. Michael Wohlgemuth ably fills this gap in chapter 21, "Has John Roemer Resurrected Market Socialism?" Roemer, in his book *A Future for Socialism* (1994) and elsewhere, claims to have created a model of market socialism immune to the devastating criticisms leveled by Ludwig von Mises and F. A. Hayek that economic coordination requires comprehensive private-property rights, free-market pricing, profit-and-loss incentives, and unhampered private capital markets. Roemer's book, according to Wohlgemuth, is saturated with contradictions and misunderstandings—all based on the profoundly mistaken belief that market competition can be made compatible with coercive egalitarianism.

MEETING THE CHALLENGE OF LIBERTY

We began this introduction by suggesting that books expressing ideologies can have enormous influence in the real world even when they do not enjoy wide readership among the general public. The discussion of influential political ideas in *The Challenge of Liberty* buttresses this argument. It suggests not only that works by such friends and foes of liberty as John Locke, Adam Smith, John Stuart Mill, Karl Marx, Ludwig von Mises, John Maynard Keynes, F. A. Hayek, and others have had a disproportionate influence relative to the size of their limited readership but also that those works have profoundly influenced readers who have found the great thinkers' ideals so engaging and persuasive that they have sought to transform those ideals into reality. *The Challenge of Liberty* provides the reader with a deeper understanding of the works of political and economic analysis in which the perceptive contributors to this volume have found substantial insights into how the world works and should work. Readers will compound their benefit from reading this volume if they proceed to study seriously the great works of classical liberalism. Although readers will certainly find the study of classical liberalism rewarding in its own right, they may also find themselves moved to contribute to that still-vital corpus of ideas and ideals—and hence to promote the future of freedom.

REFERENCES

Berggren, Niclas. 2003. The Benefits of Economic Freedom: A Survey. *The Independent Review* 8 (Fall): 193–211.

Bethel, Tom. 1999. *The Noblest Triumph: Property and Prosperity through the Ages*. New York: Palgrave Macmillan.

Boaz, David. 1997. *The Libertarian Reader: Classic and Contemporary Writings from Lao Tzu to Milton Friedman*. New York: Free Press.

Caldwell, Bruce. 2003. *Hayek's Challenge: An Intellectual Biography of F. A. Hayek*. Chicago: University of Chicago Press.

Caplan, Bryan. 2001. Libertarianism against Economism: How Economists Misunderstand Voters, and Why Libertarians Should Care. *The Independent Review* 5 (Spring): 539–63.

Cassidy, John. 2000. The Price Prophet. *The New Yorker*. February 7.

Conway, David. 1998. *Classical Liberalism: The Unvanquished Ideal*. New York: St. Martin's.

Ebenstein, Alan. 2001. *Friedrich Hayek: A Biography*. New York: Palgrave/St. Martin's.

———. 2003. *Hayek's Journey: The Mind of Friedrich Hayek*. New York: Palgrave Macmillan.

Hayek, F. A. 1944. *The Road to Serfdom*. Chicago: University of Chicago Press.

———. 1960. *The Constitution of Liberty*. Chicago: University of Chicago Press.

———. 1973, 1976, 1979. *Law, Legislation and Liberty*. 3 vols. Chicago: University of Chicago Press.

Hicks, Stephen R. C. 2004. *Explaining Postmodernism: Skepticism and Socialism from Rousseau to Foucault*. Tempe, Ariz.: Scholargy.

Higgs, Robert. 1987. *Crisis and Leviathan: Critical Episodes in the Growth of American Government*. New York: Oxford University Press.

Hocutt, Max. 2003. Compassion without Charity, Freedom without Liberty: The Political Fantasies of Jean-Jacques Rousseau. *The Independent Review* 8 (Fall): 165–91.

Kuran, Timur. 1995. *Private Truths, Public Lies: The Social Consequences of Preference Falsification*. Cambridge, Mass.: Harvard University Press.

Manent, Pierre. 1995. *An Intellectual History of Liberalism*. Translated by Rebecca Balinski. Princeton, N.J.: Princeton University Press.

Mises, Ludwig von. [1922] 1981. *Socialism: An Economic and Sociological Analysis*. Translated by J. Kahane. Indianapolis, Ind.: Liberty Fund.

———. [1927] 1996. *Liberalism: In the Classical Tradition*. Translated by Ralph Raico. Irvington-on-Hudson, N.Y.: Foundation for Economic Education.

Pipes, Richard. 2000. *Property and Freedom*. New York: Vintage Books.

Pollock, Lansing. 1996. *The Free Society*. Boulder, Colo.: Westview.

Raico, Ralph. 1996. Mises on Fascism, Democracy, and Other Questions. *Journal of Libertarian Studies* 12 (Spring): 1–27

Rasmussen, Douglas B., and Douglas J. Den Uyl. 2005. *Norms of Liberty: A Perfectionist Basis for Non-Perfectionist Politics*. University Park, Pa.: Pennsylvania State University Press.

Roemer, John E. 1994. *A Future for Socialism*. Cambridge, Mass.: Harvard University Press

Samuelson, Paul A. 1971. Understanding the Marxian Notion of Exploitation: A Summary of the So-Called Transformation Problem between Marxian Values and Competitive Prices. *Journal of Economic Literature* 9 (June): 399–431.

Shearmur, Jeremy. 2003. Commitment, Scholarship, and Classical Liberalism. *The Independent Review* 7 (Spring): 575–85.

Shirley, Mary M. 2005. Why Is Sector Reform so Unpopular in Latin America? *The Independent Review* 10 (Fall): 195–207.

Sturgis, Amy H. 1994. *The Rise, Decline, and Reemergence of Classical Liberalism*. The LockeSmith Institute. Available at http://www.belmont.edu/lockesmith/essay.html.

Yergin, Daniel, and Joseph Stanislaw. 2002. *The Commanding Heights: The Battle for the World Economy*, rev. and updated ed. New York: Free Press.

PART I
Is Classical Liberalism Still Vital?

cal devices without any understanding of their souls, the organizing principles of their operation. I do not personally know or need to know the principle on which the computer allows me to put the words on the page.

Compare this stance of ignorance and awed acceptance before the computer with that of an ordinary participant in the economic nexus. The latter may, of course, simply respond to opportunities confronted, as buyer, seller, or entrepreneur, without so much as questioning the principles of the order of interaction that generates such opportunities. At another level of consciousness, however, the participant must recognize that this order is, in itself, artifactual, that it emerges from human choices made within a structure that must somehow be subject to deliberative change through human action. And even if a person might otherwise remain quiescent about the structure within which he carries out his ordinary affairs, he will everywhere be faced with pervasive reminders offered by political agitators and entrepreneurs motivated by their own self-interest.

It is only through an understanding of and appreciation for the animating principles of the extended order of market interaction that an individual who is not directly self-interested may refrain from expressive political action that becomes the equivalent of efforts to walk through walls or on water (for example, support for minimum wage laws, rent controls, tariffs, quotas, restrictive licensing, price supports, or monetary inflation). For the scientist in the academy, understanding such principles does, or should, translate into reasoned advocacy of classical liberal policy stances. But, for the reasons noted, the economic scientists by themselves do not possess either the formal or the informal authority to impose on others what may seem to be only their own opinions. Members of the body politic, the citizenry at large, must also be brought into the ranks. And they cannot, or so it seems to me, become sophisticated economic scientists, at least in large enough numbers. The expectation that the didactic skills of the academic disciplinarians in economics would make scientists of the intelligentsia, the "great unwashed," or all those in between was an expectation grounded in a combination of hubris and folly.

WHEN POLITICAL ECONOMY LOST ITS SOUL

What to do? This challenge remains even after the manifest collapse of socialism in our time. And it is in direct response to this challenge that I suggest invoking the soul of classical liberalism, an aesthetic-ethical-ideological potential attractor, one that stands independent of ordinary science, both below the latter's rigor and above its antiseptic neutrality.

I am admittedly in rhetorical as well as intellectual difficulty here, as I try to articulate my intuitively derived argument. Perhaps I can best proceed by historical reference. Classical political economy, in the early decades of the nineteenth century, particularly in England, did capture the minds of many persons who surely did not qualify even as amateur scientists in the still-developing science of economics. The "soul" of classical liberalism somehow came through to provide a vision of social order that was sufficient to motivate support for major institutional reform. The repeal of the Corn Laws changed the world.

After midcentury, however, the soul or spirit of the movement seems to have lost its way. The light did not fail in any manner akin to the collapse of the socialist ideal in our time. But the light of classical liberalism was dimmed, put in the shadows, by the emergent attraction of socialism. From the middle of the nineteenth century onward, classical liberals retreated into a defensive posture, struggling continuously against the reforms promulgated by utilitarian dreamers who claimed superior wisdom in discovering routes to aggregate happiness, as aided and abetted by the Hegel-inspired political idealists, who transferred personal realization to a collective psyche and away from the individual. The soul of socialism, even in contradiction to scientific evidence, was variously successful in capturing adherents to schemes for major institutional transformation.

VISION AND "SOCIAL" PURPOSE

What I have called the soul of a public philosophy is necessarily embedded in an encompassing vision of a social order of human interaction—a vision of that which might be, and which as such offers the ideal that motivates support for constructive change. The categorical difference between the soul of classical liberalism and that of socialism is located in the nature of the ideal and the relation of the individual to the collective. The encompassing vision that informs classical liberalism is described by an interaction of persons and groups within a rule-bound set of behavioral norms that allow each person or agent to achieve internally defined goals that are mutually achievable by all participants. And, precisely because those goals are internal to the consciousness of those who make choices and take actions, the outcomes produced are not either measurable or meaningful as "social" outcomes. There is, and can be, no social or collective purpose to be expected from the process of interaction; only private purposes are realized, even under the idealized operation of the structure and even if collectivized institutions may be instruments toward such achievements. To lay down a "social" purpose, even as a target, is to contradict the principle of liberalism itself, the principle that leaves each participant free to pursue whatever it is that remains feasible within the limits of the legal-institutional parameters.

The soul about which I am concerned here does involve a broad, and simple, understanding of the logic of human interaction in an interlinked chain of reciprocal exchanges among persons and groups. As noted previously, however, this logical understanding need not be scientifically sophisticated. It must, however, be basic understanding accompanied by a faith, or normative belief, in the competence of individuals to make their own choices based on their own valuation of the alternatives they confront. Can a person properly share the soul of classical liberalism without sharing the conviction that values emerge only from individuals? In some ultimate sense, is classical liberalism compatible with any transcendental ordering of values? My answer is no, but I also recognize that a reconciliation of sorts can be effected by engaging in epistemological games.

Classical liberals themselves have added confusion rather than clarity to the discussion when they have advanced the claim that the idealized and extended market order produces a larger "bundle" of valued goods than any socialist alternative. To invoke the efficiency norm in so crude a fashion as this, even conceptually, is to give away the whole game. Almost all of us are guilty of this charge, because we know, of course, that the extended market does indeed produce the relatively larger bundle, by *any* measure. But attention to any aggregative value scale, even as modified to Adam Smith's well-being of the poorer classes or to John Rawls's share for the least advantaged, conceals the uniqueness of the liberal order in achieving the objective of individual liberty. To be sure, we can play good defense even in the socialists' own game. But by so doing we shift our own focus to that game rather than our own, which we as classical liberals must learn to play on our own terms, as well as getting others involved. Happily, a few modern classical liberals are indeed beginning to redraw the playing fields as they introduce comparative league tables that place emphasis on measuring liberty.

HEAT AND LIGHT

As I recall, it was A. C. Pigou, the founder of neoclassical welfare economics, who remarked that the purpose of economics and economists was that of providing heat rather than light, presumably to citizens-consumers as ultimate users. What I understood Pigou to be saying was that the economist's role is strictly functional, like the roles of dentists, plumbers, or mechanics, and that we could scarcely expect either ourselves or others to derive aesthetic pleasure from what we do. He seemed to be suggesting that nothing in economics can generate the exhilaration consequent upon revelation of inner truths.

Empirically, and unfortunately, Pigou may have been correct, especially in relation to the political economy and economists of the twentieth century. The discipline as practiced and promulgated has been drained of its potential capacity to offer genuine intellectual adventure and excitement in the large. This characteristic was only partially offset during the decades of the cold war, when the continuing challenge of socialism offered Hayek and a relatively small number of his peers a motivation deeper and more comprehensive than that of the piddling puzzle-solving that economics has become. Absent the socialist challenge, what might evoke a sense of encompassing and generalized understanding? And, further, what may be required to bring forth such a sense in those who, themselves, can never be enrolled among the ranks of the professionally trained scientists?

Let me return to Ronald Reagan and his "shining city on a hill." What was the foundational inspiration that motivated that metaphor for an idealized American society? Reagan could not solve the simultaneous equations of general-equilibrium economics. But he carried with him a vision of a social order that might be an abstraction but which embodied elements that contained more light than heat. This vision, or that of classical liberalism generally, is built on the central, and simple, notion that "we can *all* be free." Adam Smith's "simple system of natural liberty," even if only vaguely understood, can *enlighten* the spirit, can create a soul that generates a coherence, a unifying philosophical discipline, that brings order to an internal psyche that might otherwise remain confused.

A motivating element is, of course, the individual's desire for liberty from the coercive power of others—an element that may be almost universally shared. But a second element is critically important: the absence of desire to exert power over others. In a real sense, the classical liberal stands in opposition to Thomas Hobbes, who modeled persons as universal seekers of personal power and authority. But Hobbes failed, himself, to share the liberal vision; he failed to understand that an idealized structure of social interaction is possible in which *no* person exerts power over another. In the idealized operation of an extended market order, each person confronts a costless exit option in each market, thereby eliminating totally any discretionary power of anyone with whom such a person might exchange. Coercion by another person is drained out; individuals are genuinely "at liberty."

Of course, this characterization is an idealization of any social order that might exist. But, as an ideal, such an imagined order can offer the exciting and normatively relevant prospect of a world in which all participants are free to choose.

Much has been made of the American spirit or soul as influenced by the availability of the territorial frontier during the first century of the United States' historical experience. Why was the frontier important? The proper economic interpretation of frontier lies in its guarantee of an exit option, the presence of which dramatically limits the potential for interpersonal exploitation. There has been a general failure to recognize that the effectively operating market order acts in precisely the same way as the frontier; it offers each participant exit options in each relationship.

The classical liberal can be philosophically self-satisfied, because he has seen the light, because he has come to understand the underlying principle of the social order that might be. It is not at all surprising that those who seem to express the elements of the soul of classical liberalism best are those who have experienced genuine conversion from the socialist vision. I entitled my lecture in the Trinity University series "Born Again Economist."[1] In that lecture, I tried to summarize my experience in 1946 at the University of Chicago, where exposure to the teachings of Frank Knight and Henry Simons converted me to classical liberalism from the ranks of flaming socialism, and in a hurry. For me, there was light not heat on offer at Chicago. I cannot, personally, share in an experience that does not include the creation of my classical liberal soul. I remain puzzled by how it would feel never to have seen the light, to have understood all along what the liberal vision embodies but without the excitement of the experience.

CONSTITUTIONALISM AGAIN

A necessary critical step is to draw back from a stance of active advocacy in the discussion of policy alternatives as confronted in ordinary politics. There is, of course, a liberal position on almost any of the alternatives. But classical liberals do, indeed, "get their hands dirty" when they engage with the policy wonks within the political game as played. Again, the distraction of debate works against focus on the inclusive structure—"the constitution"—within which the debates are allowed to take place and from which decisions are forthcoming.

Political "victory" on a detail of legislative policy (for example, rent control) or even electoral success by those who, to an extent, espouse the relevant principles (for example, Margaret Thatcher or Reagan) is likely to produce an illusion that classical liberalism, as an underlying philosophical basis for understanding, informs public attitudes. Classical liberals who do have an appreciation of the soul of the whole two-century enterprise quite literally went to sleep during the decade of the 1980s, especially after the death of socialism both in idea and in practice. The nanny-state, paternalist, mercantilist, rent-seeking regimes in which we now live emerged from the vacuum in political philosophy.

it makes people better but that it provides the information and motivation (incentives) for ordinary people to cooperate with those for whom they bear little interest or regard.

These classical liberal understandings give economics a clear advantage in arguments based on logic, but they put it at a disadvantage when the case is made on the basis of soul.

LACK OF EMOTIONAL UPLIFT

Economics does not lack important ingredients of a message that includes soul and romance. The economist's concern for improvement and progress, and the central role of obstacles to that progress, would seem to make it possible to communicate economic insights compellingly. Most of us are touched emotionally by stories of struggles against obstacles, struggles that sometimes end in success but often in failure. But seldom do the economic narratives convey much, if any, of the human drama that draws people into sympathy with the lesson being taught. The compelling element missing in the stories economists tell is the human urge to improve oneself, to grow in virtue and to transcend the ordinary. Economists emphasize the advantage of economizing on virtue by the establishment of incentives that motivate good conduct with a minimum amount of noble human traits. This perspective was best expressed by Dennis Robertson when he said, "If we economists mind our business, and do that business well, we can, I believe, contribute mightily to the economizing, that is, to the full but thrifty utilization, of that scarce resource Love" (1956, 154). In other words, let's make the most of the economic man.

Economists are content with *Homo economicus* because they understand that he is capable of doing enormous good when faced with the right incentives. Unfortunately, *Homo economicus* does little to inspire trust, love, concern for others, or any of the other nobler feelings that are an important part of the human experience. As Kenneth Boulding observed, "No one in his senses would want his daughter to marry an economic man, one who counted every cost and asked for every reward, was never afflicted by mad generosity or uncalculating love, … economic man is a clod" (1969, 10). Visions that focus on the capacity of economic man to do good, no matter how great the good, will never have the emotional uplift of those that see good flowing from the moral elevation of the people.

We can appreciate this difference by contrasting two stories, one based on a historical event and the other purely fictitious. First the historically based story.

In the early 1800s, many prisoners were being shipped from England to Australia. The British government contracted with ship captains to provide the transportation, and paid them a specified amount per prisoner. Unfortunately, the survival rate of prisoners was only about 50 percent. This death rate was almost entirely the result of overcrowding and poor treatment, and it prompted many moralizing appeals in favor of more humane treatment. But the moralizing appeals had no effect. The survival rate remained about 50 percent. Finally, an economist, Edwin Chadwick (1862), struck an effective blow for decent treatment of prisoners by accepting that ship captains were economic men and recommending a change in incentives. Instead of paying the captains for the number of prisoners who walked onto ships in England, Chadwick recommended paying for the number who walked off the ships in Australia. The change was made, and the survival rate jumped immediately to 98.5 percent.[3]

Everyone is familiar with Charles Dickens's story *A Christmas Carol*. In the opening chapter, Ebenezer Scrooge is described as "a squeezing, wrenching, grasping, scraping, clutching, covetous old sinner!" Although some economists might disagree, this passage is not a bad description of economic man, at least as understood by most people. In due course, as a result of Scrooge's encounter with the ghosts of his former business partner and the spirits of Christmas past, Christmas present, and Christmas future, he experiences a moral awakening and becomes a thoroughly decent human being, anxious to help those less fortunate than himself. The poignancy of Scrooge's transformation is highlighted by the change in his attitude toward his employee Bob Cratchit and Cratchit's family. Initially, Scrooge is concerned only with how much work he can squeeze out of Cratchit at the small cost, and he has no sympathy for Cratchit's financial inability to obtain desperately needed medical care for his crippled son, Tiny Tim. But having been allowed by the Ghost of Christmas Present to secretly observe the Cratchit family's Christmas dinner, Scrooge becomes deeply concerned about Tiny Tim's prospects, asking the spirit "with an interest he had never felt before" if Tiny Tim would live (Dickens [1843] 1997, 52).

This story is emotionally powerful, far more so than the story about sea captains treating prisoners more humanely, even though the real-world sea captains clearly did more good than the fictitious Scrooge. But imagine that an economist had written *A Christmas Carol*. The story would have ended with Scrooge paying for Tiny Tim's operation, not because he became a better person but because of a change in the tax code allowing more generous write-offs for charitable contributions. What a story that would have been! Does anyone suppose it would still be selling well more than 160 years after it was first published?

MORE "SOUL" AND SUBSTANCE

I am not arguing that classical liberals should abandon the very foundation of our ideology to increase its appeal. Nothing would be gained by destroying the value of our worldview in order to gain its acceptance. There is real virtue in recognizing the power of the incentives created by the social institutions of constitutionally constrained government, private property, and market exchange to lead economic men, clods that they may be, to generate social outcomes far better than the most virtuous people could generate without those institutions. And there is real virtue in struggling to protect and promote classical liberal social orders by advocating increased reliance on market incentives to accomplish good.

One must recognize, however, that staying faithful to classical liberal principles does limit our ability to instill those principles with soul. The statists will always have the advantage in competing on the basis of soul. The reality-based implications of sound economics will never appeal to those searching for little more than easy inspiration and emotional uplift. And those implications are easily dismissed by demagogues as the unwarranted conclusions of people who lack compassion and concern. The one thing that can be done better by selectively ignoring the limits of scarcity is the construction of a vision of social possibilities that will seem far more humane and inspire far more emotional fervor (have more soul) than any vision based on scarcity.[4] Nonetheless, while continuing to recognize unavoidable limits, we can do more to infuse classical liberalism with soul.

Consider some of the ways that economists unnecessarily shove the soul out of their message. Remember that many of our persuasive efforts are aimed at young people, who are full of surging hormones and vivid enthusiasms and alive to the possibilities of romantic quests, heroic achievements, and "making a difference." Yet the message they hear in economic classes is that they are deluded in their aspirations, that they will never be very important or accomplish much. There are no heroes in the economic models presented; evidently no one makes a significant contribution to making the world a better place. All the heavy lifting is done by the market that coordinates the actions of millions, generating a wonderful pattern of productive cooperation, but a pattern in which no one person makes a noticeable difference.

For example, to emphasize the importance of specialization and exchange, economists like to tell their students that none of them, nor anyone else, can make something as simple as a pencil (Read 1958). When hearing from economists about the perversities of the political process, each student is informed that his vote doesn't count—with virtual certainty it will have no effect on the outcome of an election. And economists commonly dismiss the contributions of those credited with major achievements. For example, Robert Paul Thomas has argued that "individual entrepreneurs, whether alone or as archetypes, *don't matter!*" (1969, 141, emphasis in original). Using Henry Ford to illustrate his case, Thomas claims that if Henry Ford had never been born, someone else would have responded to the prevailing technological knowledge and market incentives by developing the assembly-line techniques for producing automobiles at about the same time that Ford did.

Long after most students have forgotten the significance of the intersections and tangencies in the blizzard of graphs thrown their way, they will remember the message of their venality and economic impotence, a message they resist and resent.

I acknowledge the important insights contained in these examples of the insignificance of individuals and the power of market incentives. I have used them myself when teaching economics, and I will continue to do so. But economic insights can be developed without squeezing most of the humanity out of the activities and outcomes being explained. By putting some of the humanity (soul) back into economics, we can make it more appealing and more realistic.

Economics, properly understood, is not a study of automatons responding mindlessly to external incentives, but a study of human action motivated by a broad range of aspirations, ideals, and concerns that make life meaningful. All accomplishments require individuals with vision and ambition animated by emotions and values never completely provided by market incentives, individuals who can inspire and motivate others with more than the incentives provided by market exchange narrowly defined. Indeed, markets as such don't do anything (Lee 1996). All actions are taken by people. Markets enhance the importance of individuals by allowing each to make the most of his talent and ambition through productive cooperation with others.

True, no one can make a pencil by acquiring and processing all the inputs required and combining them properly. But that sort of limitation should not cause us to lose sight of what an individual can accomplish. Manuel Ayau, a scholar-entrepreneur in Guatemala, cannot make a pencil. Yet he has accomplished something far more impressive through his dedication, skill, and sheer force of will. In the 1960s, Ayau had what everyone thought was an impossible dream, to establish a private university in Guatemala that would attract the best students in the country with a rigorous curriculum in the major academic disciplines, coupled with a strong grounding in classical liberalism. At the time, private universities were almost nonexistent in Guatemala: almost all university students attended large, publicly supported institutions that charged only nominal tuition and offered a curriculum dominated by socialist thought and advocacy. Today, the Universidad Francisco Marroquín, located on a beautiful campus in the heart of Guatemala City, is the most prestigious university in Guatemala, enrolls the brightest students in the country from every social class, graduates future leaders of Guatemala who understand classical liberalism, and stands as a testimony to what one person can accomplish. Manuel Ayau didn't make anything needed for the construction and operation of Guatemala's premier university, not even a pencil. He had to enlist the cooperation of many others in the pursuit of his dream, but without him there would be no Universidad Francisco Marroquín.

An individual's vote may not determine the outcome of an election, but that does not mean that individuals are politically impotent in the face of special-interest politics and statist-inspired government initiatives. Ideas have consequences for good and bad, and individuals can wield enormous political influence by developing and popularizing ideas. As John Maynard Keynes famously observed, "The ideas of economists and political philosophers, both when they are right and when they are wrong, are more powerful than is commonly understood. Indeed the world is ruled by little else. Practical men, who believe themselves to be quite exempt from any intellectual influences, are usually the slaves of some defunct economist" ([1936] 1965, 383). Unfortunately, Keynes's observation accurately assessed his own influence. But the influence of statist ideas has been checked and, one hopes, is now being reversed not only because a few scholars "saved the books" and "saved the ideas" of classical liberalism but also because they further developed those ideas and promoted them within and beyond the academy. James Buchanan, Milton Friedman, and F. A. Hayek have never cast a decisive vote at the ballot box, but through their writings and teachings they have probably done as much as, or more than, any politician in the last half of the twentieth century to improve the human prospect by changing the political landscape.

We can recognize the importance of market incentives in encouraging and directing entrepreneurial activity while also recognizing the heroic and the human aspects of entrepreneurs. Individual entrepreneurs *do* matter, and they are seldom motivated by considerations as narrow as those that animate *Homo economicus*. For example, everyone knows that Alexander Graham Bell invented the telephone, but few know about Bell's concern for the deaf. In fact, it was Bell's early work on the transmission of sound, motivated by his desire to improve hearing aids, that resulted in his invention of the telephone, and Bell continued to work with the deaf long after making that invention. Maybe someone else would have invented the telephone at almost the same time if Bell had never existed.[5] But who knows for sure that the lag would have been short or the approach as fruitful? We do know that important progress flowed from the efforts of one man motivated by a sensitive human concern for those who have special handicaps (Mackay 1997).

This theme is most pervasive and best developed in the work of three theorists, one from each of the last three centuries: Adam Smith in the eighteenth century, Carl Menger in the nineteenth, and F. A. Hayek in the twentieth. These three theorists belong to a continuous line of intellectual inquiry that constitutes a distinct approach to social analysis and to the discovery of the most desirable political order. As their work shows, a spontaneous-order approach to the study of human action leads to a focus on three issues: the limits of human reason arising from the inarticulate nature of much human knowledge, the institutional arrangements that evolve to enable humans to make use of dispersed and tacit knowledge, and the processes that hamper or foster the evolution of such institutions.

THE SPONTANEOUS-ORDER RESEARCH PROGRAM OF SMITH, MENGER, AND HAYEK

As a research program, liberalism in the spontaneous-order tradition attempts to understand how social formations can arise as the unintended consequences of human action. At a more philosophical level, it offers reasons why we should expect to find that those social formations are the results of human action but not of human design. The conception of the individual shared by the most important thinkers in this tradition suggests that the limits to human knowledge and reason necessitate the use of social institutions to achieve social order. At a less general level, this version of liberalism tries to understand how current and past social institutions have arisen as spontaneous orders and how they have served to coordinate human actors' diverse plans and preferences. Research in this tradition offers explanations of the operations of such institutions in terms of their enabling us to overcome the limits to our individual knowledge and shows how such institutions have emerged and evolved historically.

Adam Smith

This tradition began in the eighteenth century with the original group of thinkers associated with the Scottish Enlightenment: Adam Smith, Adam Ferguson, David Hume, Bernard Mandeville, and others. Smith's much maligned metaphor of the "invisible hand" has become the most commonly recognized emblem of the reasoning associated with the tradition. In fact, though, Smith used the term *invisible hand* only three times in his major works. However, the same idea appears explicitly in the work of Ferguson and Mandeville, and it is strongly suggested in various places by Hume and the other Scottish thinkers. All these thinkers shared the conviction that people could be taken as they are and that, with the appropriate institutions, society could both ensure against people's worst behavior and channel their self-interest so that it would benefit others, if only unintentionally. In the famous passage invoking the invisible hand, Smith argued:

> By preferring the support of domestic to that of foreign industry, he intends only his own security; and by directing that industry in such a manner as its produce may be of the greatest value, he intends only his own gain, and he is in this, as in many other cases, led by an invisible hand to promote an end which was no part of his intention. Nor is it always the worse for the society that it was no part of it. By pursuing his own interest, he frequently promotes that of the society more effectually than when he really intends to promote it. ([1776] 1976, 477–78)

In Smith's view, the need to rely on self-interest as a motivator for desirable unintended consequences increases as social relationships become less personal and more anonymous. In dealing with people one knows well, sympathy and fellow feeling would be stronger, and one would know more about what sorts of things would benefit the other. Prior to his famous discussion invoking "self-love" as the elicitor of the products provided to us by the butcher, the baker, or the brewer, Smith offered an explanation of why appeals to self-interest are necessary:

> A puppy fawns upon its dam, and a spaniel endeavours by a thousand attractions to engage the attention of its master who is at dinner, when it wants to be fed by him. Man sometimes uses the same arts with his brethren, and when he has no other means of engaging them to act according to his inclinations, endeavours by every servile and fawning attention to obtain their good will. He has not time, however, to do this on every occasion. In civilized society he stands at all times in need of the co-operation and assistance of great multitudes, while his whole life is scarce sufficient to gain the friendship of a few persons. ([1776] 1976, 18)

The appeal to self-interest is our best way to convince others to do what we wish when we do not know them well enough to appeal to their fellow feeling for us.

Altruism is often discussed as a motive for individuals to act in ways that benefit others. A bigger issue faced in an anonymous social order, however, is how one gains knowledge of what would best serve the interests of others. In a face-to-face group, such as an extended family or a tribal group, such knowledge can be readily obtained, but in the more anonymous world of "civilized society," direct knowledge about the "other" is almost always unavailable. For this reason, Smith found appeals to self-interested exchange both necessary and beneficial.

It is also of note that Smith linked the "propensity to truck, barter, and exchange" with the "faculties of reason and speech" ([1776] 1976, 17). Both are forms of persuasion. For Smith, the problem was how to convince others to do what we wish. Reason and speech are one means, a very useful one when the other person is known to us and within speaking or writing range. Inducing the other to act out of self-interest is another means, a necessary one when the other we seek to convince is among the many anonymous others of a broad social order. (Smith was speaking here of what both he and Hayek [1973] called "the Great Society.") As we shall see in the much later work of Hayek, the notion of market exchange as a form of communication became central to Hayek's version of the liberalism that emerged from the Scottish Enlightenment. However, from the beginning of this tradition, it was clear that the issue of how to ensure social order in an anonymous world was central. "In this sense, Smith's entire program may be viewed as his trying to understand how people construct morals and institutions which make self-interested cooperation among distant strangers a productive and beneficial activity" (Young 2000, 108).

It is important to note that Smith and the other Scots did not think that the beneficence of the invisible hand operated in all circumstances. Rather, the channeling of self-interest into the social good would occur only with the right social institutions. Self-interest could, and in fact did in the mercantilist systems Smith was criticizing, lead to harmful consequences. Where, in Smithian terminology, the positive law does not conform with the laws of justice, the possibility exists that self-interest will cause social harm. As Young argues, "Indeed bringing positive law into conformity with the laws of justice is the central policy problem of *The Wealth of Nations*" (2000, 105). When that conformity obtains, the benefits of a self-interested division of labor will be fully reaped.

Despite Smith's crucial insights, his ability to understand and explain the spontaneous-ordering processes of society and the role of institutions in facilitating them was limited by the constraints of classical economics, especially by the cost-of-production theory of value. Escape from that limitation had to wait another hundred years.

Carl Menger

The next major advance in this tradition came with the work of Carl Menger, writing in Vienna in the 1870s. As the history of economics is normally told, Menger, simultaneously with William Stanley Jevons in England and Léon Walras in Switzerland, discovered the principle of marginal utility. Of the three, Menger gave the greatest emphasis to the role of subjective evaluation. Whereas Jevons and Walras focused on marginal utility as a mathematical concept (the first derivative of a total utility function), Menger concentrated on explaining how human valuation set in motion the competitive discovery process of the market. In his *Principles of Economics* ([1871] 1981), Menger clearly explained how market prices, as well as other market phenomena, emerge as unintended consequences of subjective evaluation processes. In his account, he showed how the market arrived at prices, rather than positing possible prices and constructing demand and supply schedules from them, as in the modern practice. As the economist Hans Mayer ([1932] 1994) argued, Menger's theory is a theory of price formation, not of price determination.[2] It pertains to the market process, not to a mathematical equilibrium.

In his *Investigations into the Method of the Social Sciences with Special Reference to Economics* ([1883] 1985), Menger defended this approach as part of a broader research program in the social sciences. For that contribution, he deserves to be considered the outstanding nineteenth-century representative of the spontaneous-order tradition of liberalism that originated with the eighteenth-century Scots. In *Investigations*, he posed what is sometimes called the "Mengerian" question: "How can it be that institutions which serve the common welfare and are extremely significant for its development come into being without a common will directed toward establishing them?" ([1883] 1985, 146). This is but a somewhat amplified statement of the Scots' invisible hand idea. Menger sought to provide what he termed "compositive" explanations of social and economic institutions, as opposed to "pragmatic" explanations, which focus on how particular institutions have been intentionally designed for particular purposes.

Menger's famous theory of the origin of money serves as a paradigmatic spontaneous-order explanation. It deserves a brief review because it illustrates several key parts of the Mengerian approach to social science and also exemplifies what Mayer called a "genetic-causal" theory rather than a "functional" theory ([1932] 1994, 57). People who wish to trade but have no money will first attempt to barter, but the absence of a double coincidence of wants will make barter difficult. Eventually, some actors realize that they will be more likely to make trades if they can acquire goods that *other* people desire. So begins a process of cultural interpretation in which various people attempt to understand the subjective preferences of others. Those who acquire goods that have greater subjective value to more "others" will make more exchanges more easily and thus become "wealthier." As they do, their choices will be observed and imitated by others, who will also start trying to use those same goods as media of exchange. As the number of media becomes smaller, the demand for each grows, making each one that much more suitable as a medium of exchange. After some time, this process converges to one good (or maybe two) that is subjectively highly desired and can meet the minimal physical requirements of a money (relatively scarce, storable, portable, divisible). Ultimately, the good that remains is considered a generally acceptable medium of exchange, or money.

Notice the spontaneous-order elements of this account. Money is a product of human action, not human design. The only behavioral assumptions we need to make are that people will trade to acquire the goods they wish to consume and that they prefer to make those trades as easily as possible. The actors need never be conscious of the fact that they are helping to create money. In fact, how could they be, if they do not even know what money is? The institution of money is thus an unintended consequence of human action (exchange). Or, more precisely, human action initiates a discovery process that results in the creation of an institution that none of the actors could have intended or perhaps even imagined. Menger's theory starts with the notion that valuation arises from the subjective perceptions of individuals and ends with an emergent institution that is thoroughly social. Once money emerges, it, like all other institutions, constrains behavior by virtue of the advantages of participating in an intersubjectively created institution.

Although Smith and his Scottish colleagues understood this process in its broadest outlines, Menger began to fill in some of the details. In particular, Menger bridges the gap between Smith and Hayek by reorienting Smith's discussion of economic progress away from the division of labor alone and toward knowledge more broadly. In the opening chapter of *Principles*, he begins his discussion of the causes of economic progress with a review of Smith, then points out that the division of labor alone cannot explain all economic progress. He concludes that discussion by arguing, "Nothing is more certain than that the degree of economic progress of mankind will still, in future epochs, be commensurate with the degree of progress of human knowledge" ([1871] 1981, 74). With that recognition, Menger pushes the Scottish tradition forward toward Hayek.[3]

F. A. Hayek

F. A. Hayek would carry this tradition even further in the next century. His extension of the main ideas would take two important forms. First, he provided an epistemological backdrop for spontaneous-order explanations, and for liberalism more broadly, at which the Scots and Menger only hinted. Second, he clarified the role played by economic institutions, particularly market prices, in bringing about the spontaneous-ordering processes of the market and of the social world more broadly.

Hayek's main contribution to the liberal tradition begun by the Scots was to emphasize the epistemic limits to humanity's ability to design and direct our institutions and their outcomes consciously. For Hayek, the problem of creating an economic or social order arises from "the fact that the knowledge of the circumstances of which we must make use never exists in a concentrated or integrated form but solely as the dispersed bits of incomplete and frequently contradictory knowledge which all the separate individuals possess" (1945, 77). Knowing precisely how resources should be allocated or what sorts of social practices or norms would serve us best would require that we bring together in one place the bits and pieces of knowledge that separate people, families, or firms possess. Hayek argued that the relevant knowledge they possess simply *cannot* be centralized in the hands of one person or group who could then make determinations of what is better or worse. To the contrary, what is needed is a set of institutions that enable the possessors of knowledge to make that knowledge socially available for use by others in forming their own plans and intentions. For Hayek, the problem of social and economic order is a problem of communication, and the human condition is one of partial, fragmentary, and often incorrect knowledge. We need ways of communicating that allow us to learn from each other and through such learning processes to discover progressively better ways of doing things. This vision accords with Smith's insight, noted earlier, that exchange is an extension of reason and speech.[4]

Hayek complicated this view, however, by adding another level. He argued, especially in his work after World War II, that some of the knowledge required for, say, optimally allocating resources exists in a form that cannot be communicated by means of statistics or language. As part of his lifelong criticism of those who wished to apply the methods of the natural sciences uncritically to the question of social order, Hayek pointed out that objective, articulable knowledge, including economic statistics, was not the only kind of knowledge relevant for economic activity. He first made this point clearly in 1945, when he emphasized the role of "the knowledge of the particular circumstances of time and place" (80). Much of the knowledge relevant for social coordination is, in Hayek's view, inherently contextual.

In his later work, Hayek added that much of the relevant knowledge might be tacit and therefore not even potentially articulable. For example, most people know how to keep their balance on a bicycle. In doing so, they are implicitly solving some fairly complex physics equations, yet hardly anyone can articulate, much less solve, those equations as he rides. More mundanely, consider that even young children can speak grammatically correct sentences without having been explicitly taught any rules of grammar. At issue here is Gilbert Ryle's famous distinction between "knowing how" and "knowing that." Knowledge of the former sort pervades the social world. The problem is to find a means, even though neither natural language nor mathematics can serve to do so, of making such knowledge available to others so that they can make use of it.

In the context of economics, Hayek showed that competition within well-structured legal and political institutions provides a way for this communication process to take place because the prices generated by market competition serve as socially accessible proxies for tacit as well as objective knowledge. When actors make decisions to buy and sell, they are communicating—through action rather than by means of written or spoken words or numbers—their knowledge and preferences concerning the goods in question. The movement of prices in one direction or the other provides indirect access to other people's knowledge and allows actors to coordinate their behavior with that of others without the need for centralized direction. As Hayek argued in 1945, market prices bring "about the solution which (it is just conceptually possible) might have been arrived at by one single mind possessing all the information which is in fact dispersed among all the people involved in the process" (86). In other words, the price system enables us to generate order spontaneously by providing us with an institutional process for overcoming the unavoidable dispersion, context specificity, and tacitness of our knowledge.

THE ROLE OF INSTITUTIONS IN THE SCOTTISH TRADITION

The role of institutions has become a central topic of modern work in the spontaneous-order tradition emerging out of the Scottish Enlightenment. Smith, Menger, and Hayek recognized that because the size and anonymity of modern society preclude our gaining detailed knowledge of all but a few others, we need to coordinate our social behavior by the use of norms, rules, and institutions. In the words of Ludwig Lachmann, "Institutions, as understood in the Weberian tradition, enable each of us to rely on the actions of thousands of anonymous others about whose individual purposes and plans we can know nothing. They are nodal points of society, coordinating the actions of millions whom they relieve of the need to acquire and digest detailed knowledge about others and form detailed expectations about their future action" (1971, 50). Lachmann ties the role of institutions into our previous discussion of fragmented and context-specific knowledge. He suggests that Weber's theory of institutions represents all economic and social institutions as communication processes that make our diverse, often tacit knowledge socially usable.

This aspect of institutions figures prominently in modern work that views institutions as "interpersonal stores of coordinative knowledge" (Langlois 1986c, 237). Institutions limit what we need to know in order to act successfully; they allow us to form more accurate expectations about the behavior of others without detailed knowledge of them. If everyone agrees—whether explicitly or tacitly—on a particular practice, we no longer have to outguess or outstrategize other actors. The classic example of such so-called coordination problems is deciding which side of the road to drive on. As long as all agree, the particular choice is irrelevant. A rule about which side to drive on reduces the need to make a fresh choice on a case-by-case basis. By removing some elements of social interaction from conscious deliberation, institutions free us to focus on other matters that lack institutional solutions: "The existence at higher levels of institutions that stabilize the environment and reduce environmental entropy effectively frees behavioral entropy for use at lower levels. In a stable regime, the agent's reliability is high enough that he can add new actions to his repertoire ... at lower levels" (Langlois 1986a, 186–87). By serving as coordinative nodes, institutions reduce the knowledge needed to execute our plans and therefore enhance our ability to execute those plans successfully.

How do institutions come into being? Many emerge as the unintended consequence of successful individual rule following. That is, not only do institutions contribute to the larger spontaneous order of society, they are themselves often spontaneous orders. In trying to improve their conditions, individuals construct plans of action and attempt to carry them out. They will continue to use modes of behavior that are successful and will treat them as "rules of action" for how to behave in certain circumstances. To the extent that others can observe the ways of behaving exhibited in the successful plans, they will imitate those ways, increasing the number of actors behaving in those particular ways. As this imitation process continues and the number of users of particular rules increases, people learn to expect similar behavior from others. A larger number of rule followers makes using the rule more attractive to potential newcomers because more users implies more opportunities to use the rule as a predictor of behavior, enhancing the likelihood of coordinated outcomes.[5] When the behavior in question is so widespread that we can call it "generally accepted," the rule has become a social institution. As Lachmann explains, "Successful plans thus gradually crystallize into institutions.... Imitation of the successful is, here as elsewhere, the most

Speaking of how the Scottish thinkers used the term *self-interested*, Hayek argued in 1946: "These terms [*self-love or selfish interests*], however, did not mean egotism in the narrow sense of concern with only the immediate needs of one's proper person. The 'self' for which alone people were supposed to care, did as a matter of course include their family and friends; and it would have made no difference to the argument if it had included anything for which people did in fact care" (13). Hayek continued with an explanation of why it still made sense to assume that humans are self-interested in a *broad* sense: "Far more important than this moral attitude ... is an indisputable intellectual fact which nobody can hope to alter and which by itself is a sufficient basis for the conclusions which the individualist philosophers drew. This is the constitutional limitation of man's knowledge and interests, the fact that he *cannot* know more than a tiny part of the whole society and that therefore all that can enter into his motives are the immediate effects which his actions will have in the sphere he knows" (1946, 14). The phrase "sphere he knows" is understood to include family, friends, and the like, not just the "self" narrowly construed. Once again, this appreciation of the "sphere he knows" harkens back to Smith and the continuum he laid out between how one acts toward those one knows well and how one acts toward anonymous others. In our interactions with those close to us, we can more easily invoke fellow feeling and other relevant dispositions that are less reliable as we move toward interactions with those less known to us or not known at all.

Moreover, unlike neoclassical economics and the traditions of liberalism that make use of it, liberalism in the spontaneous-order tradition does not rest on any belief about the rationality of human actors. In fact, the case for this kind of liberalism is predicated on our ignorance. Because so much of our knowledge is tentative, fragmented, and tacit, we require the use of spontaneously evolved social institutions to generate social order. Spontaneous-ordering processes are communication procedures that enable us to overcome our very narrow and partial views of the world and to make use of the differently partial and narrow knowledge that others possess. In this tradition, it is not the individual actors that are best described as "rational," but the processes in which they operate.

LIBERALISM AS A POLITICAL POSITION

The liberalism of the Enlightenment, sometimes called *classical* liberalism and today best expressed by the term *libertarianism*, holds that in order to create "the wealth of nations" or to better the condition of individuals in other ways, it is not necessary for the state do anything more than protect rights to life, liberty, property, and the pursuit of happiness. State intervention beyond those limits is counterproductive and, by violating the stipulated rights, will diminish people's ability to achieve their own ends. In short, state intervention makes people worse off.

In contrast to other classical liberal or libertarian writers, relatively few in the Scottish tradition have posited a priori natural rights. Modern libertarianism— which remains largely rooted in the Lockean and Hobbesian, more English, variant of the Enlightenment—is dominated by related rights talk: state intervention is bad because it violates one's right to X. For many libertarians of this school, once one has made a case for individual rights, then state intervention is ipso facto bad because it immorally violates those rights.

For writers in the Scottish tradition, the central issue is not rights but consequences. Smith argued for free trade because it would increase the wealth of nations and, in so doing, would make people better off. He also wrote about rights and the system of "natural liberty," but they are seen as desirable because they produce good consequences; they are not inviolable in all circumstances. At many places in *The Wealth of Nations*, Smith deviated from the system of natural liberty because he regarded the consequences of natural liberty as problematic. Moving forward in this tradition, we encounter almost no discussion of rights, certainly not natural rights, in Menger's work. Like Smith, Menger was interested in economic development and how markets would promote it and the larger betterment of humanity. Hayek's mentor in economics, Ludwig von Mises, who was a much more ardent opponent of state intervention than Hayek, concurred with Jeremy Bentham's characterization of natural rights as "nonsense on stilts." And Hayek himself—although constantly torn between his Scottish heritage, in the form of a Humean love of the empirical, and his Germanic debts to Kant, in the form of a real concern with freedom and generalizable rules—rarely talked about rights.[6] In the Scottish tradition, the arguments for free markets, freedom of expression and association, and international peace are consequentialist: allowing spontaneous-ordering processes to do their job is desirable because such processes *work*; they make for a more prosperous, happier world than do the alternatives.

The key guiding political principle for this branch of liberalism is a recognition of the limits of human rationality and of our ability to design top-down solutions to social problems. It might seem somewhat ironic that a branch of Enlightenment liberalism would treat the limits of reason and rationality as foundational, but this view traces back to Hume's claim that he wished to "use reason to whittle down the claims of reason."[7] Nothing in the ideal of the Enlightenment commits one to applying the methods of physical and biological science—so powerful and productive in the material domain—to the social world. The mind-set of the scientist or the engineer is inappropriate for solving human problems. The social world is constituted by the subjective evaluations of human actors, often based on their inarticulable or time- and place-specific knowledge and informed by their oft-conflicting values. To believe that certain people, themselves uniquely conditioned by context and history, might successfully design a top-down, one-size-fits-all solution for millions of other people stretches the imagination beyond its limits.

Instead, solutions emerge in multiple forms as a result of the bottom-up activities of people with the sort of detailed, context-specific knowledge that enables them to serve the needs of those around them in finely tailored ways. More important, according to the spontaneous-order tradition, when we allow the competitive forces of markets and culture to generate solutions, we can rely on the feedback mechanisms of those spontaneous-ordering processes to weed out the failures and to select what actually meets people's needs.

One of the major differences between the liberalism of Smith and Menger and the liberalism of Hayek is that Hayek had access to and was an important participant in one of the great intellectual debates that brought together the research program and political concerns of the liberal tradition: the debate over the possibility of economic calculation under socialism that took place in the years between the two world wars.

In response to the arguments of earlier socialists such as Karl Marx and of twentieth-century writers such as Otto Neurath, Ludwig von Mises ([1920] 1935) launched the debate with his article on economic calculation in the socialist commonwealth. He argued that without private property in the means of production, socialist planners, whether a small group or a more democratically organized polity, would have no way to determine how effectively they were using resources. In the absence of private property in capital, there would be no market for capital goods and therefore no prices for capital; hence, planners would be deprived of an irreplaceable guide in determining what to produce and how to produce it. In deciding how to apply a particular capital good to produce various consumer goods or how to produce a given consumer good by using various capital goods, planners without genuine market prices determined by exchanges of private property would be groping in the dark. Mises's argument cut to the heart of socialist claims about the productive superiority of planning. Whereas socialists had long seen the market as irrational and anarchic, Mises's argument showed how the seeming anarchy of production gave rise to a rational economic order when actors could make use of market prices to guide their decisions.

Later refinements of this argument by Hayek and contemporary economists working in the spontaneous-order tradition have stressed the same sorts of epistemological issues raised in the discussion of liberalism as a research program. These economists claim that when government officials intervene in the market, they do so largely blind to the intricate details and context-specific and tacit knowledge that shape the market. As Smith wrote in the paragraph after his reference to the invisible hand: "What is the species of domestic industry which his capital can employ, and of which the produce is likely to be of the greatest value, every individual, it is evident, can, in his local situation, judge much better than any statesman or lawgiver can do for him. The statesman [would] assume an authority ... which would nowhere be so dangerous as in the hands of a man who had folly and presumption enough to fancy himself fit to exercise it" ([1776] 1976, 448).[8] Clearly, the focus on the context specificity of knowledge and the difficulties of communicating such knowledge "to the top" dates back to the earliest contributions to the Scottish Enlightenment.

In this tradition, markets are a communication process that enables us to extend human communicative action beyond language and mathematics to the realm of the tacit. Market prices perform a semiotic function in communicating the kinds of knowledge we often have difficulty articulating. Interfering with or eliminating market processes deprives participants of the full benefits of the market "conversation." In modern terms, markets are "communicatively rational." As the philosopher Gary Madison has noted, "The market economy can be said to be irrational only to the extent that one entertains an overly *rationalistic* conception of rationality, one which in fact reduces reason to mere instrumental, means-end (utility maximizing) rationality.... Monetary transactions are of a communicatively rational nature; they are not ... purely utilitarian and instrumentalist. Monetary transactions are an extremely important way in which citizens of a civil society carry on their society-constituting interactions with one another" (1998, 135, 137, emphasis in original). The argument that planners would not be able to engage in economic calculation in the absence of money prices suggests that what market processes do is to generate orderly outcomes, without design, by the use of those prices.

The Misesian critique of planning presupposes a vision of the market radically different from that associated with both mainstream economics and the other strands of Enlightenment liberalism. The market is not the arena in which atomistic maximizers blindly collide, hoping against hope to produce some sort of optimal static equilibrium outcome. Rather, it is part of the human conversation, a process through which we overcome the limits of our minds and engage in cooperative behavior to create, produce, and exchange. By providing others with indirect knowledge via market prices, we allow them to make use of that knowledge and construct their plans accordingly. This process permits the ever finer degrees of division of labor and knowledge associated with economic growth. Those finer divisions of labor and knowledge require that increased amounts of cooperation must take place in order for consumer goods to be produced. In this light, the Mises-Hayek argument against planning can be seen also as an extension of Smithian insights about the progressive division of labor, refined by both the epistemological issues raised by the subjective theory of value and the importance of monetary calculation as stressed in the calculation debate.[9]

CONCLUSION

The liberalism rooted in the Scottish Enlightenment points toward a different conception of both the task of the social sciences and the most desirable economic and political order. Unlike the more rationalistic conceptions of humans and their social world associated with other strands of liberalism, the Scottish variant recognizes human fallibility and the subjective, tacit, and context-specific nature of much of our knowledge. It further recognizes the inherently social nature of human beings: in order to survive, we must cooperate with others. However, adherents of the spontaneous-order tradition argue that such cooperation need not and to a high degree *cannot* be intentional, planned cooperation. They emphasize how much of our social world has emerged as unintended consequences of human action. The social world arises from "human action but not human design." The market is the foremost example. In the Scottish tradition, the market is seen as a set of institutions that facilitates our (often erroneous) attempts at social coordination. It is in that way an outgrowth of our faculties of reason and speech, as Adam Smith argued more than two hundred years ago. The market allows us to communicate with millions of anonymous others in ways that extend our human capacity to persuade others in direct face-to-face encounters and by the use of language.

NOTES

1 My task in this chapter is not to explore and contrast all the various strands of the Enlightenment, although doing so would be a valuable project. Here, I aim simply to explore the continuity among the thinkers associated with the Scottish tradition and to defend that tradition against some of the criticisms I have noted.

2 See the discussion in Vaughn (1994, 26, n. 21) and the sources cited there.

3 Menger also connects to the Scottish political economists of the early twentieth century, who, with a deep interest in the Austrian tradition spawned by Menger—studying, for example, translations of Eugen von Bohm-Bawerk's publications—continued to work along Smithian lines. I thank Alastair Dow for bringing this point to my attention.

4 The idea of monetary exchange as an extension of language is explored in greater depth in Horwitz 1992.

5 This process of learning through experience reflects the broadly empiricist view of knowledge that all three thinkers held. The point is expressed most clearly by Hayek (1952), who views mental categories as the product of human interaction with the external world. Both Hayek and Smith were quite "Humean" in their epistemologies. The links between Hayek's view of the mind and his work in political economy are explored in Horwitz 2000.

6 See Kukathas 1990 for more on Hayek's attempts to reconcile Hume and Kant.

7 As Hayek wrote, "By 'reason properly used' I mean reason that recognises its own limitations and, itself taught by reason, faces the implications of the astonishing fact, revealed by economics and biology, that order generated without design can far outstrip plans men consciously contrive" (1988, 8).

8 See also Smith's famous "chessboard" passage in *The Theory of Moral Sentiments* ([1759] 1976, 233–34).

9 For an interpretation of the calculation debate that stresses the role of money, see Horwitz 1998.

REFERENCES

Hayek, F. A. 1945. The Use of Knowledge in Society. Reprinted in *Individualism and Economic Order*, 77–91. Chicago: University of Chicago Press, 1948.

———. 1946. Individualism: True and False. Reprinted in *Individualism and Economic Order*, 1–32. Chicago: University of Chicago Press, 1948.

———. 1948. *Individualism and Economic Order*. Chicago: University of Chicago Press.

———. 1952. *The Sensory Order*. Chicago: University of Chicago Press.

———. 1973. *Law, Legislation and Liberty*. Vol. 1. *Rules and Order*. Chicago: University of Chicago Press.

———. 1988. *The Fatal Conceit: The Errors of Socialism*, edited by W. W. Bartley III. Chicago: University of Chicago Press.

Hodgson, Geoff. 1993. *Economics and Evolution: Bringing Life Back into Economics*. Ann Arbor: University of Michigan Press.

Horwitz, Steven. 1992. Monetary Exchange as an Extra-Linguistic Social Communication Process. *Review of Social Economy* 50, no. 2 (Summer): 193–214.

———. 1998. Monetary Calculation and Mises's Critique of Planning. *History of Political Economy* 30, no. 3 (Fall): 427–50.

———. 2000. From *The Sensory Order* to the Liberal Order: Hayek's Non-rationalist Liberalism. *Review of Austrian Economics* 13, no. 1: 23–40.

Jaffe, William. 1976. Menger, Jevons, and Walras De-homogenized. *Economic Inquiry* 14 (December): 511–24.

Kukathas, Chandran. 1990. *Hayek and Modern Liberalism*. Oxford: Clarendon.

Lachmann, Ludwig M. 1971. *The Legacy of Max Weber*. Berkeley, Calif.: Glendessary.

Langlois, Richard. 1986a. Coherence and Flexibility: Social Institutions in a World of Radical Uncertainty. In *Subjectivism, Intelligibility, and Economic Understanding*, edited by Israel M. Kirzner, 171–91. New York: New York University Press.

———. 1986b. The New Institutional Economics: An Introductory Essay. In *Economics as a Process: Essays in the New Institutionalist Economics*, edited by Richard Langlois, 1–25. Cambridge: Cambridge University Press.

———. 1986c. Rationality, Institutions, and Explanation. In *Economics as a Process: Essays in the New Institutionalist Economics*, edited by Richard Langlois, 225–55. Cambridge: Cambridge University Press.

Madison, Gary. 1998. *The Political Economy of Civil Society and Human Rights*. New York: Routledge.

Mayer, Hans. [1932] 1994. The Cognitive Value of Functional Theories of Price. Reprinted in *Classics in Austrian Economics*, vol. 2, edited by Israel M. Kirzner, 55–168. London: Pickering and Chatto.

Menger, Carl. [1871] 1981. *Principles of Economics*. Reprint. New York: New York University Press.

———. [1883] 1985. *Investigations into the Method of the Social Sciences with Special Reference to Economics*. Reprint. New York: New York University Press.

Mises, Ludwig von. [1920] 1935. Economic Calculation in the Socialist Commonwealth. Reprinted in *Collectivist Economic Planning*, edited by F. A. Hayek, 87–130. Clifton, N.J.: Augustus M. Kelley.

Smith, Adam. [1759] 1976. *The Theory of Moral Sentiments*. Reprint. Indianapolis, Ind.: Liberty Fund.

———. [1776] 1976. *An Inquiry into the Nature and Causes of the Wealth of Nations*. Reprinted from the 1904 edition, edited by Edwin Cannan. Chicago: University of Chicago Press.

Vaughn, Karen. 1994. *Austrian Economics in America*. New York: Cambridge University Press.

Veblen, Thorstein. [1898] 1919. Why Is Economics Not an Evolutionary Science? *Quarterly Journal of Economics* 12: 273–97. Reprinted in *The Place of Science in Modern Civilization*, 56–81. New York: W. B. Huebsch.

Young, Jeffrey T. 2000. Adam Smith's Two Views of the Market. In *Knowledge, Division of Labour, and Social Institutions*, edited by Pier Luigi Porta, Roberto Scazzieri, and Andrew Skinner, 95–110. Cheltenham, U.K.: Edward Elgar.

Acknowledgments: Reprinted from *The Independent Review*, 6, no. 1 (Summer 2001), pp. 81–97. Copyright © 2001. A version of this chapter was given as the 1999 Frank P. Piskor Lecture at St. Lawrence University. I thank my SLU colleagues Ansil Ramsay and Jeff Young, as well as Peter Boettke, Karen Vaughn, Don Lavoie, and participants at the J. M. Kaplan Seminar in Political Economy at George Mason University, for comments on earlier drafts of the lecture version. Comments on the present version were happily received from Alastair Dow and other participants at the 1999 History of Economics Society meetings in Greensboro, N.C.

4

Liberalism, Loose or Strict
Anthony de Jasay

Political doctrines can be understood and interpreted in many ways, but in order to survive and prosper, each doctrine needs an irreducible, constant element that represents its distinct identity and that cannot change without loss of the doctrine's essential character. Nationalism must hold out sovereignty, the safeguarding and, if possible, the expansion of a territory, a language, and a race as the chief goals of policy. If it does not, it will be no longer nationalism but something else. Socialism appears in many guises, but all its versions have at least one common, unalterable feature: the insistence that all wealth is created by society, not by its individual members. Therefore, society is entitled to distribute wealth in whatever way fits its conception of justice. Common ownership of the means of production and equality of well-being are derivatives of this basic thesis. Liberalism, I maintain, has never had such an irreducible and unalterable core element. As a doctrine, it has always been rather loose, tolerant of heterogeneous components, easy to influence, open to infiltration by alien ideas that are in fact inconsistent with any coherent version of it. One is tempted to say that liberalism cannot protect itself because its "immune system" is too weak.

Current usages of the words *liberal* and *liberalism* are symptomatic of the protean character of what the names are meant to signify. "Classical" liberalism is about the desirability of limited government and what goes by the name of laissez-faire, combined with a broad streak of utilitarianism that calls not for limited government, but for active government. American liberalism now is mainly concerned with race, homosexuality, abortion, victimless crimes, and in general "rights." In mid-Atlantic English, a liberal is what most Europeans would call a Social Democrat, and in French *liberal* is a pejorative word, often meant as an insult, and liberalism is a farrago of obsolete fallacies that only the stupid or the dishonest have the audacity to profess. These disparate usages do not have much in common. It should not surprise us that they do not.

LOOSE DOCTRINE ON LOOSE FOUNDATIONS

Much of liberalism's lack of a firm identity is explained by its foundations. At its deepest, the doctrine seems to spring from the love of liberty. In more philosophical language, liberty is a value, final or instrumental, that we hold dear. The superstructure of liberalism is made to rest on this easily acceptable value judgment. However, liberty is not the sole value, not even the sole political value. It has many rivals: security of person and property, security of subsistence, equality of many kinds, protection for the weak against the strong, the progress of knowledge and the arts, glory and greatness; the list might be virtually endless. Many if not most of these values can be realized only by curtailing freedom. It is contrary to the liberal spirit of tolerance and love of liberty to reject these values and to dispute anyone's freedom to cherish some of them even at the expense of freedom. The love of liberty allows trade-offs between itself and other things. The amount of freedom that should be given up for a certain amount of security or equality or any other worthy objective that at least some people want to achieve is obviously a subjective matter, my values against yours, my argument against yours. Disagreement is legitimate. From this foundation, therefore, the evolution of the doctrine tends toward allowing rival values more and more lebensraum, to incorporate and cooperate with them. What results is a variable mishmash, all things to all men.

UTILITARIANISM AND THE HARM PRINCIPLE

This evolution, almost predestined by the doctrine's dependence on value judgments, was pushed further forward by the teachings of the three most influential theorists of classical liberalism, Jeremy Bentham, James Mill, and John Stuart Mill. They made one-man-one-vote and the good of the greatest number into imperatives of political morality, establishing a wholly arbitrary, if not downright self-contradictory, linkage between democracy and liberalism. This linkage has since achieved the status of a self-evident truth. It is being repeated with parrot-like docility in modern political discourse, and it is doing much to empty liberalism of any firm identity.

These three theorists also bear much of the responsibility for endowing liberalism with a utilitarian agenda. Liberal politics became the politics of betterment in all directions. There is always an inexhaustible fund of good ideas for improving things by reforming and changing institutions, by making new laws and regulations, and perhaps above all by constantly adjusting the distribution of wealth and income so as to make it yield more "total utility." John Stuart Mill explicitly laid down that whereas the production of wealth is governed by economic laws, its distribution is for society to decide. Utilitarianism made such redistribution not only legitimate but mandatory because by failing to increase total utility by redistributing incomes, we fail to do the good that we can do. A mandate for overall betterment is, of course, a sure recipe for unlimited government.

Many defenders of classical liberalism interpret Mill's famous harm principle as the safeguard against precisely this tendency of utilitarian thought. The principle looks like a barrier to the state's boundless growth. "[T]he only purpose for which power can be rightfully exercised over any member of a civilised community against his will," states Mill, " is to prevent harm to others" (*On Liberty*, chap. 1, para. 9). However, what constitutes harm and how much harm justifies the use of state power are inherently subjective matters of judgment. There is a vast area of putative or real externalities that some people regard as grounds for government interference, whereas others regard them as simply facts of life, best left to sort themselves out. The harm principle, being wide open to interpretation, is progressively expanding its domain. Today, omission is amalgamated with commission. "Not helping someone is to harm him"; certain modern political philosophers invoke the harm principle to make it mandatory for the state to force the well-off to assist those who would be harmed by the lack of assistance. Strong arguments may exist for forcing some people to help others, but it is surprising to find one that is supposed to be quintessentially liberal.

Observing the effects of good intentions is often a matter for bitter irony. Locke tried with his innocent-looking proviso to prove the legitimacy of ownership and succeeded in undermining its moral basis. John Stuart Mill thought that he was defending liberty, but he ended up shackling it in strands of confusion.

STRICT LIBERALISM

To prevent liberalism from becoming indistinguishable from socialism, unprincipled pragmatism, or just plain ad hockery, it must become stricter. It needs different foundations, and its structure must be made minimal and simple, so as to resist better the penetration of alien elements. I suggest that two basic propositions, one logical and one moral, suffice to construct a new, stricter, liberal doctrine capable of defending its identity: one is the presumption of freedom, the other the rejection of the rules of submission that imply the obligation of political obedience.

The Presumption of Freedom

The presumption of freedom should be understood to mean that any act a person wishes to perform is deemed to be permissible—not to be interfered with, regulated, taxed, or punished—unless sufficient reason is shown why it should not be permissible.

Some deny that there is, or ought to be, such a presumption (notably Raz 1986, 8–12). However, the presumption is not a matter of opinion or evaluation that can be debated and denied. It is a strict logical consequence of the difference between two meanings of testing the validity of a statement—namely, falsification and verification.

An indefinite number of potential reasons may speak against an act you wish to perform. Some may be sufficient or valid, others (perhaps all) insufficient or false. You may falsify them one by one. No matter how many you succeed in falsifying, however, some may still be left, and you can never prove that none are left. In other words, the statement that a particular act would be harmful is not falsifiable. Because you cannot falsify the statement, putting on you the burden of proving that the act would be harmless is nonsensical, a violation of elementary logic. In contrast, any specific reason that objectors may advance against the act in question is verifiable. If they have such reasons, the burden of proof rests on them to verify that some or all of those reasons are in fact sufficient to justify interference with the act.

All this seems trivially simple. In fact, it is simple, but not trivial. On the contrary, it is of decisive importance in conditioning the intellectual climate, the "culture" of a political community. The presumption of liberty must be affirmed vigorously, if only to serve as an antidote against the spread of "rightsism" that contradicts and undermines liberalism and that has done so much to distort and emasculate liberalism in recent decades. "Rightsism" purports solemnly to recognize that people have "rights" to do certain specific things and that certain other things ought not to be done to them. On closer analysis, these "rights" turn out to be the exceptions to a tacitly understood general rule that everything else is forbidden, for if such were not the case, announcing "rights" to engage freely in certain acts would be redundant and pointless. The silliness that underlies "rightsism" and the appalling effect it has on the political climate illustrate how far current liberal thought has drifted away from a stricter structure that would serve the cause of liberty instead of stifling it in pomposity and confusion.

The Rule of Submission

"The king in his council has expressed his will, and his will shall be obeyed by all" is a rule of submission. So are the rules that required the citizens of Venice to obey the Signoria, which gave the power to make laws to a majority of a legislature and the power to elect legislators to a majority of voters. The latter rules are more "democratic" than the former, but they all share the same essential feature: the obligation of all in a community to submit to the decisions of only some of them. Moreover, every such rule imposes the obligation to submit in advance to decisions that certain persons reach in certain ways, before a community knows what those decisions are in fact going to be.

Reasons of practical expediency can be found why such submission must prevail if the business of government is to be transacted. The reasons may be good ones, but the rule they call for is no less outrageous for all that. Submission can be morally acceptable if it is voluntary, and voluntary submission by rational individuals is conceivable on a case-by-case basis, on the merits of particular propositions. As a general rule that amounts to signing a blank check, however, submission can hardly be both voluntary and rational. If a general rule of submission is necessary for governing—and it may well be—then the legitimacy of government, any type of government, turns out to be morally indefensible.

Does this inference mean that strict liberals cannot loyally accept the government of their country as legitimate and that in effect they should advocate anarchy? Logically, the answer to both parts of the question must be "yes," but it is a "yes" whose practical consequences are necessarily constrained by the realities of our social condition. Orderly social practices that coordinate individual behavior so as to produce reasonably efficient and peaceful cooperation can be imposed by law and regulation. Today, many of our practices are in fact so imposed—many, but not all. Some important and many less vital yet useful practices are matters of convention.

Unlike a law that must rely on the rule of submission, a convention is voluntary. It is a spontaneously emerging equilibrium in which everybody adopts a behavior that will produce the best result for him, given the behavior that he anticipates everybody else will adopt. In this reciprocal adjustment, nobody can depart from the equilibrium and expect to profit by doing so because he will expect to be punished for it by others' departure from the equilibrium. Unlike a law that depends on enforcement, a convention is thus self-enforcing. Its moral standing is ensured because it preserves voluntariness.

David Hume was the first major philosopher systematically to identify conventions in general, including two especially vital conventions, of property and of promises, in particular. F. A. Hayek's fundamental idea of the "spontaneous order" can be understood best in terms of conventions. We owe the rigorous explanation of the self-enforcing nature of conventions to John Nash, and more recent developments in game theory show that conflict-ridden social-cooperation problems formerly believed to be "dilemmas" requiring state intervention in fact have potential solutions in conventions.

THE STRICTLY LIBERAL AGENDA

It is easy to describe plausible scenarios in which spontaneous conventions emerge to suppress torts and to protect life and limb, property and contract (Jasay 1997, 192–212). However, such scenarios are written on a blank page, whereas in reality the page is already covered with what the past has written on it. In the West, at least two centuries of ever more elaborate legislation, regulation, taxation, and public services—in short, repeated recourse to the rule of submission—have bred a reliance on the state for securing social cooperation. Society therefore has less need for the old conventions, and its muscles for maintaining old conventions and for generating new ones have atrophied.

In the face of this reality, it is probably vain to expect the collapse of a state to be followed by the emergence of ordered anarchy. Perhaps the likeliest scenario is the emergence of another state, possibly nastier than its predecessor.

This reality limits strict liberalism's practical agenda. Despite the logic of the thesis that the state is intrinsically unnecessary and the attractiveness of ordered anarchy, it is hardly worth the effort to advocate the abolition of the state. It is worth the effort, however, constantly to challenge the state's legitimacy. The pious lie of a social contract must not be allowed to let the state complacently take its subjects' obedience too much for granted. Democracy has a built-in mechanism for the state to buy support from some by abusing the rule of submission and exploiting others. Loose liberalism has come to call this practice "social justice." The best that strict liberalism can do is to combat this state intrusion step by step at the margins, where some private ground may yet be preserved and where perhaps some ground may even be regained.

REFERENCES

Jasay, Anthony de. 1997. *Against Politics: On Government, Anarchy, and Order*. London: Routledge.

Raz, Joseph. 1986. *The Morality of Freedom*. Oxford: Clarendon.

Acknowledgments: Reprinted from *The Independent Review*, 9, no. 3 (Winter 2005), pp. 427–432. Copyright © 2005.

PART II
Freedom and the Moral Society

5

On the Nature of Civil Society
Charles K. Rowley

The collapse of the Soviet Empire and the efforts made in Central and Eastern European countries to construct or reconstruct civil society as the salvation of their nations have inspired Western intellectuals to reconsider the concept of civil society and to ask whether it may also help us to understand the condition of Western societies. In both cases, the crisis of socialism, as an ideology and as a practical experience, has proved to be the fulcrum of this search for alternative concepts. For the most part, the concept of civil society is viewed by those active in its renaissance as an attractive combination of domestic pluralism and a continuing role for extensive state regulation and guidance. As such, it offers a broad tent capable of sheltering a multitude of diverse political systems. So broad indeed is this tent that it may be defined more appropriately as an *empty shell* (Rowley 1996, 6).

In this chapter, I shall review briefly the history of the concept of civil society and evaluate its relevance for classical liberal political economy. I shall suggest that the concept of civil society advanced by John Locke, the young John Stuart Mill, and other like-minded classical liberal scholars best encapsulates the classical ideal and provides an intellectually rigorous basis for defining the appropriate role of government, for protecting individual liberties, and for stimulating those private associations of individual citizens, all of which, in combination, constitute the fundamental basis for human flourishing and the wealth of nations.

THE CONCEPT OF CIVIL SOCIETY IN HISTORICAL PERSPECTIVE

Until the end of the eighteenth century, the term *civil society* was synonymous with the state or political society. In this respect, the term reflected precisely its classical origins as a translation of Aristotle's *Koinonia politike* or of Cicero's *so-*

cietas civilis. In this conception, civil society expresses the growth of civilization to the point where society is civilized as classically expressed in the Athenian polis or the Roman republic. It represents a social order of citizenship in which men (more rarely women) regulated their relationships and settled their disputes according to a system of laws, where civility reigned, and where citizens took an active part in public life (Kumar 1993, 377; Ferguson 1991; Roepke 1996).

Following directly in this tradition, John Locke ([1690] 1991) employed civil government as a synonym for civil or political society, Kant defined *bürgerliche Gesellschaft* as that constitutional state toward which political evolution tends, and Rousseau defined the *état civil* simply as the state. In all these usages, civil society is contrasted with the uncivilized condition of humanity in a hypothetical state of nature or under an unnatural system of government that rules by despotic decree rather than by laws.

In *Democracy in America*, Alexis de Tocqueville narrowed the concept of civil society along sociological lines by delineating three realms of society. First, there is the state, which comprises the system of formal political representation, with its parliamentary assemblies, courts, bureaucracies, police, and army. Second, there is civil society, which essentially comprises the system of private and economic interests. Third, there is political society with its political associations such as local government, juries, and political parties and its civil associations such as churches, schools, scientific societies, and commercial organizations.

The life of all these associations, the "super-abundant force and energy" they contribute to the body politic, constitutes political society. Political society supplies "the independent eye of society" that exercises surveillance over the state. It educates us for politics, tempers our passions, and curbs the unmitigated pursuit of private self-interest.

In the postcommunist order, Tocqueville's third category, political society, has become the principal fulcrum for the reconstructed concept of civil society. The tendency has been for ex-Marxists and non-Marxists alike to stress the specifically noneconomic and nonstate dimensions of civil society and to focus attention on civic, cultural, educational, religious, and other organizations operating at the periphery of the capitalist system, yet essentially autonomous from the state itself.

In a sense, this preoccupation is entirely understandable, though misguided, among the intellectuals of Central and Eastern Europe, where prior to 1989 the elevation of civil society was perceived not as constituting a new relationship between state and society, but rather as an uncoupling of that relationship. Because the state could not be effectively challenged, it was to be ignored. The supporters of civil society aspired to make it an alternative society, a parallel society coexisting for the time being with a delegitimized and weakened official state (Kumar 1993, 386). Nothing better illustrated this parallel than Solidarity in Poland, which remained cohesive from the late 1970s until the collapse of communism but thereafter fragmented into sectorial squabbles and personal rivalries and became incapable of evolving the institutions necessary for a safe transition to constitutional democracy.

In no small part because intellectuals had evaluated civil society above the state, viewing it as the solution to all problems accumulated by socialism, they evinced a serious lack of concern after 1989 with regard to the reconstitution of the state and the private economy from the broader perspective of civil society in its classical conception. This lack of concern was especially serious (Klaus 1996) because communism was not defeated but simply collapsed, leaving weak and inefficient markets and weak and inefficient democracies, conditions that continue to plague the entire postcommunist order, the Czech Republic included. As Tocqueville noted, politics spreads "the general habit and taste for association," not vice versa. In the absence of an appropriately formulated polity, civil society in both its broad classical sense and its narrow, late-twentieth-century conception simply will not exist.

Much less excusable, and at least equally misguided, has been the post-1989 reaction of too many Western intellectuals. By claiming "the end of history" (Fukuyama 1992) and assuming too easily that the collapse of communism implied the success of U.S.-style capitalism, the large majority of Western intellectuals forgot the maxim that "eternal vigilance is the price of liberty" and focused attention excessively on the resurrection of civil society in the narrow "political association" sense of Tocqueville.

By inferring the final victory of democracy and capitalism over autocracy and socialism, these Western intellectuals proclaimed, at least implicitly, that any preoccupation with classical political economy was unnecessary and suggested instead that the results of majoritarian democracy represented the highest level of politicoeconomic achievement (Nozick 1989; Gray 1989, 1993). These judgments were (and are) misguided.

Certainly, the free society rests upon and is intended to nurture a solid foundation of competent, self-governing citizens, fully capable of and personally responsible for making the major political, economic, and moral decisions that shape their own lives and those of their children. Certainly, such personal qualities are nurtured and passed on to future generations by healthy families, churches, neighborhoods, voluntary associations, and schools, all of which provide training in, and room for, the exercise of genuine citizenship. Certainly, this expansive understanding of citizenship is challenged in the late-twentieth-century United States, as it was not when Tocqueville wrote *Democracy in America*, by contemporary forces and ideas that regard individuals as passive and helpless victims of powerful external forces.

It is a fundamental error, however, to assume that these contemporary forces and ideas are exogenous elements of the state of nature to be counteracted by some narrow retreat into civil society or by some program that seeks directly to reinvigorate and to reempower the traditional local institutions that provide the environment for the exercise of genuine citizenship. In truth, the forces and ideas that now erode good citizenship emanate from the consequences of an ill-directed twentieth-century political economy, not from any neglect of civil society in its narrow late-twentieth-century form.

BEFORE RESORTING TO POLITICS

"Why does anyone want to resort to politics, and why does anyone put one kind of political order above another?" Anthony de Jasay (1996) suggests that those who are both very earthy and very frank approve the political order that they believe is doing the most good for them. Such a "grand criterion" of political hedonism has no prospect of generating basic agreement about the respective merits and consequences of political systems except for the lowest common denominator of democracy, namely, the shared redistributive advantage of a winning over a losing coalition.

What is true in this crude and obvious way about the system of political hedonism in which the state caters to some interests and neglects others is also true, if less conspicuously, about any other political order that fosters one value and neglects others. Not all values are compatible; most compete with one another. A political order reveals a hierarchy of values by what it promotes and demotes, by the marginal rates of substitution between them that it establishes through policy interventions.

Predictably, the value-orientated political order will be an imperfect match for those who live within it if the citizens are heterogeneous with respect to the values they uphold. No discernible mechanism would make global choice coincide with the best available choice of each individual consistent with the best available choice of every other—the equilibrium condition of ordered anarchy. Value neutrality, where there is not too much of one thing and too little of another, can be achieved by individuals for themselves, but not by a political order for many, let alone for everybody (Jasay 1996, 5).

Jasay (1996, 7) notes the pronounced danger for the equilibrium condition of ordered anarchy posed by the narrow consequentialism of utilitarian philosophy when promoted through the political process. Within the logic of consequentialist ethics, it is all but incoherent to want to limit the scope of government. Limiting government on purpose would be rational only if the scope for doing good were itself limited, which no doubt it is not.

Yet the utilitarian ethic as deployed in its late-twentieth-century form ignores its own value judgment, namely, the impossibility of comparing utilities across individuals. If alternatives are incommensurate, no balance can be struck between the good and the bad consequence, and consequential reasoning is simply out of place. This difficulty leads Jasay (1996, 10) to deploy his first warning to those who would resort to consequentialist politics: *first, avoid doing harm.*

In this view, a political authority simply is not entitled to employ its power of coercion for imposing value choices on society. Its sole guiding principle in all such cases can only be: *when in doubt, abstain.* This principle can be applied retrospectively to dismantle polities that have become suffused with consequentialist ethics as well as prospectively, in the state of nature, to prevent such a suffusion from ever occurring.

One implication of this guiding principle for political ethics is that applying coercion is legitimate only when it is positively invited by those who will be coerced. Assuming that property rights are given, the only circumstances in which rational individuals might choose coercion would be if transaction costs, default, and free-rider and hold-out temptations obstructed the solution of bargaining problems. In such circumstances, Jasay (1996, 7) suggests that hypothetical invitations to be coerced have no better standing than hypothetical contracts. Those who will be coerced must actually invite coercion. Only then do certain tasks become duties that the state must assume.

Circumstances endow each individual with a set of actions that are feasible from a material perspective. Some of these actions are inadmissible because they would harm others in a way that would constitute a tort by the conventional norms of the society. Other actions are inadmissible because individuals have contracted with others not to choose them. To choose such actions would constitute a default or a breach of an obligation. Every other feasible act is admissible (Jasay 1996, 29–30).

With torts and obligations taken care of, the set of admissible actions becomes a residual. Harm and obligations together constitute the full set of valid objections, establishing a strong presumption that all other actions should be allowed.

Coercion by the state fits well into this categorization of feasible actions. Applied to the inadmissible subset, coercion functions to deter tortious harms and contract breaches. State coercion applied to the admissible subset of actions prima facie is illegitimate. It deforms the value of rights and liberties by threatening or committing a tort (in principle, if not by social convention). Only by the explicit invitation of those who are coerced can this presumption conceivably be over-ruled. Doubt about an issue creates a presumption to abstain from resolving it by state coercion (Jasay 1996, 54).

OF PROPERTY

For those who accept this delineation of the role of politics, the twentieth-century view that notions of fairness call upon the state to play a deliberately redistribu-tive role seems mistaken. Redistributive politics clearly creates gainers and losers. Therefore, it necessitates a balancing of the good of some and the bad of others. If such a balancing is ruled inadmissible, redistribution cannot serve as a warrant for the use of coercion. If consequentialism is disallowed, politics can play no legitimate role with regard to redistribution.

Fundamental to this thesis is the presumption that property is partitioned before resorting to politics, that it is not some common-pool resource the use of which and the partitioning of which remain permanently under the control of the political process. This presumption runs counter to late-twentieth-century prac-tice, which emphasizes a redistributionist ideology. The only difference between this redistributionist ideology and socialism is that the former still pays lip service to efficiency gains and accepts on consequentialist grounds some limited version of the exclusion principle implied by private property, whereas the latter does not. The tragedy of the commons overhangs all societies in which property is not strictly partitioned among private individuals, quite independently of whether such societies are redistributionist or socialist, autocratic or democratic.

In the view of John Locke ([1690] 1991), even prior to the social contract that establishes political or civil society, every individual has a property in his own person and a right to the product of his own labor. In addition, individuals create property rights out of the common pool of available resources by mixing their labor with such resources and thereby annexing them. These rights are natural rights, at least if the Lockean proviso is satisfied:

> Whatsoever then he moves out of the State that Nature hath provided and left it in, he hath mixed his *labour* with, and joyned to it something that is his own, and thereby makes it his *Property*. It being by him removed from the common state Nature placed it in, it hath by this *labour* something an-nexed to it, that excludes the common right of other Men. For this *Labour* being the unquestionable Property of the labourer, no Man but he can

have a right to what that is joyned to, at least where there is enough and as good left in common for others. (288)

It is important to note that this natural right to property is not an inalienable right, at least in the sense I shall outline. For this reason, the founders of the United States, who were influenced greatly by Locke's writings, failed to list property as one of the inalienable rights in the preamble to the Constitution. If we define an inalienable right as a right that cannot be lost in any way, then such a right would incorporate both a disability and an immunity: the possessor of the right would not be able to dispose of it voluntarily or involuntarily, nor would any other person, group, or institution be able to dispossess him of it. Property clearly does not fall into this category of a right, as it can be given away or exchanged voluntarily (*alienated*) and it can be lost involuntarily through negligence or wrongdoing (*forfeited*).

The natural right to property does imply, however, that it cannot be taken away by some other party, including a government (*prescribed*). In this sense, we may denote the natural right to property as an *imprescriptible right*. What revolutionary authors such as Locke had in mind was not that no government could take away the right to property, but rather no state legitimately could take away this right without the owners' consent. The force of this claim can be appreciated only when we remember that Locke wrote his *Treatises* under the influence of contractarian accounts of government authority (Simmons 1993, 107).

> The Supreme Court cannot take from any Man any Part of his Property without his own consent. For the preservation of Property being the end of Government, and that for which Men enter into Society, it necessarily supposes and requires, that the People should *have property*, without which they must be suppos'd to lose that by entering into Society which was the end for which they entered into it, too gross an absurdity for any Man to own. (Locke [1690] 1991, 360)

The Lockean assertion that each individual is born free in the state of nature correctly recognizes that we are not born into political communities. We are not naturally citizens; we must do something to become citizens. Locke clearly depicted the state of nature as one of "*perfect freedom* to order their Actions, and dispose of their Possessions, and Persons, as they think fit, within the bounds of the law of Nature, without asking leave, or depending on the Will of any other Man" (bk. 2, para. 4). The state of nature has a law to govern it, which obliges every individual: no individual "ought to harm another in his Life, Health, Liberty or Possessions" (bk. 2, para. 6).

The enclosure worsens their situation even though it does not violate their rights. If the unowned resource has been used regularly by identifiable individuals, common-pool ownership may be implied, and these individuals should be paid compensation in the form of reliance-based damages. Enclosure itself is not a tort. It constitutes a clash of two liberties, not a clash of liberty and a right. If exclusion is successful and just claims for compensation on grounds of reliance are satisfied, the resource passes legitimately into the ownership of the finder-encloser.

THE LAW OF NATURE AND HUMAN FLOURISHING

The state of nature, as earlier defined, is not a state of license, even though people in that state have an uncontrollable liberty to dispose of their property. The state of nature has a law of nature to govern it, which obliges everyone (Locke [1690] 1991, bk. 2, para. 6). As every individual is equal and independent under that law, no one ought to harm another in his life, liberty, or possessions. In the state of nature, the law of nature provides that every man has a right to punish the transgressions of that law to such a degree as may hinder its violation. All who are damaged by the unlawful act have a particular right to seek reparation from the transgressor. In this sense, every individual has executive power in the state of nature.

Because men are free, equal, and independent by nature, no one can be subjected to the political power of another without his own consent. Why would people give such consent? Locke's answer is that although in the state of nature men have such rights, the enjoyment of them is uncertain and constantly exposed to the invasion of others (Locke [1690] 1991, bk. 2, para. 123). People create civil society mainly for the mutual preservation of their lives, liberties, and estates, which Locke calls by the general name *property*.

Although man gives up the executive power to protect his own property when he enters into civil society, he does so only to better preserve his property. The power of civil society is constrained to secure everyone's property by providing against the defects inherent in the state of nature. Even if, as Locke supposed, majority rule governs society, it does so subject to the strict requirement that every man's life, liberty, and estates must be protected at least as well as he could protect them in the state of nature. Evidently, such an outcome can be achieved only by the *minimal state*, that which exists solely to determine and defend property rights against potential internal and external aggression. Note that this definition of the minimal state permits a state whose size may vary according to the nature and scale of the forces of aggression it is obligated to resist.

I shall now argue that human flourishing occurs best in the environment provided by the minimal state; that political societies composed of individuals with diverse interests predictably stifle human flourishing unless the state takes no action except to uphold the negative natural rights of all citizens. This argument follows in the lineage of classical liberal scholars perhaps best epitomized by John Locke ([1690] 1991), Wilhelm von Humboldt ([1791] 1969), and John Stuart Mill ([1859] 1989).

It is instructive to initiate this analysis of human flourishing with Aristotle's concept of *eudaimonia*, which describes a state of individual well-being induced by living rationally or intelligently and characterized by self-actualization and maturation. Use of the term eudaimonia in no sense implies an endorsement of Aristotle's ethics, which does not embrace the notions of natural rights and individual liberty central to this chapter.

Although eudaimonia is usually translated as "happiness," this is misleading if not qualified. Here, happiness should be understood not simply as the gratification of desire, but rather as the satisfaction of right desire—the desires and wants that will lead to successful human living (Rasmussen and Den Uyl 1991, 36). Of course, man is not only a rational being but also an animal with the biological capacity and need for sensory experiences. Emotions play a significant role in achieving eudaimonia. Nevertheless, human flourishing requires that the emotions be controlled by man's capacity to reason. For a successful life, man must live so that he achieves goals that are rational for him not only from an individual perspective but also as a human being (Machan 1975, 75). In so doing, he controls his animal passions.

In a society of diverse individuals, the outcomes of human flourishing will reflect that diversity. Human flourishing is unlikely to lead to a consensus about the good, despite much modern consequentialist reasoning to the contrary. Value pluralism, which so concerns conservatives and communitarians, will be dealt with later, and I shall argue that it constitutes a problem only within the context of the nonminimal state.

Human flourishing or eudaimonia must be attained through a person's own efforts. It cannot be achieved as the result of forces beyond his control. If a human is to flourish, the cardinal virtue is rationality, which can develop only when an individual has full responsibility for his own choices. Individuals cannot flourish or grow when others make choices for them or when they are not held responsible for the choices they make, because the human faculties of perception, judgment, mental activity, and even moral preference are exercised only in making a choice:

He who lets the world, or his own portion of it, choose his plan of life for him, has no need of any other faculty than the ape-like one of imitation. He who chooses his plan for himself, employs all his faculties. He must use observation to see, reasoning and judgment to foresee, activity to gather materials for decision, discrimination to decide, and when he has decided, firmness and self-control to hold to his deliberate decision. And these qualities he requires and exercises exactly in proportion as the part of his conduct which he determines according to his own judgment and feelings is a large one. It is possible that he might be guided in some good path, and kept out of harm's way, without any of these things. But what will be his comparative worth as a human being? It really is of importance, not only what men do, but also what manner of men they are that do it. (Mill [1859] 1989, 59)

Of course, the laws of nature do not guarantee that every human being will flourish. Some will not seize the opportunity provided by liberty to fulfill their lives to the limit of their respective capacities. Many will evade the burdens and constraints of choice and make their way in life through imitation or servitude rather than creativity. Others will be overwhelmed by their passions, discarding rationality in favor of purely sensory pleasures. The laws of nature offer only opportunities, not a guarantee of utopia. They also protect individuals from the choices by others that threaten their lives, liberties, or property. The freedom to flourish is not a license to behave in ways injurious (in this sense) to others. Fundamentally, the law of property, of contract, and of tort, effectively enforced, would control the injurious impulses incidental to human flourishing.

In the Lockean tradition of negative natural rights, the natural right to private property arguably is its most controversial component. This controversy extends to the relationship between property rights and human flourishing (Rawls 1971). This relationship, therefore, requires particular attention. Individuals are material beings, not, as Rawls supposes, disembodied ghosts. Being self-directed or autonomous is not some psychic state but pertains to actions in the real world and often involves material resources. By using and manipulating material resources, autonomous individuals, in large part, develop and exercise their creativity under conditions of liberty.

For individuals to flourish, they need to maintain control of what they have pro¬duced (Buchanan 1993; Rasmussen and Den Uyl 1991, 116) and to retain or dispense their accumulated resources according to their own judgment. In this respect, the imprescriptible right to property takes its full place with the inalienable rights to life and liberty as the strongest foundation for human flourishing.

THE NONPROBLEM OF VALUE PLURALISM

John Gray (1989, 1993) has argued for what he calls *plural realism in ethics* along the following lines: because there are definite limits on the varieties of human flourishing and there are many forms of social life, often involving divergent and uncombinable goods, in which human beings may flourish, no one form is the one right way of life for man. Plural realism thus differs sharply from Aristotelian ethics, which claims that the one best form of life for the human species can be rationally discovered. Plural realists, in contrast, argue that human well-being can be realized in many, diverse, and incompatible forms of social life. With this assessment I have no quarrel; indeed, it is the essence of the political philosophies of both Locke and Mill (Waltzer 1994).

Gray (1993), however, deploys plural realism as a weapon to attack classical lib¬eral ethics, most certainly the brand of ethics I have advanced in this chapter. He claims that pluralism fells classical liberal meliorism, which ranks societies by the degree to which they approximate a classical liberal order; that it overwhelms the notion that all human beings are endowed with rights, because highly strati-fied societies may give rise to some form of human flourishing; that it destroys Kant's notion that only persons have intrinsic value, because elements of a "rich cultural environment" may enter into autonomous choice constitutively rather than instrumentally.

In passing this judgment, Gray lays claim to intellectual support from Isaiah Berlin, in his view the most compelling liberal political philosopher of the twen-tieth century (Gray 1996). At the heart of Berlin's thought, he claims, is value pluralism, an idea of enormous subversive force. If there is no single master-value and some values are not necessarily compatible or harmonious, no single moral theory can guide our conduct when we face moral dilemmas that force us to forsake one good for another. No metric enables us to make trade-offs. In such circumstances, classical liberal institutions have no universal authority.

Whether Gray is accurate in his reflections on Berlin—and there is a lot of evidence that Berlin is a fox who knows many things rather than a hedgehog who knows one big thing (Kukathos 1996)—he wields these reflections to attack classical liberal political orders, arguing that they have no general superiority. In Gray's view, value pluralism dictates pluralism in political regimes and under-mines the claim that only classical liberal regimes are fully legitimate. Gray finds a wide range of past and present societies that are far distant in nature from classi-cal liberal orders to be compatible with his concept of civil society.

In my view, the argument from value pluralism strengthens rather than weak-ens the case for a political society grounded either on the law of nature or, equiva-lently, on Jasay's maxims set out in *Before Resorting to Politics* (1996). For only in such a society, where the negative rights of individuals are strictly enforced, will value pluralism withstand public-choice pressures to conform either to the values of transient majorities or to the dictates of an autocrat. In his critique of classical liberal political orders, Gray falls into a categorical error of assuming that the whole of society is politicized; that the supposed monism of classical liberal values will be imposed on all aspects of an individual's life.

This assumption is not the case. By definition, a classical liberal order constrains politics to its minimal form, leaving individuals free to form their own associations and groups and to pursue their own goals subject only to the laws of property, contract, and tort, uninhibited by political pressures. Ultimately, it leaves individuals free even to abandon the order itself should they so choose. Classical liberals will not force individuals to be free (Rowley and Peacock 1975). Citizens who flourish within the framework of classical liberalism, however, will not easily choose to deny themselves the advantages they enjoy.

A FLAWED CONCEPT OF CIVIL SOCIETY

Gray (1993) claims that classical liberalism, as a doctrine taken to have universal prescriptive authority, is dead; its philosophical foundations are in a state of collapse. All that remains is "the historic inheritance of civil society that has now spread *to most parts of the world*" (314). Civil society, as defined by Gray, superficially conforms with the basic tenets of a classical liberal order, although on a closer examination this conformity is discovered to be a mirage.

By civil society, Gray (1993) means a number of things. First, it is a society tolerant of the diversity of views, religious and political, that it contains and in which the state does not seek to impose any comprehensive doctrine. In this sense, Calvin's Geneva was not a civil society, nor were any of the societies characterized by twentieth-century totalitarianism.

Second, it is a society in which both government and individual citizens (Gray significantly refers to them as its subjects) are restrained in their conduct by a rule of law. A state in which the will of the ruler is the law cannot contain a civil society. In consequence, civil society presupposes an omnipotent but limited government.

Third, civil society is characterized by the institution of private property. Societies in which property is vested in tribes or most assets are owned or controlled by governments cannot be civil societies. Private property is defended as an enabling device whereby individuals with radically different goals can pursue such goals without recourse to a collective decision-procedure that must be highly conflictual. Private property, in Gray's view, is compatible with a wide range of political institutions.

These institutions need not conform to classical liberal predilections. Nor need they contain the culture of individualism. Nor need they embrace the institution of market capitalism, which in Gray's opinion is not the only market institution compatible with private property. In Russia and Japan, for example, municipal, village, and cooperative forms of property ownership are likely to prove greatly superior to the capitalist form (Gray 1993, 316).

The criteria set out by Gray as the defining characteristics of civil society are capable of defining a narrow or a broad tent, depending on how the words are interpreted. By his selection of societies, he categorizes as civil societies, Gray unequivocally chooses the broad-tent definition. The societies of North America and Western Europe clearly qualify, although Gray is not uncritical of the growth of government in these countries, especially during the second half of the twentieth century. One senses that something is seriously awry, however, when Gray (1993) adds to this list of civil societies a range of past and present political orders radically different from the great democracies: Czarist Russia, Meiji Japan, Bismarckian Prussia, Duvalier's Haiti, Singapore, Hong Kong, South Korea, and Taiwan. None of these has demonstrated great tolerance for diversity of opinions and lifestyles; none has provided great security for private-property rights, recent indexes of economic freedom (Gwartney, Lawson, and Block 1996) notwithstanding; and none has protected the lives and liberties of citizens by restricting government through any recognizable rule of law enforced by an independent judiciary.

It would be easy to take advantage of Gray's poor judgment to ridicule the concept of civil society advanced in his recent writings. It is more instructive, however, to review a stronger contestant for his lists in order to demonstrate the flawed nature of his broad concept. Certainly, many of the citizens of the United States claim preeminence for their political order as the leading example of civil society in the modern world. The concept of the new world order advanced by Presidents Bush and Clinton essentially involves a commitment to reshaping all nations in the American image. Evaluated by the criteria of classical liberalism, however, the United States is not now a civil society, although it probably was at its founding in 1787 except for the evil institution of slavery.

In the late twentieth century, the United States has the highest murder rate of all advanced nations; clearly, it is not protecting the lives of its citizens. It also has the highest incarceration rate of all advanced nations, as a consequence of extremely interventionist legislation and administrative regulations that further erode the liberties of its nonincarcerated citizens. Its taxes and regulations significantly encroach on the private-property rights of its citizens, and its takings of private property for public use in no sense honor the wording of the Fifth Amendment to the Constitution. There is no imprescriptible right to property in the United States.

These characteristics are no accident of fate. They are entirely predictable consequences of the expansion of government beyond the limits of the minimal state, of the abandonment of either natural rights or Jasay's maxims "before resorting to politics." In many ways, Tocqueville anticipated the likely regression of American democracy away from liberty and civil society and toward equality and noncivil society in volume 2 of *Democracy in America*.

Tocqueville warned that "the type of oppression which threatens democracies is different from anything that has ever been in the world before" ([1840] 1969, 691).

He envisaged "an innumerable multitude of men, alike and equal, consistently circling around in pursuit of the petty and banal pleasures with which they glut their souls" (692). In such a society, a man "exists in and for himself, and though he may still have a family, one can at least say that he has not got a fatherland" (692). In a prophetic passage, Tocqueville sets out the implications for the political order of this state of affairs:

> Over this kind of men stands an immense, protective power which is alone responsible for securing their enjoyment and watching over their fate. That power is absolute, thoughtful of detail, orderly, provident, and gentle. It would resemble parental authority if, fatherlike, it tried to prepare its charges for a man's life, but on the contrary, it only tries to keep them in perpetual childhood.... It provides for their security, foresees and supplies their necessities, facilitates their pleasures, manages their principal concerns, directs their industry, makes rules for their testaments, and divides their inheritances. Why should it not entirely relieve them from the trouble of thinking and all the cares of living? (692)

The process of subjugation of such a population is subtle rather than brutal as in totalitarian orders:

> It does not break men's will, but softens, bends, and guides it; it seldom enjoins, but often inhibits action; it does not destroy anything, but prevents much being born; it is not at all tyrannical, but it hinders, restrains, enervates, stifles, and stultifies so much that in the end each nation is no more than a flock of timid and hardworking animals with the government as its shepherd. (692)

Much of what Tocqueville feared in 1840 for democracy in America has come to pass with consequences for civil society that manifest themselves in high crime rates, high rates of incarceration, a cult of property theft by middle-income groups through the process of government, and a decline in thrift, manliness, civility, toleration, duty, self-sacrifice, service, fidelity, self-control, fortitude, honesty, honor, trust, mutual respect, diligence, discretion, and self-improvement (Anderson 1992).

For the most part, these qualities of civil society may seem more psychological and sociological than economic. My central hypothesis is that they depend not on the perfectibility of man but on sound political economy as enunciated by the great classical liberal scholars whose ideas form the basis of this chapter. These lost values will return, if at all, only through a return to the minimal state obligated to preserve and protect the lives, liberties, and properties of the citizens who create and effectively control it. Only in such a society will human beings flourish and assume for themselves duties and obligations they have currently abandoned in an ever-escalating demand for unjustified rights and privileges.

THE RESTORATION OF CIVIL SOCIETY

In his *History of the Decline and Fall of the Roman Empire* ([1787] 1974), Edward Gibbon describes the gradual emergence and consolidation of classical civil society throughout the Roman Empire over some six hundred years during the period of the Great Republic (SPQR). He chronicles the disastrous consequences of monarchy and the collapse of SPQR following the assassination of Julius Caesar, the subsequent civil war between Octavianus Caesar and Marc Antony, the final victory of the former at the battle of Actium (34 BC), and the crowning of Octavianus as the Emperor Augustus Caesar. He relates the slow but inexorable decline and fall of this once great empire during the following several centuries as it was ravaged from within by internecine battles for the Imperial Crown, always involving the Praetorian Guard and the Roman Legions, and from without by the barbarian hordes waiting at the boundaries for any perceived weakening of imperial resolve.

Following the final collapse, "the greatest, perhaps, and most awful scene in the history of mankind" (Gibbon [1787] 1974, 6:2441), the institutions of civil society disappeared completely for the greater part of a millennium. Later Great Britain freed itself from the Stuart dynasty in 1688 and accelerated the slow process of evolution of the institutions of civil society, which eventually were to extend far beyond its own frontiers to encompass much, although by no means all, of its own extensive empire. The twentieth century witnessed the decline and fall of the British Empire and, with it, the erosion of classical liberal civil society, ravaged alike by two world wars and the follies of unlimited democracy. If this process of erosion is not checked, a new Dark Age beckons from which, given the destructive power of modern weaponry, mankind is unlikely to reemerge.

Now that government has grown so large, both in absolute size and in the range of its functions, in all Western nations, the public-choice constraints obstructing any rapid return to the minimal state are formidable. The advance of the welfare state has created a culture of dependency that manifests itself at the polls even as it corrodes human flourishing among the individuals addicted to its offerings. The politicization of society that accompanies the growth of government has essentially destroyed the rule of law and, in doing so, has weakened the protection accorded the lives, liberties, and property of individual citizens. This weakening of protection, in turn, has curtailed human flourishing even among the more independent individuals in society, lowering the degree of vigilance on which the law of nature depends for its continued existence.

In such circumstances, public-choice predictions for the restoration of the minimal state are less than propitious. Without the minimal state, the prospects for the restoration of civil society are as bleak as they were in the dying years of the Roman Empire.

It is instructive in this regard to switch attention from the fundamental characteristics of classical civil society as outlined in this chapter to the complex of interlocking institutions and individual dispositions on which civil society may be expected to flourish in a twenty-first-century environment. Insights are available concerning these interrelationships from the experience of Great Britain during the late eighteenth and early nineteenth centuries. The freedom of British citizens at that time stemmed, as Michael Oakeshott (1991) has noted, not from separate rights, laws, or institutions but from many mutually reinforcing liberties:

> It springs neither from the separation of church and state, nor from the rule of law, nor from private property, nor from parliamentary government, nor from the writ of *habeas corpus*, nor from the independence of the judiciary, nor from any one of the thousand other devices and arrangements and characteristics of our society, but from what each signifies and represents, namely, the absence from our society of overwhelming concentrations of power. (1991, 387)

In this perspective, individuals considered themselves free in classical liberal Britain because no one was allowed unlimited power—no leader, faction, party, government, church, corporation, trade or professional association, or trade union. Instead, power was diffused through what Oakeshott refers to as a *civil association* in which each individual acknowledges the authority in which he lives. Respect for the authority of law did not imply that every individual supported every law. The law itself was a slowly changing spontaneous order (Hayek 1973) that garnered respect not just for what it was but also for what it promised to become, always within the framework of the rule of law. In a civil association, the government "is an instrument of the people, charged with keeping in good order the institutions which allow people to pursue their self-chosen ideals" (Green 1993, 9).

The twentieth century witnessed major retreats by all such civil associations as illiberal nation-states have abandoned the minimal state and have reconstituted their citizens into what Oakeshott (1991) refers to as *enterprise associations*. Nation-states constituted as enterprise associations are composed of individuals related by their pursuit of a common interest or objective. There is but one sovereign purpose. The task of leaders "is to manage the pursuit of this goal and to direct individuals as appropriate" (Green 1993, 8). Communism and national socialism were ultimate forms of the enterprise association. However, late-twentieth-century social democracy evolved as a less extreme form of this perversion of the civil association, unfortunately much better entrenched than either of its totalitarian close relations.

Hayek (1973) has demonstrated that the classical liberal experiment with democracy failed because the institutions chosen to preserve liberty proved inadequate. In particular, faith placed in the separation of powers—legislative, executive, and judicial—was not justified even in the most sophisticated experiment, the U.S. Constitution.

The U.S. Supreme Court, although equal in status to the Congress and the president, had been designated as the crucial check against politicization of the law. It played this role effectively until, in 1937, a majority of its justices rendered themselves unlawful in the case of *West Coast Hotel Co. v. Parrish*, caving in to pressures from the White House to subvert the Constitution in favor of unconstitutional New Deal legislation. Thereafter, periodic coalitions between Congress and presidents effectively destroyed the separation of powers and the rule of law.

In large part, classical liberal scholars underestimated the capacity of the state to subvert society by shifting it from the civil to the enterprise association because they failed to anticipate the shift from the law of *Nomos* to the law of *Thesis*, from the common law to law making by the state (Hayek 1973). The idea that the law was immune from interference by government, that it was discovered and not made, was fundamental to natural law, or the law of God, indeed was the fundamental contribution of Judeo-Christian religion to the seventeenth- and eighteenth-century concept of civil society. That view was swept away by the extension of the franchise in the nineteenth and early twentieth centuries and the "philistinization" of the majority vote in most advanced democracies.

What was swept away had taken many generations to evolve. It cannot be reestablished by constitutional decree but only by another slow process of evolution. From a public-choice perspective, such an evolutionary process faces formidable obstacles in the form of special interests that control the enterprise association. In a civil association, the law must not be the instrument of special interests or the tool of government. It must constitute a body of moral and prudential rules binding on everyone (Green 1993, 122). How can law making be restored as the making of impartial rules of just conduct in an environment subverted by the forces of public choice? How can it be established in environments that have never experienced the rule of law?

One route to such reform is the weakening of central government through a process of devolving power (including the power to tax) to the states or provinces in a federalist system or to the local level in nonfederalist systems. In and of itself, such devolution does not guarantee a shift away from Leviathan in favor of the minimal state. In some instances, where the population is highly dependent on the state, devolution may shift the balance even further in favor of Leviathan.

Nevertheless, locally ruled communities would then be free to experiment (at their own cost) with differing forms of government. To the extent that such experimentation steers clear of contamination by the spending and taxing interventions of central government, communities that are more successful in encouraging human flourishing signal the existence of a better way to those that are less successful. Given the powerful forces ranged against such reforms by the central government, if civil associations are once again to replace enterprise associations, devolved competition may be the only feasible mechanism.

REFERENCES

Anderson, D. 1992. *The Loss of Virtue: Moral Confusion and Social Disorder in Britain and America*. London: Social Affairs Unit, National Review Book.

Buchanan, J. M. 1993. *Property as a Guarantor of Liberty*. Shaftesbury Papers, no. 1. Aldershot, U.K.: Edward Elgar.

Ferguson, A. 1991. *An Essay on the History of Civil Society*. New Brunswick, N.J.: Transaction.

Fukuyama, F. C. 1992. *The End of History and the Last Man*. New York: Free Press.

Gibbon, E. [1787] 1974. *The History of the Decline and Fall of the Roman Empire*. 6 vols. New York: Easton.

Gray, J. 1989. *Liberalisms: Essays in Political Philosophy*. New York: Routledge.

———. 1993. *Post-Liberalism: Studies in Political Thought*. New York: Routledge.

———. 1996. *Isaiah Berlin*. Princeton, N.J.: Princeton University Press.

Green, D. G. 1993. *Reinventing Civil Society*. London: IEA Health and Welfare Unit.

Gwartney, J., R. Lawson, and W. Block. 1996. *Economic Freedom of the World: 1975–1995*. Vancouver, Canada: Fraser Institute.

Hayek. F. A. 1973. *Law, Legislation and Liberty*. Vol. 1. *Rules and Order*. London: Routledge and Kegan Paul.

Humboldt, W. von. [1791] 1969. *The Limits of State Action*. Cambridge: Cambridge University Press.

Jasay, A. de. 1996. *Before Resorting to Politics*. Shaftesbury Papers, no. 5. Aldershot, U.K.: Edward Elgar.

Klaus, V. 1996. *Transforming toward a Free Society*. Vienna: Mont Pelerin Society Meeting.

Kukathos, C. 1996. What's the Big Idea? *Reason* (November): 66–70.

Kumar, K. 1993. Civil Society: An Inquiry into the Usefulness of an Historical Term. *British Journal of Sociology* 44 (3): 375–401.

Locke, J. [1690] 1991. *Two Treatises of Government*. Edited by P. Laslett. Cambridge: Cambridge University Press.

Machan, T. 1975. *Human Rights and Human Liberties*. Chicago: Nelson-Hall.

Mill, J. S. [1859] 1989. *On Liberty and Other Writings*. Cambridge: Cambridge University Press.

Nozick, R. 1989. *The Examined Life: Philosophical Meditations*. New York: Simon and Schuster.

Oakeshott, M. 1991. *Rationalism in Politics and Other Essays*. Indianapolis, Ind.: Liberty.

Rand, A. 1961. *The Virtue of Selfishness*. New York: New American Library.

Rasmussen, D., and D. Den Uyl. 1991. *Liberty and Nature: An Aristotelian Defense of Liberal Order*. La Salle, Ill.: Open Court.

Rawls, John. 1971. *A Theory of Justice*. Cambridge, Mass.: Belknap Press of Harvard University Press.

Roepke, W. 1996. *The Moral Foundations of Civil Society*. New York: Transaction.

Rowley, C. K. 1996. What Is Dead and What Is Living in Classical Liberalism. In *The Political Economy of the Minimal State*, edited by C. K. Rowley. Aldershot, U.K.: Edward Elgar.

Rowley, C. K., and A. T. Peacock. 1975. *Welfare Economics: A Liberal Restatement*. London: Martin Robertson.

Simmons, A. J. 1993. *On the Edge of Anarchy*. Princeton, N.J.: Princeton University Press.

Tocqueville, A. de. [1835/1840] 1969. *Democracy in America*. New York: Harper and Row.

Waltzer, M. 1994. Multiculturalism and Individualism. *Dissent* (Spring): 185–91.

Acknowledgments: Reprinted from *The Independent Review*, 2, no. 3 (Winter 1998), pp. 401–420. Copyright © 1997. This chapter is a revised version of the introductory chapter in *Classical Liberalism and Civil Society*, edited by Charles K. Rowley and published by Edward Elgar Publishing (1997). Permission to republish is gratefully acknowledged. I wish to express deep appreciation to the Lynde and Harry Bradley Foundation for financial support for this project. I am also grateful to Robert Higgs for sound editorial advice and to Maria Pia Paganelli for research assistance.

6

Liberty, Dignity, and Responsibility
The Moral Triad of a Good Society
Daniel B. Klein

In *The Constitution of Liberty*, F. A. Hayek wrote, "The belief in individual responsibility ... has always been strong when people firmly believed in individual freedom" (1960, 71; see also 1967, 232). He also observed that during his time the belief in individual responsibility "has markedly declined, together with the esteem for freedom." In surveying the twentieth century, noting the ascent of the philosophy of entitlement, the doctrines of command and control, and their institutional embodiments—the welfare state and the regulatory state—one can only respond, "indeed." Lately, perhaps, a reversal has begun.

We might advance the reversal if we better understood responsibility and its connection to liberty. We speak often of responsibility, but vaguely, even more so than when we talk of liberty. When Hayek refers to "the belief in individual responsibility," does he mean the striving by the individual to be admirably responsive in his behavior, to be reliable, dependable, or trustworthy? Or does he mean the belief that individuals ought to be held to account, to be answerable or liable for their actions? A drunken watchman can be held accountable for trouble that occurs during his shift; he is then both irresponsible and responsible. Indeed, the two kinds of responsibility tend to occur together, but they are conceptually distinct. As moral philosophers, we usually have the reliability notion in mind; as political philosophers, the accountability notion. To make the terminological distinction clear, I shall call the personal trait of being admirably responsive *personal responsibility*, and the social-relations trait of holding the individual to account *individual responsibility*.

Individual responsibility fosters personal responsibility. Policy affects morals. And personal responsibility enhances the appeal of individual responsibility and of liberty. Morals affect policy. Putting policy and morals together, we get feedback loops and multiplier effects.

I shall attempt to clarify the moral dimension of our statist ways. But moral philosophy here is handmaiden to political philosophy. I do not aim to persuade the individual to find or affirm certain moral outlooks or personal habits. I aim to persuade members of the polity to change government policy. One of the most important, if subterranean, arguments for changing government policy, however, is that doing so affects individuals' moral outlooks and personal habits, which in turn affects. . . .

CLARIFYING LIBERTY AND INDIVIDUAL RESPONSIBILITY

My usage of *liberty* has a common recognition and acceptance. By liberty, I refer to private-property rights, consent, and contract. By private-property rights, consent, and contract, I mean what traditional common-law conventions have meant. Of course, there are gray areas here—what is the precise scope of private-property rights? what of implicit terms in agreements?—and one must consider the senile, children, and other hard cases. But as a famous jurist once said, that there is a dusk does not mean there is no night and no day. Some things are gray, but most are either black or white. Despite its areas of ambiguity, the principle of liberty is cogent and well established. In the United States, it is most consistently and most completely advocated by the libertarian movement. National and state policies that clearly encroach on the principle of liberty include drug prohibition, drug prescription requirements, drug approval requirements, restrictions on sexual services, licensing restrictions, wage and price controls, health and safety regulations of private-sector affairs, antitrust policies, import restrictions, laws against discrimination in private-sector affairs, and gun control. On the truly local level, such policies might be viewed as acceptable because we might grant town government the status of contract, as for a proprietary community. The point here is not that liberty is everywhere good and desirable, only that it is reasonably cogent.

Let us think of liberty as conceptually distinct from individual responsibility. Libertarians often speak in terms of the liberty dimension, disregarding the responsibility dimension. The point is familiar with respect to the welfare issue. The taxes, which libertarians deem an encroachment on liberty, are only part of the complaint. Suppose that instead of our current national and state welfare systems, we had the following: governments at the national and state levels continued to collect the same taxes but instead of providing welfare payments, they gathered all the tax dollars into a huge paper mountain, doused it with gasoline, and set it on fire. This hypothetical arrangement encroaches on liberty just as much as the existing system does. Libertarians may instinctually prefer the bonfire, but they cannot explain this preference with reference to the liberty dimension. The government distribution of welfare payments is itself objectionable, and for reasons aside from government ineptitude. The difference between the welfare system and the bonfire lies in the dimension of responsibility.

We can analyze government policy better by distinguishing liberty from individual responsibility. The dole is one thing: that the dole is financed by confiscatory taxation is another. Historically and practically, however, liberty and individual responsibility are intertwined. They are, especially, morally intertwined.

"Individual responsibility" means accountability; more specifically, it means government-administered systems of accountability for citizens. Both liberty and individual responsibility, then, pertain to the citizens' relationships with government. Hence, in my usage, one citizen's crime against another is not an encroachment on liberty, and the practices of a philanthropic organization, even if arbitrary, are not departures from individual responsibility. I shall sometimes abbreviate "individual responsibility" as just "responsibility."

Think of liberty and responsibility as one-dimensional continuous variables. For the sake of setting the benchmark, we can describe the absolute liberty and absolute responsibility that constitute the Libertarian Utopia. Absolute liberty would be the freedom of private-property rights, consent, and contract among private parties. Government would maintain and enforce the legal order and not burden citizens with tax levies beyond those necessary to pay for these protective services. This arrangement is the classical Nightwatchman State, the utopia of Wilhelm von Humboldt, Frederic Bastiat, Herbert Spencer, William Graham Sumner, Albert Jay Nock, and other classical liberals. Here the government holds people accountable for their transgressions of private-property rights, consent, and contract—punishing criminals, enforcing restitution where possible, and adjudicating a thick-skinned tort doctrine—but it provides no other benefits to citizens. (Again I hedge on the question of local government because local government services beyond the Nightwatchman functions may occupy a gray area between ordinary contract and state power.) In the Libertarian Utopia, summarized in the middle column of figure 1, the variables "liberty" and "individual responsibility" both have their extreme values.

Departure from responsibility—indulgence—takes various forms, as summarized in the first column of the figure. In interactions between citizens and government, government acts with indulgence when it gives benefits to citizens—welfare payments, medical care, housing, schooling, freeways, and so on. In its policing of interaction among private parties, government engages in indulgence in making inadequate punishment of criminals (meaning burglars, not pot dealers). In its adjudication of civil disputes, government engages in in-

	INDULGENCE Departures from Responsibility	LIBERTARIAN UTOPIA Nightwatchman State	COERCION Departures from Liberty
Govt. Practice in Govt.- individual Interaction	welfare-state benefits; free govt. services	taxation to finance the nightwatchman state	confiscatory taxation; conscription
Govt. Practice toward Private Activity	inadequate punishment of consent violators	freedom for consensual and protections from nonconsensual activities	restrictions, regulations, or prohibitions on consensual activities
Govt. Practice in Civil Disputes	frivolous awards to plaintiffs; failure to make judgments against malfeasant defendants	thick- skinned tort doctrine	frivolous awards to judgments; failure to make awards to aggrieved plaintiffs

FIGURE 1. Departures from responsibility and from liberty, in relation to the
libertarian utopia

dulgence by failing to make tort judgments against truly malfeasant defendants
or by making tort awards to frivolous plaintiffs, for example, in liability, discrimination, or sexual harassment suits beyond the bounds of a thick-skinned
tort doctrine.

Encroachment of liberty—coercion—takes the forms of confiscatory taxation (in excess of funding the Nightwatchman), conscription, any kind of restric-
tion on consensual private activity, excessive punishment of criminals or detainment of suspected criminals, making frivolous judgments against defendants in
civil disputes, and failing to make tort awards to truly aggrieved plaintiffs in civil
disputes. (Again, these delineations apply in the context of state and national
government; at the level of truly local government, the contours of liberty and
individual responsibility are much fuzzier.)

Having clarified the concepts of liberty and responsibility, let us now consider
their interdependence.

INTERACTION BETWEEN LIBERTY AND INDIVIDUAL RESPONSIBILITY

Government must be small and circumspect if society is to enjoy a high degree of liberty and a high degree of individual responsibility. To explain the magnitudes of these two variables in terms of the people's general attitude toward government—by whether or not they view it as wise and efficacious—we might say that liberty and responsibility vary together because they depend alike on the popular attitude toward government. Where people distrust government, they choose politically to have much liberty and much responsibility. A serious shortcoming of this approach, however, is that most people lack cogent views in political philosophy. Rather, their views on public issues are, if existent at all, superficial, inconsistent, piecemeal, and highly fickle.

Taking a more marginalist approach to the interaction of liberty and responsibility (economists might call it "comparative statics"), one asks: How do marginal encroachments on liberty affect responsibility? And how do departures from responsibility affect liberty? I shall briefly mention the more obvious connections only, then take up some subtler morals-based connections.

Before proceeding, however, we should acknowledge another dynamic: diminutions of liberty today can lead to further diminutions of liberty tomorrow, and likewise for responsibility. Recognized aspects of this dynamic include the slippery slope, the force of precedent—"How come they have protection from discrimination and we don't? How come they get subsidies and we don't?"—lock-in and status quo biases in government policy, the prehensile government agency, the ratchet effect, and the intervention dynamic (Mises 1978, 75ff.). These factors help to explain how liberty and responsibility, each as a historical variable, undergo self-reinforcing changes—hence the famous saying of the Revolutionary Era about eternal vigilance being the price of liberty. A fuller treatment of how liberty and responsibility evolve through time would include discussion of these recursive processes. Here the focus is on how liberty and responsibility influence one another over time.

Much of the connection is direct and obvious. Welfare benefits and free government services, listed in the left column of figure 1, must be paid for by confiscatory taxation, listed in the right column. A similar direct symmetry appears in the bottom row, with regard to government practice in civil disputes: frivolous awards to plaintiffs imply frivolous judgments against defendants.

Other connections flow from the political economy of the matter. Commentators often point out the public-charge connection between diminished responsibility and diminished liberty. If taxpayers pay the doctor bills for repairing the motorcyclist's fractured skull, then there is a reason beyond paternalism for requiring him to wear a helmet. This argument arises often, in matters ranging from drug use to schooling. Hayek (1960, 286) not only acknowledged the point, he employed it in calling for a requirement that individuals purchase insurance for "old age, unemployment, sickness, etc." (though he opposed a unitary government institution). Thus, by accepting restricted individual responsibility as a premise, Hayek concluded by endorsing an encroachment on liberty.[1] The same dynamic appears in the argument that immigration must be curtailed because the newcomers expand the costs of welfare programs.

Other political-economy connections also exist. In *The Road to Serfdom* (1944) Hayek explains that government planning necessitates encroachments on liberty and departures from responsibility, as the planning promotes the breakdown of the rule of law and the expansion of arbitrary government. Thus, "the more the state 'plans,' the more difficult planning becomes for the individual" (76). Government's operation of the school system, for example, may well lead to restrictions on private schooling, in order to keep "the plan" viable. Government often favors its indulgence programs by hobbling the competition.[2] Thus, departures from responsibility lead to encroachments on liberty. Another connection ties the breakdown of the tort system to the rise of regulation (Wildavsky 1988, chaps. 4, 8) with a dynamic that results in an encroachment on liberty. In general, a breakdown of the rule of law leads to encroachments on liberty. Once individual responsibility loses force, liberty can turn into a riot of license. A stark example is the curfew imposed during actual urban riots. The influence runs in the opposite direction as well: restrictions on liberty cause poverty or the suppression of voluntary institutions, leading to government programs to supply what has been suppressed.

Clearly, liberty and responsibility exhibit acute fragilities, vulnerabilities, and instabilities. Yet none of the foregoing considerations takes into account the moral dimension, where we find an affinity between the morality of indulgence and the morality of coercion.

A SHIP OF SELVES, BUT A SINGLE CAPTAIN

Thomas Schelling (1984, chaps. 3, 4) has portrayed the individual as a bundle of multiple selves, often in conflict. Schelling describes how one self can foil another by acting strategically. The long-term self that wants to quit smoking might foil a short-term self by flushing the unsmoked cigarettes down the toilet. The long-term self that wants to keep his wife makes heartfelt promises to be more attentive. We all experience regrets and the tribulations of self-command. Is each of us merely a bundle of ephemeral impulses ever struggling among themselves for control without an inner judge? I think not.

For when we reflect on our behavior, we may find it coherent, even spiritually moving. Certain impulses receive inner support or admiration. Thus, it may be that when we are tranquil, our true self, an inward eye, tries to sort out who we are and who we ought to be.

If only it were so. For when we examine the inward eye—with an eye yet further inward?—we find that it also is multiple and constantly in self-conflict. Our most personal reflections, most searching judgments, most decided resolutions are—yet more impulses! Perhaps the impulse to smoke belongs to a dual long-term self that wants to be the being that certain exciting achievements enable him to be, and those achievements can come only from the steady nerves that smoking a cigarette produces. Perhaps the impulse to neglect one's wife belongs to a dual long-term self that wants ample freedom to pursue dangerous adventures, to complicate and enrich life's loves. Even our thoughts are actions of a sort, carried out by impulses or selves. True, they are impulses operating at a deeper level, perhaps with a powerful influence over whole sets of shallower impulses, yet somewhat alien and suspect nonetheless. We cannot escape bitter struggle and sorrow even within the deepest level of consciousness.

Must we endure an amoral existence, the product of a mere struggle of opposing forces based on historical contingency, none worthier than the rest? No heroes to root for, no romances to experience, just hungers in conflict and transient gratifications?

Perhaps not. First of all, no one ever said transient. Some sentiments breathe and rejoice for a lifetime.

As for worthiness, even here we need not surrender. If consciousness, even in its farthest reaches, cannot reveal to us reliable indications of the worthy, let alone the worthiness algorithm itself, we still have the subconscious. After all, the conscious must emerge from somewhere. Even within economic philosophy, Michael Polanyi (1958) tells of tacit or inarticulate knowledge, which forms the roots of our ideas and the basis of our beliefs, and Israel Kirzner (1985, chap. 2) describes entrepreneurial discovery, a component of human action beyond mere choice-making.

But in the realm of tacit knowledge and the subconscious, do we again find multiplicity and conflict, a lack of unitary essence telling us what is worthy? Must we reach yet farther to satisfy our yearning for a sense of worthiness that guides our actions and gives meaning to our lives? How do we ever come to say that a story has a moral?

In the end, we come to a fundamental question of existence, to which the answer must be action, not explanation. Time to act. If we must, let us believe in the soul. If the soul does not exist, let us invent it. A sense of worthiness is itself worthy. I simply affirm that I belong—my soul belongs—to the force for affirming the sense of worthiness and meaning. Happily, you belong to that force, too.

The ship of selves, then, is in the hands of a multitude of crew members, each trying to pull the ship's course this way or that—or neglecting it altogether—to satisfy its special limited desire. But the ship's course results not merely from this diffuse process of conflict and negotiation among crew members. There is a captain, too. Though he keeps to his cabin below deck, he works his influence on the crew members. Some he feeds; others he starves. Some he tutors into new becomings, refining them to specialized tasks for specialized moments. He cajoles and disciplines, hoping to get them to work together. He is constant. He wills but one thing. He has a destiny, ever distant, and he strives to manage the crew so as to follow the course that now seems to him best calculated to make his approach. He is neither Good nor Bad; he simply is. His being makes things good or bad. He judges worthiness and he gives meaning to the journey.

Some may rejoin, "What a plush tale you tell! And what makes it so? What evidence can you give? You offer us mere myth."

Myth indeed, but better a myth than a vacuum. For this myth is worthy. And I doubt that anyone will dispute its worthiness.

The plea is to try always to end on a note of hope of character integration. Figure 2 shows the spiral of disintegration and reintegration of character. On top are notions of the integrated self. The arrows on the right side bring the disintegrative challenges of multiplicity and inner conflict. The arrows on the left side affirm a deeper resolution, restoring integration. The spiral shows the soul as the limit, impossible to reach or reveal, and shows that being human has two sides: one to be accepted candidly for the reality it is, the other affirmed and made real by hope, struggle, and pain.[3]

I use the metaphor of the ship crew to represent self-multiplicity and conflict at one level, and that of the ship captain to embody the integrative force of a deeper, encompassing self. This crew-captain relationship is recursive; hence "the captain" is not the soul, but merely the hope of progression to character integration and, for the time being, resolution.

SELF-ESTEEM, SELF-RESPECT, AND DIGNITY

The feeling of self-esteem is one of good cheer among the crew in action, of solidarity among themselves, of satisfaction and pride in the ship they serve. It often comes from outward recognition of achievements to their credit. Although self-esteem comes from positive reinforcement, the feeling is always somewhat illusory, for self-satisfaction naturally fuels self-striving. Self-esteem occurs at the

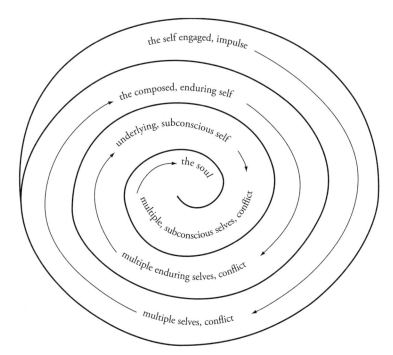

FIGURE 2. The spiral of the self: disintegration and reintegration of character

shallow levels of the ship of self, and fluctuates with the ebb and flow of achievement and recognition. A compliment from an admired soul will send it soaring; a criticism or rejection will make it sink.

Self-respect runs deeper. John Rawls (1971) speaks of two aspects of self-respect. "First of all, … it includes a person's sense of his own values, his secure conviction that his conception of the good, his plan of life, is worth carrying out. And second, self-respect implies a confidence in one's ability, so far as it is within one's power, to fulfill one's intentions" (440). We might interpret as follows: First, self-respect requires a feeling that one has a coherent moral force within oneself, that the judging faculty—the captain—exists. Second, self-respect requires hope among the crew that the captain can maintain his command and keep his mission alive. Together these two elements cause the crew to respect the captain. Out of respect, a crew member will sacrifice himself in response to the captain's will. Personal responsibility is a corollary of self-respect.[4]

But a respectful crew member does not always feel good cheer in his work. There can be respect without esteem. The crew member might question, negotiate, or even rebel. Inner conflict, turmoil, and inconsistency belong to a process of regeneration of the crew, a process of self-search and self-creation. "A foolish consistency is the hobgoblin of little minds" (Emerson 1951, 41). The captain's will to travel ever onward might mean that some crew members who have served their function must now be disposed of, and they, being habits of the mind and the heart, will resist. Inconsistency, disappointment, disillusionment, and pain accompany self-search, the process of reaching back to find a deeper understanding that will reconcile or resolve conflict. The search may yield the disappointing discovery of one's limitations—so some crew members in charge of hope must die—or the terrifying resolution that the hopes can live but only by the grueling sacrificial slayings of other parts that are old and dear. From the search for self-respect comes both gratification and despair.

A steady feeling of self-esteem, or satisfaction, is not possible for the normal aspiring person, so it is not any sort of ideal. Unflagging self-respect may be an ideal, but self-respect is an attitude about oneself projected inward, so it is not generally possible or even meaningful for an observer to gauge self-respect in others. Self-respect remains very personal and individual. Individuality makes like actions differ among individuals; in each case the action plays a unique role in a unique story. Self-respect is a question not only of our own voyages but of our own destinations.

The observer cannot peer into the private ocean of another, but the observer can gauge the extent to which someone comports himself in relations with others so as to afford himself self-respect. In a word, we can form an idea of the extent to which the individual comports himself with dignity. Dignity is a social phenomenon. It is not about how one behaves in the exclusive company of oneself, but about one's outward behavior in relations with others.

We value dignity in our fellows because their example and standard aid us in behaving with dignity ourselves, which helps us to respect ourselves. By behaving with dignity, we take possession of ourselves, sort out our impulses, measure the worthiness of one impulse against another, clean ship if necessary, and on the whole give ourselves a more coherent and enduring sense of mission. The captain nourishes the crew members, but he is nourished in turn by them.

Let us place dignity then in the footlights along with liberty and responsibility. Dignity measures a certain quality in the behavior of the members of the society. That quality has two aspects: first, the extent to which they guard their own self-respect, or preserve their own dignity, in their social behavior; second, the extent to which they accommodate the self-respect of others, or preserve the dignity of others with whom they interact.

In preserving our own dignity, each of us says:

My struggles are a necessary part of me, emerging from my personal drama. You may hear a crew member indicating a desire to be treated in a belittled fashion, but now I indicate that I will welcome no such treatment. I have validity and method in my being; don't tread on me. My drama is mine. I am its author and judge. I create its meaning. By showing self-possession, I show that I possess my story, and therefore you do not. It is my property, and you have no right to use it for your purposes except with my welcome and consent, in which case I make interaction with you part of my being.

In preserving our own dignity, we affirm the myth of the captain and his mission. We oppose those who would use our being without due regard for our own story, our own meaning. In preserving dignity, we oppose those who would demean us by denying, disdaining, or belittling the captain, the integrative moral force, of our being.

In acting so as to preserve the dignity of others, we presume that the individual is conducting his affairs as he sees fit, no matter how mad the method may seem. We respect his individuality. We do not dwell on, pity, or patronize someone's apparent weakness or disadvantage. We do not attempt to rescue when no rescue has been sought. We do not judge or even draw attention to, except insofar as doing so is a part of the relationship the other has willfully entered into. We honor an ethic of MYOB—Mind Your Own Business. We in no way question the captain's judgment or his command. Acting so as to preserve the dignity of others might also be called acting with common decency.

The relationship between the two aspects of societywide dignity—guarding one's own self-respect and accommodating the self-respect of others—will not be considered here, but it would seem that the two go hand in hand, based on a sense of universal human likeness, or brotherhood.

Although liberty and individual responsibility have been defined narrowly within relations involving government, the same political orientation does not hold for the definition of societal dignity. I am considering dignity as exhibited by individuals throughout society, in all sorts of social interaction.

Dignity is a worthy goal for a political or social movement, perhaps the worthiest. But my present goal is not to celebrate dignity or to recommend a plan for its achievement. Rather, I have introduced dignity to show the moral mechanism linking liberty and responsibility. If liberty and responsibility each has a reflexive relationship with dignity, then they have a reflexive relationship with each other.

THE INTERDEPENDENCE OF DIGNITY AND LIBERTY

If the individual consists of multiple selves, the question arises: Should the government protect Dr. Jekyll from Mr. Hyde, just as it protects the innocent citizen from the criminal? If the individual is multiple, then in a way his actions are not so personal after all. One self imposes an externality on other selves, and externalities raise the issue of whether the government ought to intervene. Americans commonly make the assumption that intervention is called for with regard to opium use, gambling, Social Security, safety issues, suicide, and many other matters.

But the support for paternalism rests not only on the notion of the multiple self but on the presumption that the conflict among the selves represents a sort of moral collapse. It is rather analogous to butting into a domestic dispute. A married couple needs to learn how to respect and tolerate one another, their dispute belonging to the drama of their marriage. In the case of the multiple self, the paternalist solution can make sense only once the hope for self-respect is lost. The paternalist presumes that the crew has taken over the ship, that all respect for the captain is lost and the crew no longer responsive to him. Dignity is gone. It is time, reasons the paternalist, to sacrifice liberty, too.

Thus, low societal dignity leads to coercion. The less the citizen preserves his own dignity, the less it makes sense to say that he acts in keeping with the captain's mission. Such doubt about individuals' mastery over their own behavior is manifest in the war on smoking waged by U.S. Commissioner of Food and Drugs David Kessler. He views the decision to smoke as resting in the hands of tobacco companies. Owing to their practices, he says, "Most smokers are in effect deprived of the choice to stop smoking." Part of the reason Kessler is prepared to doubt the dignity of the people is that, in fact, their dignity is not as high as it might be. For example, John Gravett (1993) wrote a magazine column titled "Life-Long Smokers Should Welcome Hillary's 'Nico-Tax.'" Gravett declares that the First Lady's tax hike of two dollars per pack "will surely bolster my resolve to quit." "I, like so many other life-long smokers, am only waiting for a good enough reason to quit once and for all" (54). Rather than searching as an adult to come to terms with his habit, Gravett glibly asks that he (and all other smokers) be treated as a helpless child. Citizens such as Gravett lend truth and legitimacy to Kessler's presumptions.

Low societal dignity motivates Kessler's actions in another sense, too. Dignity has two sides. Kessler himself reflects low societal dignity in the sense that he is loath to preserve the dignity of others by accommodating the self-respect of smokers.

Kessler's attitude typifies what Thomas Szasz calls the therapeutic state (1963, 212–22; 1990, 253–61). Viewing personal behavior in terms of health and medical conditions, agents of the therapeutic state quickly attribute an individual's troublesome impulse to forces outside his moral being. Rather than seeing the impulse as a test of the captain's mastery over his crew, they see it as a sea monster that has attacked the ship and now must be cast off. Viewing the problem as caused by an alien force, they fancy themselves saviors stepping in to subdue the alien by restricting its powers. Rather than viewing the enjoyment of gambling, opium, or tobacco as growing out of and belonging to the being of the individual, they view it as an "addiction," an illness or disease that, like the mumps or smallpox, has descended on the individual and now warrants "treatment." Insofar as the prohibitionists regard the "illness" as a permanent constitutional condition, a "sick" part of the being, their coercive ways signal their disdain for the validity of the captain.

If eroded dignity promotes erosions of liberty, so too does eroded liberty promote erosions of dignity. Paternalist prohibitions and restrictions flatly tell the individual: "You are not competent to choose fully; we must circumscribe your choice." As Isaiah Berlin (1969b) puts it, "To manipulate men, to propel them toward goals which you—the social reformer—see, but they may not, is to deny their human essence, to treat them as objects without wills of their own, and therefore to degrade them" (149). Paternalism very plainly declares that the captain is invalid or incompetent.

Thus, the individual is invited to play the role of a child, unable to manage himself and unqualified to judge for himself. The individual must either accept the role set out for him or willfully resist the culture that presses him into that role. Such resistance can be psychologically arduous. In the culture of paternalism, the childlike role creeps up on the citizenry, compromising their dignity. Individuals begin to surrender the romantic idea that the captain is the source and author of one's own meaning. Hence, paternalist encroachments work to demean the individual's existence. This is the most tragic consequence of paternalism. Although the demeaning of individuals is a very important human consequence, rarely is it even noted in policy debates over drugs, Social Security, occupational licensing, and similar issues.

With the affront to dignity comes a loss of personal responsibility and self-possession. Berlin (1969a) explains:

> For if I am not so recognized, then I may fail to recognize, I may doubt, my own claim to be a fully independent human being. For what I am is, in large part, determined by what I feel and think; and what I feel and think is determined by the feeling and thought prevailing in the society to which I belong. (157)

Psychological research supports Berlin's claim (Rosenthal and Jacobson 1968; Merton 1957, 430–36). Paternalism demeans its subjects and becomes a self-fulfilling prophecy.

Paternalism demeans people in other ways as well. It treads on individuality. The habit of gambling, drug use, or leaving seat belts unbuckled may not even be a personal problem, a point of inner conflict. Many people roll the dice, snort, or smoke in moderation; they have no misgivings whatever about their actions. Yet paternalism tells them that the activity is bad, and therefore demands that everyone fit a common mold. "But I am an individual; I have made myself unique," responds the miscreant. Again, resistance is psychologically arduous and, weary of resisting, the individual succumbs and dignity suffers.

Paternalism also damages dignity by the brutality of enforcement. Even those who successfully reject the morality and culture of paternalism may taste the bitterness of enforcement. Detainment, questioning, handcuffing, strip searching, and imprisonment are brutal, dehumanizing experiences and, whatever one's political views, bound to challenge one's belief in one's own mastery over existence.

As Lord Acton's maxim reminds us, power tends to corrupt. Paternalist encroachment damages dignity also by rehearsing the paternalist in denying dignity to others. Coercing people at one place now, the paternalist learns to treat them with small regard for their self-respect and so becomes more inclined to coerce them at another place later. Aside from the moral corruption of the public official, the corruption works on the public at large. Most of the popular support for paternalist coercions lies in the notion that those other people need to be protected from themselves. By supporting paternalist prohibitions, we develop a habit of demeaning our fellow citizens. Thus some might say that David Kessler and his supporters suffer from an addiction, that Kessler's moral corruption issues from his "coercion dependency."

Liberty and dignity complement one another. Their mutual dependence helps to explain why the price of liberty is vigilance. Encroach on liberty this morning and you cause an erosion of dignity this afternoon, which itself will generate a new encroachment on liberty tomorrow, and so on. If we neglect this multiplier effect, we are apt to underestimate the hazards of coercion.

THE INTERDEPENDENCE OF DIGNITY AND INDIVIDUAL RESPONSIBILITY

During the 1992 Los Angeles riots, trucker Reginald Denny was dragged from the cab of his truck and beaten. As he lay prone on the street, Damian Williams bounded forward and hurled a block of concrete at his head. The videotape showed that the block was thrown with such force that it bounced off Denny's skull. At Williams's trial, the jury acquitted him of attempted murder because "he was caught up in mob violence." Williams's stay in prison did not last longer than four years. Those convicted of murder nowadays stay in prison, on average, for five and a half years. (In 2003, Williams was sentenced to life in prison for a 2000 murder.)

The jury might rationalize its decision: How can we punish Dr. Jekyll for the deeds of Mr. Hyde? We are loath to see the actions of a Damian Williams as part of an integrated moral force, to hold accountable all his impulses, including the Dr. Jekylls, for the action of a Mr. Hyde. Williams is like a child, and just as we don't accord full liberty to children, we don't put children in prison. After all, Los Angeles was suddenly transformed, the riot a whole new experience. How is one to know how to control himself in astoundingly new situations? Like a child glee-fully dropping stones from a balcony, Williams was overcome by the thrill and the turmoil. Heavy punishment would be unfair.

The discounting of dignity now pervades the criminal justice system. Lawyers invoke all manner of syndromes, disorders, and mental illnesses to argue that the defendant is not fully human, that an alien force seized his person, making the human being a mere host. California has no Department of Punishment, but a Department of Corrections. The offender is not treated as an integrated moral force that has desecrated the civil order; he is an incompetent, defective, self-con-tradictory moral force that needs correcting. He is not fully human and therefore should not be held fully to account. Indeed, the less dignity the citizens actually have, the more plausible this view becomes.

We seem sometimes to deny all human conflict and instead pretend that a sus-tainable, happy, official cooperation exists. First we deny inner conflict, regarding troublesome impulses as the result of alien "illnesses" or external circumstances. Then we deny the conflict between the offender and society, abnegating punish-ment for "caring" and "correction." As Thomas Szasz (1990) says, "We appear un-able or [un]willing to accept the reality of human conflict. It is never simply man who offends against his fellow man: someone or something—the Devil, mental illness—intervenes, to obscure, excuse, and explain away man's terrifying inhu-manity to man" (239). Do we cast ourselves as "caring" and "correcting" in order to deny the conflict within our own breast? Does it testify to our humanity or our hypocrisy that punishment goes out of fashion?

The diminishment of societal dignity erodes individual responsibility and, in turn, the diminishment of responsibility further erodes dignity. The authorities tell the criminal: "We are not going to punish you. You are blameless for what happened. You did not have the power to prevent it. It happened to you. You are a victim of circumstances." The criminal is invited to play the role of a moral invalid.

Instead, to preserve the criminal's dignity, the authorities would say: "What you have done is intolerable to us. You must be punished. That's who we are, and that's who you are. You might change who you are, but that is your business." Then the criminal might come to terms and search his soul for penance.

Danish writer Henrik Stangerup tells a tale of a demeaned society in his novel *The Man Who Wanted to Be Guilty* (1982), set in a dystopian Therapeutic State where "it's always the circumstances that dictate our actions." People there have adequate comfort, ample leisure time, and "insurances from head to toe," but no individual responsibility. When trouble arises, citizens call the Helpers, who correct the situation, sometimes with red and green pills. The character Torben is bored and disgusted with life, especially with "the ease with which everybody surrendered to the system." He and his wife had always considered themselves underground dissidents, resisters who would rear their son to know a different ethic. But their spirits have been weakening, especially hers. One evening the crisis of identity erupts in a bitter dispute between them. He recognizes her resignation and foresees a future of meaningless tedium. He becomes drunk and abusive. She calls for the Helpers. He beats her to death.

The last stitch of self-respect Torben could possibly retain lay in being held guilty of his action. But the Helpers tell him that "punishment and guilt are not concepts we use any more." They will care for his future. In Torben's world, the absence of individual responsibility causes such extreme demeaning that the only way for the hero to proclaim his dignity is to fight for his own guilt and punishment. That is his last chance to affirm the myth of the captain. The novel is a study of affirming one's dignity even when it requires the complete sacrifice of happiness.

Refusing to punish demeans the innocent as well as the guilty. "Pardoning the bad is injuring the good," says Benjamin Franklin. The good stop feeling pride in their behavior when they see the bad indulged. "Maybe they're not bad after all. But then I am no longer good. So why am I bothering?" Indulgence of criminals sends a message of moral emptiness to one and all: "Be not ashamed or proud, for if the captain exists at all he is inane and absurd. Your moral precepts are mere myths."

Indulgence carries the same message when it takes the form of welfare-state benefits. Government dispenses aid in an anonymous and arbitrary manner. The benefactors are taxpayers, forced to pay. Without voluntary contribution, there can be no gratitude; without gratitude, no generosity. No reciprocity comes about, just a doling out from above. This kind of relationship signifies moral emptiness: the faceless state provides for you regardless of your behavior; no one will ask whether you deserve your benefits. Thence arises the ethic of entitlement. With respect to education and many health benefits, government programs rest on the presumption that individuals or parents cannot care for their own needs or those of their families.

Before creation of the welfare state in America, when mutual aid was pervasive, one of the chief organs of the mutual-aid movement, *The Fraternal Monitor*, decried the rise of government welfare programs: "The problem of State pensions strikes at the root of national life and character. It destroys the thought of individual responsibility" (21 January 1908; cited in Beito 1990, 720). Welfare benefits place the recipient in the role of helpless supplicant, and the self-reliant person in the role of sucker. Again, pardoning the bad is injuring the good. In contrast, mutual aid rests on reciprocity and the refined use of superior local information. The member down on his luck receives assistance, knowing that it is temporary and given for specific reasons communally recognized as "hard luck." He is not demeaned. The institution would not render assistance to a member if he were "undeserving" (Beito 1990, 1993).

If welfare-state indulgence demeans recipients, it also springs from a collapse of dignity. As Berlin (1969a) observes, "Specific forms of the deterministic hypothesis have played an arresting, if limited, role in altering our views of human responsibility" (73). "Structuralism" has always been a major theme of reformers, from Jacob Riis to the New Deal, the Great Society, and most recently Midnight Basketball (Murray 1984, 24–40). In his 1890 tract for housing reform, *How the Other Half Lives*, Riis described tenement buildings and neighborhoods as though the physical structures themselves made residents miserable. Calling for expanded welfare statism in his 1962 *The Other America*, Michael Harrington blamed poverty on "the system." Welfare statists attribute misfortune to "society," "capitalism," "the economy," "patriarchy," "greed," and so on but rarely to the individual experiencing it. Again, as in the case of David Kessler's attitudes toward smokers, the attribution has some truth and justification. As individuals surrender their dignity, they lose ground as authors of their own existence. How can one argue with individuals who say, "Please help me, my captain has fallen overboard and drowned"? Low societal dignity leads to increases in welfare-state indulgences. In a paper titled "Hazardous Welfare-State Dynamics" (1995), the Swedish economist Assar Lindbeck argues that the entitlement ethic expands the dole and the dole enhances the entitlement ethic. This thesis also conforms to the view of Gordon Tullock (1995) that the growth of government since the 1930s has been a phenomenon of "Bismarkism," or welfare-statism.

INTERDEPENDENCIES ILLUSTRATED

If, on the one hand, liberty and dignity are interdependent and, on the other hand, dignity and responsibility are interdependent, then liberty and responsibility are interdependent by way of dignity.

Across the top of figure 3 are the connections between Responsibility and Liberty that involve not morals but the dynamics of political economy discussed briefly at the beginning of this chapter. Below are the connections that involve moral dynamics, working through Dignity. Diminished Liberty causes diminished Dignity. Diminished Dignity points straight back to further diminished Liberty, and to diminished Responsibility. Diminished Responsibility works its effects in similar fashion.

If we were to posit a sudden exogenous shock to Responsibility, the result would be substantial first-round blows to Liberty and Dignity, and then secondary or multiplier effects bouncing through the system. We can illustrate the point with another figure.

Of the connections shown in figure 3, consider only those that point in a clockwise direction: Liberty is a function of Responsibility, which is a function of Dignity, which is a function of Liberty.

Now consider the model shown in figure 4. On the morning of Day 1, Liberty checks the magnitude of Responsibility, and that evening adjusts itself to that magnitude according to the wiggly positively sloped line in the northeast quadrant of the figure. On the morning of Day 2, Dignity checks the magnitude of Liberty, and that evening adjusts itself to that magnitude according to the positively sloped line in the northwest quadrant. This adjusted level of Dignity is

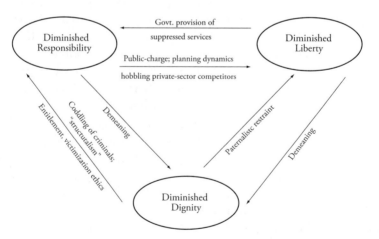

FIGURE 3. Interdependencies between liberty, dignity, and responsibility

reflected from axis to axis in the southwest quadrant; that quadrant is merely a mirror. On the morning of Day 3, Responsibility checks the magnitude of Dignity, and that evening adjusts itself to that magnitude according to the positively sloped line in the southeast quadrant. Now we've gone full circle, and Liberty is ready again to adjust to Responsibility.

At point A the system is in stable equilibrium. If we pass through the system beginning from point R_A on the Responsibility axis, we keep coming back to point A. Now suppose that somehow an exogenous event causes Responsibility to drop from R_A to R_Y. Liberty and Dignity would drop as well, but as the system cycled, eventually it would return to point A. (The exogenous shock is assumed, implausibly, to last only one period.) It is possible that wounds will heal.

But wounds can also fester and become gangrenous. Suppose that an exogenous event, say, the provision of universal governmental Social Security pensions, were to shift Responsibility from R_A to R_X. In this case, as we work through the system we do not move back to A, but rather sink further and further until finally we settle at point B. The initial blow to Responsibility amounts to the distance

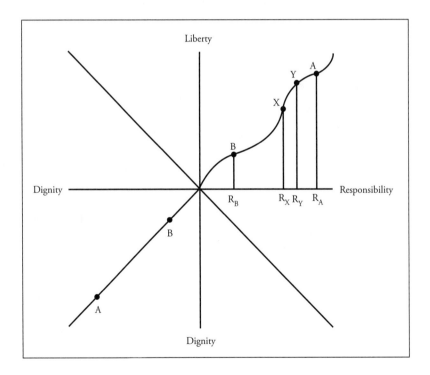

FIGURE 4. Dynamics of liberty, dignity, and responsibility.

between R_X and R_A, the secondary or multiplier effects to the distance between R_B and R_X. We have stumbled onto the slippery slope, and ultimately are stuck in a system with low Responsibility, low Liberty, and low Dignity.

WHAT HAS AMERICA BECOME?

Alexis de Tocqueville perceptively described the American character (outside the slave states) in the 1830s. His description probably continued to fit pretty well right up to the twentieth century. Much that he described Americans might well hope to shed: the naïveté, the insensibility to art and refinement, the repression of sensual and aesthetic delights, the fervent religiosity, the sanctimony, the bounderism, the oppressive conformism. But what of the goodwill, the hope, the self-reliance, the pride in oneself? Only by straining can we see in Americans today the following characteristics de Tocqueville ([1835/1840] 1945) saw in the 1830s:

> [A]s soon as the young American approaches manhood, the ties of filial obedience are relaxed day by day; master of his thoughts, he is soon master of his conduct.... [T]he son looks forward to the exact period at which he will be his own master, and he enters upon his freedom without precipitation and without effort, as a possession which is his own and which no one seeks to wrest from him.... In America there is, strictly speaking, no adolescence: at the close of boyhood the man appears and begins to trace out his own path. (2:202–3)

> Long before an American girl arrives at the marriageable age, her emancipation from maternal control begins; she has scarcely ceased to be a child when she already thinks for herself, speaks with freedom, and acts on her own impulse.... [T]he vices and dangers of society are early revealed to her; as she sees them clearly, she views them without illusion and braves them without fear, for she is full of reliance on her own strength, and her confidence seems to be shared by all around her.... Instead, then, of inculcating mistrust of herself, they constantly seek to enhance her confidence in her own strength and character. (2:209–10)

> In the United States, as soon as a man has acquired some education and pecuniary resources, either he endeavors to get rich by commerce or industry, or he buys land in the uncleared country and turns pioneer. All that he asks of the state is not to be disturbed in his toil and to be secure in his earnings. (2:263)

When a private individual meditates an undertaking, however directly connected it may be with the welfare of society, he never thinks of soliciting the cooperation of the government; but he publishes his plan, offers to execute it, courts the assistance of other individuals, and struggles manfully against all obstacles. (1:98)

When an American asks for the cooperation of his fellow citizens, it is seldom refused; and I have often seen it afforded spontaneously, and with great goodwill. (2:185)

[I]n no country does crime more rarely elude punishment. The reason is that everyone conceives himself to be interested in furnishing evidence of the crime and in seizing the delinquent. (1:99)

In the United States professions are more or less laborious, more or less profitable; but they are never either high or low: every honest calling is honorable. (2:162)

In the United States hardly anybody talks of the beauty of virtue, but they maintain that virtue is useful and prove it every day. (2:129)

Tocqueville saw a people with self-reliance and self-respect. One of the significant themes of his work is that these traits flowed from the fact that American government at the time was small, was decentralized, and permitted much freedom (see esp. vol. 1, chap. 5; vol. 2, bk. 2, chaps. 4–10).

Do Americans today retain these character traits? The Mexican American writer Richard Rodriguez (1994) remarks on the American spirit: "The notion of self-reliance. The notion of re-creation. More and more I'm sensing that that kind of optimism belongs now to immigrants in this country—certainly to the Mexicans that I meet—and less and less so to the native-born" (36).

All the talk about the breakdown of character in America indicates more than a passing media fad. The entitlement ethic, victimhood, privileges for minorities (who by one calculation constitute 374 percent of the population),[5] the assault on merit, the stigmatization of stigmatization, the proliferation of psychological "disorders," the medicalization of behavior (Szasz 1963; Peele 1989), the abandonment of guilt and punishment, the deterioration of personal responsibility—all seem to be real, and well along in their institutional entrenchment.

A study of the evolution of character in America would be an enormous, wide-ranging undertaking; the changes during just the past few generations have been stupendous. Nonetheless, sweeping aside so many stupendous things in order to air a hypothesis, I submit that the growth of government—a government that increasingly treats citizens as children—has played an important role, even a leading role, in the decline of character. Figure 5 shows federal government expenditures as a percentage of gross national product from 1850 to 1990 (with the war fiscal years 1918–19 and 1940–45 omitted). From the 5 percent range in 1930, it has climbed steadily (excluding the war years) to reach consistently more than 20 percent in recent years. Adding state and local government outlays would bring the total to about 35 percent. This trend mirrors a massive decline in individual responsibility. At the same time, the decline of liberty has been severe and extensive.

If we are to tell stories that begin with important historical moments, looking to changes in government policy is more plausible than looking to spontaneous changes in moral character. A significant change in government policy might be devised hastily and driven through to political approval; Robert Higgs (1987) has described how this process often accompanies a national crisis. Moral character is obstinate and resilient, but make no mistake: Over time moral character will be altered.

American politics gradually embraced statism, most notably in the 1930s, and major moral decline occurred with a lag. William Julius Wilson (1987, 3) and oth-

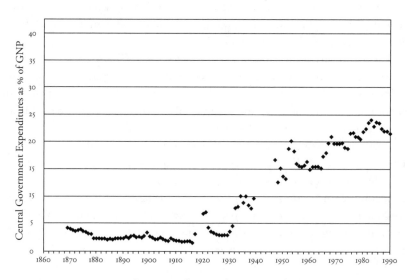

FIGURE 5. Government burgeons beginning in the 1930s.

er scholars have described how, through the 1950s, even in ghetto neighborhoods, common decency, personal responsibility, and public safety remained the norm. Only slowly did erosions of dignity take place, eventually feeding back into indulgence and coercion. Despite short-term fluctuations, it seems safe to say that liberty, dignity, and responsibility have been on a significant slide since the early 1930s and that the problem has become increasingly virulent since the 1960s.

Our problems of declining character have relatively little to do with sexual permissiveness, homosexuality, secularism, paganism, drug use, rock music, rap music, MTV, television violence, Howard Stern, or Hollywood. It is the demeaning of citizens, witnessed and experienced and perpetrated in actual human relations, and legitimized and even celebrated and glorified by officialdom, that really debases and destroys moral character, and that is what the government does on a vast scale with its programs of indulgence and coercion. Moral character is suffocated by the nanny state, which tells us constantly not to believe in ourselves for we are, and will forever remain, children. Such a fate is exactly what Tocqueville's final chapters warn democratic societies against.

A WORD TO FELLOW TRAVELERS

Liberty and individual responsibility are made of the same moral cloth. Both preserve and affirm the dignity of the individual, the myth of self-determination and self-possession, of an integrative self. By corollary, a kinship links coercion, demeaning, and indulgence. The claim by Hayek that opened this essay—that responsibility and liberty go together historically—can be defended by appeal to the moral dimension of the people. If the argument has merit, it might give pause to those who tend to favor one but not the other. The social democrat should fear for personal freedom when supporting programs of indulgence, and the tory-conservative for responsibility when supporting programs of proscription.

A REASONED VIGILANCE FOR A WORTHY MYTH

In *The Devil's Dictionary*, Ambrose Bierce defined liberty as "one of Imagination's most precious possessions." Even when we try to make her tangible by dressing her with private-property rights, consent, and contract, she remains elusive, ambiguous, half in the shadows. Responsibility is more ritual—"mere myth!"—and dignity most vaporous of all—"captain of one's soul? Ha-ha!"

The myth speaks for the complexities we cannot explain. The libertarian

American founders, such as Thomas Paine and Thomas Jefferson, knew that this triad—liberty, dignity, and responsibility—deserved an eternal vigilance because they knew that each had virtues not easily reduced to cogent argument. When subtle secondary effects abound, effects we sense but do not comprehend in detail, we fail to render their import in words. We manage only judgment, declaration, and action. Sometimes the action is a declaration of our resolve, put in terms of morality, or myths.

The myth of responsibility, for example, holds that the wrongdoer could have refrained from the wrong and hence is "at fault," "to blame," or "guilty." That is the necessary myth that serves clumsily in place of the subtler reasoning that eludes us on the spot or fails to persuade the jury. A student of the deeper reasons for maintaining a system of individual responsibility, such as Hayek (1960), knows better: "We assign responsibility to a man, not in order to say that as he was he might have acted differently, but in order to make him different.... In this sense the assigning of responsibility does not involve the assertion of fact. It is rather of the nature of a convention intended to make people observe certain rules" (75).

Myths may help because individuals must be made "to submit to conventions . . . whose justification in the particular instance may not be recognizable" (Hayek 1948, 22). To sustain the convention, to prevent massive free riding by short-term, often compassionate impulses, it must be infused with moral import, mythologized as in: "Men are endowed by their Creator with certain unalienable Rights . . . among these are Life, Liberty, and the pursuit of Happiness." In this connection, Adam Smith ([1790] 1976) wrote:

And thus religion, even in its rudest form, gave a sanction to the rules of morality, long before the age of artificial reasoning and philosophy. That the terrors of religion should thus enforce the natural sense of duty, was of too much importance to the happiness of mankind, for nature to leave it dependent upon the slowness and uncertainty of philosophical researches. (164)

He who scorns a myth merely because it is a myth misses the point, and betrays a poor understanding of his own moral being.

NOTES

1 Note, however, that Hayek (1960) uses "liberty" a bit differently than I do here; see especially pp. 20–21 and 142–44.

2 A fine example comes from the making of Social Security in 1935. Senator Bennett Clark proposed an amendment that would give companies and their employees the liberty to opt out of the public program by setting up a parallel private pension. But Senator Robert LaFollette explained that such liberty would not be tolerated by the new indulgence scheme: "If we shall adopt this amendment, the government … would be inviting and encouraging competition with its own plan which ultimately would undermine and destroy it" (quoted in Weaver 1996, 47).

3 The two sides, left and right, of figure 2 coincide with the "two different sets of virtues" described by Adam Smith ([1790] 1976):

> The soft, the gentle, the amiable virtues, the virtues of candid condescension and indulgent humanity, are founded upon the one [namely, the set of virtues that pertains to the arrows on the right side of figure 2]: the great, the awful and respectable, the virtues of self-denial, of self-government, of that command of the passions which subjects all the movements of our nature to what our own dignity and honour, and the propriety of our own conduct require, take their origin from the other [namely, the set of virtues that pertains to the left side of figure 2]. (23)

4 The discussion here has been influenced by the chapter titled "Dignity, Self-Esteem, and Self-Respect" in Murray (1988).

5 The calculation is by Aaron Wildavsky, cited in Sykes (1992, 13).

REFERENCES

Beito, David T. 1990. Mutual Aid for Social Welfare: The Case of American Fraternal Societies. *Critical Review* 4 (Fall): 709–36.

———. 1993. Mutual Aid, State Welfare, and Organized Charity: Fraternal Societies and the "Deserving" and "Undeserving" Poor, 1900–1930. *Journal of Policy History* 5:419–34.

Berlin, Isaiah. 1969a. Historical Inevitability. In *Four Essays on Liberty*. New York: Oxford University Press.

———. 1969b. Two Concepts of Liberty. In *Four Essays on Liberty*. New York: Oxford University Press.

Emerson, Ralph Waldo. 1951. Self-Reliance. In *Essays*. New York: Harper & Row.

Gravett, John. 1993. Life-Long Smokers Should Welcome Hillary's "Nico-Tax." *Excursions*, May, 54.

Harrington, Michael. 1962. *The Other America: Poverty in the United States*. New York: Macmillan.

Hayek, Friedrich A. 1944. *The Road to Serfdom*. Chicago: University of Chicago Press.

———. 1948. Individualism: True and False. In *Individualism and Economic Order*. Chicago: University of Chicago Press.

———. 1960. *The Constitution of Liberty*. Chicago: University of Chicago Press.

———. 1967. The Moral Element in Free Enterprise. In *Studies in Philosophy, Politics and Economics*. Chicago: University of Chicago Press.

Higgs, Robert. 1987. *Crisis and Leviathan: Critical Episodes in the Growth of American Government*. New York: Oxford University Press.

Kirzner, Israel M. 1985. *Discovery and the Capitalist Process*. Chicago: University of Chicago Press.

Lindbeck, Assar. 1995. Hazardous Welfare-State Dynamics. *American Economic Review, Papers and Proceedings* 85 (May): 9–15.

Merton, Robert K. 1957. *Social Theory and Social Structure*. Rev. and enl. Glencoe, Ill.: Free Press.

Mises, Ludwig von. 1978. *Liberalism: A Socio-Economic Exposition*. Kansas City, Mo.: Sheed Andrews and McMeel.

Murray, Charles. 1984. *Losing Ground: American Social Policy, 1950–1980.* New York: Basic Books.

———. 1988. *In Pursuit: Of Happiness and Good Government.* New York: Simon and Schuster.

Peele, Stanton. 1989. *Diseasing of America: Addiction Treatment out of Control.* Boston: Houghton-Mifflin.

Polanyi, Michael. 1958. *Personal Knowledge: Towards a Post-critical Philosophy.* Chicago: University of Chicago Press.

Rawls, John. 1971. *A Theory of Justice.* Cambridge, Mass.: Harvard University Press.

Riis, Jacob A. 1890. *How the Other Half Lives: Studies among the Tenements of New York.* New York: Scribner's.

Rodriguez, Richard. 1994. The New, New World: Richard Rodriguez on Culture and Assimilation. (interview). *Reason* 26 (August/September): 35–41.

Rosenthal, Robert, and Lenore Jacobson. 1968. *Pygmalion in the Classroom: Teacher Expectation and Pupils' Intellectual Development.* New York: Holt, Rinehart & Winston.

Schelling, Thomas C. 1984. *Choice and Consequence: Perspectives of an Errant Economist.* Cambridge, Mass.: Harvard University Press.

Smith, Adam. [1790] 1976. *The Theory of Moral Sentiments.* 6th ed. Edited by D. D. Raphael and A. L. Macfie. New York: Oxford University Press.

Stangerup, Henrik. 1982. *The Man Who Wanted to Be Guilty.* Translated by D. Gress-Wright. Salem, N.H.: Marion Boyars.

Sykes, Charles J. 1992. *A Nation of Victims: The Decay of the American Character.* New York: St. Martin's.

Szasz, Thomas. 1963. *Law, Liberty, and Psychiatry.* New York: Macmillan.

———. 1990. *The Untamed Tongue: A Dissenting Dictionary.* La Salle, Ill.: Open Court.

Tocqueville, Alexis de. [1835/1840] 1945. *Democracy in America.* 2 vols. Translated by H. Reeve, F. Bowen, and P. Bradley. New York: Knopf.

Tullock, Gordon. 1995. Government Growth. *Taiwan Journal of Political Economy* 1:21–36.

Weaver, Carolyn. 1996. Birth of an Entitlement: Learning from the Origins of Social Security. *Reason* 28 (May): 45–48.

Wildavsky, Aaron. 1988. *Searching for Safety.* New Brunswick, N.J.: Transaction Books.

Wilson, William Julius. 1987. *The Truly Disadvantaged: The Inner City, the Underclass, and Public Policy.* Chicago: University of Chicago Press.

Acknowledgments: Reprinted from *The Independent Review*, 1, no. 3 (Winter 1997), pp. 325–351. Copyright © 1997. I received valuable comments from D. McCloskey, A. Moore, and Thomas Szasz.

7

Moral Capital and Commercial Society

Suri Ratnapala

Modern civilization is based on laws and other institutions that allow individuals a large measure of freedom to seek profit through voluntary exchange. Indeed, but for the prospect of making profits, many transactions simply would not occur, and we would find ourselves without most of the goods and services that we now take for granted. There is not much argument these days about the role of profits in the production of goods and services. Yet the notion of profiting from dealings with others seems intuitively wrong to many people even when the profits are gained by perfectly legal transactions. The ancient Greeks had their own pejorative term for money making, *chrematistics*. Cicero thought that those who buy from merchants in order to resell immediately make no profit "without much outright lying" (qtd. in Finley 1987, 1:421). Some religions still condemn usury, and philosophers still pursue the quest begun by Aristotle for the "just price." In the present age, the bias against commerce persists, evidenced by constant pressures in democracies to restrain profit seeking and to redistribute wealth. Such thinking contains the unspoken assumption that entrepreneurship is a necessary evil whose consequences need to be mitigated.

Another way of looking at human affairs regards commerce as not only morally unimpeachable but also unsustainable without moral capital. This viewpoint is closely but not exclusively associated with the evolutionary tradition in social science that sees both markets and morals as aspects of the spontaneous order of society. In this chapter, I examine from this theoretical perspective the connections among moral capital, commerce, and economic performance. Following Adam Smith, David Hume, and later evolutionist thinkers, I argue that commerce coevolves with moral rules and leads not only to prosperity but also to the accumulation of moral capital. Conversely, depletion of moral capital can result in economic deterioration that causes further moral decline. I do not attempt here to devise ways to measure moral capital or to test the theory empirically. My aim is the more modest one of explaining the theory by clarifying some of the conceptual issues relevant to its understanding. I hope to provoke thought about what societies can do to enhance their stocks of moral capital.

The first part of this chapter contains a discussion of the concept of moral capital. I explain the sense in which the disposition to moral conduct represents a type of capital, and I distinguish the concept of moral capital from the related ideas of social capital and human capital. The main forms of morality are identified as justice, beneficence, and temperance. Whereas morality in all forms is conducive to commerce, justice has special significance. I follow a discussion of the abstract qualities of justice with an inquiry concerning the rules of justice that are indispensable for commerce. I conclude this part of the chapter with observations on the role of institutions in the accumulation of moral capital.

The second part presents a closer examination of the connection between commerce and morals. I present morals rules and commerce as aspects of the same evolutionary phenomenon and examine the dependence of commerce on moral capital against the converse proposition that commerce promotes greed and hence causes moral decline.

In the third part, I discuss the competence of the state with respect to the accumulation of moral capital and propose that the state is effective mainly in the promotion of justice and that its attempts to promote beneficence and other virtues invariably result in the erosion of justice.

I end with a summary of my principal conclusions and some ideas about ways to build moral capital.

THE CONCEPT OF MORAL CAPITAL

Morality as a factor in production may be counterintuitive, but it is both real and substantial. The most obvious ways in which morality helps production and exchange are by enhancing the security of person and property and by promoting the keeping of contracts. Laws that protect person and property and that enforce contracts rest on ubiquitous moral rules whose origins are lost in the mists of time. Legal reenactment strengthens these rules but obscures their origins. Such reenactments are of limited value unless most members of the community live voluntarily by the morals that the reenactments encapsulate.

Capital generally understood consists of resources owned by individuals or firms and applied in the production of goods and services. These resources include incorporeal assets such as goodwill, trade reputation, and training. The concept of capital has more recently been extended to conditions that help production by facilitating coordination among parties to transactions. This form of capital may or may not be "owned" by individuals or firms, but it provides them with clear advantages. Morality falls within this extended meaning of capital.

Morality as capital may be seen from the viewpoints of the individual and of society in general. It can take two forms from the individual standpoint. Persons who are habitually moral in conduct may gain a reputation for trustworthiness that induces others to deal with them. This form of capital may increase in value where institutions have become unreliable and people seek reliable trading partners. Again, habitual observation of a common set of known moral rules within a community of individuals will reduce costs of transacting with others. These costs include the costs of finding reliable trading partners and the costs of enforcement through self-help or third-party intervention in the event of breach of obligation. In contrast, persons living among rule breakers need to take costly precautions and will have to limit their transactions to a minimum. The transaction-cost saving that accrues to a person as a result of others' moral conduct represents part of that person's moral capital.

In what sense does a group possess moral capital? The number and types of transactions that occur are influenced by transaction costs (Coase 1960; Calabresi 1968). The extent to which a group's moral rules reduce transaction costs and hence facilitate mutually advantageous dealings between group members as well as between group members and outsiders represents the community's moral capital: members of the group have an economic advantage that results from the objective prevalence of the observance of certain moral rules. As explained presently, these rules owe their existence to the moral conduct of individuals.

If capital is taken to mean a factor in the production of goods and services, those moral rules that increase transaction costs do not generate moral capital. Thus, the rule against usury will not constitute moral capital. In our tribal past, it was considered perfectly moral to treat strangers harshly and to use force to take their belongings and even their lives. Coincidentally, it was a time when we were very poor and our own lives were, as Thomas Hobbes famously described them, "nasty, brutish, and short." Fortunately, we learned to extend to countless strangers some of the consideration that previously we accorded only to our own, and thereby we made civilization possible.

Moral Capital Distinguished from Social Capital

The concept of *social capital* refers to informal or voluntary social organizations and networks that engage in charitable activities or the production of public goods. The term *social capital* in this sense is aligned to the concept of *civil society*, the base structure of society that is distinguishable from the coercive order the state imposes. The term is used widely in the analysis of social factors that help or hinder communities in achieving prosperity. Among the better-known studies of social capital are Robert Putnam's (1993) on the role of civic tradition in Italian democracy, Glenn Loury's (1977) and Ivan Light's (1972) on racial income differences, James Coleman's (2000) on the creation of human capital, and Jane Jacobs's (1961) on the role of community networks in crime prevention. In contrast, moral capital refers to individual conduct. Clearly, individuals make up social networks, and hence moral capital is required for social capital formation. Conversely, social networks place constraints on individual behavior and hence contribute to moral capital. However, it is useful to distinguish these concepts not only because they are not coextensive but also because moral capital raises distinct issues whose discussion would be hindered by confusing it with social capital.

Human Capital, Work Ethics, and Moral Capital

Moral capital and human capital overlap at the margins, but the concepts are clearly and usefully distinguished. *Human capital* is regarded as the stock of skills and knowledge gained by education, training, and experience that enhances a person's earning powers and that increases the efficiency of economic decision making (Rosen 1997, 2:682). Earning power arises through improved productivity of value to oneself (as in self-employment), to a firm, or on the more general scale (Becker 1964). Sound professional education encompasses the ethical norms relevant to the profession, such as legal ethics and medical ethics. Membership of certain guilds and tradesmen's associations also requires competencies that include knowledge of relevant ethics. Thus, training can generate moral capital. Yet moral capital is a wider concept. It reaches beyond the needs of specific professions or occupations, and its accumulation depends on many more factors than education. Work ethics also overlap with moral capital to the extent that they translate to just conduct or beneficence. Thus, diligence in the discharge of contractual obligations is just conduct, and delivering more than what is bargained for amounts to beneficence.

Moral Capital Consists of Justice, Beneficence, and Temperance

Morality is conceived in both negative and positive terms. In simple terms, morality consists of do's and don'ts. On the positive side, it consists of exhortations to engage in virtuous acts, and on the negative side it consists of the observance of rules forbidding certain types of action. The more important rules on the negative side have been termed *rules of justice* (Hume [1777] 1964, 2:180; Smith [1759] 1976, 79), *rules of just conduct* (Hayek 1976, 31–33), and the *morality of duty* (Fuller 1964, 5–6). These rules guide a person's conduct in relation to others. Many of them are formally recognized as laws and are often coercively enforced. Some rules are ubiquitous, such as those against unjustified killing, willful or negligent harm to person and property, and the breaking of promises. It seems logically impossible to achieve harmonious coordination of the lives of a multitude without these rules.

Rules of temperance comprise negative norms that commend self-restraint even when conduct does not directly harm others. *Temperance* here is not used in Plato's sense of cardinal virtue but in the sense of the social unacceptability of excessive indulgence in pleasurable activities that are legal. Social disapprobation of conduct such as immodesty, alcoholism, and promiscuity offers evidence of such rules. The conduct that these rules seek to curb may be mildly offensive to some, but it does not harm others as unjust acts do. Temperance as moral capital is difficult to assess because it is a relative concept. One man's moderation in drink, for example, may be another man's excess. Conduct appropriate in one circumstance may be intemperate in another. Sometimes calculated intemperance may be an advantage, as when disorderly conduct on stage enhances the entertainment value of a rock concert. Yet it is apparent that in the commercial world, where agents seek reliable trading partners, a reputation for temperance counts for something.

Apart from these negative constraints, morality in the traditional sense also encompasses the positive virtue that Hume and Smith called *beneficence* (Smith [1759] 1976, 78–79) and that Fuller termed the *morality of aspiration* (1964, 5–6). Justice or morality of duty is expected of us: we will be condemned if we murder, rape, or steal, but we will not be praised if we don't. On the contrary, beneficence or morality of aspiration is not mandatory. We are not condemned if we fail to perform acts of great charity or to make heroic sacrifices, but we will be praised if we do. Beneficence, by this definition, consists of voluntary acts that both the giver and the beneficiary are not compelled to give or to receive. One can be just without being beneficent. As Smith wrote, "We may often fulfil all the rules of justice by sitting still and doing nothing" ([1759] 1976, 82). Not that beneficence carries no reward, however. Its payoff can take the form of psychological fulfillment, reciprocal beneficence, and enhanced reputation that fosters trust in future dealings. Society also benefits from beneficence to the extent that it promotes trust and eases dependence on the state.

Justice as Moral Capital Excludes Distributive Justice

The term *justice* is used here in a specific sense. Following a long tradition in moral philosophy, I regard justice as pertinent not to states of affairs but to responsible agents' conduct that affects others. Justice in this sense constitutes moral capital. There are other conceptions of justice, including that of *distributive* or *social justice*. Because words have no transcendentally true meanings but only meanings they acquire by convention or definition, it is not possible to deny the term *justice* to such notions. As presently explained, however, distributive or social justice does not form moral capital in the economic sense.

Moral capital excludes Aristotle's distributive justice that requires the division of riches, honors, and burdens in proportion to each person's merit, such as freeman status, nobility, or excellence (Aristotle 1980, bk. 5, chaps. 2, 3). It also excludes the modern concept of social justice. Aristotle's distributive justice arises among persons who have claims to a particular good or who have suffered a particular loss, the question being how the benefit or loss must be apportioned. Modern social justice, in contrast, is regarded as "an attribute which 'actions' of society, or the 'treatment' of individuals and groups by society, ought to possess" (Hayek 1976, 62). In this conception, responsibility is attached to society as a whole to produce "just" distributions of wealth, overcoming where necessary certain conditions for which no individual, group, or government is directly responsible. It is the old idea of distributive justice applied on the social scale.

There are a number of reasons for excluding these two notions of justice from the concept of moral capital. It is well to remember why morality is considered as capital at all. The prevalence of moral conduct on the part of members of a community reduces the costs of transacting in that community. The critical factor here is the agents' conduct, not their material resources. Wealth distribution may create capital for some at the expense of others, but that capital is not moral capital. Distributive or social justice does not preannounce rules that guide future conduct. This form of justice is achieved by retrospective adjustment of the material positions of individuals according to criteria such as strict equality, resource equality, utilitarianism, and just desert, which are all what Robert Nozick calls end-state principles of justice (1988, 155). Authorities who determine particular distributions of utilities have no way of knowing whether the distributions are just without knowing the circumstances of every individual affected by the scheme—circumstances that, of course, are ever changing. As John Rawls puts it, "The principles of justice do not select specific distributions of desired things as just, given the wants of particular persons. This task is abandoned as mistaken in principle, and it is, in any case, not capable of a definite answer" (1963, 202).

I exclude Rawls's own theory, however, for much the same reasons. Rawls opts for a conception of justice that lays down the ground rules of a just political order, with justice being equated to fairness. He seeks to elevate distributive justice to a higher level of abstraction by proposing that "social and economic inequalities are to satisfy two conditions: They are to attach to positions and offices open to all under conditions of fair equality of opportunity; and ... they are to be to the greatest benefit of the least advantaged members of society" (1993, 5–6). This so-called difference principle remains one that demands retrospective adjustment of material conditions not only to uphold the second limb of the principle but also to ensure that persons have "fair equality of opportunity" to seek positions and offices. Rawls's difference principle does not inform individuals, groups, and firms beforehand how they should conduct themselves or, more accurately, how they should not. It simply tells them that if they get too far ahead of the least advantaged, they will suffer some unspecified deprivation. In Rawls's scheme, the state can fully discharge its responsibility for justice only by reactive measures as "impermissible" inequalities come to light. Justice in this sense may equate to morality in some people's judgment, but the point at issue here is different. Such morality is not the kind that can form capital in an economic sense.

General, Negative, and Interpersonal Character of the Rules of Justice

The concept of justice relevant to moral capital cannot be defined exhaustively. It is not possible to know in advance all the possible circumstances that will raise a moral question. Because the universe is an evolving process both in its physical and its cultural dimensions, we cannot even imagine all the kinds of situations that may call for our moral judgment. Some situations may never arise, and others may arise so rarely that our established moral codes do not reveal a time-tested rule of conduct on which we can rely (for a clear example, see Sen 1999, 54–55). Fortunately, most people grasp intuitively the most important rules of moral conduct on which civilized life depends. These moral rules are inseparable from civilization because they are constitutive of it. From the evolutionary viewpoint, they were winnowed by the winds of experience. As Hume observed, "Rules of justice, like other conventional things, such as language and currency, arise gradually, and acquire force by a slow progression, and by our repeated experience of the inconvenience of transgressing it [*sic*]" ([1748] 1975, 490).

Distillation through experience is a process of generalization or abstraction. The fruits of experience are preserved "not as a recollection of particular events, or [as] explicit knowledge of the kind of situation likely to occur, but as a sense of the importance of observing certain rules" (Hayek 1976, 4). A rule of conduct can be universalized only in the negative form unless the rule relates to a very narrow type of circumstance. It is impossible to express the rules against murder, rape, theft, trespass, and nonperformance of contracts in positive terms if they are to protect all persons currently living and yet to be born. Universality can be achieved only by the "Thou shalt not" formula. Even when a rule appears to require positive action, it will be seen on closer examination to be capable of negative formulation. The rule that requires performance of contracts, for example, is a rule that prohibits actions contrary to contract. The rule that requires a surgeon to provide postsurgical care to a patient is actually an application of the rule against negligence, measured by the standard of care expected of a surgeon. Even in the rare cases in which the common law imposes positive duties, such as the seafarer's duty of rescue at sea, the duty bearer occupies a unique, hence quasi-fiduciary position in relation to the beneficiary. The law can be generalized into the injunction: "Do not abandon a person whose life uniquely depends on you, if you can save him without endangering your own life."

The test of justice is not state recognition and enforcement. Evolutionists and social anthropologists regard the rules of justice as preceding the emergence of the state. Smith finds the rules of justice originating in the instinct of sympathy and in the disapprobation of acts that offend this instinct. Whereas absence of beneficence and of justice evokes disapprobation, only unjust conduct brings forth the stronger feeling for retribution. Retribution may occur without state intervention, through social or religious pressure—including ostracism, social shunning, expulsion from associations, commercial blacklisting, excommunication, and admonishment—and in some cases through self-help measures.

Only norms that can be universalized become recognized as rules of justice, but not all such norms are so recognized. As F. A. Hayek notes, Kant's categorical imperative— to act only by rules that you will apply to all (Kant [1785] 1948)—is a necessary but not a sufficient condition of justice (Hayek 1976, 43). The difference between justice and beneficence is rooted in the very structure of the evolved complex order that is society. The rules of justice are the coordinating principles of social life without which the social structure collapses; they are determined by the nature of the spontaneous order of society. The difference between rules of justice and norms of beneficence may be seen also from another angle. Rules of justice forming the same system are generally accommodated to each other, and hence they may be enforced without violence to one another. Rules of justice also can be enforced without violence to beneficence, but, as discussed presently, beneficence cannot be enforced without violence to justice.

Rules of justice concern a person's relations with others. A rule that pertains to a thing will be a rule of justice insofar as it also involves some other person. Thus, the rules against pollution are rules of justice where they prevent harm to others. However, the state has a history of legislating rules that prohibit conduct where the harm to others is not clear. Examples include prohibitions of pornography and alcohol consumption. Strictly speaking, these prohibitions are attempts to enforce temperance rather than justice.

Substantive Content of Justice

Justice has two aspects, but, like the sides of a coin, they are inseparable. One aspect is the presence of a rule, and the other its observance. Rules of justice are not corporeal things. Even the fact that a "rule" is written in a book does not make it a rule. A rule owes its objective existence to its observance as an obligatory norm by a group of interacting persons. Rules of justice that precede legislative authorization may be regarded as spontaneously formed out of coincidence of behavior. Once a rule begins to crystallize, reliance on it increases, causing it to be stabilized as part of the overall social structure. Although the genesis of a rule is in the conduct of individuals, considerable time may pass before the members of the society can articulate the rule clearly (Campbell 1965, 32–33; Ferguson [1767] 1966, 34, 122; Smith [1759] 1976, 159; Hume [1739–40] 1978, 490; Hayek 1973, 17–19).

As society evolves, so does its stock of moral and legal rules. Yet we notice that all societies that extend beyond the small family group share a set of basic rules of just conduct. An extended society without these rules is difficult to conceive, and there is no historical evidence that any society has existed without them. Functioning societies display what Hume termed "the three fundamental laws concerning the stability of possession, translation by consent and the performance of promises" ([1748] 1975, 541). In legal terms, these laws confer the right to hold property, the liberty to deal with property as the owner pleases, and the right to have contracts performed. We must add to this list the rule of justice that prohibits violence to person. Hume considered this rule presupposed in the rules concerning property and contract. Rights are meaningless without self-ownership because they exist in relation to persons, and the first requirement of personhood is personal integrity.

The basic rules that secure personal security, property, and contractual freedom are simple and few (Epstein 1995), yet their maintenance depends on many other rules and subrules. The rule that contracts must be observed cannot be sustained without subsidiary rules concerning misrepresentation and fraud, mistakes, frustration, and quantification of damages, as well as the important rule of justice that in disputes one does not judge one's own cause but accepts the judgment of an impartial arbiter. John Stuart Mill considered impartiality a distinguishing characteristic of justice ([1863] 1999, 90). Contracts are unlikely to be made where these complementary rules of justice are unobserved. Similarly, property is secured by the rules against theft, trespass, and other willful and negligent acts that cause damage to property. Thus, it is evident that rules of justice do not exist in isolation, but only as parts of an interlocking and interacting system of rules. They include rules that secure just conduct by parties to disputes and by those who assist in the resolution of disputes, such as police (public or private), lawyers, and judges. What is critical for justice is that the rules are complementary and harmonious. Thus, just conduct by a judge qua judge consists in upholding the rules of justice as they apply to the case. A judge who issues a decree contrary to such rules undermines the system. Likewise, legislators act unjustly when, in the name of justice, they create powers to adjust arbitrarily the consequences that result from the application of the rules of justice.

Institutions and Moral Capital

Institutions are important in several ways to the accumulation and retention of moral capital. The value of morality as capital depends on reputation for moral conduct. Because people cannot read minds, they predict behavior through observation. In granting a loan, for example, bankers rely more on the customer's credit history than on their moral convictions. Even this kind of knowledge is unavailable in most commercial transactions. People live in societies of many millions of individuals, and they have direct and personal knowledge of only a few persons within this multitude. Yet their daily activities depend on the coordination of the actions of vast numbers of strangers. This coordination is made possible not by personal knowledge of others, but rather by reliance on observable constraints on unjust conduct. These constraints are *institutions*, a term economists use to signify all the constraints that give structure to social life, including laws and less formal rules such as customs, social practices, moral rules, and all forms of self-restraint that people voluntarily assume (North 1990, 3). Institutions are not corporeal. They consist of patterns of action that arise from the coincidence of individuals' behavior. Individuals, in turn, rely on these patterns of action in the conduct of their own affairs. Not all institutions are humanly devised. Some are, to use Adam Ferguson's memorable epigram, "the result of human action but not the execution of any human design" ([1767] 1966, 122). Institutions are not independent and self-sustaining, but exist as parts of a complex web of interacting constraints.

Moral rules are institutions, but not all institutions constitute moral rules. Some institutions are morally neutral, such as the rule in England that motorists must drive on the left side of the road or the rule that a contract by postal communication is concluded when the acceptance of the offer is put in the post rather than when it is received. They are moral only in the sense that they supply a rule that allows people to coordinate their actions and to avoid conflict. In continental Europe, opposite rules apply with equally beneficial effects. Though regarded as moral, some institutions may actually increase transaction costs by regulating or prohibiting particular kinds of transactions altogether (for example, bans on alcohol consumption and sales or on Sunday shopping), and hence they do not help to build moral capital.

Institutions encapsulate moral capital to the extent that they represent rules of justice or standards of beneficence. Morality is constitutive of these institutions because the coincidence of individuals' moral conduct creates and sustains the institutions. Once formed, institutions shape conduct by providing moral guidance and by signaling more clearly the costs and benefits of the choices we make. A rule can exist despite its violation by individuals. Unlike physical laws, human rules by their very nature are violated from time to time. However, normative rules require a critical level of observance to persist. We cannot foretell what this level is, but we recognize when it is reached.

In early society, institutions were closely aligned with moral rules. What was legally wrongful was practically indistinguishable from what was morally wrongful. Traces of this fusion are found in many languages in which one word continues to refer to both kinds of right. The Latin *ius*, the English *right*, the German *Recht*, the Italian *diritto*, the Spanish *derecho*, and the Slavonic *pravo* are a few examples (Vinogradoff 1913, 61; Mill [1863] 1999, 91–92). As Fritz Kern observes, "The medieval world was filled with theoretical respect for the sanctity of the law—not the prosaic, dry, flexible, technical, positive law of today, dependent as it is upon the State, but for a law which was identified with the sanctity of the moral law" (1968, 155). In times of absolute monarchy, rulers claimed the power to make law and did make law in derogation of the common law of the land, yet law making did not occur on the modern scale.

In modern democracies, many laws reflect distributional outcomes that result from complex public-choice processes. They are moral only in the dubious sense that they satisfy the demands of particular interest groups. In fact, many such laws directly violate Humean justice concerning the security of property and the sanctity of contract. Even leading legal positivists concede, however, that a legal system is unsustainable unless it embodies a minimum content of morality (Hart 1994, 193). The economic cost of maintaining the legal system grows in proportion to the extent that its rules deviate from the community's morals. Laws that give expression to the rules that members of a society observe as part of their traditional modes of conduct need little enforcement. State laws that are inconsistent with such morality, in contrast, entail high enforcement costs.

INTERDEPENDENCE OF MORALS AND COMMERCE

The preceding discussion of morality as capital has revealed the dependence of commerce on morality. The converse proposition, that morality is strengthened by commerce, requires further examination. In this section, I argue that commerce was a major force in the emergence of the rules of justice, and I reject on logical and empirical grounds the common claim that commerce corrupts morals.

Coevolution of Justice and Commerce

The critical role of commerce in shaping justice was first clearly perceived by the eighteenth-century evolutionist thinkers. This breakthrough resulted from their skeptical investigation of the nature of human knowledge and institutions, which led them to the conclusion that accumulated experience, not reason, was the source of moral rules. Given the premise that man has no foresight of the future, Hume argued that reason alone could never give rise to any original idea ([1739–40] 1978, 157). Adam Smith found "altogether absurd and unintelligible" the idea that we can derive from reason the first principles of right and wrong ([1759] 1976, 320). Adam Ferguson memorably declared that "every step and every movement of the multitude ... are made with equal blindness to the future; and nations stumble upon establishments, which are the result of human action, but not the execution of any human design" ([1767] 1966, 122). Morality, from this perspective, is seen to emerge spontaneously and unintentionally through the coincidences of behavior and the retention by communities of practices that conferred advantages on them (Campbell 1965, 32–33).

How does this experience come about? Smith maintained that human beings have "original passions" that lead to moral conduct, including sympathy or fellow feeling, about which he wrote that "we derive nothing from it except the pleasure of seeing it" ([1759] 1976, 9), yet it is not a wholly unselfish passion. We have sympathy for others because we need the sympathy of others; hence, we try to judge others as we like them to judge us—as impartial spectators (Otteson 2002, 84–85). Whatever the nature of sympathy, it cannot of its own force translate into moral rules. Rules of conduct can result only from the experience of interaction with others. This experience springs from two other instincts: one is "the desire for bettering our condition," which "comes with us from the womb, and never leaves us till we go into the grave" (Smith [1759] 1976, 341); the other is the "propensity to truck, barter and exchange one thing for another." The division of labor arises "as the necessary, though very slow and gradual consequence" of this propensity and not as the product of human wisdom that foresees the great advantages (Smith [1776] 1981, 1: 25). People learn the rules of justice through the experience of barter and exchange (Otteson 2002, 20). People do not discover already existing rules of justice in the course of exchanging, for that process, too, is unintelligible from the evolutionary standpoint. Rather, the rules are formed by practice, and their existence and value dawn on people even as the rules emerge in consequence of their practice. Only the action of exchanging reveals what exchange is like and what conditions make it work.

What would the first fumbling attempts at exchange reveal? The first lesson must be that it is difficult for a person to exchange anything that is not acknowledged by others as belonging to him. It is in the interest of the party giving and of the party receiving that the giver have title. Thus, exchange requires the stability of possessions that Hume saw as a necessary condition of civil society. John Locke considered the proposition "where there is no property there is no justice" as certain as any demonstration in Euclid ([1690] 1924, 18). The second lesson is that exchange is possible only when promises are kept. Early trade was seriously constrained by lack of trust, as is evident from practices such as hostage taking as insurance and face-to-face exchanges, the latter still surviving in town bazaars and village fairs. To break out of these constraints and to transform themselves into civilizations, early communities had to acquire new moral capital in the form of just treatment of strangers (Hayek 1976, 88). Commercial societies eventually comprised many millions of individuals linked by common rules of justice but with no personal knowledge of each other. For this development to happen, justice had to be institutionalized, and commerce was the driving force of the process. As Smith wrote, commerce can seldom flourish long in any state that does not enjoy a regular administration of justice—a state "in which the people do not feel themselves secure in the possession of their property, in which the faith of contracts is not supported by law, and in which the authority of the state is not supposed to be regularly employed in enforcing the payment of debts from all those who are able to pay" ([1759] 1976, 910).

Once established, rules of justice continue to gain strength from commerce. Smith was convinced of the moral superiority of the commercial class over the land-holding feudal aristocracy ([1763] 1978, 538). He claimed that feudal landlords who enjoyed wealth and security by birthright had little interest in industry or commerce and sought aggrandizement through plunder and warfare, thus "interrupting the regular execution of justice" (421). In contrast, "Whenever commerce is introduced into any country, probity and punctuality always accompanied it" (538). His explanation of the cause of this propensity anticipated a much later theory of how the problem of defection from rules is overcome: "Where people seldom deal with one another, we find that they are somewhat disposed to cheat because they can gain more by a smart trick than they can lose by the injury which it does to their character ... wherever dealings are more frequent, a man does not expect to gain so much by any one contract as by probity and punctuality" (538).

Does Commerce Corrupt Justice?

That commerce coevolved with justice suggests that each facilitated the growth of the other in a quasi-symbiotic manner, yet the charge is often heard that commerce creates a culture of greed and bestows on some people the bargaining power to corrupt the institutions of justice. The argument implies that commerce carries the seeds of its own destruction. If so, commerce has become independent of justice. Such independence is not possible, however, because property rights and contractual freedom are essential to commerce, and only justice can secure them. If justice dies, commerce dies with it.

If commerce has an effect on how people behave, it does so through cultural rather than biological change. If evolutionary psychology has any credence, commerce has not been around long enough to change our adapted minds (Barkow, Cosmides, and Tooby 1992, 3–15). Hence, commerce could not have implanted greed in the human psyche, as some contend (see, for example, Booth 1994, 658). What is not at issue is the capacity of commerce to shape people's customs and institutions. It has also made the pursuit of profits, whether out of greed or other impulse, an acceptable form of behavior. It does not follow necessarily that commerce made it acceptable to profit by unjust conduct.

The Humean notion of justice concerning the security of person, property, and contract appears more stable in societies that have achieved high levels of prosperity through commerce than in societies that are biased against commerce. Strong evidence of this relation is provided by surveys such as the *2003 Index of Economic Freedom* (Heritage Foundation and *Wall Street Journal* 2003). This is hardly surprising, given that commerce expands the range of opportunities available for persons to satisfy their needs and desires by just means. Commerce allows me to obtain through trade those things I could have gained only by plunder in precommercial society. There is no reason to think that wealth increases incentives for unjust conduct, especially if the costs of unjust conduct are high as a result of effective law enforcement. It is more often people's inability to satisfy their needs and desires through just conduct that drives them to injustice. Unjust behavior may occur in times of extreme scarcity. Here, too, commercial society has a better record of responding to catastrophic short-ages than command economies (Sen 1999). Injustice in the Humean sense is much more likely to result directly or indirectly from state action. The state directly outlaws just conduct and sanctions injustice by legislation that abrogates property rights, limits contractual freedom, and displaces the principle of fault-based liability. By weakening justice, the state weakens commerce and thereby further erodes justice even more.

Economic studies of crime tend to attribute rising crime rates (a useful yardstick of injustice as understood here) to combinations of causes, such as economic decline, demographic factors, weakening deterrence, and social disruptions (Becker 1968; Fukuyama 2000, 80–85; Deadman and MacDonald 2002, 13; Wynarczyk 2002, 34–35). The state bears primary responsibility for weakening deterrence. Official policy in many countries even rejects deterrence as an aim of criminal justice. Social disruption (of which drug abuse, family breakups, single parenting, truancy, falling school standards, and welfare dependency are symptoms) is attributable to combinations of factors, yet persuasive studies identify as major causes the perverse incentives and moral hazard created by the welfare state itself (Becker 1981; Murray 1984).

Does Commerce Hinder Beneficence?

Whereas Adam Smith believed that commerce unambiguously favors justice and temperance, he was pessimistic about its effect on beneficence (Rosenberg 1990). His pessimism arose from what he believed to be the direct and indirect negative consequences of commerce on beneficence. The direct harm he feared sprang from the effect of specialization on the education of the working class. The indirect consequence had to do with the diminishing opportunities for beneficence that result from the strengthening of justice.

Smith thought that the growing division of labor has a tendency to make some classes "stupid and ignorant" as their working lives become confined to "a few simple operations." Of the man of labor, he wrote, "The torpor of his mind renders him, not only incapable of relishing or bearing a part in any rational conversation, but of conceiving any generous, noble, or tender sentiment, and consequently of forming any just judgment concerning many even of the ordinary duties of private life" ([1759] 1976, 782). In contrast, a member of precommercial society was versatile, "capable of doing, almost every thing which any other man does or is capable of doing (783). Smith's point was that in precommercial society a person had wider but shallower knowledge, whereas the person in the age of specialization has deeper knowledge over a much narrower field. Although this specialization confers tremendous advantages on human civilization, he feared that "all the nobler parts of the human character may be, in a great measure, obliterated and extinguished in the great body of the people" (783–84). He advocated universal education "for reward so moderate that even a common labourer can afford it" (785). The payoff for government was that an educated electorate would make more mature political judgments and be less prone to manipulation by interested factions (788).

History has shown that Smith's fear was misplaced. In fairness to Smith, it is most unlikely that when he suggested that the "nobler parts of the human character" will be debased by the type of work people do, he was thinking of changes in human nature. He believed that human nature consists of certain "original passions," of which sympathy is one ([1759] 1976, 9). As mentioned earlier, human psychology is not malleable over the relatively short period in which commercial society has existed. Smith had in mind the weakening of the capacity for moral judgment as a result of lessening life experience. He was mistaken on this count. The division of labor has distributed wealth in ways that no one anticipated, and the typical unskilled person today has much more and broader knowledge than the typical peasant of preindustrial society. This knowledge is imparted not only by formal education but also by the incessant transmission of information that characterizes technologically advanced economies. Smith also did not foresee that the modes of production that he rightly or wrongly associated with the moral decline of the working class—the large factory, the labor-intensive mine, and so forth—would be themselves only transitory. The extreme specialization that those modes engendered are being superseded by the more general and multiskilled attributes demanded by manufacturing, trading, and service sectors of modern economies. Missing from Smith's calculations was the role of technological change in institutional development.

As regards the indirect effects of commerce on beneficence, Smith reasoned that when justice prevails and security from violence improves, the need for communal solidarity is lessened, and he thought that the decline of this interdependence would reduce opportunities for beneficence. Here he is closer to the mark. Opportunities for beneficence are diminished when people become prosperous and secure in their personal liberties and possessions. In prosperous welfare states, this interdependence has been reduced by a combination of private wealth generated by commerce and state-provided welfare. These conditions may make people less aware of the opportunities and needs for beneficence, but it is improbable that the human capacity and propensity for beneficence have declined as a result of economic independence. Certainly, no one has produced reliable data that indicate they have. On the contrary, everything that we know about evolution tells us that if beneficence was part of human nature two hundred years ago, it must still be part of human nature now simply because much more time is required for environmental changes to alter human psychology (Mithen 1996, 223). The upsurges in private aid in times of catastrophe and the large scale of private charity flowing from the rich to the poor countries contradict the view that prosperity diminishes beneficence as a human quality.

THE STATE AND MORAL CAPITAL

Can the State Be Beneficent?

The state can be just by observing the rules of justice and by maintaining institutions for the administration of justice. Can it also be beneficent, however? This question needs to be separated from the question of whether the state can enforce beneficence on the part of its citizens. It must be distinguished also from the capacity of rulers to be beneficent with their private wealth or the wealth at their disposal by virtue of constitutional prerogative. The capacity of the state to engage in beneficence in its own right depends on the resources that belong to it. I cannot be beneficent by giving away your money. Similarly, it is misleading to say that the state can be beneficent by taking one person's wealth to give it to another.

The state can be beneficent in a meaningful sense only if it has wealth that it has not taken coercively from citizens and does not hold as the citizens' agent or fiduciary. The modern state has very little, if any, such wealth. When the state provides public goods out of tax revenue, it acts more like a party to a contract to provide public goods. Where the citizens agree unanimously or according to an agreed constitutional process to authorize the state to carry out some beneficent act on their behalf, the state simply acts as their agent. When the state gives away public lands, for example, it is granting lands that it holds in trust for the people. Even when the state acquires wealth through commercial enterprise, it does so with capital taken from citizens. Hence, it is not very useful to talk of the beneficence of the state in its own right. More pertinent is the question of whether it can make the citizens themselves beneficent.

Can the State Enforce Beneficence?

Adam Smith argued that although the absence of beneficence excites disapprobation, attempts to extort it would be even more improper: "To neglect it altogether exposes the commonwealth to many gross disorders and shocking enormities, and to push it too far is destructive of all liberty, security, and justice" ([1759] 1976, 79, 81). Smith realized that although beneficence is highly desirable, it cannot be exacted without jeopardizing the more fundamental morality that is justice. Beneficence is the "ornament which embellishes" the building, whereas justice "is the main pillar that upholds the whole edifice" (86). Although both justice and beneficence contribute to society's moral capital, the state can be effective only in the promotion of justice. It can promote beneficence only by "advice and persuasion" (81).

The modern democracy, typified by the member states of the Organization for Economic Cooperation and Development (OECD), is a welfare state that has assumed a wide range of social security functions. It is also characterized by direct and indirect wealth transfers through taxation and regulation of economic activity. Coercive wealth transfers do not constitute acts of beneficence by the state or by the persons from whom the wealth is transferred. It can hardly be said that I engage in a beneficent act when I give that which I am forced to give. If I choose to distribute my wealth, I will be beneficent, but only because the rules of justice do not require me to do so. A private citizen who coerces me to give away my wealth commits a serious crime. When the state compels me to part with my wealth, it may be acting lawfully, but it is still acting contrary to the rules of justice.

Most members of a society are likely to agree that every member should have an economic safety net for coping with misfortune. There is an element of beneficence in such an arrangement, although it is also in everyone's self-interest as a form of universal insurance against catastrophe. However, in the age of democracy, the welfare state has extended itself far beyond this objective. Elected governments, in particular those whose powers are not carefully circumscribed by constitutional rules, cannot ignore the distributional claims of critical sections of the voting public on whom its fate depends. As Hayek wrote, "An omnipotent democratic government simply cannot confine itself to servicing the agreed views of the majority of the electorate," but will be forced "to bring together and keep together a majority by satisfying the demands of a multitude of special interests, each of which will consent to the special benefits granted to other groups only at the price of their own special interests being equally considered (1979, 99). The argument that wealth transfers resulting from the electoral process and the discretionary powers of government have little to do with genuine collective choice is well supported by public-choice studies (Buchanan and Tullock 1962;

Olsen 1965, 1982; Buchanan 1975, 1986; Tullock 1976). Even if it is conceded that such transfers deserve to be called beneficence on the occasions that they benefit the genuinely destitute, there is no way to determine accurately the winners and losers in the overall political scramble. It is difficult to disagree with Wilhelm Ropke's comment that the welfare state has degenerated "into an absurd two-way pumping of money when the state robs nearly everybody and pays nearly everybody, so that no one knows in the end whether he has gained or lost in the game" (1971, 164–65). Indeed, as Brennan and Buchanan remind us, "The implementation of political transfers will always be such that the direction of transfer is away from the minority and toward the decisive majority, and the poorest cannot be expected to be in the decisive majority any more often than anyone else" (1985, 128). In the absence of genuine community consensus, the coercive redistributions effected in the name of social welfare transgress the rules of justice.

These observations are not meant to understate the value of beneficence as a moral good or as moral capital. Acts of beneficence as understood here benefit both giver and recipient. They rarely have externalities if performed in accordance with rules of justice. As previously stated, beneficence increases trust and reduces transaction costs. A society without beneficence will also be one in which all those in need are dependent on the state. In such a society, justice will be in increasing jeopardy from the continual interventions of state. A society rich in beneficence more than likely will be a society rich in justice because beneficence requires a stability of possessions that only justice secures.

State and Temperance

Temperance is traditionally promoted by social disapprobation, religious beliefs, and commonsense adoption out of self-interest. However, the modern state has a record of attempting to compel temperance by law. Restrictions on alcohol and tobacco sales and consumption, prohibition of many recreational drugs, regulation of prostitution, and censorship of erotica are prominent examples of temperance-related limits on liberty. Legislators seek to justify these laws on the grounds that such laws protect not only the consumer but also others. Yet these laws deviate radically from traditional tort principles. Tort law allows freedom of action but compels reparation if harm results from intentional or negligent conduct. It does not ban activities beforehand, but rather lays down duties of care toward others. Modern laws designed to enforce temperance or abstinence prohibit activities that may never harm another. They erode justice by diminishing self-ownership, property rights, and contractual freedom, and they impose significant costs by limiting choice. Admittedly, there are difficult issues at the edges. Preemptive action is necessary in the face of clear and present danger to the public, but intemperance rarely poses such danger—thus, the notorious ineffectiveness of such laws.

CONCLUSIONS

There is no tension between morality and commerce when morality is understood as pertaining to the conduct of human agents as distinguished from end states. On the contrary, just conduct is a necessary condition for commerce. Justice is the foundation of beneficence, for justice alone secures the personhood, property, and contractual freedom that make true beneficence possible. The argument that commerce per se promotes a culture of greed and hence corrupts morals I reject on logical grounds. I also reject it, as Peter Bauer would say, on the evidence of the senses that suggests endemic corruption is associated for the greater part with poorer societies in which state action severely curtails economic and political freedoms (2000, 20).

There is, however, much tension between commerce and justice when justice is understood as an end state. Social justice is an end-state conception that departs from the idea of morality as an attribute of conduct. It demands particular patterns of wealth distribution that can be achieved only through coercive wealth transfers. It contradicts the notion of justice as just conduct and unsettles the institutional framework of commerce. End-state justice requires an agent with power—in a word, the state—to make adjustments continually in people's material condition. Thus, the state in its present interventionist form is a major source of injustice.

The state can contribute to the accumulation of moral capital by nurturing and strengthening the institutions of justice. Again, as commerce and justice are interdependent, the removal of obstacles to commerce is a logical means of promoting justice. However, justice cannot be maintained solely by force of law. It needs to take root in the culture of the people. In industrialized democracies, the culture of "playing by the rules" has been weakened. As Becker, Murray, Fukuyama, and others have pointed out, much of this weakening has resulted from misguided social engineering. The weakening of property rights, the undermining of contractual certainty, and the abandonment of the fault basis of liability through numerous legislative interventions and discretionary powers have not only distorted rules of justice directly but have also led to a general decline of the culture of responsibility for one's own conduct. The extension of the welfare state beyond the provision of a safety net has disrupted the traditional institutions that nurtured the culture of justice and beneficence, such as family, church, and school. Fukuyama sees in late-twentieth-century statistics an encouraging process of social and moral rebuilding (2000, 271). Such revitalization of norms may prove unsustainable, however, without the withdrawal of the state to a much narrower province.

The problem of depletion of moral capital is more acute in poorer nations. The institutions of justice are weak in these countries, and commerce is greatly hampered by the arbitrariness of government, nepotism, cronyism, state patronage, excessive regulation, lack of transparency and accountability of public authorities, and inherited cultural constraints on market processes. These problems will not be overcome without the liberalization of their political and economic systems. As the success of the so-called Asian Tiger nations and more recently of China have shown, commerce can drive political and legal reform. This process can be catalyzed by the industrialized democracies through the removal of barriers to trade. Trade barriers limit the property rights and contractual freedom of those living at home and abroad; hence, their elimination will promote justice everywhere.

REFERENCES

Aristotle. 1980. *Nicomachean Ethics*. Translated by D. Ross. Oxford: Oxford University Press.

Barkow, H., L. Cosmides, and J. Tooby, eds. 1992. *The Adapted Mind: Evolutionary Psychology and the Generation of Culture*. New York: Oxford University Press.

Bauer, P. 2000. *From Subsistence to Exchange and Other Essays*. Princeton, N.J.: Princeton University Press.

Becker, G. 1964. *Human Capital*. New York: Columbia University Press.

———. 1968. Crime and Punishment: An Economic Approach. *Journal of Political Economy* 76:169–217.

———. 1981. *A Treatise on the Family*. Cambridge, Mass.: Harvard University Press.

Booth, W. J. 1994. On the Idea of the Moral Economy. *American Political Science Review* 88, no. 3: 653–67.

Brennan, G., and J. M. Buchanan. 1985. *Reason of Rules*. Cambridge: Cambridge University Press.

Buchanan, J. M. 1975. *The Limits of Liberty*. Chicago: Chicago University Press.

———. 1986. *Liberty Market and State*. Brighton, U.K.: Wheatsheaf.

Buchanan, J. M., and G. Tullock. 1962. *The Calculus of Consent*. Ann Arbor: University of Michigan Press.

Calabresi, G. 1968. Transaction Costs, Resource Allocation, and Liability Rules: A Comment. *Journal of Law and Economics* 11:67–73.

Campbell, D. T. 1965. Variation and Selective Retention in Socio-Cultural Evolution. In *Social Change in Developing Areas: A Reinterpretation of Evolutionary Theory*, edited by H. R. Barringer, G. I. Blanksten, and R. W. Mack, 19–49. Cambridge, Mass: Schenkman.

Coase, R. 1960. The Problem of Social Cost. *Journal of Law and Economics* 3: 1–44.

Coleman, James. 2000. Social Capital in the Creation of Human Capital. In *Social Capital: A Multifaceted Perspective*, edited by P. Dasgupta and Ismail Serageldin, 13–36. Washington, D.C.: World Bank.

Deadman, D., and Z. MacDonald. 2002. Why Has Crime Fallen? An Economic Perspective. *Economic Affairs* 22, no. 3: 5–14.

Epstein, R. 1995. *Simple Rules for a Complex World*. Cambridge, Mass: Harvard University Press.

Ferguson, A. [1767] 1966. *An Essay on the History of Civil Society 1767*. Edinburgh: Edinburgh University Press.

Finley, M. I. 1987. Chrematistics. In *The New Palgrave: A Dictionary of Economics*. Vol. 1, 421–23. London and Basingstoke: Macmillan.

Fukuyama, F. 2000. *The Great Disruption: Human Nature and the Reconstruction of Social Order*. London: Profile.

Fuller, L. L. 1964. *The Morality of Law*. New Haven, Conn.: Yale University Press.

Hart, H. L. A. 1994. *The Concept of Law*. 2d ed. Oxford: Clarendon.

Hayek, F. A. 1973. *Law, Legislation and Liberty*. Vol. 1, *Rules and Order*. London: Routledge and Kegan Paul.

———. 1976. *Law, Legislation and Liberty*. Vol. 2, *The Mirage of Social Justice*. London: Routledge and Kegan Paul.

———. 1979. *Law, Legislation and Liberty*. Vol. 3, *The Political Order of a Free People*. London: Routledge and Kegan Paul.

Heritage Foundation and *Wall Street Journal*. 2003. *2003 Index of Economic Freedom*. http://cf.heritage.org/index/indexoffreedom.cfm.

Hume, D. [1777] 1964. *Essays Moral, Political, and Literary*. Edited by T. H. Green and T. H. Grose. Darmstadt, Germany: Scientia Verlag Aalen.

———. [1748] 1975. *Enquiries Concerning Human Understanding and Concerning the Principles of Morals*. 3d ed. Oxford: Clarendon.

———. [1739–40] 1978. *A Treatise of Human Nature*. 2d ed. Oxford: Clarendon.

Jacobs, J. 1961. *The Death and Life of Great American Cities*. New York: Vintage.

Kant, I. [1785] 1948. *Groundwork of the Metaphysic of Morals*. Translated by H. J. Paton. London: Hutchinson's University Library.

Kern, F. 1968. *Kingship and Law in the Middle Ages*. New York: Harper and Row.

Light, I. H. 1972. *Ethnic Enterprise in America*. Berkeley and Los Angeles: University of California Press.

Locke, J. [1690] 1924. *Essay Concerning Human Understanding*. Oxford: Clarendon.

Loury, G. 1977. A Dynamic Theory of Racial Income Differences. In *Women, Minorities, and Employment Discrimination*, edited by P. A. Wallace and A. LeMund. Lexington, Mass.: Lexington.

Mill, J. S. [1863] 1999. *Utilitarianism*. Oxford: Oxford University Press.

Mithen, S. 1996. *The Prehistory of the Mind*. London: Phoenix.

Murray, C. 1984. *Losing Ground*. New York: Basic Books.

North, D. 1990. *Institutions, Institutional Change, and Economic Performance*. Cambridge, U.K.: Cambridge University Press.

Nozick, R. 1988. *Anarchy, State, and Utopia*. Oxford: Basil Blackwell.

Olson, M. 1965. *The Logic of Collective Action*. Cambridge, Mass.: Harvard University Press.

———. 1982. *The Rise and Decline of Nations*. New Haven, Conn.: Yale University Press.

Otteson, J. R. 2002. *Adam Smith's Marketplace of Life*. Cambridge, U.K.: Cambridge University Press.

Putnam, R. 1993. *Making Democracy Work: Civic Traditions in Modern Italy*. Princeton, N.J.: Princeton University Press.

Rawls, J. 1963. Constitutional Liberty and the Concept of Justice. In *Nomos VI: Justice*, 98–125. New York: Atherton.

———. 1993. *Political Liberalism*. New York: Columbia University Press.

Ropke, W. 1971. *A Humane Economy: The Social Framework of the Free Market*. Chicago: Henry Regnery.

Rosen, S. 1987. Human Capital. In *The New Palgrave: A Dictionary of Economics*. Vol. 2, 681–90. London: Macmillan.

Rosenberg, N. 1990. Adam Smith and the Stock of Moral Capital. *History of Political Economy* 22:1–17.

Sen, A. 1999. *Freedom as Development*. Oxford: Oxford University Press.

Smith, A. [1759] 1976. *The Theory of Moral Sentiments*. Oxford: Clarendon.

———. [1763] 1978. *Lectures on Jurisprudence*. Oxford: Oxford University Press.

———. [1776] 1981. *An Inquiry into the Nature and Causes of the Wealth of Nations*. 2 vols. Indianapolis, Ind.: Liberty Classics.

Tullock, Gordon. 1976. *The Vote Motive: An Essay in the Economics of Politics, with Applications to the British Economy*. London: Institute of Economic Affairs.

Vinogradoff, P. 1913. *Common-Sense in Law*. London: Thornton Butterworths.

Wynarczyk, P. 2002. Ethical Limitations on Criminal Participation. *Economic Affairs* 22, no. 3: 29–36.

Acknowledgments: Reprinted from *The Independent Review*, 8, no. 2 (Fall 2003), pp. 213–233, Copyright © 2003. This chapter was researched and completed during my fellowship at the International Center for Economic Research, Turin, Italy. I gratefully acknowledge the contributions of Professor Enrico Colombatto, Stefano Chiadò, and the editor and anonymous referees of *The Independent Review*.

8

Liberalism and the Common Good

A Hayekian Perspective on Communitarianism

Linda C. Raeder

*In the end, given liberty to learn, men will find out
that freedom means community.*

—William Aylott Orton

In recent years, a spirited exchange between certain critics and defenders of liberalism has engaged the interest of many North American political philosophers. Although the philosophical differences between the two camps
should not be exaggerated, the so-called new communitarians (Gutmann 1985,
308) clearly part company with their liberal cousins over one fundamental issue:
the new communitarians are convinced that liberal public philosophy is undermining the social foundations of "the good society." Under its influence, they
claim, inhabitants of contemporary liberal society have grown ever more isolated,
asocial, selfish, calculating, and spiritually barren. Preoccupied by their blind
pursuit of trivial and arbitrarily chosen "private goods," modern men no longer
recognize the existence of, let alone an obligation to pursue, a comprehensive
common good that transcends mere personal interest. The new communitarians
include Charles Taylor, Alasdair MacIntyre, Michael Sandel, Benjamin Barber,
Michael Walzer, Roberto Unger, and others. Antiliberalism is not new, of course;
it is a critical tradition that extends back at least as far as Joseph de Maistre. The
new communitarian critique of liberalism, however, may be distinguished from
earlier variants in that its proponents have drawn their inspiration primarily from
Aristotle and Hegel, rather than Marx, Rousseau, or Nietzsche. Following Aristotle, they conceive of political society as a "community whose primary bond is a
shared understanding both of the good for man and the good of th[e] community"; and, following Hegel, they regard the "free[,] ... rational, [and autonomous]
being[s]" who people the pages of rationalist-liberal tracts as mere figments of the
philosophical imagination (Gutmann 1985, 308).

The new communitarians are united by their common apprehension that our sense of community—the recognition that we are a people bound by shared values, meanings, traditions, purposes, and obligations—is being destroyed by an "atomistic" liberalism (Taylor 1985, 187–210) that trumpets the "rights" of the individual at the expense of social cohesion, fellowship, and the pursuit of the common good. Although they may offer different remedies for the social ravages allegedly wrought by the liberal creed, the new communitarians all agree that we must seek to transform the stridently individualistic "politics of rights" that presently dominates public discourse and practice into a more fraternal and morally elevated "politics of the common good" (Sandel 1984, 93; 1992, 222).

Liberals have always been suspicious of calls for "community." Calvin, Rousseau, Marx, and Hitler have cast a long shadow on communitarian dreams. Moreover, liberals regard appeals to the common good warily because historically such rhetoric has accompanied various dangerous or oppressive sentiments—religious intolerance, nationalism, militarism, and the like. Indeed, "far from being innocent," writes Stephen Holmes (1989), "the idea of the common good was traditionally implicated in the justification of privilege, hierarchy, and deference" (240). Ever since Aristotle distinguished between master and slave by asserting the former's superior ability to recognize and comprehend the common good, there has been no shortage of potential rulers claiming a special insight into its nature and seeking to impose their exclusive conception of goodness or virtue on the social order.

Despite such abuse, however, few theorists, liberal or otherwise, would challenge the principle that in a free society, governmental coercion may legitimately be employed only in the service of the common good. Of course, the ambiguity of the concept "common good" (general welfare, public interest) generates seemingly intractable difficulties and lack of consensus regarding the proper application of that principle. However, the rise of the new "party of the common good" (Sandel 1992, 224), with its antiliberal rhetoric, underlines the importance of characterizing the common good if we are to preserve our liberal heritage and its institutions of freedom.

HAYEK'S DEFENSE OF CLASSICAL LIBERALISM

The social and political philosophy of F. A. Hayek yields insights into the nature of the common good in an advanced liberal society that help to clarify what is at stake in the current communitarian/liberal debate. Hayekian theory generates a precise conception of the nature of the common good in liberal society, an explication of the institutional means by which it may be realized, and a set of criteria by which we may test whether a public policy is conducive to its realization. Thus it dispels some of the fog surrounding one of political theory's most nebulous yet indispensable concepts.

Hayek fits in neither the communitarian nor the modern-liberal camp; Hayekian liberalism simultaneously supports and refutes various aspects of both the communitarian and modern-liberal perspectives. Although Hayek must certainly be considered a liberal theorist, his classical liberalism is strongly at odds with the rationalistic, rights-based liberalism espoused by the theorists who are the object of communitarian criticism. Hayek and the modern liberals do share a commitment to certain traditional liberal values—universal justice, tolerance, peace, individual liberty—but the moderns typically reject the severely circumscribed public sphere implied by Hayekian theory. Having "made ... peace with concentrated power" (Sandel 1992, 93), the dominant liberal philosophy of our time represents a clear departure from the classical liberalism espoused by Hayek.

On the other hand, Hayek's devotion to individual liberty, the free society, and the rule of law distinguishes him from the communitarians, for whom neither liberty nor justice necessarily has the highest value. Moreover, neither the modern liberals nor the communitarians share Hayek's respect for the ordering function of the market mechanism; indeed, both groups exhibit a certain antipathy toward market-governed exchange. This may explain why both camps give short shrift to Hayek's views even though Hayekian liberalism rests on precisely the sort of social theory that the communitarians claim liberal theory both sorely lacks and requires.

Indeed, the major communitarian criticisms of liberalism simply do not apply to Hayekian theory. Communitarians maintain, for instance, that liberalism ignores or discounts the influence of social factors on the formation of individual identity and purpose and that this flawed conception of selfhood undermines its validity. Unlike contractarian and rights-based theories, however, Hayek's defense of the liberal political order is free from the ahistorical rationalism criticized by both Hayek and the new communitarians and is, as mentioned, firmly grounded in a comprehensive social theory. For Hayek, individualism and individual liberty depend on a thoroughgoing immersion in social reality. As one commentator put it, for Hayek, "individualism is a social theory" (Kukathas 1989, 216).

In short, Hayek's defense of the liberal order meets the communitarian challenge on communitarian terms. Hayekian liberalism neither presupposes the existence of human "atoms," entails the destruction of human community, nor denies the existence of a transpersonal common good. In fact, the liberal Hayek is as concerned as the communitarians to revive a "politics of the common good." If Hayek is right, however—if individual liberty is both the product of a liberal society and the source of that society's continuing progressive evolution—then personal liberty and the pursuit of the common good are not only compatible but, in a sense, inseparable.

HAYEK ON SOCIAL LIFE, LAW, AND THE COMMON GOOD

Although the communitarian/liberal debate raises many issues that may fruitfully be explored from the Hayekian perspective, I shall consider specifically the following: Does liberal society possess a common good distinct from the private goods of its members? If so, how may that good be identified and realized? What are the nature and function of law and justice within the liberal community? Will our need for justice really become less pressing as our communitarian sympathies expand (as certain communitarians argue)? To answer such questions, I shall examine Hayek's views on the nature of law and the common good, as well as the relation between them, in advanced liberal society.

Liberal Society Is a Spontaneous Order

Because Hayek's political prescriptions are inseparable from his general theory of the nature and operation of complex social formations—the theory of spontaneous order—this must be our point of departure. According to Hayek, Western liberal society is the unintended outcome of the widespread observance of certain "nonrational" traditions—rules, practices, and values—that prevailed not because anyone foresaw the consequences of observing them but because groups that observed them proved more successful than other groups. Once this order had come into existence, however, one could retrospectively investigate its structure and principles of operation. The result of these investigations, first undertaken by the philosophers of the Scottish Enlightenment and significantly extended and developed by Carl Menger and his followers in the Austrian school, was the formulation of what Hayek terms the theory of spontaneous order.

A spontaneous order is a self-generating and self-maintaining order, an abstract, purpose-independent pattern (system, structure) of stable and predictable relations that emerges as an unintended consequence of the regular, rule-governed behavior of the individual elements forming it.[1] An example of a spontaneous ordering process in the physical realm may help us understand how such forces function in the social realm. To induce the formation of a crystal, one must create the conditions in which the individual elements will arrange themselves so that the overall structure of a crystal will emerge. One cannot deliberately arrange the several elements to produce the desired formation. In the appropriate conditions, however, each rule-governed element, adapting itself to its initial position and particular circumstances, will arrange itself in a way consistent with the formation of the relatively more complex structure. Hayek sees liberal society as such a spontaneous order.

The character of the spontaneous order of liberal society may be seen more clearly in contrast with a second type of social order also found in modern society—organization, or "made order." An organization is an end-dependent order created by the *deliberate arrangement* of its several elements according to the conscious intention of a designing mind.[2] An example from the physical world is a watch or a computer microchip, in which each component is deliberately positioned in accordance with the maker's knowledge and purpose. Because someone constructs an organization by putting its elements in their places or directing their movements in order to fulfill a particular purpose, organization is an ordering technique indispensable for achieving known aims.

The purpose-independent spontaneous order of liberal society consists of both individuals and organizations—business corporations, governmental institutions, and voluntary associations of all kinds deliberately created to pursue particular ends. The coordination of the activities of the individuals and organizations within society, however, comes about through the spontaneous ordering processes generated and governed by the observance and enforcement of certain types of rules. I shall discuss the attributes and function of law later. For now, notice that the operation of spontaneous ordering processes depends crucially on the observance of *certain kinds of rules* by the individual elements, because not all rule-following behavior will result in the formation and maintenance of a complex spontaneous order.

The Constitution of the Common Good

Every society exhibits an orderly pattern of activities—otherwise, "none of us would be able to go about our affairs or satisfy our most elementary needs" (Evans-Pritchard 1951, 49). Hayek emphasizes that we pursue our aims within a comprehensive order of abstract social relations that most of us take more or less for granted. Although we may not be consciously aware of the existence of this "background order," the realization of all our plans depends on its smooth functioning.

The order to which Hayekian theory refers manifests itself as the matching, or "coincidence," of plans and expectations among persons who are necessarily ignorant of most of the concrete circumstances prevailing throughout society and the concrete aims pursued by their (mostly unknown) fellows. Why do strangers who have no explicit knowledge of our concrete needs and wants provide the means we require to realize both our transitory ends and our enduring values? How is the evident order we experience in our daily affairs generated and maintained even though most persons are only tacitly aware of its existence and do not deliberately aim to produce it? Such questions lead one to the Hayekian notion of the common good.

This consists in securing the abstract conditions that allow the activities of millions of persons who do not and cannot know one another's concrete circumstances and intentions to fit together rather than come into conflict. As previously mentioned, such conditions arise from the observance of certain rules—perceptual, behavioral, moral, and legal—that structure the operation of the ordering mechanism we call the "market."

The Ordering Principle of the Market

The "market," of course, comprises a complex of social relations, institutions, and practices. Hayek maintains that the market represents historically evolved solutions to the "central problem" any advanced society must solve: how to generate, utilize, and coordinate knowledge that *only and always* exists fragmented and dispersed among the numerous members of any complex society. The "price system" should be conceived as an evolved "medium of communicati[on]" allowing people to bypass their ignorance of most of the facts that determine the success of their actions (the concrete circumstances prevailing throughout society) and to integrate the actions of individuals and groups into a coherent overall order (Hayek 1976, 125). The ability to use abstract thought and symbols such as prices, Hayek explains, enables humans to overcome their inability to master the infinite complexity of the environment. Prices serve as an indispensable guide to action. Without this guidance, persons could not know how to employ their efforts in a manner compatible with the plans and actions of their fellows. Without the guidance of prices, human activity would have to be directed by command. But in the absence of undistorted prices that reflect the reality of current circumstances, no one can know how resources "should" be employed.

For Hayek, the cultural achievements of Western civilization reflect not superior knowledge per se but the evolution of a method of coordination that encourages the generation and utilization of more knowledge than any other method yet discovered. No mind or group of minds could consciously assimilate or coordinate the vast knowledge and information that daily enters the social process via the market mechanism. Indeed, much of that knowledge cannot be consciously communicated or articulated. Knowledge, Hayek reminds us, consists not merely of explicit, systematized theories and data but also of the inarticulate "know-how" embodied in "techniques of thought," habits, dispositions, and customs and of the fleeting local knowledge of specific times and places, whose utilization is so essential in the functioning of a complex social order. In short, Hayek contends that certain epistemological facts render the "automatic" coordination achieved via the market process far superior to any method of coordination based on conscious direction. Nonmarket ordering devices, such as governmental planning or majoritarian decision making, must necessarily restrict the knowledge employed to that possessed by a relatively few limited minds and therefore prevent that flexible adaptation to ever-changing concrete circumstances whereby the order as a whole maintains itself.

According to Hayek, then, the common good in a "great society" such as an advanced liberal society—one characterized by an extensive division of labor and knowledge and integrated by common economic, legal, and moral practices—consists in the fulfillment of the fundamental value implicitly held by all its members: the preservation of the social order as a whole, the abstract, enduring structure within which all individual and organizational activities must occur. Such a good is realized, moreover, by securing the general conditions that ensure the smooth functioning of the automatic coordination mechanism we call the market. Government has a critical role to play in securing the common good, one that is primarily juridical in nature: to maintain and develop the institutional (essentially legal) framework indispensable to the operation of the ordering process itself. It does so by enforcing certain abstract, evolved "rules of just conduct."

Hayek seems to believe that once we recognize the function served by law in relation to the operation of the spontaneous order that is liberal society, we shall recognize our common interest in preserving a particular kind of legal framework—an abstract, purpose-independent framework that all persons and groups employ (implicitly and explicitly) in pursuing their own aims. He maintains, then, that the common good can be discerned through comprehending the nature of the liberal order and that the conditions essential to its realization can be consciously cultivated, but he denies that the common good is, properly speaking, an object of political determination.

The Common Good Is an Abstract Value

For Hayek, the common good in an advanced liberal society is necessarily an *abstract* value—the preservation of a certain abstract pattern of social relations—

not the fulfillment of particular concrete ends. He contends that we can establish certain general conditions that "improve as much as possible the chances of any person chosen at random" (Hayek 1973, 114) to fulfill his or her goals and values, but we cannot simultaneously secure those abstract conditions and enact legislation designed to achieve concrete outcomes. A purpose-independent spontaneous order (society) and an end-dependent organization (government) are conceptually and functionally distinct types of order, and they operate according to different rules and irreconcilable principles. The simultaneous application of irreconcilable principles—self-organization versus deliberate arrangement—can never produce a rational, coherent order.

One of Hayek's main concerns, then, is to repudiate any conception of the common good that entails the imposition of a preconceived *concrete* pattern of distribution on the social order. Although the intellectual poverty of socialism is now widely recognized, the moral and epistemological views that underlie socialist doctrines still inspire demands for "social justice," "industrial policy," protectionism, and so on—demands for all sorts of piecemeal interventions in the market process. For Hayek, the fulfillment of such demands can never serve the common interest. If our world is one of scarcity and if all persons benefit from the efficient use of scarce resources, then any attempt to override the results of spontaneous ordering processes or to impose a preconceived material distribution on the social order must work against the long-term common good.

Moreover, all plans to override the results of the spontaneous ordering processes in the name of an alleged common good must require persons to serve concrete ends determined by the planners. Consequently, the indispensable incentive to discover and employ one's particular knowledge—for example, the necessity to integrate oneself into the overall order by choosing one's occupation—is removed, so potentially valuable knowledge is lost to the social process.

For Hayek, the decision to promote the common good by maintaining a particular legal framework can be a conscious and rational decision—that is, we can understand the rationale and requirements of the liberal order and deliberately shape the legal framework in accordance with them. The common good itself, however, is not a product of intellectual design, "reasoned debate," or extensive political participation but is generated, one might say, by the circumstances of human existence, the permanent limits of the human mind, and the nature of the liberal order. Moreover, the abstract rules of justice that compose the liberal legal framework have this same character. We turn now to explore how, according to Hayek, the rules that government should enforce in liberal society—those that promote the common good by facilitating the aims of all persons—are determined.

THE ABSTRACT LEGAL FRAMEWORK

Law: The Grammar of Practice

"The aim of jurisdiction," Hayek (1973) tells us, "is the maintenance of an ongoing order of actions" (98). Thus he reminds us that all law tacitly presupposes the existence of and refers to an ongoing factual order of activities—the comprehensive "back-ground order" whose character I discussed earlier.

According to Hayek, law in the sense of enforced rules of conduct is coeval with society, for the de facto observance of common rules is what constitutes even the most primitive social group.[3] Prevailing rules will not necessarily be recognized or explicitly treated as rules but will manifest themselves as habitual perception or behavior, as customs and conventions. Those who practice certain inherited customs may not be aware that in so doing they contribute to the maintenance of the social order; they may merely "know" that certain actions are taboo or "just not done." Yet those who attempt to articulate the enforceable rules will have a more or less conscious awareness that the rules "refer to certain presuppositions of an ongoing order which no one has made but which nevertheless is seen to exist" (Hayek 1973, 96).

The rules that structure liberal society, then, refer to certain presuppositions and requirements of that *kind* of social order; these presuppositions and "inchoate rules" are bound up with the prevailing "sense of justice." An analogy drawn from language may clarify this relationship. As one's "feeling for language" enables one to recognize the appropriateness or inappropriateness of a spoken or written word without explicit knowledge of the rule applicable to the case at hand, so one's "sense of justice" enables one to recognize an inappropriate (or unjust) rule or action without necessarily being able to articulate the rule of justice that has been violated. As the task of the grammarian is to articulate the general rule that governs a particular linguistic usage, so the task of the jurist is to "discover" the general rule that (implicitly or explicitly) governs the case at hand. The rules of both law and grammar belong to that abstract structure of rules "found" to be governing the operation of the mind.[4]

The task of the jurist, then, is not to invent good law but to bring to conscious awareness the general principle or rule that, once expressed, will be recognized as just (or at least not unjust)—which means, more or less, in conformity with the implicit rules that have customarily guided spontaneous interaction in a given society. The law that emerges from the law-finding efforts of jurists always emerges, in other words, as a result of "effort[s] to secure and improve a system of rules which are already observed" (Hayek 1973, 96). The law that structures the spontaneous order of liberal society is, according to Hayek, of this nature.

He is concerned, then, to show that evolved social phenomena such as law and language exhibit certain similarities. First, law, like grammar, refers to a factual overall order (or abstract pattern) of which actors and speakers are only tacitly aware. Second, the legal rules whose observance generated liberal society were as little the product of rational design or deliberate invention as were the rules of grammar. They emerged through the ongoing efforts of jurists to articulate, develop, and interpret the (implicit and explicit) rules that structured a preexisting order of actions.

The development of law, in other words, always proceeds within a *given* framework of values, rules, and practices on which the integrity of the overall order depends. The task of the jurist, although certainly an intellectual one, cannot be accomplished through engaged participation in public affairs or a revival of communal affection. In resolving disputes, the judge is, in effect, asked to clarify which of the conflicting expectations will be treated as legitimate, a determination that depends on the requirements of the overall order and not on the judge's or anyone else's preferences. Justice is necessarily an impersonal virtue.

The Attributes of Law

One of Hayek's fundamental contentions is that the law whose observance generated and maintains liberal society necessarily possesses certain attributes. He further con-tends that all law (and legislation—deliberately constructed, or "made," rules) enforced by government in a liberal order should possess those same attributes, because only rules of a particular type can sustain the operation of the complex social formation that is liberal society.

Hayek identifies two conceptually and functionally distinct types of legal rules that prevail in contemporary liberal society, the *nomos* (private law) and the *thesis* (public law). Hayek regards only the former as true *law*, the evolved rules of conduct that define justice and secure spontaneous order. The latter consists of the rules that govern organizational structures (especially the organization of government)—directives and commands designed to realize particular purposes determined by the director(s) of the organization. The distinction between private and public law is one between standing general rules that all must obey and specific orders to be executed by government officials. One cannot, of course, execute, or carry out, a rule of conduct.

The *law*, or *nomos*, the historically evolved rules whose observance formed and maintains the liberal spontaneous order, generally takes the form of negative prohibitions that delimit a private sphere within which individuals are guaranteed a free range of action protected from the arbitrary interference of others.[5]

According to Hayek, the negativity of liberal rules follows from the progressive universalism of liberal morality: the gradual extension of a uniform legal code over an extended spatial area necessitated the gradual attenuation of specific positive obligations; it is impossible to fulfill a positive moral duty to assist someone if one has no personal knowledge of his concrete needs or even of his existence.

The function of *the law* is to create a secure and stable framework of expectations so that persons may know which features of their environment they may count on in making their plans. It tends to reduce conflict, establish certainty, and allow for the smoothest possible mutual coordination of activities. It also allows for the fullest use of dispersed knowledge: although each person must take the general rules into ac-count in pursuing his own ends, he is free to act upon his particular knowledge, bound only by general negative prohibitions. For Hayek, the enforcement of the *law*, or *nomos*, constitutes the only good that all persons in liberal society can truly be said to possess in common.

A HAYEKIAN CRITIQUE OF COMMUNITARIAN JUSTICE

One of the themes that runs throughout much of the communitarian literature is that a society governed by abstract, impersonal rules—the "procedural Republic" that is the liberal order—is not only cold and harsh but morally suspect. The communitarians seem to long for something "warmer," more personal, and more morally elevated than what abstract liberal justice can provide. They long for a community whose laws reflect the "shared self-understandings" of the members of various groups, laws that take into account the particular characteristics and social affiliations that constitute a person's identity, laws indifferent to neither the "real problems of concrete men" (Crowley 1989, v) nor the intrinsic moral worth of their actions and ends. They suggest that a society governed by general, impersonal rules that subordinate a person's substantive "good" to some abstract "right" and disregard the concrete and contingent character of social reality is somehow unworthy of a truly human existence.[6]

Certain communitarians argue, in short, that liberal justice—the strict application of universal rules to persons who vary widely in personal and social characteristics and circumstances—is unjust. Because individuals are not "uniform atoms," they must be judged not in accordance with an abstract and universal standard but in accordance with the "standards of behavior applicable to their ... situation,... [standards that] vary with [their] circumstances" (Crowley 1989, 244, 253). The only conception of justice worthy of the name is one that dictates an acknowledgment of man's historical particularity and a concern for his substantive needs.

The communitarian wish for a personal justice, which takes account of both the intrinsic moral worth and substantive outcomes of particular actions, is irreconcilable with the maintenance of the complex spontaneous order that constitutes an advanced liberal society. A legal framework consisting of particular laws for particular persons or groups, by which legislators seek to bring about specific outcomes, is the very antithesis of the rule of law—the foundation and core value of the liberal order. And the communitarian polemic is characterized by a curious and disturbing inattention to the concrete institutional manifestations a renewed "communal" spirit might assume and to the consequences that would flow from the abandonment of the abstract liberal legal framework.[7]

More particularly, the communitarians seem completely oblivious to what Hayek has called the "role of law in an ordering mechanism," which I have attempted to describe; they do not seem to recognize that the sort of personal and outcome-based justice they crave would undermine the legal foundation of liberal society. As they typically portray themselves as moderate agents of cultural renewal and their prescriptions as "supplements" to the liberal order (Holmes 1989, 22), not replacements for it, one must assume that they are simply unaware of the radical consequences of the abandonment of abstract, universal justice in favor of personalized and particular "laws." Abstract liberal laws are not arbitrary, mean-spirited injunctions indifferent to the human good, but the indispensable framework that sustains the overall order on which all persons rely in pursuing all their ends, crass or sublime.

The moral issue raised by the call for a "desert-based justice" is whether anyone has the right to alter the existing order fundamentally or to replace it with one of his choosing. In Hayek's view, no one has such a right (or, indeed, such an ability). Every person, he points out, is born into a given value framework and a given working social order that no one created and no one has the power or authority to alter at will. The extent to which one can deliberately reform or change existing rules is limited, both morally and pragmatically, by the reality that the "existing factual order of society exists only because people accept certain values" (Hayek 1978, 21).

> All rules of conduct serve ... a particular kind of order to society.... Though such a society will find it necessary to enforce its rules of conduct in order to protect itself against disruption, it is not society with a given structure that creates the rules appropriate to it, but the rules which have been practiced by a few and then imitated by many which created a social order of a particular kind. (Hayek 1979, 166)

No individual has the power to change [this order] fundamentally; because such change would require changes in the rules which other members of the society obey, in part unconsciously or out of sheer habit, and which, if a viable society of a different type were to be created, would have to be replaced by other rules which nobody has the power to make effective. (27)

Although liberal society, like all others, is far from perfect and ever in need of improvement and reform, the only legitimate criticism, in Hayek's view, is what he calls "immanent criticism"—criticism of "particular rules within standards set by . . . the aggregate structure of well-established rules" (Barry 1989, 279). Because the replacement of impersonal liberal standards by standards varying with persons' circumstances would destroy the liberal order, the communitarian critique of liberal justice may be less benign than is generally assumed.

"Dialogue," "Participation," and the Common Good

Hayek's conception of the common good also runs counter to that associated with another political tradition sometimes invoked by the communitarians, the neo-Aristotelian view that politics is the "process by which one both discovers and affirms oneself as a moral and social being" (Crowley 1989, 8). Those who conceive politics as an intrinsically ennobling and civilizing activity, who wish to restore the value of "participation in rule for its own sake" (Taylor 1989, 179), who believe the common good "is realized in the very process of debating its meaning" (Dobuzinski 1989, 253–54), seem to suggest that both the substantive content of law and a morally compelling hierarchy of common concrete ends can and should be determined by widespread political participation, extensive discussion, and "reasoned debate." Hayek insists, on the contrary, that no amount of "participatory self-rule" or "dialogue" can determine either the law that serves the common good or the concrete ends that all should be compelled to serve in its name.

For Hayek, the rules that structure liberal society arise not from achieving consensus or explicit agreement among rational men but from the structural requirements of the liberal order—from how society "works," or what earlier jurists referred to as the "nature of things." The lawmaker has a pointed intellectual task: to discover the rules that cohere with the overall body of accepted rules governing a working social order. This task must be undertaken by persons well versed in both jurisprudence and social theory, as well as intimately acquainted with the tacit dimensions of their society. According to Hayek, the correct rules are, in a sense, determined by the rationale and requirements of the existing order.

"Dialogue" and "participation" no more assist in determining the rules appropriate to the operation of liberal society than they do in determining the rules of grammar.

Of course, discussion may facilitate the discovery of the correct rules. The growth of knowledge always depends on the interplay of many minds. In Hayek's view, the development of law, like the development of scientific or any other knowledge, proceeds by a trial-and-error process of elimination (of wrong or unjust rules and refuted hypotheses, respectively). Any judge may err or fail in the endeavor to find or articulate the correct rule, and the opinions of peers and critics are indispensable. But this process differs from that advocated by adherents of the "dialogue and participation" school of thought.

Hayek denies that the liberal legal framework is an object of political determination. It is, in his view, an outcome of a transpersonal evolutionary process in which rules that secured the overall order and best contributed to human flourishing were selected and transmitted over time. Members of liberal society must, he argues, observe certain rules even though those rules have not been deliberately chosen by engaged participants or anyone else and their significance may not be fully transparent to the reasoning mind. The realization of the common good requires not greater participation in politics but the willingness to honor the rule of law and forgo the gratification of particular desires, including and especially the desire for a personal justice that acknowledges the particular "social roles" and "shared self-understandings" of various groups and seeks preconceived substantive outcomes.

Hayek denies the existence of a general principle by which we may objectively determine the relative importance of conflicting concrete ends. No amount of deliberation or discussion can produce agreement on the particular *concrete* manifestation our complex social order should assume if no such agreement exists at the outset. To compel persons to serve some hierarchical scale of concrete ends in the name of the "common good" can mean only that "common ends are imposed upon all that cannot be ... more than the [arbitrary] decisions of particular wills" (Hayek 1976, 32). Thus, for Hayek, the issue of an abstract versus a concrete common good is also a moral one: whether persons have a moral obligation to submit to political decisions concerning the pursuit of substantive ends that can never be more than arbitrary commands of the politically powerful.

All we can truly have in common with our fellows in a great society, and thus the only basis for a genuine agreement regarding the common good, are certain shared *abstract* values and opinions regarding the "kind of society" in which we would like to live, as opposed to opinions about the particular manifestations it should assume. Commitment to such shared general values, not the pursuit of common concrete purposes, constitutes social cohesion in a great society. No one can possess the concrete knowledge required to justify a rational pursuit of common concrete ends. The common knowledge we do possess is confined to certain *abstract* features of our social and physical environment (we share knowledge of the *kind* of clothing we wear, the *kind* of food we eat, the *kind* of literature we enjoy, and so on). Most of the innumerable and ever-changing facts and circumstances that determine the concrete shape of our fellows' lives in the spatially extensive contemporary liberal order are and must forever remain unknown to us.

Regardless of how disinterested, just, intelligent, and altruistic we may be, we can never rationally design a nonarbitrary hierarchy of concrete ends that all persons should pursue, for those ends depend on concrete facts and circumstances that no human mind or group of minds can grasp. Should I buy a Bible or a loaf of bread? It depends on my needs, values, and desires, on the decisions of all the other persons in society (reflected in relative prices), and on prevailing concrete circumstances (relative scarcities). The most appropriate *concrete* pattern can only be continually rediscovered as persons employ their knowledge to adapt to the concrete circumstances encountered within their local environments. Such knowledge emerges only if persons are permitted to pursue self-chosen objectives. For Hayek, the "best" concrete pattern arises from the most comprehensive utilization of all the knowledge of particular conditions dispersed throughout a society, knowledge unavailable as a whole to anyone.

According to Hayek, abstract liberal rules prevailed precisely because they serve to bypass both the limits of the human mind and the need to reach consensus on concrete goals before taking action. By ignoring these epistemological considerations, one misunderstands the "whole rationale" (Hayek 1976, 9) of a liberal society, that is, a free society in which persons may choose the ends they will pursue. Hayek's fundamental objection to any conception of the common good that seeks to employ the power of government to achieve particular concrete goals is that any such scheme must inhibit the generation and employment of knowledge, especially the knowledge of concrete circumstances known only and perhaps only tacitly to the countless individuals who compose a society of any degree of complexity. If the common good entails the effective functioning of the overall order and is meant to foster the long-term well-being of every person and the preservation and growth of civilization, then, Hayek argues, any scheme that inhibits the utilization of such knowledge cannot be in the general interest.

Hayek (1960) argues that "all institutions of freedom [law, markets, money, morals] are adaptations to [the] fundamental fact of ignorance" (30), to the irremediable limits of the human mind. If somehow we could know the "best" concrete manifestation for a "good society" to assume, the case for liberal institutions would collapse. If omniscient human beings could direct each person's activities toward his own and others' best fulfillment, we would not require the trial-and-error process whereby we *discover* the pursuits that fulfill our values (and what, in fact, those values are). Human fulfillment—the good of all—cannot be predetermined by "participatory self-rule."

Peace and the Common Good

I conclude by drawing attention to the relationship between the common good as Hayek conceives it and that "currently most neglected" (Kukathas 1989, 222) value in political philosophy—peace. One cannot exaggerate the value classical liberals of the Hayekian stripe place on securing the conditions that allow persons with widely varying purposes and values to live in harmony. Indeed, for Hayek (1976), the "greatest discovery mankind ever made" was the "method of collaboration" (that is, market-governed exchange) that enables people to live together "in peace and to their mutual advantage without having to agree on common concrete ends" (3, 136). If the members of liberal society all value the peaceful reconciliation of mutually conflicting purposes, then, Hayek argues, government's responsibility to secure the general welfare entails maintaining the only mechanism that permits such reconciliation—the abstract market mechanism.

Because no one can know the relative importance of the innumerable particular ends pursued by the inhabitants of an advanced society, any endeavor to impose some concrete conception of the common good on the social order can be no more than an attempt to compel many persons to serve purposes in which they are not the least interested and of which they may not approve; the result must surely be perpetual social discord and an unbearable politicization of social life. However great our aspirations for solidarity or community, Hayek (1988) maintains, social cohesion within our complex "extended order of cooperation" (134) cannot be achieved by the common pursuit of known visible purposes without dramatically altering the character of our social order and repudiating most of the values—the inviolability of the person, individual freedom, justice—responsible for its existence. On the other hand, he has shown that the reconciliation of individuality and community, of creative exploration and social stability, of individual rights and common good, does lie within our grasp.

NOTES

1 Hayek (1973) defines the concept of order as a "state of affairs in which a multiplicity of elements of various kinds are so related to each other that we may learn from our acquaintance with some spatial or temporal part of the whole to form correct expectations concerning the rest, or at least expectations which have a good chance of proving correct" (36). The relations that structure a spontaneous social order include such abstract social relations as buyer and seller, lessor and lessee, lender and borrower, producer and consumer, judge and litigant, and so on.

2 According to Hayek, his conceptions of spontaneous order and organization are more or less equivalent to Michael Oakeshott's conceptions of the "nomocratic," purpose-independent "civil association" (*societas*) and the "teleocratic," end-dependent "enterprise association" (*universitas*). For further discussion of Oakeshott-Hayek comparisons, see Rowley 1998, 417–18.

3 Contrary to Thomas Hobbes and others, early man did not know solitude; man always and only existed as a member of a group. "The savage is not solitary, and his instinct is … collectivist.… [In the beginning] a solitary man would have been a dead man" (Hayek 1988, 12). Both the "state of nature" and the "social contract" are myths.

4 According to Hayek, the human mind itself consists of a system of abstract rules, which govern both perception and behavior regardless of whether they have been recognized or expressed in words. Some persons may better articulate the rules that underlie personal behavior and social interaction, but such rules govern the operation of the mind whether or not they have been explicitly stated or discursively described. Hence, Hayek maintains that the rules of justice are found, not made.

5 Hayek maintains that *the law*, or *nomos*, that governs the spontaneous order of liberal society exhibits the following properties: Each law is an abstract (general) rule intended to apply to unknown persons in an unforeseeable number of future circumstances; it is known, certain, and intended to be perpetual; it is the same for all persons (the ideal of "equality under the law"); it generally takes the form of a negative prohibition delimiting the protected domain ("property") of each person; it serves to regulate the relations between private persons or between such persons and the government; it is part of a system of "mutually modifying rules"; and it possesses no specific purpose except the "purpose" of the system of rules as a whole—that is, to maintain the overall social order.

6 The communitarian conception of "shared self-understandings" is problematic, to say the least. Members of the most antisocial groups (the Ku Klux Klan, for instance) certainly share a self-understanding, as do members of all economic special-interest groups (farmers, teachers, doctors, etc.). Why the political claims of such groups should be privileged is unclear; the gratification of the special "sinister" interests has long been regarded as inimical to the general welfare.

7 The communitarian dream has an oddly unrealistic and romantic aspect. As David Levy (1989) points out, the "new communitarians" seem curiously unaware that government is a coercive agency and not the agent of self-expression and ecstatic communal experience.

REFERENCES

Barry, Norman P. 1989. The Liberal Constitution: Rational Design or Evolution? *Critical Review* 3:267–82.

Crowley, Brian Lee. 1989. *The Self, the Individual, and the Community: Liberalism in the Thought of F. A. Hayek and Sidney and Beatrice Webb*. Oxford: Clarendon.

Dobuzinski, Laurent. 1989. The Complexities of Spontaneous Order. *Critical Review* 3:241–66.

Evans-Pritchard, E. E. 1951. *Social Anthropology*. Glencoe, Ill.: Free Press.

Gutmann, Amy. 1985. Communitarian Critics of Liberalism. *Philosophy and Public Affairs* 14:308–22.

Hayek, F. A. 1960. *The Constitution of Liberty*. Chicago: University of Chicago Press.

———. 1973. *Law, Legislation and Liberty*. Vol. 1, *Rules and Order*. Chicago: University of Chicago Press.

———. 1976. *Law, Legislation and Liberty*. Vol. 2, *The Mirage of Social Justice*. Chicago: University of Chicago Press.

———. 1978. *New Studies in Philosophy, Politics, Economics, and the History of Ideas*. Chicago: University of Chicago Press.

———. 1979. *Law, Legislation and Liberty*. Vol. 3, *The Political Order of a Free People*. Chicago: University of Chicago Press.

———. 1988. *The Fatal Conceit*. Chicago: University of Chicago Press.

Holmes, Stephen. 1989. The Structure of Antiliberal Thought. In *Liberalism and the Moral Life*, edited by Nancy L. Rosenblum. Cambridge, Mass.: Harvard University Press.

Kukathas, Chandran. 1989. *Hayek and Modern Liberalism*. Oxford: Clarendon.

Levy, David. 1989. Liberalism, Politics, and Anti-Politics. *Critical Review* 3:336–47.

Orton, William Aylott. 1945. *The Liberal Tradition: A Study of the Social and Spiritual Conditions of Freedom*. New Haven, Conn.: Yale University Press.

Rowley, Charles K. 1998. On the Nature of Civil Society. *Independent Review* 2 (Winter): 401–20.

Sandel, Michael. 1984. The Procedural Republic. *Political Theory* 12:91–112.

———. 1992. Morality and the Liberal Ideal. In *Justice: Alternative Political Perspectives*, edited by James P. Sterba. Belmont, Calif.: Wadsworth.

Taylor, Charles. 1985. Atomism. In *Philosophy and the Human Sciences: Philosophical Papers* 2. Cambridge: Cambridge University Press.

———. 1989. Cross-Purposes: The Liberal-Communitarian Debate. In *Liberalism and the Moral Life*, edited by Nancy L. Rosenblum. Cambridge, Mass.: Harvard University Press.

Acknowledgments: Reprinted from *The Independent Review*, 2, no. 4 (Spring 1998), pp. 519–535. Copyright © 1998.

PART III
Securing Freedom

9

Securing Constitutional Government
The Perpetual Challenge
Suri Ratnapala

Every country in the world claims to have a constitution, but only some have constitutional government, and most of the world's people do not live under constitutional government. The term *constitution* once was synonymous with constitutional government that meant a particular type of political order in which the rulers' authority, including their legislative power, was limited through appropriate institutional devices, and both rulers and citizens were subject to the general law of the land. However, the term has been so debased that the *Encyclopaedia Britannica* (1987 edition), the most widely read encyclopedia, informs its readers that in the simplest and most neutral sense every country has a constitution no matter how badly or erratically it may be governed.

Constitutional government is an ideal, and like all ideals it can be achieved only as an approximation. Even the countries that appear to be near the ideal are revealed on examination to be not so near. Constitutional government, to the extent it is achieved, reflects a state of affairs that remains under constant threat from power seekers, ideological opponents, ill-informed social engineers, and manipulative special interests. It is also being eroded in the postindustrial era through a serious depletion of social capital, weakening the institutional foundations of constitutional government (Fukuyama 2000). In the more unfortunate countries, economic circumstances, cultural constraints, and entrenched ruling classes create seemingly intractable obstacles to the attainment of acceptable levels of constitutional government. This predicament harms seriously not just the unfortunate people of these countries but also the industrialized democracies of the world.

Deepening our understanding of the conditions that make constitutional government possible thus remains an intellectual task of the highest priority. In the past two decades, scholars have done a tremendous amount of work in this regard. My aim in this chapter is to make a modest contribution along these lines. I argue specifically that nations achieve constitutional government in the sense used in this chapter to the extent that they realize the following conditions: (1) prevalence of this particular conception of constitutional government as a dominant ideology, (2) an official constitution in written or customary form that adopts this conception of constitutional government, (3) an institutional matrix that sustains the official constitution and translates it into the experience of the people, and (4) a healthy economy that supports the institutional foundation of constitutional government. It is immediately evident that the third and fourth conditions are interdependent, each being a cause of the other. There is nothing unusual in nature or in culture about reciprocal causation. However, it raises important questions about prospects for breaking and reversing vicious cycles that grip countries whose economic conditions undermine institutions in ways that cause further economic decline. I consider some of these questions and propose that the integration of these countries into the market economy and hence into the liberal constitutional order is an unqualified good for both the industrialized democracies and the Third World.

F. A. Hayek called the ideal of constitutional government under discussion here the *constitution of liberty*. Its pedigree traces back to the evolutionist thought of the eighteenth century. In *The Constitution of Liberty* (1978), Hayek presented a restatement of the principles of a free society. He completed this restatement in his monumental three-volume intellectual defense of the rule of law and individual freedom, *Law, Legislation and Liberty* (1973, 1976, 1979). These treatises together explain the constitution of liberty: the logic and the institutional framework of the political order that sustains human freedom. The constitution of liberty is not a specific constitution but a coherent set of general principles that characterize a constitution capable of securing freedom. At the heart of the constitution of liberty is the supremacy of general laws over all authority, public or private. Its modalities include the rejection of sovereign authority, even of elected assemblies, and the effective separation of the executive and legislative powers. The term *constitutional government* as used in this chapter refers to this set of principles. I do not undertake the futile task of defining constitutional government or the constitution of liberty, but I try to make its essential attributes clearer as my discussion proceeds. I use the terms *constitutionalism* and the *constitution of liberty* interchangeably with *constitutional government*.

IMPORTANCE OF THE THIRD WORLD

Some libertarians may question why we need to concern ourselves with the destinies of other peoples who in some sense have brought their condition on themselves and whose choices we have no right to interfere with or question. This question raises interesting philosophical issues that I cannot deal with here. I do maintain that coercive interference in the affairs of other countries can be justified only on grounds unequivocally and universally recognized by public international law, such as self-defense and the prevention of humanitarian catastrophe. Still, it is important to inquire what, if anything, can be done within liberal principles to encourage the economic and political transformation of countries toward the liberal ideal and what compelling moral and economic reasons exist for doing so.

The countries with the greatest institutional deficits are also the ones least capable of coping with humanitarian catastrophes, whether manmade or natural (Sen 1999). Democratically elected governments of the Organization for Economic Cooperation and Development (OECD) countries cannot ignore such catastrophes, nor should they. However, the upshot is that the taxpayers of these countries continue to bear the cost of the follies of other national governments. Catastrophes aside, the economic and political inhospitableness of these countries creates a welfare burden on the industrialized democracies through large wealth transfers in the form of aid and concessionary loans granted directly by developed countries and indirectly through international agencies, as well as through migration of persons fleeing destitution and oppression at home. Although compelling arguments exist for accepting such refugees, it is certainly much more desirable if people have no cause to flee their homes and if migration takes place voluntarily in an orderly and secure manner for mutual advantage.

It is hardly disputable that illiberal regimes are breeding grounds of international terror. My liberal Muslim friends argue persuasively that a liberal Saudi Arabia would not have engendered the al Qaeda movement. The costs of terrorist actions for liberal democracies hardly need itemization. The greatest cost inflicted by terrorism, however, is not in the lives and property lost (though these costs are horrendously unacceptable), nor in increased defense spending, but in the jeopardy of the rule of law that results from the extraordinary powers that the state gains in times of national emergency. Terrorists cause more harm to free societies through the reactions they precipitate than by the physical destruction they wreak.

A deeper reason to encourage the liberalization of the Third World is grounded in the very nature of the market economy and hence also in liberal constitutionalism. The term *globalization* is the popular catchword to suggest a new phenomenon. Though only recently discovered by the popular press and social commentators, this process has been coextensive with the emergence of the market economy from its misty origins. The market economy emerged in consequence of the growth of trade among strangers that gave rise to the institutions of private property, the sanctity of contract, and in general the extension of the protection of the law to all. Civilization as we know it is a result of increasing exchanges between individuals that consolidated tribes into larger communities and thence into cities, nations, and the international community. Thus, trade has brought peoples together progressively and enriched them economically and culturally through specialization and exchange, creating what Hayek termed the extended order of human interaction or civilization (1991, 39–47; see also Bauer 2000, 6). This civilization is an unfolding process that has bestowed great benefits, none so great as the rule of law providing security of life, liberty, and property. Yet more than half the world's population remains unconnected or tenuously connected to it although their integration into it would be an unqualified good.

Constitutional government cannot be legislated into existence or thrust upon a community. Its attainment and maintenance even in approximate form require appreciation of its nature, much hard work, and a great deal of good fortune. As mentioned earlier, it requires intellectual acceptance of a particular conception of constitutional government, official adoption of this conception in the form of a national constitution, a supporting institutional substratum, and a favorable economic climate.

PREVALENCE OF A PARTICULAR CONCEPTION OF CONSTITUTIONAL GOVERNMENT

The proposition that the achievement of constitutional government requires its proper understanding may seem self-evident and even faintly tautologous. The fact, though, is that even in countries where constitutional government is relatively strong, a continuing struggle rages over what it takes to have constitutional government. I maintain that only a particular notion of constitutional government is self-sustaining in the longer term and that other notions, however fashionable today, give rise inevitably to conditions that even their present advocates fail to recognize as constitutional government in any meaningful sense. These faulty conceptions are, to borrow Hayek's expression, "roads to serfdom." Constitutional government as understood here requires its appreciation and acceptance by critical sections of the intellectual community—persons whose actions and decisions shape higher-order institutions as well as others who influence them strongly. This community includes government ministers, legislators, judges, senior civil servants, statutory authorities, trade union heads, leaders of important nongovernmental organizations, and powerful business people, as well as opinion shapers such as university professors, clergy, journalists, authors, producers, directors, and entertainers of various kinds.

The faith in democracy as a sufficient condition for constitutional government is alive and well. Republicans and liberals from Cicero to Machiavelli, Locke, Montesquieu, Hume, Smith, Madison, Menger, Mises, and Hayek have counseled against this faith, however—this myth that we thought public-choice analysis had laid to rest. A greater obstacle to the commitment to constitutional government is the continued dominance within critical intellectual circles of a conception of society that fails to recognize its complex, emergent, and adaptive nature. The other side of this misunderstanding is the belief that society may be radically redesigned or at least continually adjusted and micromanaged toward some optimal state that is predeterminable through foresight and reason. This conception of society relegates a constitution to a set of pliable rules to be observed to the extent and in a form that it does not impede the pursuit of preferred social and economic outcomes. The idea that ends justify unconstitutional means establishes itself in political and legal culture. The culture loses what James Buchanan terms the "constitutional way of thinking." To appreciate the seriousness of the intellectual challenge of reenthroning the classical idea of constitutional government, we must understand how it was dethroned.

RULE OF LAW: BEDROCK OF CONSTITUTIONAL GOVERNMENT

The bedrock of the classical ideal of constitutional government, and hence of freedom, is a particular conception of the rule of law—namely, the subordination of all public and private power to general norms of conduct. It is said that the rule of law is a necessary condition of freedom but not a sufficient one. This proposition sounds logical inasmuch as certain laws may diminish the liberty of all while ostensibly remaining faithful to the rule-of-law ideal. For example, prohibition of alcohol consumption in some countries limits everyone's choice. We need to examine these examples carefully, however. Such laws are likely to be kept in place only by derogations from the rule of law in other respects. Prohibition laws typically are maintained by elevating certain religious or moral opinions above others. Some also claim that abhorrent institutions such as apartheid and slavery can be implemented consistently with the rule of law provided that the disabilities are imposed by laws that do not confer arbitrary discretion on authorities. This claim is much more problematic. In such cases, the legislators themselves are acting arbitrarily in both establishing and maintaining the institutions. The proscription of arbitrary determinations by the rule of law applies equally to the legislature. Such laws are general only in a very perverse sense.

The concept of generality implicit in the rule of law does not require that all laws have universal application. (It does not require children and adults to have the same contractual capacity or the same level of criminal responsibility, for instance.) However, the rule of law does require a rational and nonarbitrary basis for differential treatment of individuals or groups. Questions concerning the rationality and legitimacy of legislative classifications are often controversial. Hence, in some states constitutional bills of rights attempt with varying degrees of success to bar specific types of laws by placing certain civil liberties and in some cases property rights beyond the power of legislative derogation.

From the Rule of Law to the Rule by Law: The Public-Choice Perspective

The clear distinction between law and royal command was the foundation of the ancient constitution of England from which modern constitutionalism was born. The power to give binding commands existed within the narrow province of matters concerning the government. It was the ancient power of *gubernaculum*. These commands were mainly administrative orders generalized for efficiency and directed to civil servants—what Hayek called *thesei*. The law itself lay beyond the arbitrary power of the ruler and resided in the community, to be changed only with their actual or putative consent. Such change was made by the exercise of *jurisdictio*, the power to alter the rights and duties under the common law (McIlwain 1947, 77). The critical point to observe is that the *jurisdictio* could not be constitutionally transferred or delegated to the monarch, though for a while Henry VIII managed to bully Parliament into doing so. The so-called Henry VIII clauses under which Parliament grants the executive the power to make laws, including laws that override Parliament's own acts, were never accepted as constitutionally proper.

It was obviously perilous to hand any part of the *jurisdictio* to the unelected monarch. Indeed, the constitutional history of England and Great Britain until the twentieth century in many ways was the story of the struggle by the coalition of the common-law courts and Parliament to keep the *jurisdictio* from the grasping hands of the Crown. Then came the Great Reforms and mass democracy. The source of executive power moved from the monarch to the electorate, from prerogative to parliamentary confidence. The repository of executive power shifted from the monarch to elected leaders who controlled Parliament, hence also public finance. Members of Parliament and the electorate lost their traditional fear and mistrust of the executive, for now it was removable at periodic elections. Executive power eventually became tradable through its capacity to create benefits in exchange for votes. However, before governments could start creating tradable goods on a significant scale, they had to overcome a central tenet of the rule of law—namely, that citizens should be subjected only to general and impersonal laws. It is possible to win votes by offering principled changes to the general law of the land, but it is much easier to win votes by offering benefits to particular constituencies, whether they are seekers of wealth transfers or pursuers of public causes such as conservation. The demands of these constituencies are difficult to meet through general law. They require specific allocations and deprivations as well as constant adjustment of entitlements in ways that defeat the rule of law.

Jurisprudential Errors Concerning the Rule of Law

The decline of the rule of law in the classical sense cannot be explained solely through application of the economics of public choice. The ideal of the rule of law was too entrenched in the political culture to be repudiated explicitly. It needed to be maintained as an ideology but reformulated to accommodate the new state that was emerging through the electoral process.

Part of the means of this reformulation was already present in the form of the reductionist jurisprudence of legal positivists that sought to define all law in terms of the will of a legislator. Hobbes, Bentham, and Austin were the principal authors of this theory, but the twentieth century produced its own influential positivists in Hans Kelsen, H. L. A. Hart, Joseph Raz, and their numerous followers. The rule of law in the sense used in this chapter is the rule of the law as understood from antiquity—namely, general norms of conduct as opposed to the rule of *commands*. According to this view of the law, commands are lawful only in the sense and to the extent that they are authorized by law. Commands themselves were not law. This distinction dissolved in positivist thought. Any "ought" proposition, provided the authorities effectively enforced it, came to be regarded as law. In Kelsen's pure theory of law, even commands devoid of normative content were regarded as legal norms if they were validated by a hierarchy of norms ultimately grounded in political fact (*Grundnorm*).

The result of the positivist consensus was to regard as law all measures recognized and enforced by authorities, including Parliament and courts (Hayek 1976, 50). The question "What qualities must an instrument possess to be regarded as law?" was answered by the tautology that a law is what is enforced as law by the authorities. In contrast, during his famous debates with Hart on the possibility of separating law and morals, Lon Fuller observed that there were eight ways to fail to make law, corresponding to the failure to endow enactments with the following eight qualities: generality, prospectivity, promulgation, clarity, consistency (within and among laws), constancy (infrequency of rule changes), possibility of compliance, and congruence between proclamation and enforcement (1964, chap. 2). These qualities traditionally gave law its status and the rule of law its meaning. The consequence of classifying all types of state interventions under the rubric of law was to destroy the basis of government under law—namely, the limitation of Parliament and courts to making or declaring general rules and the subordination of executive actions to such general rules. The new conception of law meant that whosoever has legislative power has authority not only to change the general laws of the land but also to determine the law for the particular case. According to this view, the legislator or its delegate could annul or modify contracts, expropriate property, confer special benefits, impose deprivations on individuals and groups, and generally make the law at the very point of its enforcement. The theory rejected the classical constitutional model of the separation of powers in favor of the model of sovereignty under which the effective will of the ruler is law. This construction was thought to accord with the British Constitution but was based on a misreading of its key features. The British Constitution is customary in nature, and the courts of England do not invalidate acts of Parliament for violating the indispensable principles of common law. Yet, as A. V. Dicey (1964) maintained, the British Parliament was not absolved from the duty to maintain the rule of law. The fact that no court would enforce this norm did not mean that it was not a constitutional rule.

The rule of law as classically understood requires (1) that all public and private actions are, in general, subject to law conceived as general and impersonal norms that are end independent in the sense that they are not directed to the achievement of specific outcomes; and (2) that citizens, in general, are not compelled to obey any dictate that does not take the form of a general, impersonal, and end-independent norm in the preceding sense.

These two elements are fundamentally linked; one cannot exist without the other. A great conceptual error in constitutional theory resulted from the belief that the first element could be maintained while the second was abrogated. An official who has power to coerce a citizen by arbitrary command cannot at the same time be subject to a general law with respect to the province of that power. The power of arbitrary command can be generated only by the displacement of a general law. An official who fixes the price of goods does so without the guidance of an impersonal norm, and his determinations displace the norm that contracts freely concluded must be observed. The official who prohibits trade by denial of a license displaces the freedom of con-tract that not so long ago was a common-law doctrine. Derogations from the second element are automatically derogations from the first element because the officials who have power of arbitrary command are placed above the law. It is wrong to say that such officials act under the law. They make law for the individual case in derogation of general law. It is not sufficient for the rule of law that officials always act under the authority of the legislature. It is necessary that the legislature be constrained from authorizing arbitrary action.

REVISION OF THE IDEAS OF LIBERTY AND JUSTICE

The reformulation of the rule of law was further driven by the revision of two other concepts embodying values that are inextricably associated with and indeed possible only under the rule of law: liberty and justice. These two concepts are indispensable requirements of civilization based on the market economy. Democracy is a means of securing liberty and justice. Ironically, the sheer power of these ideas over the human mind makes them prime targets of those who seek to reshape society and the redefinition of them has caused incalculable harm to the rule of law and hence to constitutional government.

Human thought is mediated by language. Even if we reject Jacques Derrida's contention that nothing exists outside texts, it is hardly disputable that language not only limits what we can express but also structures our thought. Language is the product of convention. In evolutionary terms, it is the outcome of the convergence of understanding within a linguistic community. When we say the word *elephant*, most English-speaking people will have a pretty good idea of what we mean. Yet when we mention the word *justice*, they seriously disagree concerning its meaning. Some terms have more settled meanings than others. Meanings are more likely to be contested and are more susceptible to manipulation when they are politically or economically significant. I have no great incentive to destabilize the meaning of the word *elephant*. In contrast, a significant payoff may accrue if I can establish that my claim for a higher wage is a claim of *justice* because justice is a universally held value and claims clothed in the rhetoric of justice are more difficult to resist. Hayek understood better than most liberals the susceptibility of liberal ideals to erosion through imprecise language (1976, 12–15, 62–66). His efforts to restore conceptual clarity to the ideas of liberty, justice, law, and democracy illuminated the constitution of liberty and helped others to perceive more clearly the new forces arrayed against it.

Redefinition of Liberty

Liberty in the traditional sense meant the absence of arbitrary interference by human agents as distinguished from the physical constraints that limit choice. Thus, I do not consider myself unfree simply because I cannot evade the law of gravity. This distinction between freedom in the physical (alethic) sense and freedom in the human-relational (deontic) sense is of the highest importance in the constitution of liberty. However, in the twentieth century, the distinction faded in political discourse, with drastic consequences for liberty and for the rule of law. The question "How can one be free if one has no means to enjoy freedom?" took center stage in political and philosophical debate. Freedom and the capacity to enjoy freedom became fused in leftist political thought.

This argument, advanced by those who include within freedom the positive capacity for its exercise, has two aspects. The first is that freedom is diminished not only by the arbitrary coercion of others but also by a person's lack of material resources to exercise the freedom. Freedom needs to be available legally before anyone can exercise it, but the argument is that if physical constraints prevent the exercise of freedom, it is of no avail. This aspect of the argument by itself is weak because no law can remove physical constraints for which no specific person is responsible. We cannot legislate away the law of gravity or the second law of thermodynamics. Hence, the need for the second aspect of the argument.

The revisionists assert that certain physical constraints, such as the lack of material resources, are not purely the results of chance, but are the cumulative effects of the actions of many. Hence, it is alleged, society as a whole bears responsibility for diminishing some people's freedom. The inference from these assertions is that the enhancement of freedom requires the coercive adjustment of social and economic relations, which in turn entails necessary infringements of some freedoms, such as the freedom to hold property and the freedom of contract, in order to increase the overall level of freedom in society. This argument, represented as a freedom-based case against freedom, and its variants have resonated widely, particularly among the less-endowed sections of society. Yet wherever the argument has succeeded in influencing policy, people have become poorer. The proposition has been falsified by the history of the twentieth century.

Redefinition of Justice

Closely linked to the revision of the concept of liberty has been the expansion of the concept of *justice*. The older idea of justice as the observance of the general rules of just conduct was extended to include the notion of just distribution of the social product. Poverty, even when no individual or group was responsible for its creation, came to be regarded as an unjust condition, not merely an unfortunate one. In the Marxian socialist doctrine, just distribution was represented by the condition of material equality based on the principle "to each according to his need, from each according to his means." Social democrats, though they subscribed to this ideal, pursued it by piecemeal adjustments of economic relations aimed at moderating material inequalities. The goal of achieving just allocations included use of the term *social justice*, which created a major problem for the constitution of liberty.

Philosophers from antiquity onward have sought unsuccessfully the objective means of ascertaining just material distribution. The principle "to each according to need, from each according to his means" requires highly subjective determinations of the needs and means of countless persons. Even the more modest social democratic goal of reducing economic inequalities requires a high degree of discretionary and hence arbitrary government. General laws cannot produce or maintain specific material conditions. Even if the law succeeded in equalizing the wealth of all persons, such equality could not be maintained except by continuous microadjustments of wealth distribution through discretionary power. The pursuit of the egalitarian ideal invariably subverts the rule of law by the displacement of general rules of conduct with inherently arbitrary impositions of authority in the particular case. It strikes at the heart of the constitution of liberty.

The ideal of social justice under discussion here is not the same as social security. The latter may be provided by an income safety net in the form of a minimum income guaranteed to all persons. Social security in this sense does not require discretionary income adjustment and hence is compatible with the rule of law in the classical sense, provided that it serves as a universal form of insurance rather than as a device for wealth redistribution. In fact, most classical liberal thinkers see no harm and much merit in universal safety nets.

In the industrialized democracies, the first condition for constitutional government—the prevalence of the understanding of constitutionalism in the classical sense within the community immediately responsible for the maintenance of constitutional government—has been severely eroded. The fact that constitutional government remains relatively healthy in these countries owes much to the corrections that the spontaneous order of civilization has imposed on the constitutional systems of these countries and to the heroic efforts of a minority of intellectuals.

AN OFFICIAL CONSTITUTION DEDICATED TO CONSTITUTIONAL GOVERNMENT

An official constitution is not easy to ascertain, even in countries that possess written constitutional documents having paramount force over other law. A written constitution has no life of its own. Its words have no magical quality. It gains meaning from the way it is understood, construed, observed, and enforced by officials who form the government in its many manifestations. The same text might be construed to facilitate arbitrary rule or to restrain it.

The U.S. Constitution was intended to set up a government of divided and limited powers functioning under law. The great panoply of devices—including the separation of legislative, executive, and judicial powers; the territorial dispersal of power among the states; the commerce clause; the bans on bills of attainder and takings without compensation; the due process and equal protection clauses; the entrenchment of the representative principle; and the independence of the judiciary—was intended to prevent, directly or indirectly, arbitrary government and to promote the rule of law in the classical sense. This intention is the clear and consistent message of the *Federalist Papers*. The words of the Constitution are perfectly capable of being understood as establishing just such a model of government. Yet its divisions and limitations have been blurred substantially by legislative, executive, and, most important, judicial action since its inception. The rule against the delegation of excessive legislative power to the executive branch, though judicially recognized, is seldom enforced, creating a rich source of arbitrary power for government. The commerce clause, meant to facilitate free trade among the states, has become, despite the 1995 *Lopez* ruling, a general source of power to regulate not only the economy but much else. The general-welfare clause, meant to impose a general-welfare test for taxation and spending, has been claimed as a charter for wealth redistribution.

The Australian Constitution, which was inspired by the U.S. model of limited and divided power, has suffered a similar fate at the hands of Parliament and the High Court. The Court has obliterated the rule against the delegation of legislative power, allowed ad hominem legislation, emasculated the free-trade clause, expanded the industrial relations clause to permit tribunals to determine "the just wage" and in general to regulate the labor market, tolerated gerrymander at state level, and weakened the federal structure through expansive interpretation of commonwealth powers (Ratnapala 2002; Ratnapala and Cooray 1986).

The countries with so-called flexible constitutions, where the supreme legislative bodies have both legislative and constituent power, such as the United Kingdom and New Zealand, are instructive with respect to the problem of ascertaining the official constitution. The U.K. constitution is traditional, and the limits of Parliament's power are not clear. Hence, most British constitutional lawyers tend to consider its power to be (legally speaking) limitless, despite Britain's treaty obligations to observe European Union law. This absence of limitation exists because the courts, ever since the removal of Chief Justice Coke, have never claimed the power to invalidate an act of Parliament, although they often dilute the effect of oppressive acts through interpretation. New Zealand's Constitution Act may be changed by a simple majority of its Parliament. In many other countries, the legislature may change the constitution by a special majority, the most common being the two-thirds majority. In Malaysia, Singapore, and Zimbabwe, governments have enjoyed two-thirds majorities and hence have had the capacity to change their constitutions at will.

In countries with flexible constitutions, the constitution is defined to a large extent by unwritten constraints that the political culture imposes. Governments in Singapore, Malaysia, and Zimbabwe have used their two-thirds majorities to make frequent changes to their constitutions to extend their own hold on power. In contrast, in Britain and New Zealand, where parliaments have much greater constituent power, individual governments' attempts to perpetuate their power are rendered impossible by the practical limits that the political culture imposes on government. Yet in the latter countries, people lack one of the more important safeguards of the rule of law—namely, the ability of an aggrieved individual citizen to challenge a law in a judicial forum on the ground of its inconsistency with a declared norm of the constitution. This constitutional deficiency has been offset in part by the heroic efforts of the courts in these countries to enforce both procedural due process and the standards of natural justice against administrative action. However, if the offending law does not affect the rights of a significant group, it is unlikely to trigger the kind of public reaction and media attention that can lead to its repeal through the force of public opinion.

I am not suggesting that countries such as the United States, Canada, the United Kingdom, Australia, and New Zealand have no constitutional government. On the contrary, on a scale of constitutional achievement, they are closer than most to the ideal of constitutionalism. We need to guard against excessive pessimism. The basic structures of the constitutions of these nations have proved much too robust for radical change, but they also have enabled corrections to occur. Recent decisions of the Fifth and Eleventh U.S. Circuit Courts of Appeal that reject the pursuit of cultural diversity in student populations as a legitimate aim of affirmative action provide a good example of such corrections. The stability of these constitutions has much to do with the strength of their institutional underpinnings.

THE INSTITUTIONAL MATRIX OF CONSTITUTIONAL GOVERNMENT

Ultimately, a constitution exists in the experience of the people. The best-intentioned constitutional instrument cannot deliver constitutional government if the patterns of official action do not correspond to its norms or if officials engage in patternless projections of authority. The constitutional text, together with interstitial legislation and judicial constructions, provides guidance to official action, and hence it is an important determinant of the living constitution. However, the extent to which officials in fact are guided by constitutional norms depends on many more constraints and conditions than the psychological effects that constitutional texts provide. Therefore, a lawyer's sole preoccupation with the constitutional law of the books is seriously misconceived and dangerous to constitutional government.

The concept of an institution has been likened to the constraints that make up the rules of the game, as opposed to the players who engage in the game (North 1990, 3). Institutions are distinct from organizations that belong with the players. The term *institutions* is elastic enough to include constraints of all kinds that influence human behavior, including legal and moral rules, etiquette, cultural constraints (such as those concerning reputation), superstition, other more personal and less understood values that guide action (such as parental and filial affection and compassion toward fellow beings).

There are, of course, more constraints on political actors than those imposed by institutions as defined here. Nonnormative physical constraints of various kinds exist. Strong central government is more feasible in city-states such as Singapore than in large states such as the United States of America. Afghanistan is thought by some to be ungovernable from one location because of its terrain and its diverse regional ethnicities. Montesquieu thought that climate had much to do with English liberty. Ethnic and religious diversity can necessitate forms of federalism, as in the Russian Federation, India, and Nigeria.

Some types of organizations and organizational alliances also provide powerful determinants of constitutional governments, including a vocal and independent press, trade unions, business associations, and various other interest groups. Their impact on constitutional government can be positive or negative, but on balance constitutional government owes much to their existence. They mobilize opinion and provide avenues of action. Favorable institutions make their activities possible, and in turn these organizations effect institutional change.

A norm has no independent existence. It can exist only as a part of an extended matrix of norms. The ancient legal norm *pacta sunt servanda* (contracts should be observed) is supported by many other norms, such as those concerning respect for person and property, truthfulness, the impartiality of third-party arbiters (in case of breach), and the integrity of law enforcement officials. The cardinal constitutional norm of independence and impartiality of the judiciary, so essential to the rule of law, depends critically not only on the norms of judicial ethics and responsibility but also on the acceptance of judicial decisions by officials and citizens adversely effected by them. Such acceptance is the outcome of numerous other norms that create the overall culture of "playing by the rules."

One of the great dangers to constitutional government—a danger that has not received sufficient attention from lawyers and economists—arises from what Francis Fukuyama describes as the Great Disruption. A majority of classical liberal constitutional theorists (myself included), in their justifiable preoccupation with official threats to the rule of law, failed to hear conservative alarm bells about the corrosion of the social foundations of the free society. It is not easy for lawyers schooled in black-letter law and economists trained in neoclassical theory to connect constitutional government with what happens in households, classrooms, boardrooms, factories, and neighborhoods. Nevertheless, the connections are real and substantial. Lawyers tend to think only in terms of norms enforceable in courts of law, as they should when they give professional advice to clients. Yet it is time that lawyers who set themselves the wider goal of understanding, advocating, and defending the rule of law in general—including lawyers who serve as academics, judges, legislators, and responsible public servants—show greater appreciation of what it takes to realize the rule of law. Likewise, economists who limit themselves to what is quantifiable and who distrust intuition and conventional knowledge should heed Peter Bauer's advice to wake up from their disregard of the evidence of the senses and to return to "the traditional sequence of observation, reflection, inference, tentative conclusion, and reference to established propositions, and to findings of other fields of study" (2000, 20).

The interconnections between family breakups, single-parent upbringing, drug abuse, street crime, truancy, lack of essential life skills, decline in trust, more litigation, welfare dependence, and many other symptoms of social disorder cannot be established with the kind of empirical precision that some social scientists demand. Nor can we find monocausal explanations for why all these unhappy events are occurring. However, the coincidence of the rising statistics in these areas (Fukuyama 2000, chap. 2, appendix) raises a very strong suspicion that they are parts of a broader phenomenon that swept the industrialized democracies in the second half of the twentieth century.

Social disorder affects constitutional government in a number of different ways, some more obvious than others. The dishonor of contracts as well as crimes and civil wrongs against person and property are inconsistent, by definition, with the rule of law, but they are inevitable in societies of imperfect souls. Law-governed societies cope with these problems through law enforcement resulting in punishment or reparation. However, when such transgressions occur frequently, they seriously threaten the existence of the rule of law because legal systems are not designed and indeed cannot be designed to cope with widespread lawlessness. When offenses are committed against person or property, the injury is apparent and the victim usually known. Another category of delinquency seems to be regarded as victimless or at any rate not blameworthy in the sense of causing harm to others. This category includes drug abuse and calculated welfare dependence. These delinquents themselves are often thought of as victims rather than wrong-doers. The borderline between preventable and unpreventable dysfunctionality is difficult to draw in some cases, but palpable in many others. The welfare state passes on the cost of this kind of delinquency to people who play by the rules. The arbitrary behavior of others thus subjects to vitiation the rule followers' property rights, a situation that directly contradicts the rule of law. Also, in the welfare state, social disorder, by increasing persons' dependence on the state, generates more discretionary state activity. The greater the momentary adjustments of wealth, the greater the damage to the rule of law as conceived by classical liberals.

More important, social disorder is also disorder of the matrix of rules that supports constitutional government. Rules exist through observance. It is a fatal mistake to think that the rule of law and constitutional government could be legislated into existence and maintained solely through the coercive power of the courts and the police. The conditions of the rule of law and constitutional govern-ment prevail because most people observe the rules of the social order most of the time, including important unwritten ones. It is not possible to destabilize some rules without affecting others in the system. As rules become frayed through nonobservance, people cease to count on them. Mistrust of people transfers to mistrust of institutions. People take other precautions. They fortify their homes, keep their children away from the public parks, abandon entire neighborhoods (which then become more lawless), increase insurance coverage, and begin to ste-reotype people defensively. As standards fall, corruption spreads to government. The economic cost of such disorder is incalculable and takes the ultimate toll on the institutional matrix of constitutional government.

We may be witnessing an institutional revival in the Western democracies through the self-correcting processes of open societies. The increases in crime, divorce, and illegitimacy rates seem to have decelerated in the 1990s (Fukuyama 2000, 271), and the importance of personal responsibility is now acknowledged frankly in public debates, with more voices from the left joining the traditional voices of the right in lamenting its decline.

One of the most remarkable developments in this regard in Australia concerns the changing complexion of the public debate about the plight of the country's indigenous population. The aboriginal people of Australia have suffered the fate of many other indigenous peoples who found themselves in the path of European colonization and settlement, a fate that included dispossession, large-scale exter-mination, loss of children through forced adoption, destruction of traditional habitats, cultural dislocation, discrimination, and alienation from mainstream society. The rule of law simply passed them by. The aborigines lead the nation in every statistic on social disorder, including crime, family breakup, and drug abuse. By the admission of aboriginal leaders themselves, domestic violence against women and children is a huge problem among aborigines. Education and health conditions in some communities are worse than in many parts of the Third World. These conditions persist despite enormous welfare spending and preferential arrangements by commonwealth and state governments.

Throughout the last three decades of the twentieth century, aboriginal leaders and the Australian left directed their efforts toward obtaining more government assistance and the reclamation of indigenous land rights, the latter supported correctly by many on the right. In the early 1990s, a combination of judicial rulings and consequential legislation brought about a settlement of the native title question, but the social problems remained intractable.

Then, in the past two years, a different set of voices has risen above the traditional chorus of blame and claim. Indigenous leaders such as Noel Pearson, a hero of the left in the 1990s, have asked their communities to look within themselves to identify their problems and to find their own solutions. His argument is that nothing can erase the past injustices inflicted on them, but that if they understand the present causes of social decay in the context of current realities, they can revive their fortunes. Pearson and others are asking for no less than the restoration of the underpinnings of the rule of law—responsibility for one's self and one's family and respect for others' rights. They realize that the guilt-ridden white governments cannot help native peoples with endless patronage. Their message is that the indigenous people need to rebuild their own institutions and reestablish the rule of law in order to become economically independent and to achieve equality with the rest of the nation.

At the Ben Chifley Memorial Lecture of 2000, a highlight of the left intellectual calendar in Australia, Pearson declared to the dismay of many left commentators:

> The truth is that, at least in the communities that I know in Cape York Peninsula, the real need is for the restoration of social order and the enforcement of law. That is what is needed. You ask the grandmothers and the wives. What happens in communities when the only thing that happens when crimes are committed is the offenders are defended as victims? Is it any wonder that there will soon develop a sense that people should not take responsibility for their actions and social order must take second place to an apparent right to dissolution? Why is all of our progressive thinking ignoring these basic social requirements when it comes to black people? Is

it any wonder the statistics have never improved? Would the number of people in prison decrease if we restored social order in our communities in Cape York Peninsula? What societies prosper in the absence of social order? (Pearson 2000)

There is no consensus about the causes of institutional decay. The standard leftist argument is that social disorder springs from poverty or, alternatively, from income inequality. The obvious problem with this line of reasoning is that it disregards the causes of poverty and hence overlooks the problem of reciprocal causation. Others have pointed to causes such as the lessening interdependence of individuals in consequence of growing wealth and welfare safety nets (Yankelovich 1994) and to the perverse incentives and moral hazard created by the welfare state itself (Becker 1981; Murray 1984). Whatever the causes may be, the problem for liberal constitutionalism is to repair its institutional foundations without violating its own principles.

ECONOMIC CONDITIONS AND CONSTITUTIONAL GOVERNMENT

However we look at constitutional government, it is apparent that economic conditions form a major factor in its success. The emergence of the market economy converts society from one in which the benefits of the law are extended only to members of one's tribe or group to one in which everyone has the protection of abstract and impersonal rules. The recognition of the benefits of trade, hence of the right to hold and dispose of several property, caused the emergence of the system of abstract rules that secure freedom and order (Hayek 1991, 30). Markets based on the observance of such shared rules created a new form of trust among strangers. This is not trust of the individual stranger but trust of the rule system—a reliance on institutions more than reliance on individuals. Repeated transactions based on abstract rules strengthen such rules. Where markets shrink, for whatever reason, the strength and reach of abstract law will weaken as exchange among strangers lessens and trust diminishes.

Poverty by itself does not destroy the rule of law, but it limits the strength and reach of such rule. History shows that impoverished communities often have very stable general laws. In these communities, the gain from observing the law and the harm from violating the law are palpable. The rule of law breaks down when the real or perceived costs of compliance are greater than the costs of noncompliance. Social security laws, for example, are difficult to enforce because of the uncertainty of the eligibility criteria and the evidentiary problems of disputing a claim. (One of the most difficult facts to establish in law is the level of a person's wealth and hence his income.) In contrast, in a society in which one's general well-being or survival in catastrophic circumstances depends on the goodwill of others, powerful incentives exist for observing the rules of the game. The problem for the rule of law in this economic context occurs when the state takes over as provider, displacing markets with regulations and entitlements.

Consider an extreme example from the political history of Sri Lanka, a country I know well. In 1948, Ceylon, as it was then known, gained independence as a constitutional monarchy under a constitution that established a Westminster-type parliamentary democracy guaranteeing universal adult franchise, independence of the judiciary, and the public service and equal protection of the law to all communities. In its first decade, the country was held up as a model of constitutional government, the living proof of the cross-cultural validity of the rule-of-law ideal. Its constitutional decline began in 1956, however, with the election of its first socialist government. This government introduced racially discriminatory laws and administrative practices to fulfill pledges to its electoral support base among the Sinhala peasantry and petit bourgeoisie. The 1972 Constitution, authored by a leading Marxist lawyer, dismantled many of the existing checks and balances in the name of the sovereignty of the people. The return to power of the right of center in 1977 brought about some reinstatement of constitutional checks, but the rot had well and truly set in, and the situation for the rule of law in some respects worsened during that government's sixteen years in office.

Although tampering with the Constitution was a factor in the decline of constitutional government, it was not the major cause. Even the 1972 Constitution had more safeguards than the United Kingdom, New Zealand, and many other functioning democracies enjoy. In Sri Lanka, however, the institutional matrix of constitutional government was destroyed by a catastrophic economic decline resulting from the conversion of the country's market economy to a socialist-type command economy. Nationalization of all key sectors of the economy—including the public-transport system, the banks, the insurance industry, wholesale trade, and, most damaging of all, the plantation industry, which was the backbone of the economy—converted the people into a population of public servants. Controls on prices, rents, house ownership, imports, and currency exchange drove foreign investors out and choked off local enterprise. As the universities and schools produced more and more unemployable general arts and science graduates, the government created more jobs to keep them off the streets. Armies of youth did little more than open doors, bring cups of tea for senior officials, and move documents from one office cubicle to the next. Real incomes declined as a shrinking economic pie was divided into ever-smaller slices. Essential goods became scarcer and dearer, and queues stretched longer. The Tamil youth suffered most. Not only did private-sector jobs dry up, but the young Tamils were also squeezed out of public-service employment through language policy. It is not difficult to imagine the impact on constitutional government of the efforts of a nation of public servants seeking to make a decent living off the government.

It is easy to destroy institutions, but much more difficult to rebuild them, as Sri Lanka has learned painfully. The rebuilding process begun in the 1980s has been dealt savage blows by the civil war and by terrorism. Now there are signs at least that an emerging national leadership understands markets and their foundation in the rule of law, and it has made progress toward establishing peace and rebuilding institutions. The Sri Lankans need all the encouragement and support they can get to become again a living example of the resilience and power of liberalism.

REBUILDING CONSTITUTIONAL GOVERNMENT

Constitutional government has reasserted itself strongly in some parts of the world, but it continues to struggle against tremendous odds in other places. Dictatorships of various kinds have been replaced by democracies of various kinds. In democracies, the withdrawal of government from some areas of the economy has restored the general law with respect to contract, tort, and property in those areas. Although the size of government measured as a percentage of gross domestic product (GDP) has not been reduced significantly or at all, the nature of government has changed in many countries. These gains owe much to the work of liberal thinkers such as Hayek, who have broken up the intellectual consensus supporting the interventionist state and provided key economic arguments for the limited and law-governed state. A certain inevitability about these corrections can be explained by the positive analysis of social systems by Hayek, Fukuyama, and other evolutionist thinkers.

As Hayek (and before him Carl Menger and the Scottish evolutionists) pointed out, the self-ordering quality of society cannot be eliminated through engineering. Even the most regulated societies, such as those under Stalinist-communist rule, could not escape the self-ordering process. New elites emerged to replace the old ones. Private exchange did not disappear even in the state-monopolized area of basic goods and services. The economy did not behave in the manner planned and decreed, nor did the people in general. Most important, the social system continued to absorb information from the outside despite the state's best attempts to insulate it. The Stalinist state was undergoing endogenous reordering long before its dramatic final collapse. Western intellectuals and media simply failed to notice it.

The corrections in the Western democracies were less dramatic but just as interesting. The welfare state produced the admirable outcomes of decolonization and international trade liberalization but could not cope with the resulting exposure to international competition from non–welfare states and from welfare states that shed their more intrusive and costly features. Countries that built short-term prosperity behind walls of protection found themselves at a serious disadvantage in competing for markets and investment. In the face of these feedback challenges, the stakes began to change in the electoral game. As the unsustainability of the overregulated state became evident, politicians began to find votes in structural reform. The same democratic systems that produced the welfare state produced President Reagan, Prime Minister Thatcher, and, later, the "Third Way" politicians. In Australia and New Zealand, the reform processes were launched not by conservatives or liberals but by labor governments, with the Labour treasurer Paul Keating famously warning the electorate that without reform Australia was heading for banana republic status. The welfare state in its more ambitious forms probably was unsustainable even without exposure to international competition, but that competition certainly made it so. When social democrats championed the Third World cause for market access to the West, they hardly meant to unleash forces that would destroy some of their cherished accomplishments. Yet such destruction is precisely what they brought about. The lesson of all this is that we cannot foresee, much less control, the outcome of our designs in a dynamic spontaneous order. Although we can provide design inputs, the environment will select what is preserved and determine the shape and form in which these elements are preserved.

The fact that societies are self-ordering systems does not suggest that we should stand by passively and watch its spontaneous readjustments. Waiting for society to correct itself is not a promising option. Eternal vigilance remains the price of freedom. It is a serious mistake to think that the politics of wealth distribution has gone away. Redistribution will always remain one of the keys to elective office. Hence, the containment of this electoral game remains an ongoing challenge for constitutional government.

Efforts to defend and foster constitutional government must focus on the four conditions discussed earlier. First, the intellectual struggle over the meaning of the rule of law must continue at all levels, with a view to restoring the ascendancy of the classical understanding of it as the supremacy of general laws over public and private power. Second, the classical understanding of the rule of law needs to inform constitutional interpretation, legislative activity, and public administration so that the official constitution conforms more closely to the classical ideal. In this respect, lawyers have important roles to play as advisers, advocates, legislative draftsmen, legislators, tribunal members, and judges. Third, social disorder must be dealt with both legally and economically in ways that are consistent with the rule of law. A solution here requires restoration of the integrity of the law in areas where it has been whittled away, so that responsibility for personal conduct rests with the person and is not spread around the community, whether it be with respect to contracts, due diligence toward others, or family relations. It requires the gradual withdrawal of the welfare state to its essential role in providing a safety net to those who genuinely cannot look after themselves. Trust needs to be regenerated through the bonds of the market economy, which will require the progressive elimination of arbitrary powers over the economy that have accumulated over more than half a century. Restoration of the basic rules of the law, such as those ensuring the sanctity of contract and the fault basis of tort liability, is essential. Real tax reductions must follow the scaling back of the foster state, returning money to the people whose private transactions are the substratum of the market economy and hence also of constitutional government.

Globalization has come to the aid of constitutional government in exposing constitutional systems to competition. The greatest payoff from globalization, perhaps, takes the form of the enhanced prospects for extending constitutional government to people in parts of the world that hitherto have not enjoyed its benefits. As argued previously, this development is not only an unqualified good in itself but also a necessary step for maintaining the long-term security of constitutional government in the developed parts of the world. For decades, Peter Bauer argued without success that internal trade, not external aid, would deliver the Third World from abject poverty. The subtext of his argument was that the institutional settings that enable internal trade to occur—namely, constitutional government in the classical sense—are indispensable to solve this problem. Bauer's vision is finally becoming a reality as countries are inexorably exposed to the global marketplace and as both local elites and international agencies begin to understand what it takes to be a successful player in this market.

Still, we need to consider whether globalization might pose threats of its own to constitutionalism. Constitutional government subjects both public and private power to the general laws of the land. The question is whether the constitution of liberty can govern the conduct of the actors in global markets through the reach of its laws and institutions. This reach is limited both by jurisdictional boundaries and by the impracticalities of cross-border law enforcement. To what extent do these conditions constitute a challenge to the rule of law? For centuries, merchants have managed their own disputes with minimal assistance from state apparatuses, mainly through their own arbitrators who applied their own *lex mercatoria*. Their common interests in maintaining ongoing trading relationships and their membership in a close-knit trading community allowed this informal system to operate successfully. In the ages past, few transnational consumer transactions, as distinct from merchant-to-merchant dealings, took place. Today's global market is characterized by increasing numbers of consumer transactions across borders through the Internet and other means. There is a clamor among academics and policy makers for international consumer-protection laws modeled on domestic versions of such laws. These appeals may or may not eventuate in new laws, and if they do, they may have little impact. The optimistic view is that informal market-driven institutional mechanisms will emerge to take care of the matter. The problems are not peculiar to transnational trade. Much consumer trade takes place on the basis of trade reputation anyway, and there is no reason to suppose that similar patterns of trader-consumer relations will not emerge in transnational trade.

Some observers also fear that globalization leads to the increasing power of multinational corporations, which may engage in unlawful activity with impunity because of their capacity to relocate business. Governments, the argument goes, may become so beholden to mobile capital that they will sacrifice the public interest and indeed the rule of law. These fears ultimately are fears of institutional failure. Capitalists are not angels, and we should not expect them to behave like angels. Successful constitutions rest on the conviction memorably expressed by Hume that "in contriving any system of government and fixing the several checks and controls of the constitution, every man ought to be supposed a knave, and to have no other end, in all his actions, than his private interest" (1964, 1:117–18). As the recent Asian financial crisis showed, there is no good substitute for stable, transparent, and open institutions if a country is to attract and retain capital in the long term.

What can industrialized democracies do within liberal principles to encourage constitutional government elsewhere? The one great noninterventionist tool at their disposal is trade. I have argued here that constitutional government needs to be grounded in a supporting institutional substratum and that positive economic conditions will promote favorable institutions. The gradual emergence of constitutionalism in countries that have built prosperity based on markets (most notably the so-called Asian Tigers) lends credence to this argument. The industrialized democracies can provide a powerful impetus to constitutional government by removing the substantial remaining barriers to international trade. The World Bank estimates that the removal of such barriers will boost income in poor countries by $1.5 trillion (Panitchpakdi 2002). These barriers not only deny people in poor countries the freedom to trade what they produce but also effect arbitrary wealth transfers among groups of citizens in rich countries. Hence, their elimination represents a major challenge in the perpetual struggle for constitutional government throughout the world.

REFERENCES

Bauer, P. 2000. *From Subsistence to Exchange and Other Essays*. Princeton, N.J.: Princeton University Press.

Becker, G. 1981. *A Treatise on the Family*. Cambridge, Mass.: Harvard University Press.

Dicey, A. V. 1964. *Introduction to the Study of the Law of the Constitution*. 10th ed. New York: Macmillan.

Fukuyama, F. 2000. *The Great Disruption: Human Nature and the Reconstitution of Social Order*. London: Profile.

Fuller, L. 1964. *The Morality of Law*. Rev. ed. New Haven, Conn.: Yale University Press.

Hayek, F. A. 1973. *Law, Legislation and Liberty*. Vol. 1, *Rules and Order*. London: Routledge and Kegan Paul.

———. 1976. *Law, Legislation and Liberty*. Vol. 2, *The Mirage of Social Justice*. London: Routledge and Kegan Paul.

———. 1978. *The Constitution of Liberty*. Chicago: University of Chicago Press.

———. 1979. *Law, Legislation and Liberty*. Vol. 3, *The Political Order of a Free People*. London: Routledge and Kegan Paul.

———. 1991. *The Fatal Conceit: The Errors of Socialism*. Chicago: University of Chicago Press.

Hume, D. 1964. *Essays Moral, Political, and Literary*. Vols. 1 and 2. Edited by T. H. Green and T. H. Grose. Darmstadt, Germany: Scientia Verlag Aalen.

McIlwain, C. H. 1947. *Constitutionalism, Ancient and Modern*. Ithaca, N.Y.: Cornell University Press.

Murray, C. 1984. *Losing Ground*. New York: Basic Books.

North, D. 1990. *Institutions, Institutional Change, and Economic Performance*. Cambridge: Cambridge University Press.

Panitchpakdi, P. 2002. Enemies of Poverty Should Seek Lower Tariffs. *The Australian* 15 (November): 15.

Pearson, N. 2000. Ben Chifley Memorial Lecture. www.australianpolitics.com /news/2000/00-08-12a.shtml.

Ratnapala, S. 2002. *Australian Constitutional Law: Foundations and Theory*. Sydney: Oxford University Press.

Ratnapala S., and M. Cooray. 1986. The High Court and the Constitution: Literalism and Beyond. In *Commentaries on the Australian Constitution*, vol. 6, edited by G. Crave, 203–25. Sydney: Legal.

Sen, A. K. 1999. *Development as Freedom*. Oxford: Oxford University Press.

Yankelovich, D. 1994. How Changes in the Economy Are Reshaping American Values. In *Values and Public Policy*, edited by H. J. Aaron, T. E. Mann, and T. Taylor, 16–53. Washington, D.C.: Brookings Institution.

Acknowledgments: Reprinted from *The Independent Review*, 8, no. 1 (Summer 2003), pp. 5–26. Copyright © 2003. This chapter was researched and written at the International Center for Economic Research, Turin, whose generosity I gratefully acknowledge. I am pleased also to acknowledge the valuable research assistance of Stefano Chiado. An earlier version was presented in London at the 2002 General Meeting of the Mont Pelerin Society.

10

The Primacy of Property in a Liberal Constitutional Order
Lessons for China
James A. Dorn

China's march toward a market economy, which began in 1978, has been slow but steady. In 1980, China rated very low on the Economic Freedom of the World (EFW) index, achieving a score of only a 3.7 out of 10, in contrast to Hong Kong, which scored 8.7 and was ranked number one in the world. Hong Kong has continued to be ranked the freest economy in the world, with a score of 8.8 in 2000 (the last year for which data are available), whereas China's score has increased to 5.3 (Gwartney and Lawson 2002, 83, 110). China, however, is a huge country, and its dynamic, market-oriented coastal areas, when scored separately, reflect greater economic freedom than for the country as a whole (Fan, Wang, and Zhang 2001).

The liberalization of foreign trade has helped to transform Chinese industry and has exposed China to new ideas and new markets. China's recent entry into the World Trade Organization (WTO) will deepen economic reform and strengthen civil society.

Economic freedom is multidimensional. Its basic features, as measured by the EFW index, are "personal choice, voluntary exchange, freedom to compete, and protection of person and property" (Gwartney and Lawson 2002, 5). That China ranks 101st out of 123 countries in terms of overall economic freedom reflects the lack of secure private-property rights and the strong government presence in the economy.

In the future, China will need to develop its constitutional and institutional infrastructure to protect property rights better and to limit government intervention if it is to achieve the credibility needed to comply with WTO rules and to create real capital markets. China can learn much from Hong Kong's success. If the constitutional order of freedom characteristic of Hong Kong can spread to China, then China's future will be bright.

In this chapter, I focus on the primacy of property rights for a free society. As Milton Friedman notes, "Property rights are not only a source of economic freedom. They are also a source of political freedom" (2002, xvii). I begin by defining property rights and showing their moral and practical significance for a liberal constitutional order. The legitimate function of government is to protect property and thereby to ensure justice. Once government safeguards persons and property under a rule of law, a spontaneous market-liberal order can emerge to coordinate economic activity and to create new wealth. I show how the idea of spontaneous order, which lies at the heart of a liberal constitutional order, is fully compatible with China's ancient culture, as seen in the writings of Lao Tzu. China must move from market socialism to "market Taoism"—from constitutional fiat to constitutional freedom. That is why property rights and limited government are so important for its future.

PROPERTY, FREEDOM, AND JUSTICE

Property is often thought of only in physical terms, but that conception of it is misleading. A more accurate portrayal of property is as a bundle of rights and correlative obligations that are consistent with individual freedom. Indeed, according to James Madison, the main architect of the U.S. Constitution, "In its larger and juster meaning, it [property] embraces every thing to which a man may attach a value and have a right; and *which leaves to every one else the like advantage*" ([1792] 1906, 101, emphasis in original).

Under the rubric of property, Madison included "a man's land, or merchandize, or money," as well as the property a person has in "his opinions and the free communication of them" and especially the property a person has "in his religious opinions, and in the profession and practice dictated by them." An individual also "has property very dear to him in the safety and liberty of his person" and "an equal property in the free use of his faculties and free choice of the objects on which to employ them." In brief, "as a man is said to have a right to his property, he may be equally said to have a property in his rights" ([1792] 1906, 101).

Madison followed in the footsteps of the great classical liberal thinker John Locke. In his *Second Treatise of Government*, Locke defined property as "lives, liberties, and estates" ([1690] 1965, § 123). He questioned the so-called divine right of kings and argued that property is a fundamental human right—a moral or "natural right"—that exists prior to government. All individuals have the right to protect their property from aggressors and the correlative obligation to restrain from harming others, except in exercising the legitimate right to self-defense. Thus, everyone is equally free to pursue his or her happiness, provided everyone adheres to the basic principle of noninterference.[1]

According to Madison, the primary function of government is "to protect property of every sort; as well that which lies in the various rights of individuals, as that which the term particularly expresses. This being the end of government, that alone is a *just* government, which *impartially* secures to every man, whatever is his *own*" ([1792] 1906, 102, emphasis in original). Hence, just as *freedom* depends on the moral right to property, broadly conceived, *justice* depends on limiting the use of force—whether individual or collective—to the safeguarding of life, liberty, and estate. Justice does not refer to outcomes but to rules: to be just, rules must be applied equally and not violate our basic right to noninterference.

Justice is simple to understand in the liberal constitutional order: it is merely the absence of injustice, which is defined as the wrongful taking of life, liberty, or property. As the brilliant French liberal Frederic Bastiat wrote in 1850,

> When law and force confine a man within the bounds of justice, they do not impose anything on him but a mere negation. They impose on him only the obligation to refrain from injuring others. They do not infringe on his personality or his liberty or his property. They merely safeguard the personality, the liberty, and the property of others. They stand on the defensive; they defend the equal right of all. They fulfill a mission whose harmlessness is evident, whose utility is palpable, and whose legitimacy is uncontested. (1964, 65)

In sum, property, freedom, and justice are inseparable in the liberal constitutional order: when private-property rights are violated, individual freedom and justice suffer.

PRIVATE-PROPERTY RIGHTS, ECONOMIC FREEDOM, AND PROSPERITY

Economic freedom depends crucially on the enforcement of private-property rights, which include the exclusive right to use one's justly (freely) acquired property and the right to sell property or to partition the bundle of rights. Free markets depend on well-defined private-property rights, which means the legal system must be based on the rule of law and on limited government (Niskanen 2002).

There can be no real competitive markets—no "marketization" or capitalization—without privatization (that is, freely transferable private-property rights).[2] As Armen Alchian, a pioneer in law and economics, emphasizes, "Marketability implies *capitalization* of future effects on to present values. Thus, long-range effects are thrust back on to the current owner of the marketable value of the goods. He will heed the long-run effects of current decisions more carefully than if the rights were not transferable" (1967, 12).

The salability or transferability of private property (for example, land, shares of corporate stock, and other capital assets) means that owners can discover the present (capital) value of future expected net-income streams. It is possible to calculate those values because market interest rates can be used to discount future expected profits into their present values, as reflected in asset prices. Without competitive markets based on secure private-property rights, no one can know how to allocate capital efficiently to alternative uses based on consumer preferences. In the absence of real capital markets, investment decisions naturally will be politicized, as they are in China.

The attenuation of private-property rights lowers the market value of those rights and reduces individual freedom (Alchian 1977; Jensen and Meckling 1985). If the end and criterion of economic development are greater individual freedom, in the sense of an expansion of one's range of alternatives or choices, then any weakening of private-property rights reduces economic freedom and slows human development. Peter Bauer, in line with classical liberals going back to Adam Smith, has made a strong case for freedom of choice as the primary criterion of development: "I regard the extension of the range of choice, that is, an increase in the range of effective alternatives open to the people, as the principle objective and criterion of economic development; and I judge a measure principally by its probable effects on the range of alternatives open to individuals" (1957, 113–14).

Bastiat had that conception of development in mind when he wrote, "The best chance of progress lies in justice and liberty" (1964, 137). In his famous essay "The Law," he recognized the importance of secure private-property rights, limited government, and economic freedom for personal and economic development: "It is under the law of justice, under the rule of right, under the influence of liberty, security, stability, and responsibility, that every man will attain to the full worth and dignity of his being, and that mankind will achieve, in a calm and orderly way—slowly, no doubt, but surely—the progress to which it is destined" (1964, 94).

Bastiat saw progress as an evolutionary process in which individuals learn by trial and error. That process is enhanced by a free-market system resting on private-property rights. He understood the institutional infrastructure of a market system and recognized that competition would allow people the freedom to discover new information and to learn from their mistakes. Thus, like F. A. Hayek (1978), Bastiat viewed competition as a discovery process. He also recognized that freedom would promote social development: "Social organs too are so constituted as to develop harmoniously in the open air of liberty" (1964, 95).

History has shown that the countries with the strongest protection of private-property rights and the greatest amount of economic freedom also achieve the highest standards of living. In a study of 150 countries, Lee Hoskins and Ana Eiras (2002) found that countries with secure private-property rights have created more wealth (as measured by real gross domestic product [GDP] per capita) than countries in which private-property rights are insecure and corruption is high (see figure 1). James Gwartney and Robert Lawson (2002, 20) found a strong correlation between economic freedom, as measured by the EFW index, and income per capita, the rate of economic growth, and life expectancy. Those findings point to the importance of private-property rights and limited government not only for creating a just society in the Madisonian sense but also for alleviating poverty.

THE LAW OF LIBERTY AND SPONTANEOUS ORDER

When protection of persons and property is the overriding object of government and when people are free to choose, provided they respect the equal rights of others, then markets will coordinate economic decisions and lead to mutually beneficial exchanges. Such a voluntary or spontaneous order can arise only in a liberal constitutional order of freedom, or what Hayek (1960) called a "constitution of liberty." Equal freedom under the law of liberty is the hallmark of liberalism.

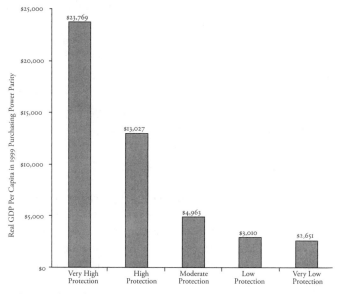

Source: Hoskins and Eiras 2002, 40.

FIGURE 1. Stronger Property Rights Equal Greater Income

"The free society," writes Roger Pilon,

> is a society of equal *rights*: stated most broadly, the right to be left alone in one's person and property, the right to pursue one's ends provided the equal rights of others are respected in the process, all of which is more precisely defined by reference to the property foundations of those rights and the basic proscription against taking that property. [Moreover,] the free society is ... a society of equal *freedom*, at least insofar as that term connotes the freedom from interference that is described by our equal rights. (1983, 175, emphasis in original)

The idea that a harmonious economic and social order can emerge spontaneously from individual action—provided government enforces just rules that protect individual rights to life, liberty, and property—is central both to liberalism and to the case for limited government. As Hayek states, "Under the enforcement of universal rules of just conduct, protecting a recognizable private domain of individuals, a spontaneous order of human activities of much greater complexity will form itself than could ever be produced by deliberate arrangement, and ... in consequence the coercive activities of government should be limited to the enforcement of such rules" (1967, 162).

China's leaders need to recognize the idea of spontaneous order. Their fear of chaos in the absence of strong government guided by the Chinese Communist Party (CCP) is misplaced. They fail to recognize that freedom under the law of justice is an alternative to unlimited freedom as well as to unlimited government. Chaos is a straw man meant to subdue the Chinese people and to keep the CCP in power. China's leaders could learn much about spontaneous order by studying the work of Adam Smith and by returning to the thought of their own Lao Tzu, who discovered the principle of spontaneous order long before Smith.

The Tao of Adam Smith

In 1776, Smith argued that if "all systems either of preference or of restraint" were "completely taken away," a "simple system of natural liberty" would evolve "of its own accord." Each individual then would be "left perfectly free to pursue his own interest his own way, and to bring both his industry and capital into competition with those of any other man, or group of men," provided "he does not violate the laws of justice" ([1776] 1937, 651).

In Smith's system of natural liberty, the government no longer would have the obligation of overseeing "the industry of private people, and of directing it towards the employments most suitable to the interest of the society"—an obligation "for the proper performance of which no human wisdom or knowledge could ever be sufficient" ([1776] 1937, 651).

Government would not disappear under Smith's market-liberal regime, but it would be limited narrowly to three major functions: (1) "the duty of protecting the society from the violence and invasion of other independent societies"; (2) "the duty of protecting, as far as possible, every member of society from the injustice or oppression of every other member of it"; and (3) "the duty of erecting and maintaining certain public works and certain public institutions" ([1776] 1937, 651).

In the private free-market system Smith advocated, people get rich by serving others and by respecting their property rights. Thus, the system of natural liberty has both a moral foundation and a practical outcome. Private property and free markets make people responsible and responsive. By allowing individuals the freedom to discover their comparative advantage and to trade, market liberalism has produced great wealth wherever it has been tried. There is no better example than Hong Kong.

The chief architect behind the Hong Kong economic miracle was Sir John Cowperthwaite, a Scot who admired the work of Adam Smith and other classical liberals. As Hong Kong's financial secretary from 1961 to 1971, Sir John constantly challenged attempts to increase the power and scope of government in that territory. Like Smith, he believed that free private markets would keep people alert to new opportunities by quickly penalizing mistakes and by rewarding success in the use of society's scarce resources. He understood that no system is perfect, but that, of all known economic systems, the market-price system, with its automatic feedback mechanism, has performed the best: "In the long run, the aggregate of decisions of individual businessmen, exercising individual judgment in a free economy, even if often mistaken, is less likely to do harm than the centralized decisions of a government, and certainly the harm is likely to be counteracted faster" (qtd. in N. Smith 1997, A14).

The idea that people have a natural tendency to make themselves better off if left alone to pursue their own interests and the notion that a laissez-faire system will be harmonious if government safeguards persons and property are the foundations of the West's vision of a market-liberal order, but they are also inherent in the ancient Chinese Taoist vision a self-regulating order—an order we properly might call "market Taoism" (Dorn 1997, 1998).

The Taoist system of natural liberty, like Smith's, is both moral and practical: moral because it is based on virtue, and practical because it leads to prosperity. The Chinese challenge is to discard market socialism and to institute market Taoism by shrinking the size of the state and expanding the size of the market, in the process recreating China's civil society.

Lao Tzu and the Principle of *Wu Wei*

China need not be confined to the ideological cage of market socialism by fear of copying Western traditions of market liberalism. The way of the market is universal. The free-market economy is, as Václav Havel has stated so elegantly, "the only natural economy, the only kind that makes sense, the only one that can lead to prosperity, because it is the only one that reflects the nature of life itself" (1992, 62). Since 1978, market liberalization has increased substantially the standard of living of millions of Chinese, and individuals are beginning to express their feeling that private property is sacred. M. Pei reports, "In a 1993 poll of 5,455 respondents in six provinces, 78 percent agreed with the statement, 'Private property is sacred and must not be violated'" (1998b, 76).

In considering what steps to take next, China's leaders should look to their own ancient culture and rediscover the principle of spontaneous order—what Nobel laureate economist James M. Buchanan has called the "most important central principle in eco¬nomics" (1979, 81–82). In the *Tao Te Ching*, written more than two thousand years before *The Wealth of Nations*, Lao Tzu instructed the sage (ruler) to adopt the principle of *wu wei* (noninterference) as the best means of achieving happiness and prosperity:

> Administer the empire by engaging in no activity.
> The more taboos and prohibitions there are in the world,
> The poorer the people will be.
> The more laws and orders are made prominent,
> The more thieves and robbers there will be.
> Therefore, the sage [ruler] says:
> I take no action and the people of themselves are transformed.
> I engage in no activity and the people of themselves become prosperous.

> (Chan 1963, 166–67)

The foregoing passage implies that the more the state intervenes in everyday life, the more corruption will occur. Alternatively, if people are left alone to pursue their own happiness, a spontaneous market order will arise and allow people to create prosperity for themselves and their country. Like Lao Tzu, China's leaders should realize that corruption stems not from freedom but from government's excessive constraint of freedom. As Nobel laureate economist Gary Becker notes, "Markets grow up spontaneously, they are not organized by governments, they grow on their own. If individuals are given freedom, they will help to develop markets for products that one cannot imagine in advance" (1996, 75).

Just as the principle of spontaneous order is central to economic liberalism, the principle of *wu wei* is fundamental to Taoism. Rulers rule best when they rule least—that is, when they take "no unnatural action."[3] Limiting government can help cultivate an environment in which individuals can pursue happiness and practice virtue (*te*). Thus, Lao Tzu writes in the *Tao Te Ching*, "No action is undertaken, and yet nothing is left undone. An empire is often brought to order by having no activity" (Chan 1963, 162).

The challenge for China is to widen the *free* market and to provide the institutional infrastructure necessary to support *private* markets (Friedman 1990, 5). The solution is to discard market socialism and to make the transition to market Taoism. As Gao Shangquan stated when he was vice minister of the State Commission for Restructuring the Economy, the challenge is to throw state-owned enterprises (SOEs) "into the sea of the market economy" (qtd. in Chang 1997, 15).

FROM MARKET SOCIALISM TO MARKET TAOISM

Although China has made significant progress in moving toward a market system, much remains to be done in terms of creating the institutional infrastructure needed for a real market economy based on private property and freedom of contract. The existence of widespread state ownership remains a major hurdle in the transition to a private free-market system. Lin, Cai, and Li have pointed to the continuing "institutional incompatibility" between plan and market and have argued that "it is essential for the continuous growth of the Chinese economy to establish a transparent legal system that protects property rights so as to encourage innovations, technological progress, and domestic as well as foreign investments in China" (1996, 226).

China needs constitutional change that enshrines the principle of freedom and depoliticizes economic life. Then real capital markets can emerge to replace centralized investment planning and government controls on capital flows. Removing government from the market will solve the problem of institutional incompatibility and reduce corruption.

A Constitution of Liberty for China

Economic and political reforms are inseparable. To depoliticize economic life, China ultimately must change its constitution from one that enshrines the CCP to one that protects persons and property. New thinking (*xin si wei*) will be required: the plan¬ning mentality will have to give way to the idea of freedom under the law. That idea, however, is not new, either in the West or in China. As Jixuan Hu writes, "By setting up a minimum group of constraints and letting human creativity work freely, we can create a better society without having to design it in detail. That is not a new idea, it is the idea of law, the idea of a constitution. Real constitutional government is a possible alternative to the dream of a perfectly designed society.... The idea is to apply the principle of self-organization" (1991, 44).

The recent amendment to Article 11 of China's constitution, which recognizes the importance of the nonstate sector and affords protection to private enterprise, is a step in the right direction. To move further toward a free society, however, China must continue to open its markets to the outside world and to abide by international law. In particular, as Pilon has emphasized, China needs "a constitution grounded in the rule of law, not in the rule of man; ... a constitution of liberty" (1998, 352).

To accept that idea, however, means to understand and accept the notion of spontaneous order and the principle of nonintervention (*wu wei*) as the basis for economic, social, and political life. China's leaders and people can turn to the writings of Lao Tzu for guidance:

> When taxes are too high,
> people go hungry.
> When the government is too intrusive,
> people lose their spirit.
>
> Act for the people's benefit.
> Trust them; leave them alone.

> (Mitchell 1991, 75)

Deng Xiaoping implicitly recognized Lao Tzu's way of thinking when he wrote,

> Our greatest success—and it is one we had by no means anticipated—has been the emergence of a large number of enterprises run by villages and

townships. They were like a new force that just came into being spontaneously.... If the Central Committee made any contribution in this respect, it was only by laying down the correct policy of invigorating the domestic economy. The fact that this policy has had such a favorable result shows that we made a good decision. But this result was not anything that I or any of the other comrades had foreseen; it just came out of the blue.[4] (1987, 189)

Although China can return to its own vision of freedom by embracing and extending Lao Tzu's thought, the idea of market Taoism can be enhanced by a deeper understanding of classical liberal economic thought and a study of free-market institutions. In breaking the planning mentality, therefore, China can learn both from its own culture and from the West.

Creating Real Capital Markets in China

The goal of creating viable *socialist* capital markets is an illusion (Nutter 1968). Modern global capital markets presuppose a transparent legal framework that protects private-property rights and allows the free flow of information. Asset prices then reflect the capitalized value of future profits. Without the right to buy and sell shares of stock freely in organized markets, and without competitively determined market interest rates, there can be no real capital markets and no way to determine true asset values.

Hernando de Soto, the author of *The Mystery of Capital*, aptly says, "Capital is that value, that additional value, that comes from things that are duly titled; . . . capital is also law" (qtd. in Fettig 2001, 23, 26). Countries remain poor when their leaders prevent privatization and fail to abide by the rule of law. Hong Kong is rich because it adheres to the rule of law and has market-supporting institutions, not because it has abundant physical capital.

The more secure are rights to future income, the more confidence individuals have in the future, the more breadth and depth capital markets have, and the more liquidity there will be. Likewise, any attenuation or weakening of private-property rights—including the rights to use, sell, and partition property—will produce less trust, less liquidity, and less wealth.

Denying Chinese entrepreneurs the freedom to specialize in ownership and risk taking will place them at a huge disadvantage in creating a financial architecture that can rival that of the West. As long as the state has a majority stake in enterprise ownership, investment decisions and managerial appointments will be politicized.

China's inclusion in the WTO has begun a process of opening its pseudo capital markets to foreign competition and expertise. Foreign banks will have full access to the local currency market within five years. Most restrictions on foreign equity holding will be relaxed, and Western legal and accounting firms will have greater market access. Geographic limits on foreign insurance firms will be eliminated, and those firms will be allowed to offer a wider range of services, including pension annuities. Other liberalization measures, especially those that allow foreign firms direct trading and distribution rights within China, will spur competition and create an ever-larger nonstate sector (Groombridge 2000, 6–7).

To create real capital markets, China must make political reforms. The state must leave the ownership of capital to private individuals who will bear ultimate responsibility for the allocation of capital assets and who will not be subject to political control. That transformation will require major changes in the institutional infrastructure and a new way of thinking about the role of property rights in China's socialist market economy. The WTO can help push China in that direction.

Beijing has propped up SOEs and created asset-management companies to take over nonperforming loans of state banks. Those measures, however, are not sufficient to cure the institutional cancer at the core of China's ownership system. Highly inefficient SOEs are starving private firms of capital. The government— that is, the CCP—remains the dominant owner of capital, and central authorities decide which firms may float shares on the stock exchanges. Recapitalizing state banks is meaningless if those banks continue to lend to SOEs and are driven by politics, not by markets. If China is to revitalize its firms and banks and is to prevent a financial meltdown, it must restructure and open its capital markets, not simply inject more funds into dying institutions. Private owners, with exclusive claims to net income and transferable shares, must be given greater scope and access to capital.

The challenge will be for the leadership to realize that China's future as a modern financial center depends on establishing trust. Foreign and domestic investors must have clearly defined rights to enterprise profits and must be guided by competitively determined rates of return and interest rates in making their investment decisions. The political challenge is to get government out of the business of allocating capital and to allow effective private ownership—something the CCP has not been willing to do except on a small scale.

The freedom to specialize in ownership and risk taking—and thus to choose among an array of assets with varying combinations of risk and reward—is an important factor promoting wealth creation (Alchian 1977, chap. 5). As private wealth grows, people will have an incentive to protect it against the state. How can the CCP be for the people if it prevents widespread private ownership?

The difficulty is to provide an incentive for China's leaders to accept private ownership as the norm rather than as the exception. Constitutional changes to give further protection to private property would be a welcome sign and would help to stem capital outflows and to attract new capital into China. As Zhong Wei, an economist at Beijing Normal University, recently stated, "The need for a constitutional amendment that adds the principle that private properties are inviolable has become quite urgent to curb private capital outflow[s]" (qtd. in Jia 2002, 5).

LESSONS FOR CHINA

Social, economic, and political order can rest on coercion or consent. The liberal constitutional order of freedom has served the world well in bringing about peace and prosperity. The failure of central planning and the collapse of communism in eastern Europe and the Soviet Union have illustrated the futility of state control as a solution to the problem of social organization. Bastiat correctly said, "The solution of the social problem lies in liberty" (1964, 94).

China's greater reliance on markets since 1978 has transformed ethical practices gradually: voluntary exchanges are replacing state controls, and people are beginning to experience the spontaneous order of the marketplace. That cultural transformation is easily seen, especially in the coastal cities. As Jianying Zha writes, "The economic reforms have created new opportunities, new dreams, and to some extent, a new atmosphere and new mindsets. The old control system has weakened in many areas, especially in the spheres of economy and lifestyle. There is a growing sense of increased space for personal freedom" (1995, 202).[5] Zhang Shuguang, an economist at the Unirule Institute in Beijing, one of China's first private think tanks, writes,

> Mandatory economy and market economy belong to entirely different ideologies and different ethics.... Planned economy is based upon some idea of ideal society and beautiful imagination, but compulsory implementation has been its only means of realization. In such a system, [the] individual is but a screw in a machine, which is the state, and loses all its originality and creativeness. The basic ethics required in such a system is obedience. In the market system, which is a result of continuous development of equal exchange and division of labor, *the fundamental logic is free choice and equal status of individuals.* The corresponding ethics in [the] market system is mutual respect, mutual benefit, and mutual credit. (1996, 5, emphasis added)

Understanding those differences is the first step in China's long march from market socialism to market Taoism and from constitutional fiat to constitutional order under the law of liberty.

In their book *China's New Political Economy*, Susumu Yabuki and Stephen Harner find "a clear tendency toward higher GDP growth rates as the proportion of non-state-owned enterprise increases" (1999, 100). Provinces with greater economic freedom grew considerably faster than those with less freedom, as indicated by the size of the state sector. For example, Fujian, Guangdong, and Zhejiang—provinces where SOEs account for less than 30 percent of industrial output value—grew at rates close to 20 percent per annum on average from 1990 through 1995. In contrast, Qinghai, Heilongjiang, and the Ningxia Autonomous Region, where SOEs are the dominant producers, experienced much slower average growth rates, in the range of 7 to 8 percent per annum (Yabuki and Harner 1999, 99–100).[6]

The importance of foreign-funded enterprises in the coastal areas and of foreign trade in general cannot be underestimated. China has benefited tremendously from the presence of alternatives to SOEs. Experimentation with nonstate ownership forms has been highly successful. The government has recognized the importance of private ownership in creating wealth. The *People's Daily* recently reported, "Zhang Dejiang, secretary of the Zhejiang Provincial Committee of the Communist Party of China, said that the contribution of the private sector in pushing forward the rapid economic growth of the province can not be overlooked" ("Chinese Private Economy" 2002).[7] It is now time to allow even greater freedom and to recognize not only the usefulness of private property but also its sanctity as a basic human right.

In an encouraging sign, the *People's Daily* also recently reported that "a new research report on China's social strata made by some scholars at the Chinese Academy of Social Sciences [CASS] says that private property will play the same role as state-owned property in forming the economic foundation and the overall national strength of socialist society" ("Chinese Private Economy" 2002). On the surface, this statement is absurd: private and state ownership are diametrically opposed—the first vests exclusive title in the individual and allows owners to sell their bundle of property rights; the second vests title in the state and its political apparatus, the CCP, and no individual has freely transferable rights. Yet, if we read between the lines, we can see that the CASS report signals that China may be ready to allow greater economic freedom by provid¬ing more security to private property. Indeed, at the 16th Party Congress, in November 2002, President Jiang Zemin boldly stated: "We need to . . . improve the legal system for protecting private property" (qtd. in McGregor and Kynge 2002, 3).

Five lessons should be carved in stone and constantly remembered as China moves from market socialism to market Taoism:

- Private property, freedom, and justice are inseparable.
- Justice requires limiting government to the protection of persons and property.
- Minimizing the use of force to defend life, liberty, and property maximizes freedom and creates a spontaneous market-liberal order.
- Private free markets are not only moral, but they create wealth by providing incentives to discover new ways of doing things and by increasing the range of alternatives.
- Governments rule best when they follow the rule of law and the principle of noninterference (*wu wei*).

The key to a successful future for China is not better government planning or more foreign aid, but rather a constitution that protects persons and property against the discretionary power of government and lays a framework for freedom under the rule of law. That is the legacy of Hong Kong and the challenge for China.

NOTES

1 On the right to noninterference as a fundamental moral right, see Pilon 1979, 1185.

2 Ludwig von Mises and F. A. Hayek were instrumental in conveying this idea. See Hayek [1935] 1975 and 1948, chaps. 7–9. On the Mises/Hayek critique of socialism, see Lavoie 1990, 76–82.

3 Wing-Tsit Chan notes that the principle of wu wei does not mean "'inactivity' but rather 'taking no action that is contrary to Nature'" (1963, 136). In essence, "wu wei . . . is the embodiment of suppleness, simplicity, and freedom" (H. Smith 1991, 208).

4 Kate Xiao Zhou describes the demise of China's collective farms and the creation of the household responsibility system (baochan daohu), with its township and village enterprises, as "a spontaneous, unorganized, leaderless, nonideological, apolitical movement" (1996, 4).

5 For a discussion of China's emerging civil society, see Pei 1998a. Kathy Chen describes the model of development in China's new urban centers, such as Shishi, as "*xiao zhenfu, da shehui*—small government, big society—which advocates less involvement by cash-strapped governments and more by society" (1996).

6 The 7 to 8 percent growth rates reported for SOE-dominated provinces are suspect because managers who are also CCP members have an incentive to overstate production and because inventories often have *little* market value. On the problem of measuring China's growth, see Rawski 2002.

7 The National Economic Research Institute (NERI) in Beijing ranked Zhejiang second in terms of its progress toward a market economy compared to other provinces in 1999. Guangdong was ranked number one. See Fan, Wang, and Zhang 2001, 10. The NERI "marketization index"

recognizes the importance of secure property rights and the rule of law in creating a market system: "One of the important aspects of market-oriented reform is the development of [a] rule of law, including the setting up of [a] legal framework for property rights protection and contract enforcement" (Fan, Wang, and Zhang 2001, 4).

REFERENCES

Alchian, A. A. 1967. *Pricing and Society*. Occasional Paper no. 17. London: Institute of Eco¬nomic Affairs.

———. 1977. Some Economics of Property Rights. In *Economic Forces at Work*, 127–49. Indianapolis, Ind.: Liberty Press.

Bastiat, F. 1964. *Selected Essays on Political Economy*. Translated from the French by S. Cain. Edited by G. B. de Huszar. Irvington-on-Hudson, N.Y.: Foundation for Economic Education.

Bauer, P. T. 1957. *Economic Analysis and Policy in Underdeveloped Countries*. Durham, N.C.: Duke University Press.

Becker, G. S. 1996. *Gary Becker in Prague*. Edited by J. Pavlík. Prague: Centre for Liberal Studies.

Buchanan, J. M. 1979. General Implications of Subjectivism in Economics. In *What Should Economists Do?* 81–91. Indianapolis, Ind.: Liberty Press.

Chan, W. T., ed. 1963. *A Source Book in Chinese Philosophy*. Princeton, N.J.: Princeton University Press.

Chang, Y. F. 1997. Temper State-Owned Enterprises in Ocean of Market Economy. Interview with Gao Shangquan, vice minister of the State Commission for Restructuring the Economy. *Hong Kong Economic Journal*, May 9, 15.

Chen, K. 1996. Chinese Are Going to Town as Growth of Cities Takes Off. *Wall Street Journal*, January 4, A1, A12.

Chinese Private Economy Seeking Wider Development Space. 2002. *People's Daily*, April 7. http://english.peopledaily.com.cn/200204/07/eng20020407_93626.shtml.

Deng, X. P. 1987. *Fundamental Issues in Present-Day China*. Translated by the Bureau for the Compilation and Translation of Works of Marx, Engels, Lenin, and Stalin under the Central Committee of the Communist Party of China. Beijing: Foreign Languages Press.

Dorn, J. A. 1997. The Tao of Adam Smith. *Asian Wall Street Journal*, August 18, 6.

———. 1998. China's Future: Market Socialism or Market Taoism? *Cato Journal* 18, no. 1: 131–46.

———. 2001a. Bastiat: A Pioneer in Constitutional Political Economy. *Journal des Economistes et des Etudes Humaines* 11, nos. 2–3: 399–413.

———. 2001b. Creating Real Capital Markets in China. *Cato Journal* 21, no. 1: 65–75.

———. 2002. The Rule of Law and Freedom in Emerging Democracies: A Madisonian Perspective. In *James Madison and the Future of Limited Government*, edited by J. Samples, 191–211. Washington, D.C.: Cato Institute.

Fan, G., X. Wang, and L. Zhang. 2001. *Annual Report 2000: Marketization Index for China's Provinces*. Beijing: National Economic Research Institute, China Reform Foundation (April).

Fettig, D. 2001. An Interview with Hernando de Soto. Federal Reserve Bank of Minneapolis. *The Region* 15, no. 2: 20–31. www.minneapolisfed.org.

Friedman, M. 1990. Using the Market for Social Development. In *Economic Reform in China: Problems and Prospects*, edited by J. A. Dorn and Wang Xi, 3–15. Chicago: University of Chicago Press.

———. 2002. Preface: Economic Freedom Behind the Scenes. *In Economic Freedom of the World 2002 Annual Report*, edited by J. Gwartney and R. Lawson, xvii–xxi. Vancouver: Fraser Institute.

Groombridge, M. A. 2000. China's Long March to a Market Economy. Trade Policy Analysis no. 10. Washington, D.C.: Cato Institute, Center for Trade Policy Studies (April).

Gwartney, J., and R. Lawson. 2002. *Economic Freedom of the World 2002 Annual Report.* Vancouver: Fraser Institute.

Havel, V. 1992. *Summer Meditations on Politics, Morality, and Civility in a Time of Transition.* London: Faber and Faber.

Hayek, F. A., ed. [1935] 1975. *Collectivist Economic Planning.* London: Routledge. Reprint. Clifton, N.J.: Augustus M. Kelley.

———. 1948. *Individualism and Economic Order.* Chicago: University of Chicago Press.

———. 1960. *The Constitution of Liberty.* Chicago: University of Chicago Press.

———. 1967. The Principles of a Liberal Social Order. In *Studies in Philosophy, Politics, and Economics,* 160–77. Chicago: University of Chicago Press.

———. 1978. Competition as a Discovery Procedure. In *New Studies in Philosophy, Politics, Economics, and the History of Ideas,* 179–90. Chicago: University of Chicago Press.

Hoskins, L., and A. I. Eiras. 2002. Property Rights: The Key to Economic Growth. In *2002 Index of Economic Freedom,* edited by G. P. O'Driscoll Jr., K. R. Holmes, and M. A. O'Grady, 37–48. Washington, D.C., and New York: Heritage Foundation and *Wall Street Journal.*

Hu, J. 1991. The Nondesignability of Living Systems: A Lesson from the Failed Experiments in Socialist Countries. *Cato Journal* 11, no. 1: 27–46.

Jensen, M. C., and W. H. Meckling. 1985. Human Rights and the Meaning of Freedom. Unpublished manuscript.

Jia, H. 2002. China Reigns in Illegal Capital Flight. *Business Weekly/China Daily* 70 (May 28–June 3): 1, 5.

Lavoie, D. 1990. Economic Chaos or Spontaneous Order? Implications for Political Economy of the New View of Science. In *Economic Reform in China: Problems and Prospects,* edited by J. A. Dorn and Wang Xi, 63–85. Chicago: University of Chicago Press.

Lin, J. Y., F. Cai, and Z. Li. 1996. The Lessons of China's Transition to a Market Economy. *Cato Journal* 16, no. 2: 201–31.

Locke, J. [1690] 1965. *The Second Treatise of Government: An Essay Concerning the True Original, Extent, and End of Civil Government.* In *Two Treatises of Government,* rev. ed., with introduction and notes by P. Laslett. New York: New American Library.

Madison, J. [1792] 1906. Property. In *The Writings of James Madison,* vol. 6, 1790–1802, edited by G. Hunt, 101–3. New York: Putnam's, Nickerbocker.

McGregor, R., and J. Kynge. 2002. China Leader Says Private Property to Be Protected. *Financial Times,* November 9, 3.

Mitchell, S., trans. 1991. *Tao Te Ching: A New English Version, with Foreword and Notes.* New York: HarperPerennial.

Niskanen, W. A. 2002. The Soft Infrastructure of a Market Economy. In *Toward Liberty: The Idea That Is Changing the World,* edited by D. Boaz, 63–68. Washington, D.C.: Cato Institute.

Nutter, G. W. 1968. Markets Without Property: A Grand Illusion. In *Money, the Market, and the State,* edited by N. Beadles and A. Drewry, 137–45. Athens: University of Georgia Press.

Pei, M. 1998a. The Growth of Civil Society in China. In *China in the New Millennium: Market Reforms and Social Development,* edited by J. A. Dorn, 245–66. Washington, D.C.: Cato Institute.

———. 1998b. Is China Democratizing? *Foreign Affairs* (January–February): 68–82.

Pilon, R. 1979. Ordering Rights Consistently: Or What We Do and Do Not Have Rights To. *Georgia Law Review* 13, no. 4: 1171–96.

———. 1983. Property Rights, Takings, and a Free Society. *Harvard Journal of Law and Public Policy* 6 (Summer): 165–95.

———. 1998. A Constitution of Liberty for China. In *China in the New Millennium,* edited by J. A. Dorn, 333–53. Washington, D.C.: Cato Institute.

Rawski, T. G. 2002. Measuring China's Recent GDP Growth: Where Do We Stand? *China Economic Quarterly* (October): 1–13.

Smith, A. [1776] 1937. *The Wealth of Nations*. Edited by E. Cannan. New York: Modern Library, Random House.

Smith, H. 1991. *The World's Religions*. Rev. and updated ed. San Francisco: HarperSanFrancisco.

Smith, N. D. 1997. The Wisdom That Built Hong Kong's Prosperity. *Wall Street Journal*, July 1, A14.

Yabuki, S., and S. M. Harner. 1999. *China's New Political Economy*. Rev. ed. Boulder, Colo.: Westview.

Zha, J. 1995. *China Pop*. New York: New Press.

Zhang, S. 1996. Foreword: Institutional Change and Case Study. In *Case Studies in China's Institutional Change*, vol. 1, edited by Zhang Shuguang, 1–18. Shanghai: People's Publishing House.

Zhou, K. X. 1996. *How the Farmers Changed China*. Boulder, Colo.: Westview.

Acknowledgments: Reprinted from *The Independent Review*, 7, no. 4 (Spring 2003), pp. 485–501. Copyright © 2003. This chapter draws on some of my earlier work (Dorn 1998, 2001a, 2001b, 2002). It was originally prepared as a lecture and translated into Chinese for Liu Junning's online workshop "The Constitutional Order of Freedom in China" (www.libertas2000.net/workshop/online/dorn.htm), supported by a grant from the Atlas Economic Research Foundation's International Freedom Project.

11

The Will to Be Free

The Role of Ideology in National Defense

Jeffrey Rogers Hummel

The practical superiority of markets over governments has become readily apparent. Only the most dogmatic of state apologists continue to deny this obvious fact—at least with respect to the production of many goods and services. Free-market economists and libertarians go much further, of course. They affirm the market's superiority in nearly all realms. Yet only a handful of anarcho-capitalists, most notably Murray Rothbard, have dared claim that a free market could also do a better job of providing protection from foreign states.[1] National defense is generally considered the most essential of all government services.

This widely conceded exception to the efficacy of markets seems to have irrefutable empirical confirmation. If private defense is better than government defense, why has government kept winning over the centuries? Indeed, the state's military prowess has more than seemingly precluded the modern emergence of any anarchocapitalist society. At one time, as far as we know, all humankind lived in stateless bands of hunter-gatherers and had done so since the emergence of modern man some fifty thousand years ago. But beginning around 11,000 B.C., a gradual transition to plant cultivation and animal husbandry—in what is variously identified as the Neolithic, Food Production, or Agricultural Revolution—fostered a steady increase in population densities. These denser, settled populations became susceptible to what the distinguished historian William H. McNeill (1992) has aptly termed *microparasites* and *macroparasites*. Microparasites are the assorted diseases and other pests that have constantly plagued civilization until (and to a lesser extent since) the development of modern medicine. And macroparasites are governments, which arose either through conquest or in reaction to the threat of conquest, until they now dominate every corner of the globe.[2]

Radical libertarians, such as Rothbard (1974, 1978), explicitly acknowledge the historical triumph of governments over primitive stateless societies when they embrace the conquest theory of the origins of the state.[3] Yet this acknowledgment boxes them into an apparent paradox. How can they attribute the origins of government to successful conquest and simultaneously maintain that a completely free society, without government, could prevent such conquest?

In the following pages, I attempt to resolve this paradox. Doing so obviously hinges on establishing a crucial difference between the conditions that permitted governments to arise in the first place and those that would characterize a future free society. So let us initially turn our attention to the first set of conditions, to ascertain exactly what aspects of the Agricultural Revolution created such fertile soil for the growth of coercive monopolies.

POPULATION GROWTH AND THE EMERGENCE OF THE STATE

Unlike the state, warfare predates the Agricultural Revolution. It was endemic among bands of hunter-gatherers. But it never led to permanent conquest. Why not? The explanation is simple enough. Hunters and gatherers could easily exit to new land. "Where population densities are very low," writes Jared Diamond, "as is usual in regions occupied by hunter-gatherer bands, survivors of a defeated group need only move farther away from their enemies" (1997, 291). This option ceases to be viable only with the higher concentrations of population supported by food production. "No doubt, if tax and rent collectors pressed too heavily on those who worked the fields," admits McNeill, "the option of flight remained. But in practice, this was a costly alternative. It was rare indeed that a fleeing farmer could expect to find a new place where he could raise a crop in the next season, starting from raw land. And to go without food other than what could be found in the wild for a whole year was impractical" (1992, 82).

In other words, hunting and gathering tends to prevail when land is relatively abundant. Yet this very abundance condemned hunting and gathering to a Malthusian dilemma. Without any serious land scarcity, hunting-gathering societies had little incentive to establish or enforce clear property rights in natural resources. Population therefore expanded, ultimately subjecting this most basic form of production to diminishing marginal returns. The most extreme manifestations of the resulting overutilization of common resources are the species extinctions that many authorities now attribute to primitive hunters. Such extinctions have their modern counterparts in the current inefficient harvesting of whales and other resources from the commonly owned oceans.

Whether humans were the primary agents in the disappearance of woolly mammoths and some two hundred other species of large mammals in the late Pleistocene is still debated, but the lack of enforceable property rights in land indisputably created a free-rider or negative-externality problem among competing bands of hunters and gatherers that caused their numbers to steadily expand. At some point, the growing population drove returns to hunting and gathering so low that settled agriculture and animal husbandry became more productive. This change in relative productivity then provided incentives for the necessary innovations in plant cultivation and animal domestication. Thus, rising population densities became both the most important cause and one of the most important consequences of the Agricultural Revolution. Migratory bands of scattered hunters and gatherers were supplanted by larger, relatively sedentary populations of farmers and herders.[4]

Property rights in land now emerged as the spread of agriculture made this resource increasingly scarce. At the same time, however, settled populations became increasingly vulnerable to both microparasites and macroparasites. Macroparasites could take the form of marauding raiders who plundered their victims and perhaps exterminated them. But "adaptation between host and parasite always tends toward mutual accommodation," as McNeill (1992, 87) puts it. The most successful macroparasites were the warriors and rulers who stumbled into some kind of long-run equilibrium with their coerced subjects. They extracted enough resources through tribute and taxation to be able to ward off competing groups of macroparasites, but not so much that they killed off their host population. They, in short, usually operated within the range of the Laffer curve apex, for those rulers who seized too much or too little wealth often suffered military defeat at the hands of other rulers. In this fashion, egalitarian bands evolved first into tribes and then into chiefdoms and finally into hierarchical states.

The free-rider problem, which economists have long presented as a normative justification for the state, is in reality a positive explanation for why the state first arose and persisted. All the earliest governments about which we have any knowledge had relatively small ruling classes dependent on wealth transfers from a much larger subject population. Why did not the more numerous subjects ever rise up and overthrow their masters? The free rider is the key. Revolutionary activity is always extremely risky, but nearly all subjects would benefit from a successful revolution, regardless of whether they participated in it or not. This condition remained an enormous obstacle to organizing the masses. Small, concentrated ruling classes, in contrast, faced fewer free-rider problems in carrying out their conquests. The history of the state, therefore, over the millennia from the Agricultural Revolution to the present has become an always dreary and sometimes horrific litany of special interests triumphantly coercing larger groups.

Numbers are not utterly irrelevant, however. All other things equal, bigger armies have an advantage over smaller ones. As governments continued the hallowed human tradition of waging war, they found it useful to motivate their subjects to fight for them. This quest helped bring about the oft-cited alliance between state and religion, between throne and altar, between Attila and the Witch Doctor.[5] All states promote some ideology, whether religious or secular, that legitimizes their rule. Legitimization makes the state's subjects more docile generally but in particular provides more willing fodder for war. It "gives people a motive, other than genetic self-interest for sacrificing their lives on behalf of others. At the cost of a few society members who die in battle as soldiers, the whole society becomes much more effective at conquering other societies or resisting attack" (Diamond 1997, 278).

Governments ruling over greater populations could more easily defeat their rivals. Even today, it is fairly obvious who would win a war between Germany and Luxembourg, between China and Hong Kong, or between the United States and Grenada. Recall, moreover, that the state owes its origins to the rising populations of the Agricultural Revolution. When ancient governments intruded on remnant bands of hunter-gatherers, the population difference was severe. Couple that with the devastating impact of the microparasitic diseases spawned and spread by denser agricultural societies on peoples not exposed long enough to have developed some natural immunity, and the population difference became even more overwhelming. Whether it was the indigenous San (Bushman) of South Africa being driven to the marginal lands of the Kalahari Desert by the cattle-herding Bantu, or the aboriginal Australians being decimated by the guns and diseases of the invading Europeans, stateless societies of hunter-gatherers were always displaced.

RESOURCE MOBILIZATION, WARFARE, AND COMPETITION AMONG STATES

Population is obviously not the only factor influencing military outcomes. A casual perusal of the intermittent warfare that has characterized the long history of governments helps us identify several others. Wealth and technology are at least as important, with wealthier or more technologically advanced societies enjoying a clear advantage. This was another factor that worked against primitive stateless societies.

The concentrated populations of the Agricultural Revolution also fostered the emergence of trade and cities, and the resulting mutual gains, as McNeill observes, "are as much a part of the historic record as are [the] exploitation and lopsided taking" by governments (1992, 75). To this contemporaneous development of markets we owe all the accouterments of civilization. "For centuries," McNeill continues, exchanges of goods and services, which were freely and willingly entered into by the parties concerned, flickered on and off, being perpetually liable to forcible interruption. Raiders from afar and rulers close at hand were both perennially tempted to confiscate rather than to buy; and when they confiscated, trade relations and voluntary production for market sale weakened or even disappeared entirely for a while. But market behavior always tended to take root anew because of the mutual advantages inherent in exchange of goods coming from diverse parts of the earth or produced by diversely skilled individuals. (75)

Over the long run, those governments that permitted trade, with its concomitant wealth creation and technological innovation, had more and better physical resources to devote to war.

Geography is another determinant of war. Rivers, bodies of water, sea lanes, and ocean barriers can play diverse roles in military maneuvers. Some countries are endowed with more easily defensible terrain because of mountains, forests, deserts, disease environments, or other natural obstacles. The geographic unity of China—bound together by two long navigable river systems, partly hemmed in by high mountains, and with a rather uniform coastline—has favored both its political unity for much of the time since 221 B.C. and its vulnerability to the barbarian invasions of horse-mounted nomads. China stands in stark contrast to Europe, which is fragmented by an irregular coastline, mountain ranges, and water obstructions that have left it politically, linguistically, and ethnically divided to this very day. The importance of geography is underscored by its role in the survival of a few isolated enclaves of hunter-gatherers well into the twentieth century, long after the world's states had staked out their territorial claims to the entire land surface of the planet.

A final factor affecting warfare is, as we have seen, the motivation of the people themselves. Ideas ultimately determine in which direction they wield their weapons or whether they wield them at all. Morale not only has directly affected military operations but also has affected indirectly the capacity of governments to impose their rule. Much successful state conquest has been intermediated through local ruling classes, who retain legitimacy among the subject population. This relationship is well exemplified in the cases of British rule over India and the Spanish conquest of Mexico. The effective dominance of would-be conquerors who possess military superiority but face the implacable hostility of an ideologically united population is more problematic. The English hold on Ireland was, owing to this factor, always tenuous, and one can find similar instances into the modern era. Cultural coherence is another advantage that hunter-gatherers and primitive agriculturists sometimes possessed in their struggles with more centralized societies. Contrast Spain's fairly rapid conquest of the Indians of Central and South America, already habituated to indigenous state rule, with the much more drawn out European campaigns against the North American Indians, who were slowly expropriated, expelled, and exterminated over several centuries but never really fully subjugated until the twentieth.[6]

We can analyze the waging of war, therefore, in a manner somewhat analogous to the economic analysis of production. The same three categories of productive factors—labor (human resources), land (natural resources), and capital goods (wealth and technology)—serve as inputs into any military endeavor, with the labor applied having both a quantitative dimension and a qualitative (human capital) dimension. The combatant who can marshal a greater input of any one of these factors, ceteris paribus, has a military advantage, although there will be numerous situations in which governments decide that actually allocating these resources to war is not worth the potential gain in territory and revenue. One might wish to expand this analysis into a fully articulated theory that allows us to predict the size and shape of states. (Preliminary attempts to do so are Boulding 1962 and Friedman 1977.) Alas, we are not even close to such knowledge, but nonetheless we can detect some crucial relationships.

Prior to the Industrial Revolution, no region of the globe experienced the sustained economic growth that has now come to be viewed as ordinary. Some places and times, perhaps ancient Rome, might have enjoyed a temporarily higher level of average wealth per person than others, but general economic stagnation, without any regular, long-run increase in output per capita, remained the prevailing condition for thousands of years after the outset of the Agricultural Revolution. It was a stagnation, moreover, in which the state's expropriations "tended to keep the peasant majority of civilized populations close to bare subsistence" (McNeill 1992, 74). Disparities among states in wealth and technology, besides those that inevitably resulted from disparities in population, consequently played a secondary role in warfare. Only with the unprecedented advances accompanying sustained economic growth did military capital become so decisive that it outweighed mere numbers and permitted handfuls of Europeans to subdue hordes of natives.

It has now become almost a commonplace observation that the Industrial Revolution occurred first in Western civilization because of Europe's political pluralism. In nearly all prior civilizations, imperial states came to encompass the entire area within which significant trade was conducted. Only in Europe did the trading area and a common culture extend beyond the borders of many small states, creating a truly polycentric legal order. The disadvantage of Europe's political fragmentation was frequent and fratricidal wars that reached their fateful culmination in the mass destruction of the two world wars. But, fortunately, every military attempt to consolidate the continent—whether by Philip II of Spain, Napoleon Bonaparte, or Adolf Hitler—proved abortive. The benefit of the competition among various jurisdictions was that it encouraged innovation, as competition always does, in this case the institutional innovations with regard to property and markets that were the prerequisites for capital accumulation and sustained economic growth.[7]

A simple way to model what happened is to conceive of long-run shifts in the Laffer curve. The short-run Laffer curve depicts the immediate trade-off between tax rates and tax revenue—or, more broadly, between the state's rate of expropriation, aggregating all forms of its exactations, and the total revenue it manages to extract from the economy.[8] Only by reducing the expropriation rate well below what will generate maximum revenue can governments lay the preconditions for secular increases in output. Over time, ironically, this leniency will shift the Laffer curve upward so that even at the same expropriation rate the government will capture more total revenue. Just as private savers must give up consumption in the present to gain more consumption in the future, governments had to give up revenue in the present in order to stimulate the growth that would make them wealthier and stronger in the future.[9] In the intensely competitive political environment of Europe, some states were finally able to discover this formula for eclipsing their rivals.

The same political competition has more recently exposed the utter economic failure of socialism. Without the dramatic comparison with the more prosperous West, the collectivist economies of the Soviet Union and China might have survived politically for eons, despite the inescapable increasing immiseration of the masses and retrogression to the stagnation of the ancient world. But, by itself, competition among states cannot account for either the Industrial Revolution or the collapse of socialism. Something must generate variation in government policies in the first place, which brings us back to the realm of ideas, culture, and legitimization. What I am suggesting is a process of natural selection among states, similar to the natural selection among living organisms. Whereas genetic mutations cause the changes and adaptations that drive the evolution of living species, the decisive causal agent for governments is ideology.[10]

A CRITICAL VARIABLE: IDEOLOGY

Ludwig von Mises was the first to explain and predict the collapse of socialism, but that forecast was just one part of his comprehensive, utilitarian defense of laissez-faire. The other part was his critique of what he called interventionism, or what economics texts used to refer to as the mixed economy and what became known historically in Europe as social democracy. Although central planning was clearly incompatible with the prosperity wrought by the Industrial Revolution, even a more limited welfare state was, in Mises's view, inherently unstable. Each specific government measure would cause such social disruption that it would either bring on further intervention or force its repeal. Society would ultimately end up with either pure socialism or laissez-faire, and because, of the two, only laissez-faire could support the living standards to which Europeans had become accustomed, the choice was obvious.[11]

Events proved Mises to have been absolutely right about central planning but wrong about interventionism. Indeed, the truth about the client-centered, power-broker state is diametrically opposite to Mises's prediction. Rather than being inherently unstable, interventionism is the gravity well toward which both market and socialist societies sink. And public-choice theory, which (in Mises's terminology) works out the praxeology of politics, has provided us with the reason. Because concentrated groups face fewer free-rider problems in seeking and maintaining government transfers and other privileges, they have an inordinate influence on policy. Today, just as at the dawn of civilization, the state's strongest incentives are to benefit special interests at the expense of the general public.[12]

Because of the rent seeking that this incentive structure encourages, not only did Britain and the United States recede after 1900 from perhaps the apogee of limited government in world history, but also Russia's rulers retreated in practice from the pure Marxist goal of abolishing all markets long before the Soviet Union's disintegration in 1991. The Brezhnev-era reign of the *apparatchiki* and *nomenklatura* was a far cry from the systematic central planning of Stalin's Five-Year Plans and even farther from the fanatical assault on all monetary exchange of Lenin and Trotsky's War Communism.[13] The macroparasitic governments in both cases had been extracting revenue well below the potential maximum of the short-run Laffer curve. And whereas Soviet special interests found that they could gain greater transfers with bribes, corruption, and other practices that in effect relaxed the government burden on the economy, the temptation for British and U.S. rulers to exploit the short-run gains in revenue by moving up the Laffer curve was too great, even at the possible cost of long-run growth.

Public-choice analysis, however, is in the awkward position of raising an across-the-board theoretical obstacle to any changes that drive the economy off this social-democratic, neomercantilist equilibrium. There must be some force causing perturbations and oscillations in government policy, or else nearly all humankind would still be slaves groaning under the pharaohs of Egypt. Most public-choice theorists simply rely on such historical accidents as wars, revolutions, and conquests to sweep away existing distributional coalitions.[14] But attributing changes to accident is simply saying that the changes are unexplained. "[T]he economic historian who has constructed his model in neoclassical terms has built into it a fundamental contradiction," concedes Douglass C. North, "since there is no way for the neoclassical model to account for a good deal of the change we observe in history" (1981, 10–11).

The missing variable is ideas. All successful states are legitimized. No government, no matter how undemocratic, rules for long through brute force alone. Enough of its subjects must accept its power as necessary or desirable for its rule to be widely enforced and observed. But the very social consensus that legitimizes the state also binds it.[15] Ideology therefore becomes the wild card that accounts for public-spirited mass movements that overcome the free-rider problem and bring about significant changes in government policy, for ideology can motivate people to do more to effect social change than the material rewards to each individual would justify. "Casual observation … confirms the immense number of cases where large group action does occur and is a fundamental force for change," writes North (1981, 10).[16] Russia was driven to the excesses of Bolshevism by a secular ideology, not by mere rent seeking. At the other end of the spectrum, classical liberalism had to generate similarly potent ideological motivation that overcame free-rider disincentives in order to roll back coercive authority in many Western nations.

We know even less about what causes ideologies to succeed than we do about what determines the size and shape of government jurisdictions. The famed zoologist Richard Dawkins has offered the intriguing proposition that ideas have striking similarities to genes. Many apparent paradoxes in biological evolution disappeared once biologists recognized that the process was driven by the success with which "selfish" genes (rather than individuals or species) could replicate themselves. Dawkins suggested that the term *memes* be applied to ideas whose capacity to replicate in other minds likewise determines their spread (1989, 189–201).[17] No matter how useful this parallel between cultural and genetic evolution may ultimately prove, it at least helps to disabuse us of the illusion that the validity of an idea is the sole or primary factor in its success.

Those who doubt that false belief systems can be tremendously influential need only glance at the worldwide success of so many mutually exclusive religions. It is not simply that they cannot all be true simultaneously; if one is true, then many of the others are not just false, but badly false. Or, to seize an example still closer to our topic, observe the tremendous popularity of invalid ideas that legitimize the state among those whom the state exploits. Other things equal, the truth of an idea might give it some advantage, but other things are rarely equal. The one consolation we can draw is that a meme-based theory implies that the spread of ideas is similarly independent of government. The state, for instance, appears to have played no part in the birth and initial growth of Christianity, and the draconian efforts that many governments devote to the suppression of dissent testifies to the threat posed by that kind of autonomous ideological development.

Successful ideologies therefore can induce alterations in the size, scope, and intrusiveness of government. The steady advance of civilization presents a succession of such surmountings of the free-rider obstacle. But the duration of any alterations has in turn rested on other factors, especially the intensity of the competition among states. Over the long run, only the changes in policy that helped a society to survive were likely to endure. Even then, however, rent seeking and ideological motivation remained in constant tension. Free-rider dynamics were always tending to unleash a process of decay, enfeebling a society's ideological sinews and ravaging its ideological immune system. Public-choice theory thus puts real teeth into the famous maxim "The price of liberty is eternal vigilance."

WHAT MAKES YOU FREE CAN KEEP YOU FREE?

For most proposed reforms, policy issues can and should be separated from strategic issues. Whether the repeal of minimum-wage laws might have desirable economic consequences, for instance, is distinct from whether the repeal of minimum-wage laws is politically attainable. But when considering protection services, this dichotomy breaks down. As I have pointed out elsewhere, protection from foreign governments is merely a subset of a more general service: protection from *any* government, whether foreign or domestic (Hummel 1990, 96–97, 117). The privatization of this service is tantamount to the abolition of the state. The territory constituting the United States is in a very real sense already conquered—by the United States government. Only when Americans have liberated themselves from that conqueror will they have effectively denationalized defense. In other words, the policy question—Can private alternatives provide more effective protection from foreign aggressors?—and the strategic question—Can any people mobilize the ideological muscle to smash the state?—are intimately intertwined.[18]

Hence, although it makes good sense to try to imagine what society would look like if minimum wages were repealed without any other change, it makes far less sense to imagine what society would look like if government were abolished— and especially to ask how such a stateless society might protect itself—without any other change. By the very act of overthrowing the domestic government, whether peacefully or forcibly, the former subjects will have forged powerful tools for protecting themselves from foreign governments. The same social consensus, the same institutions, and the same ideological imperatives that had gained them liberation from their own state would be automatically in place to defend against any other states that tried to fill the vacuum.

So let us assume that in some country, somewhere, government has become so completely delegitimized that it ceases to exist. How might such a society fare militarily in a world of competing states? The result, it turns out, still depends on the same elements noted earlier as determinants in military conflict: wealth and technology, geography, population, and motivation. With regard to wealth and technology, a modern stateless society would enjoy a major advantage. It would not only achieve more rapid increases in economic output and technological improvement with the end of government macroparasitism, but it should already have an economic edge because the most likely candidates for government abolition are countries where intervention is already minimal. The compounding effects of a higher growth rate would only enhance this potential superiority in military capital over time, so that a future free society might have as little to fear militarily from rival states as the United States currently has to fear from such economic basket cases as Mexico, India, or even Indonesia. Thus, what was one of the greatest weaknesses for hunter-gathering communities will become one of the greatest strengths of anarchocapitalist communities.

Geographic endowments, in contrast, are largely a matter of serendipity and could go either way. Population fits a similarly unpredictable pattern. A small anarchocapitalist population would be more vulnerable than a large one. This condition is just a reflection of the sad fact of reality that how much government I suffer is affected by what my neighbors believe. Even arming myself with privately owned nuclear weapons is not a strategically wise way to protect myself from taxes, so long as most of my countrymen think taxes are just and necessary. But unlike bands of hunters and gatherers, a future free society would at least not inevitably suffer from a population disparity with respect to its statist neighbors.

Nor need such a disparity be permanent, if it does exist at the outset, once the fourth military determinant—motivation—is brought into play. A people who have successfully fabricated the ideological solidarity necessary to overthrow their domestic rulers would not merely be extremely difficult to conquer, as I have already observed. Posing no threat of conquest themselves, they could tap into the sympathies of a foreign ruler's subjects better than any other opponent such rulers might take on. Would-be conquerors could find their own legitimization seriously compromised. Just as the American Revolution sent forth sparks that helped to ignite revolutionary conflagrations in many other countries, a vibrant economy free from all government would arouse such admiration and emulation that it would surely tend to expand. In short, a future stateless society would have the best prospects of enjoying beneficial ideological dynamics, both internally and externally. To switch to Dawkinesque terms, anarchy is a meme that, once having taken hold in one place, would have the potential to spread like wildfire.

Still, we cannot leave the ideological factor on a totally optimistic note. The problem of achieving a free society is similar to, but not absolutely identical to, the problem of maintaining one. Ideological fervor has waxed and waned throughout history. I can offer no guarantee that after several generations of liberty and abundance a stateless community would not suffer the same kind of decay that has afflicted so many polities in the past. Ideological motivation is difficult to keep burning strong even for a single lifetime. David Friedman has persuasively argued that anarchy would bring us to "the right side of the public good trap" (1989, 156–59). In other words, once government is gone, the underlying incentive structure is altered. People then individually gain the most from supporting "good laws" that produced net social benefits rather than "bad laws" that provided transfers at the cost of deadweight loss. But his argument may implicitly require a resolute social consensus that prevents any reintroduction of taxation.[19] Can such a consensus fend off all potential conquerors, foreign and domestic, forever?

CONCLUSION

In the distant past, the state triumphed over stateless bands of hunter-gatherers because of the favorable interaction of two major factors. The earliest governments, arising as a consequence of the Agricultural Revolution, could draw on, first, the denser, more disease-resistant populations that food production supported and, second, the superior wealth and technology that accompanied the appearance of trade and cities. Hunter-gatherers, even when they fought with steadfast morale, were easy prey unless they were also shielded by inaccessible geography.

Neither of those two factors, however, would necessarily handicap a future anarchocapitalist society. The sustained economic growth that began with the Industrial Revolution has increased the leverage of wealth and technology in military conflict. Because of the inverse relationship between the extent of government and the rate of economic growth, stateless societies would almost certainly have an advantage in military capital. Admittedly, the population of any future community without government would vary with historical circumstances. The larger its population, the greater its ability to prevent conquest.

But helping such a community both to resist invasion and to expand its area would be the motivation of its people. Settled agricultural populations were initially vulnerable to state conquest because of the free-rider problem. Large groups always face tremendous obstacles in overcoming the disincentives to organize and affect government policy. Yet the accumulation of ideological capital over the centuries and the successful instances of curtailed state power show that this problem need not be decisive. Any movement powerful enough to abolish a standing government in the modern world would thereby have demonstrated its ability to motivate ideologically a great deal of action. It would certainly be a meme capable of international propagation.

Everything said, the human species may still be unable to rid the earth of macroparasitic states, just as it may never eliminate all microparasitic pathogens. But the possibility that disease is inevitable would never be accepted as an adequate justification for abandoning the efforts of medicine against this scourge. The history of Western civilization demonstrates that great strides are feasible, both in curbing illness and in curbing government. Although we may never abolish all states, there is little doubt that we can do better at restraining their power, if only we can motivate people with the will to be free.

NOTES

1 See particularly Rothbard 1974, 1978. My own contributions to the argument for denationalizing defense include Hummel 1981, 1984, 1986, 1990, and Hummel and Lavoie 1990. Other works advocating private defense against foreign aggressors are Wollstein 1969, Tannehill and Tannehill 1970, and Hoppe 1998. Although Ayn Rand believed that national defense was a proper government function, she held that it should be funded voluntarily; see Rand 1964. A work by one of her followers who agrees is Machan 1982. In contrast, Friedman 1989 presents the views of an anarchocapitalist who questions whether a stateless society could provide effective national defense.

2 The literature on what I prefer to call the Agricultural Revolution is immense, but the three works that I have found most insightful are North 1981, 71–112; McNeill 1992, 67–100; and Diamond 1997. Of the three writers, North has the best grasp of economics and yet ironically maintains the most favorable view of the state. I have followed Diamond in using calibrated radiocarbon dates, which put the beginning of the Agricultural Revolution two thousand years earlier than the more conventional, uncalibrated radiocarbon dates put it. The date of fifty thousand years ago for the emergence of modern humans refers to the appearance of the Cro-Magnons in Europe. The origins of our species, *Homo Sapiens*, can be pushed back much further, to half a million years ago.

3 The conquest theory of the origin of the state is most notably expounded in Oppenheimer [1914] 1975, but it resonates throughout recent studies of this quintessential anthropological question, including Carneiro 1970 and 1981; Cohen and Service 1978; Otterbein 1997; and Diamond 1997, 53–66, 265–92. For an engaging account of the role of warfare in the rise of one state that occurred late enough for Europeans to observe and record it, see the first half of Morris 1966.

4 This economic analysis of the causes of the Agricultural Revolution basically follows North (1981, 72–89), who considers and critiques other hypotheses.

5 The allusion to Attila and the Witch Doctor comes from the introductory essay in Rand 1961. For a scholarly explication of the same theme, see chap. 14, "From Egalitarianism to Kleptocracy," in Diamond 1997.

6 Sowell 1998 contains several case studies of the relationship between conquest and culture.

7 Both McNeill (1992, 113–14, 117–22) and Diamond (1997, 409–19) emphasize political competition within Europe, but the author who has pushed this analysis furthest is the Marxist historian Immanuel Wallerstein (1976). On the other hand, Douglass C. North (1981, 158–86) pays more attention to the institutional developments in property rights as a factor in the Industrial Revolution. See also Kennedy 1987.

8 There seems to be no firm convention among economists about which variable belongs on which axis for the Laffer curve. I have seen texts present it both ways: with tax rates on the horizontal and tax revenue on the vertical, and vice versa. I have worded my discussion on the assumption that revenue is on the vertical axis. If one puts it on the horizontal, then the long-run curve would of course shift outward rather than upward.

9 An empirical study of the relationship between government revenue (as a percentage of gross domestic product) and the rate of economic growth (Gwartney, Lawson, and Holcombe 1998) finds that the rate of economic growth rises as government revenue falls over the entire range of observed government revenue.

10 But see Steele 1988 for some potential pitfalls in concepts of cultural evolution.

11 This analysis of both socialism and interventionism is in Mises [1949] 1966, that author's magnum opus; see particularly pages 855–61 for a summary. Mises's book-length treatment of the socialist calculation problem is Mises [1922] 1951.

12 Seminal works in the development of public-choice theory include Downs 1957, Buchanan and Tullock 1962, Niskanen 1971, Breton 1974, and Olson 1982. See also Tullock 1974.

13 Steele (1993) does the best job of charting this Marxist retreat.

14 Olson (1982) exemplifies this approach. I am reminded of a conversation I once had with Gordon Tullock in which he attributed most British liberty to the unintended effects of the completely random and therefore unexplainable adoption of trial by jury in England.

15 My discussion is deliberately vague about how many subjects is enough and how tightly they bind the state. Our theoretical understanding of government requires much development before we can systematically answer those questions. For a fascinating argument that a single social consensus may create multiple stable equilibria with respect to state power, see Kuran 1995. Such a situation would create for government policies the kind of path dependency that free-market economists have rejected as significant on the market.

16 Another economic historian who has brought ideology back in is Robert Higgs; see Higgs 1987, chap. 3.

17 Daniel C. Dennett, in his philosophical tour de force *Darwin's Dangerous Idea* (1995, 333–69), has also pursued the concept of memes. An older but not incompatible approach to the sociology of ideas is in Thomas S. Kuhn's classic *The Structure of Scientific Revolutions*, 2d ed. (1970).

18 To his credit, Murray Rothbard (1978, 238–40) perceptively recognized that defending a free society was in part a strategic question posing as a policy question.

19 The existence of this implicit ideological precondition in Friedman's analysis of a future anarchocapitalist society is suggested by his asymmetric answers to the national-defense and stability problems. Whereas he is very optimistic about protecting an anarchist society from the reemergence of a domestic state, he is very pessimistic (as observed in footnote 1) about protecting it from foreign states. I believe Friedman is too optimistic about the former and too pessimistic about the latter because I see these problems as essentially the same.

REFERENCES

Boulding, Kenneth E. 1962. *Conflict and Defense: A General Theory.* New York: Harper and Row.

Breton, Albert. 1974. *The Economic Theory of Representative Government.* Chicago: Aldine.

Buchanan, James M., and Gordon Tullock. 1962. *The Calculus of Consent: Logical Foundations of Constitutional Democracy.* Ann Arbor: University of Michigan Press.

Carneiro, Robert L. 1970. A Theory of the Origin of the State. *Science* 169 (August 21): 733–38.

———. 1981. The Chiefdom: Precursor of the State. In *The Transition to Statehood in the New World,* edited by Grant B. Jones and Robert R. Kautz. Cambridge: Cambridge University Press.

Cohen, Ronald, and Elmar R. Service, eds. 1978. *Origins of the State: The Anthropology of Political Evolution.* Philadelphia: Institute for the Study of Human Issues.

Dawkins, Richard. 1989. *The Selfish Gene.* New ed. Oxford: Oxford University Press.

Dennett, Daniel C. 1995. *Darwin's Dangerous Idea: Evolution and the Meanings of Life.* New York: Simon and Schuster.

Diamond, Jared. 1997. *Guns, Germs, and Steel: The Fates of Human Societies.* New York: W. W. Norton.

Downs, Anthony. 1957. *An Economic Theory of Democracy.* New York: Harper and Row.

Friedman, David. 1977. A Theory of the Size and Shape of Nations. *Journal of Political Economy* 85 (February): 59–77.

———. 1989. *The Machinery of Freedom: Guide to a Radical Capitalism.* 2d ed. La Salle, Ill.: Open Court.

Gwartney, James, Robert Lawson, and Randall Holcombe. 1998. *The Size and Functions of Government and Economic Growth.* Washington, D.C.: Joint Economic Committee of the U.S. Congress.

Higgs, Robert. 1987. *Crisis and Leviathan: Critical Episodes in the Growth of American Government.* New York: Oxford University Press.

Hoppe, Hans-Hermann. 1998. The Private Production of Defense. *Journal of Libertarian Studies* 14 (Summer): 27–54.

Hummel, Jeffrey Rogers. 1981. Deterrence vs. Disarmament. *Caliber* 9 (October–November): 8–10.

———. 1984. On Defense. *Free World Chronicle* 2 (January–February): 18–23.

———. 1986. A Practical Case for Denationalizing Defense. *The Pragmatist* 3 (April): 1, 8–10, and (June): 3–4.

———. 1990. National Goods versus Public Goods: Defense, Disarmament, and Free Riders. *Review of Austrian Economics* 4:88–122.

Hummel, Jeffrey Rogers, and Don Lavoie. 1990. National Defense and the Public-Goods Problem. In *Arms, Politics, and the Economy,* edited by Robert Higgs. New York: Holmes and Meier for The Independent Institute.

Kennedy, Paul. 1987. *The Rise and Fall of the Great Powers: Economic Change and Military Conflict from 1500 to 2000.* New York: Random House.

Kuhn, Thomas S. 1970. *The Structure of Scientific Revolutions.* 2d ed. Chicago: University of Chicago Press.

Kuran, Timur. 1995. *Private Truths, Public Lies: The Social Consequences of Preference Falsification.* Cambridge, Mass.: Harvard University Press.

Machan, Tibor R. 1982. Dissolving the Problem of Public Goods. In *The Libertarian Reader,* edited by Tibor R. Machan. Totowa, N.J.: Rowman and Littlefield.

McNeill, William H. 1992. *The Global Condition: Conquerors, Catastrophes, and Community.* Princeton, N.J.: Princeton University Press.

Mises, Ludwig von. [1922] 1951. *Socialism: An Economic and Sociological Analysis.* New Haven, Conn.: Yale University Press.

———. [1949] 1966. *Human Action: A Treatise on Economics*. 3d rev. ed. Chicago: Henry Regnery.

Morris, Donald R. 1966. *The Washing of the Spears: The Rise and Fall of the Zulu Nation*. New York: Simon and Schuster.

Niskanen, William A., Jr. 1971. *Bureaucracy and Representative Government*. Chicago: Aldine-Atherton.

North, Douglass C. 1981. *Structure and Change in Economic History*. New York: W. W. Norton.

Olson, Mancur. 1982. *The Rise and Decline of Nations: Economic Growth, Stagflation, and Social Rigidities*. New Haven, Conn.: Yale University Press.

Otterbein, Keith F. 1997. The Origins of War. *Critical Review* 11 (Spring): 251–77.

Oppenheimer, Franz. [1914] 1975. *The State*. New York: Free Life Editions.

Rand, Ayn. 1961. *For the New Intellectual*. New York: Random House.

———. 1964. Government Financing in a Free Society. In *The Virtue of Selfishness: A New Concept of Egoism*. New York: New American Library.

Rothbard, Murray N. 1974. War, Peace, and the State. In *Egalitarianism as a Revolt against Human Nature: And Other Essays*. Washington, D.C.: Libertarian Review.

———. 1978. *For a New Liberty: The Libertarian Manifesto*. Rev. ed. New York: Macmillan.

Sowell, Thomas. 1998. *Conquests and Cultures: An International History*. New York: Basic Books.

Steele, David Ramsay. 1988. How We Got Here. *Critical Review* 2 (Winter): 111–48.

———. 1993. *From Marx to Mises: Post-capitalist Society and the Challenge of Economic Calculation*. Chicago: Open Court.

Tannehill, Morris, and Linda Tannehill. 1970. *The Market for Liberty*. Lansing, Mich.: Tannehill.

Tullock, Gordon. 1974. *The Social Dilemma: The Economics of War and Revolution*. Blacksburg, Va.: University.

Wallerstein, Immanuel. 1976. *The Modern-World System: Capitalist Agriculture and the Origins of the European World-Economy in the Sixteenth Century*. New York: Academic.

Wollstein, Jarret B. 1969. *Society without Coercion: A New Concept of Social Organization*. Silver Spring, Md.: Society for Individual Liberty.

Acknowledgments: Reprinted from *The Independent Review*, 5, no. 4 (Spring 2001), pp. 523–537. Copyright © 2001. This chapter derives from my presentation to the Twenty-second International Conference on the Unity of the Sciences at Seoul, Korea, February 9–13, 2000. I would like to thank Michael Edelstein, Lynda Esko, Ross Levatter, Charles J. Myers, Dyanne Petersen, Jeff Singer, Tim Starr, James Stein, and Joseph Stromberg for their comments. Of course, I alone am responsible for any remaining errors.

12

The Inhumanity of Government Bureaucracies

Hans Sherrer

The media attention focused on elected officials leads many people to think of them as "the government." Such thinking diverts us from the recognition of a critical truth: politically articulated agendas are transformed into reality only by bureaucratic systems. Bureaucracies are the dominant means by which governments control and influence the daily lives of people throughout the world.

If only because of the prominent position that government bureaucracies occupy in society, we need to understand the forces bearing upon the execution of their functions. This need is heightened by the common observation that government bureaucrats routinely treat people in ways that would be decried as inhumane if that treatment were meted out by anyone else.

The human devastation wreaked by past and present political regimes has not been inflicted personally by leaders such as Joseph Stalin, Saddam Hussein, and Pol Pot, but by rank-and-file members of bureaucracies or people acting with their approval. Whoever they may be or whatever position they may hold, political leaders merely issue directives or establish general policies (Ellul 1965, 147). Those policies are executed by bureaucrats and, to some extent, acquiesced to by the general public.

Adolf Hitler himself, for example, did not bring about the Final Solution. It became a reality only because of the independently chosen decisions of tens of millions of Europeans, including bureaucrats and professional people, either to participate in it actively or to do nothing to stop it (Ellul 1965, 147–62). Although a price may have to be paid, anyone whose conscience is shocked by the inhumanity of a bureaucratic program has the option of choosing not to participate in its implementation (Bettelheim 1960, 267–300; Mayer 1966, 168–73). The successful 1943 Rosenstrasse protest in Berlin by German women, which persuaded the Gestapo to release their Jewish husbands and boyfriends from custody, illustrates that acting in accordance with one's conscience can have positive effects even in the most totalitarian of regimes during a time of war (Stoltzfus 1996).

Although the central role of government bureaucracies in ensuring the success of political policies is often overlooked, interrelated aspects contributing to the inhumanity of these bureaucracies have been exposed in numerous books, journals, and magazines. In *The Trial* ([1925] 1988), Franz Kafka immortalized the essence of bureaucratic inhumanity from the standpoint of those who experience it. Relating the plight of Josef K., *The Trial* symbolizes a person's immersion in a bureaucratic process he can neither understand nor influence. Treated as a pawn on a chessboard, Josef K. is in a state of confusion and despair after being arrested, questioned, tried, and found guilty without ever seeing his judge, without being told who his accusers are or knowing what crime he has allegedly committed. Although first published in 1925, *The Trial* eerily presaged the atmosphere of unreality that pervaded the Moscow show trials of 1936–38 (Koestler 1941).

The intense negative feelings government bureaucracies evoke in the people caught in their web not only spring from their imposing structures, impersonality, and the murky rules that guide them, but are reinforced by the sheer magnitude of the apparatus: in the United States alone, more than twenty million people have chosen employment in one of the multitude of government bureaucracies.[1] Moreover, each of those organizations is a part of a greater functioning entity. Directly or indirectly, each bureaucrat relies on the awesome power of government enforcement agencies, which undertake to ensure that the bureaucrats are funded by taxpayers, that their regulations are obeyed, that their activities go forward unimpeded. In a sense, the bureaucrats resemble the members of a shrouded society; they constitute what one might call a "bureaucratic brotherhood."

The exercise of latent bureaucratic power is a theme of Hannah Arendt's *Eichmann in Jerusalem* ([1963] 1994). Arendt uses the backdrop of Adolf Eichmann's 1961 trial in Israel to explore how bureaucratic systems facilitate unconscionably inhumane behavior by the apparently "normal" people typically associated with them. Although Eichmann was only a midlevel SS bureaucrat, his Israeli prosecutors and the world press portrayed him as Satan for his role in the Nazi regime. This media image, however, conflicted with Eichmann's single most distinguishing characteristic: he was an ordinary man who didn't exhibit any disturbing personal traits (Bettelheim 1963, 23; Kren and Rappoport 1994, 70). During the fifteen years between the end of World War II and his kidnapping in Argentina by Israeli agents, Eichmann lived a simple and quiet life with his loving family, going to work every day as people do throughout the world. His normality was unanimously confirmed by the half-dozen psychiatrists who studied him in prison during the year he awaited his trial and by the minister who regularly visited him (Bettelheim 1963, 23). Arendt subtitled her book *A Report on the Banality of Evil* precisely because Adolf Eichmann was psychologically indistinguishable from people who populate countries throughout the world.

Inhumane behavior by the evidently normal members of a bureaucracy is more in need of understanding today than it was at the time of Nazi rule in Germany. Prior to the Nazis' demonstration of the potential of bureaucracy, the destructiveness of rationally directed government bureaus was largely unappreciated. We now know, however, how easily political expediencies can mold bureaucracies into mechanisms of human destruction. This potential causes great concern because the panoply of nuclear, biological, chemical, mechanical, and psychological weapons available today provides bureaucrats with the means to act inhumanely toward large numbers of people with relative ease. In *Modernity and the Holocaust* (1989), Zygmunt Bauman has explored the inherent capability of bureaucracies as powerful instruments of destruction and control. He shows how modern methods of mass organization and production are applied to the bureaucratic control and processing of human beings as effectively as they are used in making and distributing automobile parts and office supplies (13–18, 104–6; see also Feingold 1983, 399–400).

Normal people acting within the framework of a *bureaucratic system* with access to *modern techniques* of action and control: these are the three elements that combine to enable a bureaucracy to function as a horribly destructive entity whose powers can be directed at any person or group that attracts its attention.

Serious inquiries have been made into various facets of the problem of bureaucratic inhumanity, but no single explanation suffices to explain the phenomenon. In this chapter, I discuss ten compelling factors, presented in no particular order, as a preliminary guide to understanding this important and menacing aspect of modern life.

MINDLESS OBEDIENCE TO AUTHORITY

Most people exhibit a nearly mindless obedience to authority. Stanley Milgram's experiments almost forty years ago at Yale University revealed that two-thirds of a representative sampling of Americans would inflict life-threatening high-voltage electric shocks to someone they knew was innocent of any wrongdoing, even when that person was screaming and begging for mercy (Milgram 1975; see also Kelman and Lawrence 1972). Even more disturbing, this large percentage of Americans would inflict pain on innocent people willingly and even enthusiastically upon the mere request of someone whose authority was established by nothing more than his wearing the white coat of a laboratory technician and speaking in a firm voice. These people readily substitute obedience to authority figures for the dictates of their personal moral code. They have been called "sleepers" because they can slip into and out of a state of moral blindness on command (Bauman 1989, 167).

Apart from innumerable historical examples, the stories in a major newspaper on any given day provide support for the observation that bureaucracies are predominantly if not exclusively composed of persons who belong to the large pool of morally ambiguous and obedient people identified by Milgram's experiments. Furthermore, this phenomenon is not restricted by language, geography, political system, or era. It exists as much in the United States and other countries today as it did in Germany under the National Socialists and in Russia under Stalin (Kren and Rappoport 1994, 70). The conscienceless attitude of unreflective and amoral obedience exhibited by people in a bureaucratic setting resembles Eric Hoffer's unflatteringly description of "true believers" in a political or religious mass movement (1951).

SADISTIC BEHAVIOR

Bureaucratic structures increase sadistic behavior by permitting and even encouraging it.[2] This effect is produced by the systematic lessening of the moral restraints inherent in personal agency (Kelman 1973, 52). Stanford psychology professor Philip Zimbardo's "Stanford County Prison" experiment in the early 1970s confirmed this relationship in dramatic fashion (Zimbardo, Haney, and Banks 1973). The experiment revealed that the sadism of people unhealthily obedient to authority can be tapped into and given an expressive outlet by their association with a bureaucratic organization, demonstrating that placing people in an environment in which they can freely exercise their sadistic impulses can have a liberating effect on their doing so.

Zimbardo conducted the experiment by setting up a mock jail in the basement of a building and using participants from the general public who had been selected for their normality. Those chosen to participate were randomly assigned the role of a guard or an inmate. To Zimbardo and his fellow researchers' surprise, a majority of the guards began to behave sadistically toward the inmates within hours of initiation of the experiment (1973, 87–97). Just as surprising, the inmates meekly accepted their subservient role and mistreatment. In writing about this experiment, sociologist Zygmunt Bauman noted a "sudden transmogrification of likable and decent American boys into near monsters of the kind allegedly to be found only in places like Auschwitz or Treblinka" (Bauman 1989, 167). What began as a make-believe experiment soon degenerated into an all-too-real microcosm of the interpersonal dynamics of real jails and prisons.

The universality of Zimbardo's finding is confirmed by the fact that the overwhelming majority of the heinous acts committed in Europe during the Nazi era were not perpetrated by fanatics or deranged people. To the contrary, those acts were performed by ordinary Germans, French, Poles, Czechs, and others who considered themselves to be legally authorized to act in ways that we retrospectively view as inhumane (Browning 1993, 159–89; Kren and Rappoport 1994, 70, 81–83).

The Stanford County Prison experiment had been scheduled to last two weeks, but the reaction of the inmates to their treatment at the hands of the guards forced termination of the experiment after just six days. The guards had became so psychologically immersed in their role of lording over the inmates that their inhumane behavior induced several of the inmates to suffer "acute emotional breakdowns" (Zimbardo, Haney, and Banks 1973, 89, 95). Although never repeated in an academic setting because of its legal and psychological consequences, Zimbardo's experiment is repeated every day in real prisons across America. The operation of these prisons ensures that the bureaucratically approved behavior of the sort conducted by guards at Dachau and Auschwitz is flourishing in the United States today.[3]

REINFORCEMENT OF BEHAVIORIST ATTITUDES

Bureaucracies reinforce behaviorist attitudes at odds with the idea that people are autonomous beings. Behaviorism promotes the idea that people can be conditioned to respond robotically in a predictable manner to a specific stimulus. Hence, behaviorism justifies the inhumane way in which bureaucrats view and deal with people. The inflexible rules, regulations, and mandates ad nauseam of a bureaucracy are enforced in ways that conform to the proposition that people are as behaviorally pliable as rats and pigeons (McConnell 1970; Koestler 1968, 3–18). In other words, the explicit rejection of human autonomy and the role of consciousness in human behavior is ingrained in bureaucratic systems and in the thinking of those who administer them. One of the foremost proponents of behaviorism, Harvard professor B. F. Skinner, acknowledged this relationship in the title of his 1971 book *Beyond Freedom and Dignity*.

Not by coincidence did the rise of pervasive bureaucratic institutions parallel the rise of the acceptance of behaviorist principles in psychology. In a 1913 article in *Psychology Review* that can be characterized as the manifesto of behaviorism,

John B. Watson laid the psychological foundation necessary for the increased bureaucratization of society that followed the outbreak of war in 1914. He wrote, "The time has come when psychology must discard all reference to consciousness.... Its sole task is the prediction and control of behaviour" (quoted in Koestler 1968, 6). First explicitly embraced by the Soviet bureaucracy that funded Ivan Pavlov's research, behaviorist techniques of manipulating large populations by selectively extending reward or inflicting punishment have been perfected during the past eighty years (Koestler 1968, 3–18).

Those techniques have been adopted in principle by all Western countries to the extent that behaviorism—and the hidden but very real threat of *constructive force* underlying it—dominates all interactions between members of a bureaucracy and the public. Constructive force operates on the mind and is intended to produce the same physical result and have the same effect on the affected persons as actual force applied to their bodies. When prevailing conditions suggest the potential use of physical force to gain compliance with a verbal, written, or physically or psychologically implied request or demand by a governmental entity or person, a state of constructive force exists. Needless to say, a condition of constructive or actual force exists in every encounter between someone and any form of governmental representation, whether in person by a bureaucrat or in a letter or other message received from one. In other words, in a sense there are no voluntary encounters between the government and the people considered subject to its jurisdiction.

CONFORMITY WITH PROCEDURE VERSUS INDIVIDUAL RESPONSIBILITY

Bureaucracies substitute conformity with technical procedures for individual responsibility (Bauman 1989, 98). This substitution expresses a dominant motif of the twentieth century: the replacement of human idiosyncrasies, craftsmanship, and ingenuity by the predictability of technical methods (Ellul 1964, 3–14). Henry Ford perfected the first modern factory assembly line in 1913. It was soon reflected in the assembly-line methods adopted by bureaucracies to induce politically approved human behavior. Not surprisingly, then, the enforcement of bureaucratic techniques of behavior control is carried out by people willing to adjust their own behavior to the requirements of political mandates and technical specifications.

Consequently, bureaucrats can be described as carrying out their duties "in a machine-like fashion" (Bettelheim 1960, 45). This phenomenon, however, extends beyond the bureaucracy itself. The prevalence of people throughout society who exhibit a machinelike attitude has grown as the presence of bureaucracies has increased. Conversely, the people who require the most intensive corrective bureaucratic attention are individualistic, free-spirited, and courageous men, women, and children who resistant outside pressures to conform themselves to fit a politically approved mold. In the domain of a government bureaucracy, people's uniqueness is trivialized and considered subservient to the depersonalization and anonymity of the systems and procedures of the agency.

The modern world's reduction of people to the status of things by their classification as a conglomeration of their visible and presumed characteristics was first identified in Germany. This condition was called *Karteimensch*, which loosely means someone living a punch-card existence (Bettelheim 1960, 54). Expressed in the United States by the passage of the Social Security Act in 1935, this attitude has grown to the point that the survival of vast government bureaucracies depends on the widespread categorization and inhumane treatment of human beings as numbers (Twight 1999, 169–76).[4]

CATEGORIZATION OF PEOPLE BY THEIR DEGREE OF CONFORMITY

A bureaucracy typically categorizes people outside of it in groups based on how much they conform to its standards. The more nonconforming or deviant a person or group is considered to be from bureaucratic norms, the higher the probability that person or group will be subject to dehumanization by a process known as *distancing* (Bauman 1989, 102–4)—a method of physically or mentally separating selected people from the rest of society. Those people are demonized and turned into strangers even though they may pose no threat to the public. Furthermore, mentally separating selected persons or groups by distancing often serves as a public relations precursor to their eventual physical separation. When practiced on a large scale, distancing typically degenerates into what are retrospectively described as witch hunts (McWilliams 1950, 3–23, 235–340).

One consequence of the distancing process is that it enables what ordinarily appear to be decent people to act barbarically toward those who have been dehumanized. One of the best-known examples of mental separation is the dehumanization of Jews during the 1930s by Nazi propaganda that portrayed them as the human incarnation of rats and lice (Bosmajian 1974). This action was taken to justify a legal differentiation between the Jews and the approved people in German society. The special legal status of Jews made their mistreatment by bureaucrats an activity for the patriotic general public to support.

Similarly, American soldiers in Vietnam did not kill human beings. They killed "gooks," "dinks," and "slopes." And earlier, the Americans who contributed to the dropping of atomic bombs on Hiroshima and Nagasaki did not exterminate hundreds of thousands of women, children, and old people, but a dehumanized and faceless "Jap" enemy (Keen 1991).

Distancing is actively employed in the United States. The most vivid example is the use of criminal prosecutions as a ritualistic procedure to mentally and physically distance men, women, and children labeled as criminals from the rest of American society (Blumberg 1973, 77). Distancing people through the criminalization process also serves the function of justifying the exercise of bureaucratic power as a "necessary evil" in order to assuage people's fears and insecurities about groups and individuals politically assigned the role of being a domestic enemy (Becker 1975, 96–127).

THE END JUSTIFIES THE MEANS

Obedience to the mission of a bureaucracy is given precedence by those within it over and above the means used to accomplish it. This principle is true whether the mission is issuing driver's licenses to people, imprisoning them, or herding them into cattle cars to be transported to a centralized killing ground. The end of a mission is held sacred by those within a bureaucracy. The means employed are important only to the degree that they assist in accomplishing the mission (Ellul 1965, 50–53). The idea that the end justifies the means is the very antithesis of morality, and its institutionalization as a guiding principle is one of the central features of bureaucratic systems.

Furthermore, bureaucracies reflect the image of the political institutions empowering them to act. As outlined in books such as *Amoral Politics* (Scharfstein 1995), thousands of years of experience support the idea that political institutions are fundamentally amoral.

This amorality appeared in the Nazis' claim after World War II that they couldn't be held personally responsible for their actions because they had a legal duty to achieve their politically empowered bureaucratic missions regardless of the methods they used to do so. At the Nuremberg trials, Nazis offered the following three primary defenses to justify their preoccupation with achieving the end of a bureaucratic mission to the exclusion of a concern with the means employed: I was following orders; I was obeying the law; and I did not know the consequences of my actions. Jacques Ellul observed in *The Political Illusion* that those defenses are based on anonymity and secrecy. He wrote:

> The [bureaucratic] decisions taken are anonymous. This was clearly revealed in connection with the great Nazi war crime trial after the war.

Nobody had ever made a decision. This happened again in the Eichmann trial. We must not say: "This is a lawyer's argument, a lie." On the contrary, it was the exact image of all that takes place in the modern state. All a chief [such as Hitler] can do is to give a general directive, ordinarily not incorporating concrete decisions, and therefore not entailing true responsibility for the concrete acts emerging at the other end. (1965, 147)

American judges and prosecutors involved in the trials at Nuremberg in the late 1940s summarily rejected the Nazi defense that a political end justifies the bureaucratic means used to achieve it (Harris 1954). However, in an ironic twist of fate, prosecutors, judges, and police in the United States now wholeheartedly endorse the Nazi defense.[5] These are the very people who direct the awesome power of the law enforcement bureaucracy and who are most in need of being held legally accountable for their misbehavior.

Given the human devastation and the demands for justice that the routine exercise of their power can cause, it is hardly surprising that bureaucrats everywhere tenaciously cling to the discredited Nazi defense that the end justifies the means. We hear this attitude of nonaccountability expressed every time a bureaucrat utters the chilling phrase "I am only doing my job."

PERSONAL BENEFIT

People expect to benefit personally from their association with a bureaucracy. Consequently, public proclamations by bureaucrats that they are dedicated to serving the interests of the public are little more than thinly veiled public relations ploys. People who have dealt with government agencies for any length of time are acutely aware of this reality. So-called civil servants are typically neither civil toward nor servants of the public.

Instead of serving the mythical entity known as "the people," bureaucrats are de facto mercenaries serving their own financial and professional interests. Preserving their position typically takes precedence over considerations of the impact their actions may have on people affected by them. This self-service has marked even the most extreme cases of bureaucratic loyalty we know of, such as those provided by the Nazis.

Dr. Josef Mengele committed so many heinous acts during his tenure as the chief physician at Auschwitz that he became known as "the Angel of Death." In spite of his moniker, Mengele was regarded by friends, family, and colleagues as a thoughtful and considerate man. Rather than acting out of mean-spiritedness, Mengele engaged in diabolical medical experiments on nonconsenting victims because of his desire to advance his career in the Nazi bureaucracy. A doctor who worked with Mengele at Auschwitz was quoted as saying, "He was ambitious up to the point of being completely inhuman. He was mad about genetic engineering.... Above all, I believe that he was doing this ... for his career. In the end I believed that he would have killed his own mother if it would have helped him" (Fischer 1997, 516).

Adolf Eichmann exhibited the same detachment from the human consequences of his actions as Mengele. After attending his trial, Hannah Arendt wrote: "Except for an extraordinary diligence in looking out for his personal advancement, he had no motives at all" ([1963] 1994, 287). The amoral blindness exemplified by devoted and conscientious public servants such as Mengele and Eichmann is not unusual among people involved with a bureaucracy. They hope to benefit personally from going along with a bureaucracy regardless of its inhumane policies. Thus, it is not unusual for bureaucrats to act as if their personal self-interest is intertwined with the exercise of raw power by the bureaucracy they serve.

ABSENCE OF OUTSIDE ACCOUNTABILITY

Bureaucrats are protected by a nearly complete absence of outside accountability. They can do almost anything under the color of acting as a government employee without fear of legal consequences or personal financial accountability to anyone they harm. This risk-free status is expressed by the political doctrine of qualified and absolute immunity, which protects bureaucrats from civil liability or criminal responsibility for their personally injurious and harmful actions no matter how horrible they may be (*Imbler v. Pachtman* 1976). U.S. District Court Judge Edward Lodge affirmed this doctrine in May 1998 when he dismissed criminal charges by the state of Idaho against Lon Horiuchi, an FBI sharpshooter. Horiuchi had been criminally charged for shooting an unarmed woman, Vicki Weaver, in the head while she was holding her infant daughter in her arms during the federal siege at Ruby Ridge, Idaho, in 1992. Judge Lodge ruled that under the Supremacy Clause of the U.S. Constitution federal agents cannot be criminally prosecuted by a state for violating a state law while performing their assigned governmental duties.[6]

The legal protections bureaucrats enjoy from being outside accountability place them in a privileged position similar to the one formerly occupied by aristocrats (Ellul 1990, 26). A defining characteristic of the largely self-contained aristocratic world was that its members were shielded from the enforcement of laws applying to the rabble of the general public. Thus, the bureaucrats may be seen to constitute a "new aristocracy."

BUREAUCRATIC SECRECY AND SUPPRESSION OF WHISTLEBLOWERS

A de facto code of silence contributes to hiding the illegal and amoral actions committed by members of a bureaucracy. Any sort of crisis that threatens the bureaucracy or its members triggers a closing of ranks to protect it from outside scrutiny, interference, and legal oversight. For example, for six years the Federal Bureau of Investigation, the Bureau of Alcohol, Tobacco, and Firearms, and the U.S. Department of Justice concealed from the public important facts related to possible wrongdoing by those agencies and their agents during the siege and destruction of the Branch Davidian Compound in Waco, Texas, in 1993 (Shapley 1999a, 1999b; Boyer 1999). Countless local examples reveal how the code of silence protects bureaucratic wrongdoers. The Internal Affairs Division of the Seattle Police Department concealed for three years the reported theft by a policeman of more than $10,000 in cash from a dead man at a crime scene (City 1999).

The veil of bureaucratic secrecy protecting the vile actions of its members from public exposure and scrutiny is pierced only occasionally by a courageous whistleblower (Glazer and Glazer 1990). Frank Serpico was one such whistleblower when he publicly testified in the late 1960s about widespread graft and corruption in the New York City Police Department (Maas 1973). He was rewarded for his honesty by being shot in the face after he testified. An insidious form of retaliation used to silence whistleblowers of internal government corruption or wrongdoing is their superiors' recommendation that they be psychiatrically evaluated (as reported on ABC's *20/20*, October 12, 1998). Some potential whistleblowers may be pressured to remain silent by the threat of being sued or having to pay the opponent's legal fees in an unsuccessful suit against a bureaucracy (Gavin 1999). Whistleblowers are also silenced when they die under mysterious circumstances, such as those surrounding the death of former CIA director William Colby in 1996 shortly before he was scheduled to appear on *60 Minutes*. Still other whistleblowers are punished by being forced to retire or by being transferred, demoted, or fired. An example of this latter retaliation was the IRS's attempt to fire agent Jennifer Long after her revelations during the nationally televised September 1997 Senate Finance Committee hearings on IRS abuses (Johnston 1999). Among other things, her congressional testimony revealed how the IRS selectively preys on the weak, poor, and defenseless, while ignoring people and companies "with either the resources to fight back or with friends in the agency" (P-I 1999). The IRS backtracked from its decision to fire Long only after Senator William Roth, the chairman of the Senate Finance Committee, personally protested to the commissioner of the IRS (P-I 1999).

Given the risk to the careers, the pocketbooks, and possibly even the personal safety of whistleblowers, it is not surprising that their revelations of wrongdoing in the inner sanctum of a bureaucracy are so rare that special laws have been enacted to create the impression that they are protected from retaliation. In practice, such laws do little more than enable surviving whistleblowers to sue for a cash settlement after they are forced to retire. A prominent recent example involved Frederic Whitehurst's being drummed out of the FBI after he exposed that the FBI crime lab was fabricating lab results in order to help prosecutors convict people legally presumed to be innocent. Whitehurst sued the FBI for its treatment of him, including its violations of his protections under federal privacy laws. The FBI agreed to settle Whitehurst's lawsuit for $1.16 million, contingent on his resignation. Thus, the FBI's way of dealing with the problem of operating a sham crime lab was to get rid of the one man with the knowledge and willingness to reveal to the public its unethical and unscientific practices (Cannon 1997; Glazer and Glazer 1990).

THE WORST GET ON TOP

The most amorally flexible people involved in a bureaucracy tend to rise to the top and become its leaders. Some of the reasons for this phenomenon were explored in F. A. Hayek's essay "Why the Worst Get on Top" (1944, 148–67). Bureaucracies are perfectly suited to helping the unprincipled attain positions of influence and power because a lack of scruples gives them an advantage in advancing their careers. In this sense, bureaucracies are among the most perfect forms of kakistocracy known to man.

Government bureaucracies are agencies of political power, and the accomplishment of their missions typically depends on the unreflective wielding of the power made available to their administrators. Hence, a ruthless willingness to wield an agency's power is an occupational requirement for someone to rise to the upper echelons (Hayek 1944, 159–67). As Frank H. Knight has stated, "The probability of the people in power being individuals who would dislike the possession and exercise of power is on a level with the probability that an extremely tender-hearted person would get the job of whipping-master in a slave plantation" (quoted in Hayek 1944, 152).

The attraction of power-hungry people to positions of authority in a bureaucracy can have tragic consequences for everyone affected. To some degree, everyone in society is affected when the power-oriented people who influence and control the performance of bureaucracies express their darkest and most inhumane prejudices.[7] For example, more than one in ten members of Congress as well as many federal judges are former U.S. attorneys. The power of compulsion and punishment available to U.S. attorneys and their prosecuting attorney brethren in the state courts attracts zealous people to seek these bureaucratic positions of minimal accountability. Positions in state legislatures and state courts are filled with former local, county, and state prosecutors, who infect all of the positions they fill, whether legislative or judicial, with their societally corrosive attitudes and prejudices.

CONCLUSION

Government bureaucracies lack the animating life force of a human conscience. They are the institutional equivalent of a psychopathic individual (Amado 1995), and they contribute to what sociologist Ashley Montagu has called this century's "dehumanization syndrome" (Montagu and Matson 1983).

The Final Solution was a triumph of institutional duty over morality and personal responsibility. As historian Christopher Browning noted in "The German Bureaucracy and the Holocaust" (1983), "The Nazis' mass murder of the European Jews was not only the technological achievement of an industrial society, but also the organizational achievement of a bureaucratic society.... [It was] achieved by a bureaucratic mode of operation, in which depersonalized and dispassionate behavior unprejudiced by human emotions was a fundamental and positive value of the civil service" (148).

It is a mistake, however, to view the Final Solution as an aberrant bureaucratic program. Well-planned and well-coordinated atrocities have been carried out by bureaucracies in many countries, including the United States (Rummel 1994; Courtois and others 1999).

People correctly sense that they have little or no effective defense against government bureaucracies. The most terrifying and predictive aspect of novels such as *Brave New World*, *We*, *Nineteen Eighty-Four*, *The Trial*, and *The Rise of the Meritocracy* may be their accurate portrayal of the general sense of helplessness people have against all-encompassing bureaucracies. With the continuing projection of the government's bureaucratic tentacles into ever more aspects of public and private life, it is almost redundant to observe that we now live in the "iron cage" of bureaucratic dictatorship against which sociologist Max Weber warned nearly a hundred years ago (Mitzman 1970; Beetham 1996).

Once in place, a bureaucracy projects onto society an influence peculiar to itself. As a consequence, dehumanized attitudes of conformity that are ingrained in bureaucracies are being transmitted to and absorbed by an increasing proportion of the general population. The most distinguishing characteristic of the affected people is their susceptibility to mimicking the worldview and functioning of the bureaucrats (Leinberger and Tucker 1991, 16–18). Like Pavlov's trained dogs, the bureaucratically conditioned people obey politically authorized regulations, laws, and orders in near robotic fashion because they have accepted their obligation to do so. They are among the large majority identified in Milgram's experiments as valuing conformity and obedience to authority more than the possible discomfort of a pang of conscience.

The bureaucratization of modern life is directly linked to the vast politicization of society that has occurred in the past century (Templeton 1979; Higgs 1987), displacing the moderating influences of private, voluntary personal and social relationships. The imposition of political solutions to perceived social and personal problems has become more and more accepted. Because political policies are mere words on paper unless a large group of compliant people stands willing to obey and to enforce them, bureaucratic activities and mentalities have proliferated in step with the ongoing politicization. In the wake of these developments, bureaucratic inhumanity has necessarily grown, and current developments give scant reason to expect a cessation of that growth anytime soon.

NOTES

1 As of December 1999, in the United States, 20.32 million persons were employed by federal, state, and local governments (U.S. Council of Economic Advisers 2000, 359). This figure does not include the many millions working for "private" companies under the direction or oversight of a government bureaucracy.

2 One of Zygmunt Bauman's themes in *Modernity and the Holocaust* is that the Holocaust was a product of the liberating effect a bureaucratic structure can have on inhibitions against cruel behavior (1989, 12–18). Herbert Kelman has explored areas of this theme and refers to the "processes of authorization, routinization, and dehumanization of the victim" (52) as contributing to the amoral behavior of persons acting within an authoritarian environment (1973, 38–52).

3 A recent investigative article in *Seattle Weekly* magazine exposed Washington State's practice of knowingly hiring and retaining racists and Nazi worshipers as prison guards (Vogel 1999).

4 The voluminous record keeping associated with the assignment of federal identifying numbers mandated by Social Security was one of the impetuses to the federal government's support for the development of the electronic computer.

5 See, for example, *Imbler v. Pachtman* (1976), which contains an excellent summary of the legal immunities from personal responsibility enjoyed by these "public servants." For a prosecutor's candid admission that she relies on a Nuremberg defense to justify performing tasks she may consider morally repugnant but which her superiors have ordered her to do as a part of her job, see Kaminer (1995, 164).

6 *State of Idaho v. Lon T. Horiuchi*, Case No. CR 97-097-N-EJL, Memorandum Decision and Order dated May 14, 1998 (Federal District Court of Idaho, Boise, Idaho). Judge Lodge's ruling was appealed by the Boundary County prosecutor to the U.S. Ninth Circuit Court of Appeals, and a decision is being awaited as I write. For an account of this episode by Randy Weaver's lawyer, Gerry Spence, and to see a picture drawn by FBI agent Horiuchi immediately after he shot Vicki Weaver that shows his gun sights aimed at the door behind which she was kneeling with her head visible above the door's window, see Spence (1995, 40–41).

7 For a two-thousand-year analysis of the political process that concludes that bureaucracy naturally attracts the participation and leadership of amoral people, see Scharfstein (1995).

REFERENCES

Amado, Gilles. 1995. Why Psychoanalytical Knowledge Helps Us Understand Organizations. *Human Relations* 48 (April): 351.

Arendt, Hannah. [1963] 1994. *Eichmann in Jerusalem: A Report on the Banality of Evil*. Reprint. New York: Penguin.

Bauman, Zygmunt. 1989. *Modernity and the Holocaust*. Ithaca, N.Y.: Cornell University Press.

Becker, Ernest. 1975. *Escape from Evil*. New York: Free Press.

Beetham, David. 1996. *Bureaucracy*. Minneapolis: University of Minnesota Press.

Bettelheim, Bruno. 1960. *The Informed Heart: Autonomy in a Mass Age*. Glencoe, Ill.: Free Press.

———. 1963. Eichmann; the System; the Victims. *New Republic* (June 15): 23–33.

Blumberg, Abraham S. 1973. Lawyers with Convictions. In *The Scales of Justice*, edited by Abraham S. Blumberg, 67–83. New Brunswick, N.J.: Transaction.

Bosmajian, Haig. 1974. *The Language of Oppression*. Washington, D.C.: Public Affairs.

Boyer, Peter. 1999. Burned. *New Yorker* (November 1): 62.

Browning, Christopher R. 1983. The German Bureaucracy and the Holocaust. In *Genocide: Critical Issues of the Holocaust*, edited by Alex Grobman and Daniel Landes, 145–49. Los Angeles: Simon Wiesenthal Center.

———. 1993. Ordinary Men: Reserve Police Battalion 101 and the Final Solution in Poland. New York: HarperCollins.

Cannon, Angie. 1997. Most Wanted: A Good FBI Lab. *Portland Oregonian*, February 14, A22.

Courtois, Stephanie, and others. 1999. *The Black Book of Communism: Crimes, Terror, Repression*. Cambridge, Mass.: Harvard University Press.

Ellul, Jacques. 1964. *The Technological Society*. New York: Knopf.

———. 1965. *The Political Illusion*. New York: Knopf.

———. 1990. *The Technological Bluff*. Grand Rapids, Mich.: Wm. B. Eerdmans.

Feingold, Henry L. 1983. How Unique Is the Holocaust? In *Genocide: Critical Issues of the Holocaust*, edited by Alex Grobman and Daniel Landes, 397–401. Los Angeles: Simon Wiesenthal Center.

Fischer, Klaus P. 1997. *Nazi Germany: A New History*. New York: Continuum.

Gavin, Robert. 1999. WEA seeks $1 million for "Frivolous Lawsuit." *Seattle Post-Intelligencer*, September 21, B4.

Glazer, Myron P., and Penina M. Glazer. 1990. *Whistleblowers: Exposing Corruption in Government and Industry*. New York: Basic.

Harris, Whitney R. 1954. *Tyranny on Trial: The Evidence at Nuremberg*. Dallas: Southern Methodist University Press.

Hayek, Friedrich A. 1944. *The Road to Serfdom*. Chicago: University of Chicago Press.

Higgs, Robert. 1987. *Crisis and Leviathan: Critical Episodes in the Growth of American Government*. New York: Oxford University Press.

Hirschman, Albert O. 1970. *Exit, Voice, and Loyalty*. Cambridge, Mass.: Harvard University Press.

Hoffer, Eric. 1951. *The True Believer: Thoughts on the Nature of Mass Movements*. New York: Harper and Row.

Johnston, David Cay. 1999. IRS Whistleblower Nearly Fired. *South County Journal*, Kent, Wash., April 17, A7.

Imbler v. Pachtman. 1976. 424 U.S. 409.

Kafka, Franz. [1925] 1988. *The Trial*. Reprint. New York: Schocken.

Kaminer, Wendy. 1995. *It's All the Rage: Crime and Culture*. New York: Addison-Wesley.

Keen, Sam. 1991. *Faces of the Enemy*. New York: HarperCollins.

Kelman, Herbert C. 1973. Violence without Moral Restraints: Reflections on the Dehumanization of Victims and Victimizers. *Journal of Social Issues* 29 (4): 25–61.

Kelman, Herbert C., and L. H. Lawrence. 1972. Assignment of Responsibility in the Case of Lt. Calley: Preliminary Report on a National Survey. *Journal of Social Issues* 28 (1): 177–212.

Koestler, Arthur, 1941. *Darkness at Noon*. New York: Macmillan.

———. 1968. *The Ghost in the Machine*. New York: Macmillan.

Kren, George M., and Leon Rappoport. 1994. *The Holocaust and the Crisis of Human Behavior*. New York: Holmes and Meier.

Leinberger, Paul, and Bruce Tucker. 1991. *The New Individualists: The Generation after the Organization Man*. New York: HarperCollins.

Maas, Peter. 1973. *Serpico: The Cop Who Defied the System*. New York: Viking.

Mayer, Milton. 1966. *They Thought They Were Free: The Germans 1933–45*. Chicago: University of Chicago Press.

McConnell, James V. 1970. Criminals Can Be Brainwashed—Now. *Psychology Today* (April): 14.

McWilliams, Carey. 1950. *Witch Hunt: The Revival of Heresy*. Boston: Little, Brown.

Milgram, Stanley. 1975. *Obedience to Authority*. New York: Harper and Row.

Mitzman, Arthur. 1970. *The Iron Cage: An Historical Interpretation of Max Weber*. New York: Knopf.

Montagu, Ashley, and Floyd Matson. 1983. *The Dehumanization of Man*. New York: McGraw-Hill.

P-I News Service. 1999. Whistle-blower Tax Agent Comes Close to Being Fired. *Seattle Post-Intelligencer*, April 17, B3.

Rummel, Rudolph. 1994. *Death by Government*. New Brunswick, N.J.: Transaction.

Scharfstein, Ben-Ami. 1995. *Amoral Politics: The Persistent Truth of Machiavellism*. Albany: University of New York Press.

Shapley, Thomas. 1999a. FBI's "Waco Boys" Had Role at Ruby Ridge: Same Discredited Officials Ran Both Cases. *Seattle Post-Intelligencer*, September 19, G2.

———. 1999b. Storm Clouds Gather above Waco, Texas. *Seattle Post-Intelligencer*, August 29, E2.

Skinner, B. F. 1971. Beyond Freedom and Dignity. New York: Knopf.

Spence, Gerry. 1995. *From Freedom to Slavery: The Rebirth of Tyranny in America*. New York: St. Martin's.

Stoltzfus, Nathan. 1996. *Resistance of the Heart: Intermarriage and the Rosenstrasse Protest in Nazi Germany*. New York: W. W. Norton.

Templeton, Kenneth S., Jr., ed. 1979. *The Politicization of Society*. Indianapolis, Ind.: Liberty Fund.

Twight, Charlotte. 1999. Watching You: Systematic Federal Surveillance of Ordinary Americans. *The Independent Review* 4 (2): 165–200.

U.S. Council of Economic Advisers. 2000. *Annual Report*. Washington, D.C.: U.S. Government Printing Office.

Vogel, Jennifer. 1999. Nazi Guards: The Department of Corrections Knows How to Deal with Rednecks, Racists, and Neo-Nazis: It Hires Them. *Seattle Weekly*, March 11, 22–28.

Zimbardo, Philip, Craig Haney, and Curtis Banks. 1973. Interpersonal Dynamics in a Simulated Prison. *International Journal of Criminology and Penology* 1: 69–97.

Acknowledgments: Reprinted from *The Independent Review*, 5, no. 2 (Fall 2000), pp. 249–264.

PART IV

Individualism versus "Group Think"

13

Freedom of Religion and Public Schooling
James R. Otteson

One may object to government support of education on various grounds. Here I consider two such grounds that have to do with moral consistency. First, state intervention in education, whether in the form of monetary subsidies, compulsory attendance laws, or national curriculum standards, entails violating a moral principle—freedom of conscience—that most people hold inviolable in another application, namely, in relation to religious practice. If one holds the moral principle in question to be inviolable in religious matters, then one should also hold it to be inviolable in educational matters, because the cases are analogous. Second, the same arguments typically raised against state intervention in religious practice can also be raised against state intervention in educational practice. I conclude that because, for moral argument, the cases of religion and education are essentially the same, consistency requires people who oppose state intervention in the one to oppose state intervention in the other.

FREEDOM OF CONSCIENCE COVERS RELIGION *AND* EDUCATION

I suggest that the case of government support for education is analogous to the case of government support for religion, and therefore the moral acceptability of the one is the same as that of the other. My suggestion hinges on the claim that both cases fall under the rubric of freedom of conscience, and hence both should be protected on the moral principle that everyone's private conscience is inviolable and ought therefore to be safeguarded.

One of the central freedoms protected in the classical liberal scheme of rights is freedom of conscience; indeed, many of the other protections are means to the end of protecting freedom of conscience. Private property rights, for example, can be defended not by arguing that there is something inherently special about the things owned, but rather by arguing that allowing individuals to maintain personal jurisdiction over a specified domain of things (beginning usually with themselves[1]) enables them to act on their beliefs about the good life without interference from others. Actions are, after all, the product of beliefs about the world, and so the liberal claim that *all* people should enjoy this liberty of action on private property is just an extension of the belief that people are alike in having action-guiding private beliefs. It can then be argued that the beliefs themselves should be protected because a person cannot live a truly human or truly happy life—however one ultimately fleshes out the details of such a life[2]—unless he is allowed to hold and act on his own beliefs. Because private property is necessary for maintaining and acting on one's private beliefs, it is protected as a necessary means to the end of protecting one's private conscience.[3]

A word is required about the connection between protecting one's freedom of conscience and the ability to lead a truly happy life. One might think, for example, that it is possible to be happy without exercising one's freedom of conscience: perhaps one merely accepts the beliefs of one's parents without examination, and is perfectly content to do so. Two things should be said in response. First, people who accept the beliefs of their parents, even if uncritically, are still enjoying freedom of conscience. One does not have to *examine* one's beliefs to be free to hold them, just as one does not have to cultivate one's land to enjoy private ownership of it. Having the freedom to uncritically hold one's parents' beliefs *is* having freedom of conscience, because one retains the freedom to believe something else if one should so choose. Second, the relation between freedom of conscience, on the one hand, and that freedom's being a necessary condition for leading a truly happy life, on the other, should be specified in this way: the latter is the bedrock *moral* principle, the former the bedrock *political* principle that rests on the moral principle. One cannot directly legislate that people lead a truly happy life, but one can indirectly legislate it by establishing certain protections that allow a person to develop and lead a truly happy life on his own. The most fundamental such protection, I maintain, is the protection of one's freedom of conscience.

Several other political principles follow from the foundational protection of one's private conscience. Arguments for freedom of the press, freedom of speech, and freedom of association can all be plausibly construed as the claim that the private consciences of individuals must be protected and that these various freedoms are necessary for such protection. Even rights that go beyond these so-called negative rights are typically defended for the same reason. So, for example, state-provided universal health care has been defended not because even health itself is inherently good but because it is a necessary prerequisite to leading a happy, flourishing life.[4] The connection between the two is thought to be that good health grants a person, first, the peace of mind to work out, adopt, and maintain private beliefs about the good life and, second, the soundness of body to act on those beliefs. Again, however, because the actions depend on the beliefs, the creation of a sanctuary for private beliefs is the ultimate end of supporting universal health care.

These examples license our drawing the general moral principle that most Westerners already hold dear: because of the crucial role one's private conscience plays in leading a truly happy life, it must be protected against interference; and the political structures necessary for its protection ought to be constructed. Although I subscribe to this principle, I shall not try to defend it here any more than I already have by suggesting its plausibility, but it is already widely accepted. It is explicitly at work, as previously noted, in the widespread belief in freedom of the press. Since Milton's first statement of the argument in his *Areopagitica* of 1644, the claim has been that ideas are crucially important to living a flourishing life and therefore freedom of the press must be protected as a necessary means of the expression of privately held beliefs.

More to the point here, the same moral principle undergirds the nearly universal belief in separating church and state: as a matter of private conscience, religious practice[5] must be protected; and this protection entails disallowing state intervention in religious matters. Religious practice arises from deep-seated private beliefs that, like any other such beliefs, must be protected as a matter of private conscience. Indeed, one's religious beliefs, whatever they may be, are among one's most fundamental beliefs, setting parameters for many others, including in particular one's beliefs about how one should live and what constitutes the good life. Thus, even among already safeguarded beliefs, religious beliefs enjoy a privileged place. It is for this reason that such beliefs are protected and that among those protections is the disallowance of government support or regulation of private religious practice.

Educational practice is analogous to religious practice: one's decisions about how to educate oneself and one's children also arise from deep-seated beliefs about how one should live and what constitutes the good life, beliefs that therefore fall under the scope of the moral principle enunciated earlier and hence should be safeguarded in the same way one's religious beliefs are. This protection disallows state intervention in educational practice, including subsidies drawn from taxes, compulsory attendance laws, and curriculum standards—just as, in the case of religion, it includes protection against religious subsidies drawn from taxes, compulsory church attendance, and state-prescribed religious ceremonies, rites, or doctrines. The same moral principle that debars the government from regulating or supporting any church or religious sect debars the government from regulating or supporting any school or other educational facility. Hence, what is now called "public schooling" should be abolished for the same reasons that state-enforced "public religion," wherever it exists, should be abolished.

ARGUMENTS AGAINST GOVERNMENT RELIGION

Arguments one might be inclined to marshal in favor of government regulation or support of education must, because the cases are analogous, face the objections raised against government regulation or support of religion. By bringing out the objections to government religion, we challenge government schooling as well. A note before proceeding with the following arguments: I do not necessarily endorse any of them (though I might), nor do I claim that they all fit together into a single, coherent whole, or that any of them is ultimately persuasive, or that each of them is fully distinct from my own argument given previously. My aim here is rather to capture the most common arguments presented in opposition to state-supported religion and then to show that the same arguments can, without substantive alteration, be raised in opposition to state-supported education.

Objections to state intervention in religious matters fall chiefly under three heads:[6] first, government support for religion leads to various bad consequences; second, religion is too important a matter to be left to politicians or to decisions made by political processes; third, government support for religion violates people's rights. Consider these in turn.

Government support for religion leads to bad consequences. This argument can be constructed in several ways. To begin, a religious believer might argue that true faith cannot be had by coercion: the strength of a person's faith is diminished if he is forced to believe, as opposed to choosing to believe on his own. Indeed, it may be impossible to force someone actually to hold a belief, as opposed to merely behaving as if he held the belief. This argument claims that human nature is such that a person is less likely to hold religious beliefs if he is forced against his will to act as though he believed them. A person must instead come to hold them on his own, to take responsibility for them himself. Hence, this argument concludes, government support of religion actually works against the religion by disinclining people to believe it.[7] This argument is also construed in light of the effect on parents who are (or should be) passing on proper beliefs to their children: if the government takes over the responsibility of maintaining correct beliefs, then parents tend to relax their commitment to the important job of religious education of their children.

Now it is true that supporting a religion is not the same thing as coercing belief, so one might argue that a state policy of giving money to all religions, or generic vouchers for church donations, would not be affected by this consideration. But a proponent of this argument will respond as follows: one important element in coming to hold one's own beliefs is the initial decision of *whether* to believe. If the government indiscriminately takes money from everyone by general taxation and then specifically earmarks it for support of or donation to churches, this action in a significant way preempts everyone's decision of whether to believe. *That* decision has instead been made by the government, leaving the individual only to decide which religion to support. The believer may argue, however, that it is more difficult to come to bear the proper relation to such important beliefs if this initial decision was made by someone else, and hence the government must not make that decision. The conclusion remains, then, that the government should not support religion in any way.

A believer might also be concerned that the government could support the wrong religion(s). Even though he might believe that good consequences would flow from government support of his own religion, bad—perhaps disastrously bad—consequences would flow from government support of some other, false religion. Because there can be no guarantee that the government would choose correctly, he might therefore argue that the best policy is for the government to abstain from supporting religion altogether.

On the other side, nonbelievers have at least two clear reasons for thinking that government support of religion would lead to bad consequences. First, it might propagate beliefs that the nonbeliever holds to be false, which is undesirable in itself. Second, it might have the consequence of propagating not just false beliefs but perhaps dangerous or counterproductive attitudes. It might, for example, lead people to put less stock in improving life on earth, to be less concerned with "merely temporal" injustice, or to be more inclined to believe that whatever happens is God's will (and hence not to be inclined to try to change a situation that the nonbeliever thinks should be changed). Both of these arguments apply equally to governmental systems of vouchers, credits, or other types of support.

Religion is too important to be left to politics and politicians. This argument can be and often is supported by both the believer and the nonbeliever, and bears similarities to one raised previously. It generally claims that one's religious beliefs, whatever they may be, are a foundational element of one's worldview—perhaps even the single most important element, the one that fixes and orders all the others. As such they should bear an intensely personal relation to the person holding them. If the government played an active role in supporting religion, it would tend to drive a wedge between a person and his beliefs. More particularly, it would drive a politician or political bureaucrat between a person and his beliefs.

Because of the supreme importance of those beliefs, however, we should be far more suspicious of political influence here than we might be in other, less important areas of our lives.

Often coupled with this argument is a claim about the general inefficiency, incompetence, or moral or religious failings of politicians and political bureaucrats. The idea is that even if government influence did *not* have the effect of dissociating people from beliefs to which they should be personally attached, the *last* people we should entrust with the care of matters as important as religion would be politicians and bureaucrats.[8] Here one might marshal a public-choice-style argument that such people do not have the proper incentives to encourage them actually to work in the best interest of individual people and their religious beliefs; rather, their incentives might incline them only to create work for themselves, regardless of its effect on people and their beliefs. Alternatively, one might make a Hayekian argument that the maintenance of religious beliefs can be properly provided only by people who have close, personal knowledge of the people holding those beliefs. Thus one might conclude that priests, pastors, or other personal mentors are far better equipped to handle this task than any remote stranger, as a politician or bureaucrat would necessarily be. Finally, one might make an argument based on human diversity, claiming that even if politicians and bureaucrats could somehow have all the knowledge about people that is requisite for knowing how best to maintain proper religious beliefs, it would be impossible to establish a single set of rules, laws, or programs that would simultaneously help everyone: some simplification would necessarily be required, which would in turn either not help or even actively hurt some people.[9]

Government support for religion violates people's rights. Perhaps the most powerful and (in contemporary America, at least) the most widely held argument against government support for religion is that it would violate people's rights. The rights violation can be seen in at least two forms: a violation of the right to free speech and a violation of property rights.

First, it would infringe on a person's right to free speech to make him support beliefs he does not hold. As suggested previously, one can plausibly construe the practice of religion as an instance of expressing one's beliefs commonly held to fall within the scope of speech. Requiring a person to support a religion in which he does not believe can be seen as equivalent to requiring him to support any other position, institution, or view in which he does not believe: in both cases the person's right to hold whatever beliefs he wants is violated. Because freedom of speech is protected not as an end in itself but rather as a means to protecting one's private conscience, the close connection between religious practice and "speech" licenses bringing the protection of the former within the scope of the latter. By this chain of inferences, then, requiring a person to support a religion in which he does not believe violates his right to freedom of conscience, which, in this case, violates his right to free speech. If it is true, moreover, that one's religious beliefs are of central importance to one's life, then such a violation would be especially egregious.[10]

Government support of religion can also be seen as a violation of property rights insofar as that support takes the form of money obtained involuntarily by taxation. According to a Lockean view of property rights, for example, it is illegitimate to tax a person in order to support something he does not expressly or tacitly consent to support.[11] In this case, the taxation would instead be involuntary because the other, voluntary alternative—relying on private contributions and donations—is precisely *not* what is pursued. Hence, the argument is that taking a person's money to support a religion to which he otherwise would not give his money is violating his right to do with his property as he chooses. In the Lockean view this taking amounts to the government's overstepping its legitimate authority. Even if one did not believe in the absolute sanctity of private property rights, however—if, for example, one thought that private property rights were important but could in certain circumstances justifiably be abridged—one might nevertheless argue that matters of religion are of sufficient importance that a situation would scarcely ever arise in which compulsory support of another's religion would be justified. The person arguing in favor of such support would therefore face the difficult burden of proving that the case at hand was sufficiently exceptional and important as to warrant overriding private property rights.

ARGUMENTS AGAINST GOVERNMENT EDUCATION

The same three clusters of arguments that are brought against state intervention in religion can, without substantial alteration, be brought against government support of education: government support of education leads to various bad consequences; education is too important a matter to be left to politicians or decisions made by political processes; and government support for education violates people's rights.

Government support of education leads to bad consequences. Government support of education seems to lead to bad consequences analogous to those identified in discussing government support of religion. To be specific: first, people's personal commitment to education is weakened by the government's relieving them of the responsibility of educating themselves and their own children; second, the government runs a significant risk of supporting a bad system of education; and third, the government runs a significant risk of supporting a system of education that propagates dangerous or counterproductive attitudes. Each of these charges has been leveled against government-supported schools by recent critics, including some who otherwise support government schooling.

Articulating the first charge, Sheldon Richman (1995) has argued that true education requires above all else personal initiative and commitment, and government schooling tends to deaden personal commitment by depriving people of the responsibility of providing for their own (or their own children's) education. The result, Richman argues, is that the burden of educating children tends to fall on the shoulders of people without the proper incentives or requisite knowledge to do the job well—namely, political and bureaucratic strangers.

Regarding the second charge, Allan Bloom (1987) has argued that government-supported schools from the elementary through the college levels operate under the guidance of badly flawed theories of knowledge and truth loosely based on the views of Nietzsche and Dewey. Bloom argues that these theories inform educational practices that lead students to adopt an unsophisticated moral and epistemological relativism, which severely impedes moral growth and scientific progress.

As for the third charge, Thomas Sowell (1993) has argued that public schools across the nation pursue educational policies that encourage in students the dangerous mix of high self-esteem, ignorance, and moral vacuity—which has led, quite predictably, to the amoral monsters we see increasingly often in public schools today.

My task here is not to decide whether the foregoing criticisms are justified. However, the fact that they have been raised and have received widespread, if not unanimous, endorsement[12] suggests that a considerable number of people agree that government-supported schools lead to undesirable consequences, and those consequences are strikingly similar to those regarded as evidence against government support for religion.

Education is too important to be left to politics and politicians. It is commonly held that the education of children is one of the most important tasks facing parents and communities. Yet it would seem that the same problems that beset government support of religion also plague government support of education—namely, that such support has the effect of dissociating people from something to which they should have an intensely personal commitment, and that such support is unreliable because of the inefficiency, incompetence, or moral or religious deficiencies of politicians and government bureaucrats.

A common complaint of parents involved in the operations of the public school their children attend is that disappointingly few other parents are similarly involved. Low parental involvement in public education is a chronic and chronically lamented problem. Why are so few parents involved? One plausible explanation is that when the government takes on the responsibility of providing for the education of children, parents correspondingly, and understandably, stop concerning themselves with it. The present system of government schooling—with its compulsory monetary support by taxation, its compulsory attendance, and its compulsory curriculum—attempts to control almost every aspect over which parents themselves might otherwise have had control. Parents do not decide on their own how much they are willing to pay or to whom, whether their children should or should not continue to attend school, or what the curriculum is. Even if they send their children to private schools, they must nevertheless continue to pay for the government schools, and in most states private schools either receive government support, which entails various restrictions, or are otherwise regulated by the state in such matters as attendance and curriculum. In view of the limited scope for parental responsibility, it is not surprising that parents tend to dissociate themselves from what they might otherwise treat as a matter deserving great personal attention and commitment.

Plato was perhaps the first person to make a systematic case for the crucial importance of carefully designing the educational system for children, and he made sure not to leave this matter to the people we would call politicians—indeed, in his view, it could be properly handled only by the highest of human beings, the philosophers (*Republic*, bks. 4 and 5). But Plato by no means stands alone: a succession of thinkers down to the present day has maintained the great importance of education. Various reasons are given for its importance, but most revolve around the central consideration that education is necessary for a person to live a flourishing life. But exactly the same claim is made on the behalf of religion. If both religion and education are so critically important to the success of a person's life, then they should be treated in the same way. If the importance of religion warrants that decisions regarding it not be left to the devices of politicians and bureaucrats, the same conclusion should follow for matters of education.

Government support for education violates people's rights. Finally, and perhaps most straightforwardly, government support for education commits whatever rights violations that government support for religion does. First, to make a person support an educational system with which he disagrees is an infringement of his right to free speech. If a person has beliefs about morality or politics—about, say, homosexuality or democracy—that differ from what is being taught in the government-supported school system, to compel him to support that system (let alone require him to send his children there) violates his free-speech rights in the same way as requiring him to support a religion in which he does not believe. Moreover, if taxing a person to support a religion in which he does not believe is a property-rights violation, the same violation takes place in taxing him to support an educational system in which he does not believe. Educational policies and curricula are, as I have argued, ultimately dependent on our views about deeply important matters such as human nature, the good life, and proper community relations. Whatever rights a person has that would protect his beliefs about such things in matters of religion likewise protect those beliefs in matters of education. Indeed, a person's position on religion and his position on education might rest on precisely the same set of fundamental beliefs.

BELIEF IN FREEDOM OF RELIGION IS INCONSISTENT WITH BELIEF IN GOVERNMENT EDUCATION

If my foregoing arguments are sound, the person who advocates government support and regulation of education but opposes those government actions in religion is taking an inconsistent position, because the two cases do not differ in any morally relevant way.[14]

One might raise the following objection. The two cases are in fact not analogous, because whereas everyone supports education, not everyone supports religion; therefore government support for education enjoys a prima facie justification that government support for religion does not. I suspect, however, that the widespread endorsement of "education" is the joint product of vagueness and habit. Everyone supports "education" partly because the term is vague enough to have radically different meanings to different people. The support dissipates once the details of a specific educational program are specified. The endless and ongoing battles over public-school curricula seem to demonstrate that there is in fact exceedingly little agreement about "education." In addition, since the nineteenth century an almost continuous succession of influential people, beginning with Horace Mann, Edward Ross, and John Dewey, has argued that "public schooling" is required to mold children into the kind of citizens a "modern democracy" needs (Richman 1995, chap. 3). By now most people are so thoroughly steeped in the habit of believing in the necessity of such schooling that the possibility of its abolition rarely, if ever, occurs to them. The combination of the vagueness of the term "education" and the long-standing, habitual acceptance of public schooling gives the impression of universal support for education, but that support is more apparent than genuine. I conclude that the analogy between the two cases survives this objection intact.

Another objection is that, whatever the merits of my argument, no self-respecting society should contemplate abolishing public schooling because of the disastrous effects that action would have on the poor. Public schooling gives the poor a chance; without it, only the children of the rich would get an education, and the poor would form a permanent underclass. A number of responses to this objection present themselves—entailing various ways of disputing that such bad consequences would ensue from the abolition of public schooling—but those responses require a consideration of empirical evidence that would take us too far afield. One response can be made, however, drawing strictly on the arguments made here. This objection disputes the analogy between the cases of religion and schooling in the following way: whatever may be the case with religion, schooling is simply too important to be left to the vagaries of the market, where class antagonisms, "old boy" networks, and exploitation of the disadvantaged rule. The state is therefore justified, on grounds of what might be called social justice, in intervening in educational matters.

But does the analogy really fail? After all, do not supporters of religion make precisely the same claims on behalf of religion? That is, they argue that holding correct religious beliefs is simply too important to be left to the hurly-burly processes of the market and must therefore be guaranteed by the state. What would block the religion-statist argument that would not simultaneously block the education-statist argument? Not the claim that everyone supports education but not religion, for the reasons discussed earlier. And not, importantly, the education-statist's confidence that he is correct in his estimation of the importance of education whereas the religion-statist is incorrect in his estimation of the importance of religion—for such a claim would be hotly contested, to say the least, and in any case is not shown to be true by its mere assertion. The burden of proof would be on the education-statist for holding a position that seems inconsistent and, in addition, for now claiming a certainty about human values that has yet to be justified by argument or evidence.

This last consideration leads, finally, to a more general objection, which is that I have not demonstrated that the cases of religion and education are analogous in all respects. There may be other factors that apply to one or the other that weaken the analogy sufficiently to allow a person to consistently maintain both that state regulation of one is unacceptable and that state regulation of the other is acceptable. Although I cannot think of what such considerations would be, in light of this possible objection I am willing to weaken my claim to a simple shifting of the burden of proof. That is, at the very least, the person who holds this *seemingly* inconsistent pair of views must now take it upon himself to show how they can be rendered consistent. I think such a person will fail in trying to reconcile the views, but, in any event, simply placing the burden of proof where it belongs amounts to a significant step toward breaking the habit of uncritical acceptance of state-run schooling. Until a sound argument reconciling the two views has been made, I am content to maintain the weaker thesis that state intervention in education requires, and as yet lacks, moral justification.

RELIGIOUS FREEDOM AND EDUCATION FREEDOM STAND OR FALL TOGETHER

For centuries, kings and parliaments acted on their understanding that controlling *both* the state and the religion was the key to controlling the people. Compulsory government schooling was explicitly introduced for exactly the same reason. Indeed, modern public schooling has its roots in sixteenth-century attempts by Protestant church leaders to forcibly train people in correct religious beliefs (Katz 1976).[15] As Edwin G. West (1994) has shown, controlling people—that is, instilling correct religious, moral, or political beliefs and behavior—has continued to be the driving, frequently explicit motivation behind public-school advocacy.

Now, many contemporary Americans might be inclined to agree that molding children in accordance with correct religious, moral, or political beliefs is a good idea, and hence they might be sympathetic to the motivation behind government schooling. But such sympathy no more establishes the moral acceptability of the practice than did the widespread acceptance of the king's official religion among those who happened already to believe in the king's religion. And it does not dispose of the objections I have raised to state intervention.

Here, in brief, is my claim: If it would be wrong for the government to adopt an official religion, then, for the same reasons, it would be wrong for the government to adopt official education policies. The moral case for freedom of religion stands or falls with that for freedom of education. A society that champions freedom of religion but at the same time countenances state regulation of education has a great deal of explaining to do.

NOTES

1 See, for example, Locke ([1690] 1980, chap. 5, sec. 27).

2 For reasons that will become clear, not specifying in advance what constitutes a truly happy life for a person is part of the liberal political scheme. In any case, all that is required for the argument here is that protecting one's freedom of conscience is necessary for leading such a life, regardless of what that life entails.

3 This is, in outline, Herbert Spencer's argument for protecting a sphere of private liberty (and private property within it). See Spencer ([1851] 1995, esp. part 2).

4 For a recent argument, see Fleischacker (1999, esp. chaps. 10 and 11).

5 I am construing "religious practice" broadly enough to include what we might call religious *non*practice, because atheism and agnosticism, for example, are still the products of religiously oriented beliefs. (The belief that there is no god is or entails a belief about religion.)

6 Because I am pursuing a general moral principle here, I am excluding from consideration arguments based on the U.S. Constitution.

7 This is Locke's argument in his 1685 "Letter Concerning Toleration," wherein he concludes: "How great soever, in fine, may be the pretense of good will and charity, and concern for the salvation of men's souls, men cannot be forced to be saved whether they will or no. And therefore, when all is done, they must be left to their own consciences" (42). A dissenting voice is that of Pascal, who argues in *Pensées* that "anyone who grows accustomed to faith believes it" (1966, 153).

8 For an illustration of this worry about the moral character of politicians, see Nock ([1927] 1991, 34–51).

9 For an example of this argument, see Resch (1974, 31–54).

10 This argument recalls Jefferson's famous claim in the preamble of his *Act for Establishing Religious Freedom in the State of Virginia* ([1779] 1944) that he is "well aware . . . that to compel a man to furnish contributions of money for the propagation of opinions which he disbelieves and abhors, is sinful and tyrannical."

11 The notion of "tacit" consent is a tricky one, as Locke is aware. Locke ([1690] 1980) writes, "Every man, that hath any possessions, or enjoyment, of any part of the dominions of any government, doth thereby give his *tacit consent*, and is as far forth obliged to obedience to the laws of that government, during such employment, as any one under it" (chap. 8, sec. 119; Locke's italics). It seems, however, that if a person did not enjoy the benefits of any religious institution—or, even more clearly, if he expressly renounced any such benefits—he would not in Locke's view have expressly or tacitly consented to be taxed to support it.

12 Bloom's book went on to become a number-one national bestseller.

13 Examples of important figures who have defended different educational programs on such grounds are Aristotle, Locke ([1693] 1947), and Rousseau ([1762] 1979).

14 I should perhaps point out that a person's opposition to government regulation of religion might commit him to opposing government regulation of other areas of life besides education. To pursue such possibilities would take us beyond the scope of this chapter, but I want to emphasize that my argument is not that education is necessarily unique in falling under the same protection as religion.

15 Note that Plato's justification for the scheme of compulsory education laid out in the Republic was also to control all the nonphilosophers and give them correct—though not necessarily true—beliefs. See Plato's discussion of the "noble falsehood" that the philosophers must tell everyone else in his ideal city (*Republic*, bk. 3).

REFERENCES

Aristotle. 1984. *Nicomachean Ethics*. Translated by W. D. Ross, revised by J. O. Urmson. Princeton, N.J.: Princeton University Press.

Bloom, Allan. 1987. *The Closing of the American Mind: How Higher Education Has Failed Democracy and Impoverished the Souls of Today's Students*. New York: Simon and Schuster.

Fleischacker, Samuel W. 1999. *A Third Concept of Liberty: Judgment and Freedom in Kant and Adam Smith*. Princeton, N.J.: Princeton University Press.

Jefferson, Thomas. [1779] 1944. An Act for Establishing Religious Freedom in the State of Virginia. In *The Life and Selected Writings of Jefferson*, edited by Adrienne Koch and William Peden. New York: Modern Library.

Katz, Michael S. 1976. *A History of Compulsory Education Laws*. Bloomington, Ind.: Phi Delta Kappa Education Foundation.

Locke, John. [1685] 1947. Letter Concerning Toleration. In *John Locke: On Politics and Education*. Roslyn, N.Y.: Walter J. Black.

————. [1690] 1980. *Second Treatise of Government*, edited by C. B. Macpherson. Indianapolis, Ind.: Hackett.

————. [1693] 1947. Some Thoughts Concerning Education. In *John Locke: On Politics and Education*. Roslyn, N.Y.: Walter J. Black.

Nock, Albert Jay. [1927] 1991. Anarchist's Progress. In *The State of the Union*, edited by Charles H. Hamilton. Indianapolis, Ind.: Liberty Press.

Pascal, Blaise. 1966. *Pensées*. Translated by A. J. Krailsheimer. New York: Penguin.

Plato. [c. 380 BC] 1992. *Republic*. Translated by G. M. A. Grube. Indianapolis, Ind.: Hackett.

Resch, H. George. 1974. Human Variation and Individuality. In *The Twelve-Year Sentence*, edited by William F. Rickenbacker. LaSalle, Ill.: Open Court.

Richman, Sheldon. 1995. *Separating School and State*. Fairfax, Va.: Future of Freedom Foundation.

Rousseau, Jean-Jacques. [1762] 1979. *Emile*. Translated by Allan Bloom. New York: Basic Books.

Sowell, Thomas. 1993. *Inside American Education: The Decline, the Deception, the Dogma*. New York: Free Press.

Spencer, Herbert. [1851] 1995. *Social Statics*. New York: Robert Schalkenbach Foundation.

West, Edwin G. 1994. *Education and the State: A Study in Political Economy*. 3d. ed. Indianapolis, Ind.: Liberty Press.

Acknowledgments: Reprinted from *The Independent Review*, 4, no. 4 (Spring 2000), pp. 601–613. Copyright © 2000.

14

Is National Rational?

Anthony de Jasay

Ruminating on the causes and consequences of ethnic strife, I was reminded of a young woman who at one time used to type my manuscripts. Before she learned to read my handwriting, she kept mistaking my *r* for *n*, so that when I wrote "rational" she would type "national," and vice versa. The results were sometimes quite surprising. The mistake suggests an association of ideas and a potentially serious question. Can national be rational?

Most people of liberal leanings tend to regard (and to deplore or despise) nationalism, along with the feelings that feed it, as a gut instinct, and not the most creditable one at that. It stands outside the purview of critical reason, rather like a taste we do not dispute, an ultimate preference, a Humean "passion" that can explain human conduct but that neither need nor can be explained in terms of other, more final, more basic preferences or ends.

Although I sympathize with that position, I think it gives unduly short shrift to the issue. Nationalism, whether despicable, deplorable, or not, is dangerous, potent, and important; it calls for closer consideration. One way of doing justice to the phenomenon of nationalism is to treat it counterfactually. Even if in fact it springs from sentiment fueled by historical accidents, it may be worthwhile to try to see whether nationalism could possibly be the product of rational choice. If it is, we should be able to find a theory that can explain the phenomena of nationalism *as if* they were appropriate, perhaps even the best available responses utility-maximizing individuals could make to the similarly utility-maximizing strategies of others. For present purposes, I use "utility-maximizing" in a loose sense that is almost tautological but has the merit of encompassing everything an individual thinks he should do, given his means and the information at his disposal, to get the best possible combination of all the things he values, whether they be tangible or intangible, moral or material.

If we could construct such a theory, nationalism and its principal institution, the nation-state, could be represented as instrumental, serving a purpose, comprehensible in terms of methodological individualism. We could inquire into the efficacy of nationalism in promoting the aims (maximizing the utility) of those who embrace it and subject themselves to its disciplines. In this chapter, I engage in an elementary thought-experiment. I seek to find a plausible theory that, running in terms of broadly conceived cost and benefit, could furnish elements of an answer to the question, Is national rational?

THE DIFFERENTIAL ADVANTAGE OF GROUP ACTION

For nationalism to make any sort of maximizing sense, there must exist important situations ("games") of human interaction in which the best response to the expected utility-maximizing actions of others is a group response. Impossible for any lone individual, such a response is available only to a group of individuals acting uniformly. They must form a group and then reach and submit to group decisions. In return they reap the differential advantage that, according to the hypothesis, such action can yield.

The advantage, if any, depends on at least two variables. One is group size and composition: who is in the group and who is left outside? The larger the group, the stronger it is, but perhaps the less cohesive; the larger it is, the smaller the world outside it that group action can exploit for its own advantage. The other variable is the appropriateness of the group decision to which its members conform. How is it reached? Is the process, to use simplistic categories, democratic or autocratic? How does it allocate costs within the group, and what mechanism preserves it from stupid mistakes? Needless to say, both variables go to the heart of the problem of separate nations with their processes of collective choice and enforcement.

BARGAINING AND TAKING

For present purposes, let us divide all possible interactions into four jointly exhaustive classes. One is pure cooperation. I help you, perhaps you also help me, or we both harness ourselves to a common endeavor. We are both better off as a result, but I am not trying to be even better off by haggling or pushing to make you a little less well off. The second is the kind of exchange whose ideal type is perfect competition. We engage in division of labor, we both gain; perhaps we would each like to gain more by making the other party gain less, but we are ex hypothesi "price-takers"—the terms of exchange do not depend on us and cannot be changed by any strategy. In these two types of interaction, there is no conflict: an individual's utility-maximizing behavior would not be any different if his choices were made collectively for him and all others.

The opposite is the case in the other two types of interaction, where strategy influences the gain each makes. Here it is not implausible (though it is certainly not demonstrably true) that individuals can do better by submitting to collective choice and acting as a group. One such case is any exchange that is not perfectly competitive and whose terms are bargained. The other comprises all takings by force, intimidation, or fraud. Instead of exchange, it offers gains from robbery, enslavement, blackmail, and conquest. Defense against robbery, enslavement, blackmail, and conquest is of course the integral complement of these interactions. Even if it is not—or is not always—the case that in these "games" individuals adopting a unified course of action collectively do better than if each chose his strategy for himself, the conventional wisdom supposes that group action is more efficient. Because the conventional wisdom cannot really be falsified, it is accorded near-universal credit.

NATIONS AND WHAT THEY COST

To capture the differential gain, groups must be formed and maintained. Their size, shape, cohesion, and modus operandi are bound to matter both for their efficiency in producing gains and for the cost of forming and maintaining them.

Historically, the dominant form of the collectively acting group has been the linguistic community, which fulfilled the most basic of group functions—including some and excluding others—by means of a common tongue separate from other tongues. Whether the historical dominance of language, rather than clan, tribe, race, class, or religion, as the crucial feature of group demarcation corresponds to the requirements of greatest efficiency (or least cost) is a matter of conjecture. Believers in sociobiological selection who regard the survival of a social institution as a test of its efficiency (which tends to be confused with "survival as a test of the capacity to survive") tend to think it does correspond. In any event, until comparatively recently *nation* meant a linguistic community, and only since the late eighteenth century has the word taken on a clear political connotation.

Apart from language, the group typically demarcates itself from others by means of conventions, customs, shared legends about its own history, loyalty to a center, and some degree of territorial exclusivity. All these demarcating features are costly to bring forth, live with, and uphold. The cost is probably higher the greater is the required degree of group cohesion. As a general rule, there is a cost involved in requiring conformity and forgoing the advantage of diversity *within* the group as well as in requiring diversity *between* groups that would otherwise drift toward a shared conformity.

FROM NATION TO NATION-STATE

Maximizing the putative differential advantage of group over individual action by incurring the costs of group formation and maintenance, up to the point at which marginal group gain ceases to exceed marginal group cost, is ex hypothesi collectively rational: it is the course of action that secures the greatest possible total advantage, hence also the greatest average advantage for each of the group's members. Any one member, however, can do better than the group average if he does not contribute to costs while others do. In other words, it is individually rational to take the free-rider option if it is available. If all or even most members of the group do so, costs will not be met, and individual rationality will frustrate the collectively rational outcome—the standard outcome of the inherent prisoner's dilemma that is supposed to characterize all public-good situations.

The same dilemma-generating incentive structure characterizes a nation acting as a discriminatory group that favors its members over nonmembers. Suppression of the free-rider option is thought to require the enforcing capacity of an agent placed above individuals. Hence, it is rational for the nation to transform itself into a nation-state. (How individuals are induced to make the joint effort to bring about this transformation, which is no less a public-good problem than the one it is called upon to resolve, is a question I must leave in limbo. It is not specific to the nation-state but common to all proposed cooperative solutions of a prisoner's dilemma that depend on the cooperative solution of a prior prisoner's dilemma).

The task of the nation-state is easier and the cost of its enforcing action lower, the weaker is the free-rider temptation. Weakening it, covering it with shame and guilt, is the function of patriotism in its many forms, a sentiment that it is collectively rational to foster. Hostility to and suspicion of foreigners and foreign ways, and love of one's own kind, function *as if* they were deliberately chosen means of helping to overcome the dilemma that what is collectively rational is individually irrational. It would be a functionalist fallacy, however, to conclude that the virulent and unpleasant nationalism we see around us, which is so much more vigorous than class hatred and class solidarity, is due to nationalism's capacity to help resolve a fundamental social dilemma. Nonetheless it seems that if nationalism did not exist, it would pay the nation-state to invent it.

FROM PUBLIC CHOICES TO "PUBLIC CHOICE"

The nation-state, like every other kind of state though perhaps more effectively and ruthlessly, facilitates the making of public choices for a whole group that impose losses on one part of the group and bring gains to another part. Unlike ordinary conflict outcomes in which one party gains and another loses because might makes right, the public choices effected through a nation-state's political process are generally alleged to make some net contribution to the "common good" or the "national interest." The claim is justified one way in democratic regimes, another way in autocratic or intermediate ones, but its basis is always the gratuitous assertion that, notwithstanding the redistribution, the choice generates a positive net balance of utility, welfare, or national strength. As a rule these assertions are either unfalsifiable (when they depend on interpersonal comparisons of utility) or demonstrably false, as in the case of wealth-reducing protectionist measures and most other restrictions of the freedom of contract. Public-choice theory has established beyond reasonable doubt not only that such measures are wasteful in terms of forgone wealth but more significantly that they are not accidental aberrations; on the contrary, they are the irrepressible corollaries of the individually rational, maximizing use of politics, where "politics" means simply recourse to a binding social-choice mechanism.

One possible aspect of redistributive politics peculiar to some nation-states without being uniformly true of all is a propensity to redistribute liberties, rights, and privileges from heterogeneous minorities to the dominant nationality within the state. Present-day liberal opinion considers such policies, which oppress ethnic or religious minorities, as morally more wicked than the routine redistribution of material resources from dominated to dominant subgroups. The collectively irrational, wealth-wasting effect of redistributing material resources has been well established by economic research, whereas the loss inflicted on an entire collectivity by the persecution of internal minorities is more conjectural. It is probably fair to suggest, though, that short of exterminating them, organized discrimination against minorities is collectively irrational, though individually rational, at least prospectively, for members of the dominant group.

These redistributive public choices, remote as they may seem from one another, all share the basic feature of a prisoner's dilemma, namely, that the strategy it is rational for individuals to adopt is in fact suboptimal. (In an *n*-person game where *n* is large, the solution may not be suboptimal for *all* players, but the total and the average payoff will be less than they might have been. That result qualifies it as collectively irrational.)

THE COSTLY STALEMATE

Indecisive, fruitless conflict is, I believe, the best understood of the dilemmas that entrap nationalism in collective irrationality. This hackneyed theme deserves only a brief recapitulation. The differential advantage of group action works against individuals, but if this suffices to make them form a group that ends up as a nation-state, then no individuals will be left in the types of interactions in which they could suffer differential disadvantage. All will shelter in groups of a similar type; nation-state will face nation-state.

If all adopt the same strategy, none gains from it but none can afford to abandon it. This statement will be true of individuals as well as nation-states. Individuals must seek the protection of their nation-state to preserve their liberties, property, and "identity" from other nation-states. But no additional gain can be had from doing so; indeed, some might say that entrusting one's liberty or property to the protection of the state is foolhardy, a sure way of losing some of it. Yet in the face of foreign nation-states, one risks grave losses by not doing so, too.

"Disarmament," figuratively and literally, in cultural and economic matters as well as in terms of guns and rockets, is best for all if all states do it, but irrational for any individual state both if the others disarm and if they don't. Such is the logic, purportedly (but inaccurately) derived from Hobbes, that is supposed to govern international relations among nation-states and that stops most of them from becoming anything else but nation-states—organized vehicles of wary and jealous nationalism.

It is easy to overstate this case. The logic at its base is far from being as watertight as it may look. Nevertheless, there are enough historical examples where it has worked "by the book," as Hobbes is supposed to have said that it must. The bestiality of Hutus and Serbs against their unprotected, ethnically different fellow countrymen warns us that there are even worse solutions than nation-states facing off against other nation-states in balance-of-power stalemates that, happily, neither side has the stomach to test.

TWO OF EVERYTHING

Individually rational choice provides incentives for ethnic groups of imperfectly defined identity—incipient, underdeveloped, or nascent nations—to invent themselves a history, claim mature nation status, and seek to establish themselves as sovereign political entities. That project involves secession from an existing nation-state or multinational state. If the attempt at secession is resisted, a separatist movement, often with an illegal wing employing violent means, will maintain a situation of simmering conflict. If the attempt at secession succeeds, two states and two governments will exist where only one did before.

In many cases, the separatist movement has genuine grievances, normally arising from the failure of tax-financed state education, state-controlled mass media, courts, and government offices to foster preservation of its language. This failure, a vice of omission, is sometimes hard to distinguish from a vice of commission, a deliberate centralizing, unifying policy to impose a single national majority language and cause the minority tongue to shrivel up and die. It is not altogether clear what the duties of a state are with regard to the preservation of several languages and cultures within its territory, nor what a colonial power owes to a colonized people to help it maintain its native "identity." The question is less obvious than it looks, and answering it would be a good deal simpler if the educational and other influences affecting the survival of language and ethnicity were not tax-financed products of collective choices, that is, if the state itself played a lesser or no role in shaping them. Nor is it clear when a separatist grievance is genuine and grave enough to justify secession and to brand resistance to it as tyrannical. These hard or undecidable cases all enter into the complex rights and wrongs of self-determination, which I shall confront later.

For our immediate purposes, the interesting thing to wonder at is the nature of the incentive to secede, to put two governments in the place of one, when there is no genuine grievance, in the accepted meaning of the term, when ethnic minorities are recognized by neutral observers as having equal liberties, equal rights, and "equal opportunities," whatever the latter is supposed to mean. (The neutrality of an observer who finds that an ethnic minority enjoys the same liberties, rights, and opportunities as the majority will almost certainly be contested by the advocates of the minority in question—it would take angelic fairness to accept that judgment. For the minority, just being in the minority means that its "rights" and "opportunities" are not equal to those of the majority. It is for this reason above all that the claim that Slavs were not oppressed in the Austro-Hungarian empire or that Germans and Hungarians were not unfairly treated in interwar Czechoslovakia is so contested and contestable.)

Let us, therefore, take the (perhaps somewhat idealized, perhaps actually counterfactual) case in which an ethnic group living in a state dominated by another ethnic group has no grievance other than its minority status. Why, then, does sheer "otherness" alone generate conflict? Let us even assume that the state in question is of optimal size, so that the relation of its intrinsic costs to the benefits it can procure by having individuals act collectively is as good as possible. In this case, arguably it would be collectively rational for the minority group not to secede. However, for at least some members of that group it would still be individually rational to mount a separatist movement, because of what we might label the "Paris cultural attaché" syndrome. The label looks facetious, but it is revealing.

Each government has a cultural attaché in Paris, an ambassador to the Court of St. James, a chief delegate to the United Nations, a minister of this and a minister of that at home, and so forth. The separatist movement can attract a disproportionately large number of local patriots, frustrated teachers, poets in the vernacular, and young people troubled by a mismatch between their ambitions and their abilities, all of whom harbor the fond hope of becoming their future government's cultural attaché in Paris or somebody equally enviable. It is well known that people tend to overvalue very small chances of large prizes, in the sense of betting on them at shorter odds than the true actuarial odds that would make the bet a fair one; this tendency is what makes bookmakers rich. Such behavior is perfectly consistent with (subjective) rationality as the maximization of expected utility, if the bettor either misjudges the true odds or attaches a more than proportionate increase in utility to a large increase in his wealth. (His action would be irrational if his betting in the face of known actuarial odds were inconsistent with any continuous and positively sloped utility function.) The separatist who overestimates his chances of becoming his country's cultural attaché in Paris or who attaches immense value to such glamour is presumably quite rational in militating for secession at great cost to his ethnic group, and thousands of militant separatists may all be rational even if all but one must fail to get appointed to the dream post in Paris.

The upshot, however, would be collectively irrational for all separatists taken together, and even more so for the whole ethnic group, on whose behalf the separatists militate but which contains nonseparatists as well as separatists. The horrors suffered by many if not most African peoples under vicious, corrupt, and irremediably incompetent postcolonial native governments provide a telling example of the price a liberation movement imposes on a whole collectivity for the satisfaction of the ambitions of a very few.

Evidently, not every secession produces fabulously bad government on the African model. For the horns of the dilemma between individual ambition and collective well-being to hurt, nationalism need not cause a proliferation of bad governments. A proliferation of governments is itself a wasteful phenomenon, making room for the growth of parasitism, even if the governments are just the average, indifferent sort. That the multiplication of states should give rise to two good governments where only a bad or indifferent one existed before is of course possible, but it is hard to see on what grounds one should expect such an outcome.

HOW TO DETERMINE THE SELF?

Whenever the group organized under one sovereign political authority is heterogeneous in any major respect, so that the interests and preferences of its subgroups differ, conflict arises, which governments may or may not resolve by the ordinary political processes for making public choices. I am not suggesting that the democratic process is likely to generate "good" solutions and the autocratic process "bad" ones. Everywhere in the range between the two extremes, the political process produces outcomes that reflect the might of the opposing forces in being. When, however, the heterogeneity is ethnic in nature, the resulting conflict is—or at least since World War I has been widely considered to be—subject to resolution not by the ordinary political process but by invocation and exercise of the right of self-determination: Might must yield to right.

"Right," if the word is used properly, implies that the rightholder exercises it by requiring another party to perform or suffer some act defined by the right and that the party in question has the obligation to perform or submit accordingly. The act is favorable (beneficial) to the rightholder and unfavorable (onerous) to the obligor. By exercising the right of self-determination, the "self" requires some national government to release it from that government's authority and prerogatives. Moreover, that government must release not only the person or persons who possess the right but also some part of the national territory, loosely defined as the part in which the "self" in question resides. But who is the "self"?

At a glance, one can count no less than four ambiguities in the right of self-determination, each adding to its obscurity.

The first arises from the jointness of some person or persons as the rightholder and some territory that the rightholder is entitled to take out of the territory over which the obligor (the state of the dominant ethnic group) is sovereign. Jointness means that the "self" who exercised the right to secede can hardly be a single person, for what would be the territory he was entitled to take out of the obligor country? Nor, for the same obvious reason, can the "self" be a very small number of persons. If entitlement to territory goes with residence, the smallest "self" that determines where it and its territory belong must be either large enough to populate a territory that can either make another country, with what that implies in terms of geographically and economically sensible new frontiers, or contiguous to another country to which it wishes to be joined. Some gerrymandering can ease the problem of secession, but is gerrymandering in its favor a right of the minority and consequently an obligation of the majority?

Hence arises the second major ambiguity. An ethnic group living in another ethnic group's state and large enough to claim a division of territory is seldom homogeneous. Within the territory it claims, it may be dominant, have a plurality, or even constitute an overwhelming majority. Nevertheless, minorities may live in its midst; do they also have the right of self-determination? Anglophone Canada has a francophone minority, which constitutes the majority in Quebec alongside an anglophone minority. Who in Canada is the "self" that holds the right of "self-determination"? Who in Quebec? And who in a particular area, county, or town within Quebec? The glib answer is "the majority," but why is the francophone majority in Quebec entitled to take the province out of Canada if an anglophone or just antiseparatist majority in Montreal is not entitled to take the city out of Quebec? Protestant Ulstermen formed a minority in preparation Ireland, but they constitute a majority in Northern Ireland and a minority in many areas of that territory. Similar ambiguities abound in Transylvania, the Vojvodina, Catalonia, and elsewhere. When does a minority of those living in a large territory start to enjoy the status of a majority of those living on a smaller territory, entitled to exercise a right to detach it?

A third ambiguity of self-determination is bound up with the second. If the political map is not to become a mosaic of small pieces, the "selves" who can determine themselves must be sizable multiperson ones even if, luckily, they are homogeneous and not multiethnic. However, if the rightholder is a multiperson entity, who exercises its right? Societies, communities, and groups do not decide. They have decisions made for them by some formal or informal mechanism actuated by individual decisions. It is far from evident what this mechanism should be for the right to be validly exercised. What role is to be given to "freedom fighters," militant separatists, qualified or simple voting majorities? The decision to exercise the right, to hold it in reserve, or to renounce it may change the life of generations. It is invidious for some to decide for all, whether the decision is to go or to stay. Nonunanimity is one of the great potential vices of any collective right and any collective obligation. The vice is more serious than most in the case of the right of national self-determination.

The final ambiguity is too obvious to need elaboration. Where the obligor is sovereign, enforcement of the obligation is absent by definition, a contradiction in terms; if self-determination were enforceable, the state would not be a sovereign entity. For a nation-state comprising a majority (or otherwise dominant) group and a minority, it may be collectively rational to accept self-determination as a right and to honor the corresponding obligation; likewise it may be collectively rational for the minority to retain but not to exercise the right. But it may be impracticable to share the advantages of either alternative between majority and minority in a manner that would put both in a preferred position, compared to the third alternative, which is an attempt to exercise the right and a failure to honor it, that is, unresolved conflict. Hence, it may be rational for the minority to agitate for secession and for the majority not to yield.

THE NEED FOR WAR

All dilemmas that involve individually rational conduct leading to collectively suboptimal results can be overcome by appropriate rules. This statement is obviously true of open conflicts, whether arising from rival nationalisms or not, that either fester and remain unresolved or are resolved in a fight, with escalating recourse to force by attacker and defender, in which the parties taken together incur a joint cost that leaves both victor and vanquished worse off than no solution, let alone a nonviolent bargained solution. The bargained solution, though Pareto superior to the conflict, often cannot be reached for the same prisoner's-dilemma-type reason that opposes individual to collective rationality. I use "prisoner's dilemma type" loosely, to indicate an incentive structure in which a player can rationally expect to do better by being uncooperative, nasty, obstructive, and unduly demanding both when he expects the other player to be cooperative and undemanding and when he expects him to be uncooperative and demanding. Of course, appropriate rules can always ensure a peaceful and Pareto-optimal solution—a hackneyed conclusion ceaselessly repeated in "internationalist" Wilsonian exhortations.

But if recognition of the potential benefit of rules were always sufficient to make the parties concerned adopt and obey them, then rules would hardly be needed in the first place. Right incentives would elicit right choices spontaneously. Rules that aim to neutralize the "wrong" sort of incentive structure, however, are not self-enforcing. The individually rational strategy may well be to disobey them. Making them binding requires enforcement, but nation-states live in the "state of nature," where rules are not enforced by a third party, a specialized enforcer, a world government mandated to punish transgressors. Technically, the situation is one of anarchy of *some* degree of orderliness, with occasional breaches of order.

One measure of the orderliness of international anarchy is the predominance of peaceful, negotiated solutions of conflicts between nations, as opposed to recourse to war. "War" in this context may mean a shooting war or a trade war if trade is important enough to the party refusing to yield in bargaining. War, whether economic or military, waged by a state differs from one waged by individuals in that the latter directly accept or decline the costs they would incur as a result of their choice of war or peace. In wars waged by states, costs fall on individuals who cannot decide to bear or to escape them.

However, paradoxical as it may sound, the total exclusion of war by universal military and economic disarmament would logically make negotiated solutions hard if not impossible to reach. If war were "outlawed" and the outlawing were enforced, a party to an international conflict would never gain by making any concession that would leave it worse off than its initial situation from which the bargaining started. Conflicts, therefore, could be peacefully resolved only if the initial situation was Pareto inferior, that is, if both parties could gain by moving away from it. For less benign conflicts to have a bargaining solution, it is logically necessary to introduce a dynamic factor that makes the initial situation progressively worse for the holdout party refusing to make the bargaining concession. That factor is the growing risk of war as long as the negotiation remains deadlocked. The more failure to agree looks like failure to avert war, the more the bargaining solution, with one party making the concession, resembles a move by both parties to a Pareto-superior position.

However, only the sporadic occurrence of war—that it remains, albeit distant in space or time, an event well within human experience—makes credible the risk of war that renders the failure to agree Pareto inferior. If war were either unknown or known but by some miraculous means "outlawed" or considered unthinkable in our present world, its threat could never serve to render concession in bargaining a rational strategy. Paradoxically, in a world of sovereign states, the possibility of war and its occasional occurrence are probably necessary to motivate parties to move from conflict to accommodation.

This conclusion is not cheerful, but it is a corollary of a system of groups—typically, nations organized in states whose vocation is to promote group interests. It is difficult to see how the conclusion can be avoided or attenuated, allowing peace to prevail without getting help from war, unless the institution of the state itself is avoided or attenuated.

BREAKING THE LINK BETWEEN COSTS AND BENEFITS

The sprawling argument must now be rounded up and forced into the straitjacket of a conclusion of sorts, with some pretension to generality.

Nationalism is a set of beliefs and behavioral norms designed to foster ethnic separateness and survival. By "designed" I do not mean to imply conscious calculation, but rather consistency with what calculating individuals might have rationally chosen. Nationalism is a powerful aid in capturing some advantages available for group but not for individual action.

The organized agent of nationalism is the nation-state. Its essential function is to replace individual by collective choices in any domain (over any pair of alternatives) that collective choice itself—or, as some theorists prefer to express it, collective meta-choice "at the constitutional level"—decides to preempt. On the face of it, the nation-state is a means capable of producing collectively rational outcomes that would be out of the reach of individuals acting rationally; sovereignty over individual actions must therefore rest not with individuals but with the organized collectivity. Nationalism is, among other things, a conviction that this condition is proper.

Perversely, however, the very machinery intended to impose collective rationality may produce the opposite effect. The state suppresses the basic dilemma in which individuals choose the free-rider option, evade the bearing of group costs, and as a result have no group benefits to share in, nothing to "ride free" on. But although this dilemma is suppressed, others crop up.

The stronger and more irresistible the machinery for imposing collective choices, the greater the temptation to manipulate and exploit it to individual advantage. The very ease of imposing public choices gives rise to a complex web of redistributive maneuvers within the nation-state: fiscal, regulatory, and protectionist measures, most of them wasteful and lacking the transparency that would allow them to be seen for what they are.

Moreover, although the nation-state, as initially justified, is a tool to enable an ethnic group to prevail over outsiders, its advantage disappears when the outsiders obey the same rationality and organize themselves into nation-states. The dilemma then arises that although it is individually rational for each nation to seek strength in unity and armed protection behind national frontiers, it would be collectively rational for all to dismantle the frontiers, both military and economic, and disarm.

A further dilemma appears when each ethnic subgroup aspires to be a nation and each nation seeks to have its own sovereign nation-state. There is a putative disadvantage in not having one when others have theirs. Control of the means to impose collective decisions on all is intrinsically attractive. One machinery for a large group made up of two subgroups may be the efficient solution, but it is individually rational for both subgroups to have their own governments, both sovereign, harboring two parasitic teams of office-holders where one would do. Separatist movements as well as the resistance they face, whatever their real causes, could be rationally explained by this dilemma alone. Finally, again paradoxically, the sovereignty of nationally distinct groups makes war a necessary condition of the peaceful resolution of international conflicts.

In the last analysis, these dilemmas and perverse unwelcome solutions probably have a single root cause. The making of collective choices that are binding for all, to which nationalism calls for dutiful submission, loosens if it does not break the link between benefits enjoyed and costs borne by any given individual. Then it becomes individually rational for some people to make everyone pay for something that benefits them alone; to make only some pay for the putative "common good" of all; and even to send some people to die in war, often for the good of nobody except those few whose vanity is served.

In sum, collective choice inspired by nationalism fails in its own purpose and gets entrapped in irrationality. Though not strictly within the scope of an analysis of nationalism, a plainer, blunter conclusion also imposes itself: that never mind any test of rationality or efficiency, collective choice—no matter how inspired—would have a hard time withstanding the test of morality.

Acknowledgments: Reprinted from *The Independent Review*, 3, no. 1 (Summer 1998), pp. 77–89. Copyright © 1998.

15

A Critique of Group Loyalty

Laurie Calhoun

When someone describes a person as "loyal," this description is typically thought to be a form of compliment. Approbation seems to be a part of what many take to be the very meaning of the word. However, a close look at some cases of loyalty, such as those found in Nazi Germany and during other tragic episodes in history when otherwise nonhomicidal persons were persuaded to murder fellow human beings for the sake of their group, suggests that the concept of loyalty needs to be reassessed. Although most people evince approval of what they take to be the positive character trait or virtue of loyalty, I hope to show that the notion has not been adequately scrutinized. My analysis does not presuppose moral absolutism, the thesis that there is a single true morality. What I have to say applies to the absolutist, the relativist, and the moral skeptic. I argue here that, in spite of the positive connotation of "loyalty," the concept is itself morally neutral, and remaining loyal to a group whose values one does not share is irrational.

To begin, consider whether any person should blindly obey the dictates of his group. The most obvious and nefarious case in recent history leaps immediately to mind: under Adolf Hitler, many Germans were persuaded to obey the orders of their superiors on the grounds that they belonged to the group "the Good Germans." Because of the unreflective obedience of most of the German people, millions of Jews and other innocent people were slaughtered. Clearly, a loyalty to *that* group in *that* instance was bad, insofar as it led to catastrophic consequences. In attempting to understand what happened during that episode, we quickly see that the atrocities committed by perfectly ordinary human beings resulted from a sort of domino or snowballing effect. Many people were "just doing their jobs," and they were motivated to continue "doing their jobs" by a combination of factors: commitment to what was perceived to be Hitler's "noble" aim, conjoined with, on the part of some, a generalized fear of failing to do what was demanded of them in the name of the group. As "the cause" grew stronger, the former motivation came to dominate. People were persuaded to believe that it was in their best interests to bind together with their fellow Germans in order to conquer "the evil enemy," the Jews. The power and efficacy of appeals to "loyalty" and "solidarity" are nowhere better illustrated than in the disturbing documentary film *Triumph des Willens*, directed by Leni Riefenstahl in 1934.

In retrospect, it has become obvious to thoughtful people everywhere that the Germans were swindled into adopting Hitler's megalomaniacal and arguably psychopathic telos as their own, though in a slightly different guise, which they believed to be moral. We can now see clearly how, through propagandistic appeals to loyalty and group solidarity, ordinary people were persuaded to condone and even perpetrate moral horrors. We can only lament that individual Germans, with rare exceptions, did not think for themselves. Instead, they acquiesced to a form of "ethics by authority," where the authority in question was, in the judgment of humanity, morally depraved. Undeniably, Hitler's "cause" gained strength through the erroneous interpretation of group loyalty as a virtue.[1]

Loyalty involves a commitment to go along with one's group, *even when* the group's action is something that, left to one's own devices, one would not have thought to do. In other words, loyalty is supposed to provide an *extra* reason to do what one would not otherwise do. How many of the German people, before Hitler came to power, considered murdering their Jewish neighbors? Very few, I would surmise. Despite the well-documented prejudice against Jews throughout history (Botwinick 1998), the Holocaust occurred only when people were galvanized to act en masse. The Germans were persuaded to do what they, as isolated individuals, most likely would never have done, on the grounds that loyalty required it. The general moral to draw from the story of Hitler and the Third Reich is that no one should submit to the dictates of a group when they conflict with one's own personal moral convictions. It is no one's duty to acquiesce to the will of a group.

GROUP DYNAMICS

The "convictions" of a group emerge from a bargaining process in which compromises are made and amoral and sometimes irrational forces act upon agents seeking one another's support. In bargaining processes the lowest common denominator may prevail and, when the momentum of the group is forceful, persons often end up "jumping on the bandwagon" for morally irrelevant reasons, for example, out of a fear of rejection or ridicule. This outcome gives the group the appearance of holding a stronger, more stable commitment to the alleged interests of the group than is in fact the case, for part of what appears to be the group's enthusiasm derives from purely psychological fears, which are egoistic and therefore amoral (unless, of course, ethical egoism—the thesis that prudence and morality coincide—happens to be true).

Human beings are by and large social animals, who generally enjoy being liked and appreciated by others. People tend to care what other people think about them and to coalesce into like-minded groups. Those who speak out against the status quo or the prevailing opinion represent an adversarial position vis-à-vis the group, which stigmatizes them as enemies to be maligned (or worse). Throughout history very few people have had the courage to stand up against the reigning opinions of their groups, even in instances where, in retrospect, it has become obvious that the group was making grave mistakes.

The compelling argument against submitting to the dictates of a group is that the group might be wrong. Either it was morally permissible to treat blacks as beasts of burden, or it was not. Either it was morally permissible to slaughter the Jews, or it was not. In any such conflict, only one of the sides can be right. (If moral relativism is true, then "everything is permitted," so the law of the excluded middle still holds.) If a morally corrupt person is leading one's group, then the principles of the group will be derivatively immoral, as was plausibly the case with Nazi laws. Persons who act against their own conscience, in favor of the dictates of a group, betray their erroneous belief that they are less able to render judgments about moral matters than are other members of the group, namely, those with whom they disagree.

Those who surrender in situations of group conflict fail adequately to appreciate the following question: What qualifies one to be a moral authority? When we look closely at "ethics by authority," we see that no rational grounds exist for believing that other people are better equipped to discover moral truths than are we. One of the serious problems with holding group loyalty as a paramount value exemplifies the problem with any ethics by authority. In this case the "authority" in question is the group reified into an institutional structure that its members are enjoined to obey. To appreciate the gravity of this problem, we must now consider the general problem with ethics by authority.

THE PROBLEM WITH "ETHICS BY AUTHORITY"

An ethics by authority responds to the fundamental question of moral philosophy— "What should I do?"—with a simple, univocal answer: "Do what you are told to do." The voice of some institutional (for example, familial, religious, governmental, educational) authority is accepted as a *moral* authority. The theory is deontological insofar as it exacts obedience regardless of the reasonably foreseeable consequences of obedience. A commitment to an ethics by authority betrays a faith in the superior moral vision of the alleged authority. Each version of ethics by authority proves dubious, however, because of the epistemological problem raised by the question, What grounds can we ever have for believing that another human being is a moral sage?

Consider the sorts of people to whom we often defer in moral matters. Our parents serve as our moral authorities throughout our childhood. But the qualifications for being a parent are quite minimal: fertility and sexual desire. What do these properties have to do with moral sagacity? Nothing. Still, as children, we are obliged to obey our parents, and habits of submission, regrettably, become for some people habits for life.

Throughout our grade school and high school educations, we obey the moral dictates of our teachers and school administrators (in addition to those of our parents). But the qualifications for being a teacher—holding a university degree and being conversant with a specific subject matter—have little if anything to do with the capacity for making sound moral judgments. Likewise, academic administrators are trained to manage schools, not to ascertain moral verities. To the extent that administrators serve as prudential managers of groups, their activities can be viewed as purely amoral.

In society most people heed the moral authority of their governmental leaders. When leaders deem it necessary to go to war, the vast majority of people submit to their wishes unreflectively, under the assumption that the leaders are in a superior position to render judgments on such matters. In fact, however, the properties requisite to a successful political career have, at best, nothing to do with the ability to make sound moral judgments. Some would even claim that the sorts of skills often exemplified by those who succeed in politics—for example, duplicity, sycophancy, and chameleonic malleability—are the antitheses of the qualities one would expect to be the character traits of genuine moral leaders.

To take another common case of ethics by authority, consider the religious authorities to whom millions of people turn for moral guidance. Religious authorities are human beings with a particular interest in religious matters. They might have become educators, restaurant owners, real estate brokers, or politicians. Instead, they have opted to devote themselves to the religious life, spending vast amounts of time with religious texts, in religious convocations, or in various religious exercises. Are religious leaders *moral* authorities? Admittedly, of the candidates considered so far, they seem prima facie the most concerned with morality. However, because "the word of God" (assuming, for the sake of argument, that

God exists) is necessarily mediated by human interpretations, when we defer to the authority of religious leaders, we are accepting that their interpretive faculties are somehow better attuned than are ours to receive "the word" as transmitted by God through some medium. Why should their having had the desire to communicate with God give us any grounds for believing that self-proclaimed religious authorities have in fact developed a surer method for doing so? What rational grounds can we have for accepting religious leaders as moral authorities?

As cynical as this analysis may appear, the fact that many charlatans have been exposed in the religious domain of contemporary society (for example, Tammy Faye and Jim Bakker, Charles Manson, and a variety of other cult leaders) lends inductive support to my contention. Assuming that our laws are intended to reflect our commonsense views of morality, then if these self-proclaimed religious authorities are criminals, they are prima facie morally reproachable as well and, therefore, far from obviously well suited to offer anyone else guidance in moral matters.[2] But we need not adduce the most sensational cases of recent history to make the general point about the dubiousness of appeal to religious authorities for moral guidance. A consideration of the Inquisition would suffice.

When we elevate the group to the status of a reified thing to serve as our moral authority, we encounter all of the problems of any ethics by authority, only in a much more severe form. Consider the case in which one's own opinion differs from that of one's group. If one submits to the "will" of the group, that is, the majority opinion, then one is exalting to the status of moral authority some group of individuals whose opinions differ from one's own. Capitulating to the opinion of a group is tantamount to submitting to the opinion of some one member of the group whose opinion diverges from one's own.[3] But what rational grounds do we have for believing that *that* person is a moral authority? If the foregoing analysis is correct, we have none whatsoever. In submitting to this authority, we commit precisely the error of the Germans with respect to the Nazi regime.

LOYALTY AND RELATIVISM

Some will claim that the whole point of forming groups is to make cohabitation more successful. We bind together in order to further our own interests, and this process sometimes requires a willingness to compromise on the part of the individual members of the group. According to a conventionalist view of morality, it does appear that conformity to the dictates of one's group is a part of the agreement entered into whenever we decide to become members of a group. We cannot expect all of our idiosyncratic desires to be met, but some of them will be easier to satisfy than they otherwise would have been, owing to our association with this group. In Thomas Hobbes's view, we have agreed to band together in order to avoid a "solitary, poor, nasty, brutish, and short" life in "the state of nature."

If moral relativism is true, then it is a mistake to think that some moral reality exists beyond appearances. In that case, might makes right, so in any moral dispute whoever gets the last word, whoever gets his way, makes his way the "morally right" way. Here, acceptance of an ethics by authority serves as a practical means of deciding what to do, a simple, straightforward, virtually mechanical procedure for determining the right course of action. To the question "What should I do?" the answer is unproblematic: "I should do what I am told to do." And the grounds for such acceptance must ultimately lie in the increased efficiency achieved by living as a member of a group rather than facing life as a rugged individualist. It is a sociological platitude that dissenting individuals are automatically branded by groups as "other," "deviant," "bad," and sometimes even "insane." And it is undeniably much more difficult to achieve one's mundane goals when one has forsaken the "I'll scratch your back, you scratch mine" approach, which yields so many benefits for so many people, all of whom have recognized that cooperation is crucial to success, if not survival, in society.

In other words, a commitment to a value of loyalty may seem, on the face of it, legitimate for the staunch moral relativist, who sees morality as nothing more than a set of conventions agreed upon by members of a community in order to make cohabitation more pleasant and efficient (Harman 1975, 1984). Even then, however, at some points a further commitment to the values of one's group will impede or even undermine one's fundamental projects and plans. Then, loyalty to the group must be renounced, on pain of irrationality, because the relativist's only reason for associating with a group is to benefit from that association. Therefore, even the relativist must ultimately depend upon himself as the final arbiter in moral matters, for the dynamics of his group evolve over time. Only the individual himself can determine the point at which association with the group has greater costs than benefits to him. In other words, the relativist must, on every occasion when his values come into conflict with those of his group, decide on his own once again to remain in the group or go his own way. In a later section, I investigate in some detail a concrete example of the problem relativists have with loyalty.

LOYALTY AND NONRELATIVISM: A WAGER ARGUMENT

What attitudes toward loyalty are reasonable for the absolutist and the moral skeptic? For the absolutist, it is easy to see how the arguments against the putative moral authority of another merely human being, no matter what his pretensions may be, apply to any alleged group authority. The rational response to conflicts between one's own moral conscience and one's group is to defer ultimately to one authority alone, namely, one's own conscience.

Consider the following "wager argument." Suppose that a person's intuition about a policy conflicts with the prevailing opinion of his group. Then he has the following choices:

Case 1: Go along with the group   The group is right   The group is wrong
Case 2: Divorce oneself from the group   The group is right   The group is wrong

In the first case, if the group is right, then the agent does the right thing but deserves no credit for doing so, because he is swayed only by amoral considerations. Alternatively, if the group is wrong, then the agent does the wrong thing, and he commits the error of rationality diagnosed in the previous analysis of ethics by authority. Either way the agent fails: morally, intellectually, or both.

In the second case, in which the absolutist opts to divorce himself from the group from which he dissents, the group again may be right or wrong. If the group is right but the individual desists from acting in accordance with it because of his moral scruples, then he is mistaken in his judgment, but if *ought* implies *can*, and he acts on the best evidence available to him, after careful assessment of the facts of the case, then he cannot be blamed, morally or rationally speaking, for his mistake. If, in contrast, the group is wrong and the agent acts rightly in desisting from going along with the group, then, by heeding his own conscience, the agent acts with both moral and intellectual integrity.

This analysis shows that the rational approach to any moral conflict with one's group is to heed one's conscience, because if one does the right thing only fortuitously or for nonmoral reasons, then one's action has no moral value worth acknowledging.[4] Suffice it to say that, in any view of morality according to which intentions have moral relevance, the preceding wager argument applies.[5]

Having considered the situation of the moral relativist, who affirms that might makes right and therefore that the prevailing opinion is the right opinion, and the absolutist, who in contrast affirms the possibility of being mistaken about moral matters in a substantive sense, let us now turn to the moral skeptic. The moral skeptic is agnostic on the absolutism-relativism issue. Is there a single true morality? Do any moral principles apply to all people at all times, regardless of where and when they live and regardless of the circumstances in which they find themselves? To these questions, the skeptic gives no answer beyond an expression of his unwillingness to take a stand one way or another. But this answer implies that the skeptic, no less than the absolutist, holds open the possibility of a substantive sense of moral fallibility among human beings, and that is all that is necessary for the preceding wager argument to apply. So long as the moral skeptic accepts the *possibility* of being morally mistaken, then all of the same options remain real for him. In other words, for the moral skeptic no less than for the absolutist, loyalty to a group whose moral judgments and policies conflict with his own may be both morally and intellectually reproachable.

LOYALTY AND INSTITUTIONS

Beyond its irrationality, the value of loyalty becomes decidedly dangerous because of the potential for corrupt institutions, the administrators of which are human beings and therefore fallible. Consider for a moment the nature of administration. The purpose of an administration is to manage an institution. Those in positions of power have that power by virtue of their having been appointed by the relevant community to act as agents for those affected by the institution (Calhoun 1994). One obvious problem with an exhortation to group loyalty is that it leads to the reification of institutions: the club, the university, the government, the military. The institution acquires an importance above and beyond its purpose to protect and further the interests of those who banded together to form it and appointed certain individuals to head it. Anarchists are particularly sensitive to this problem, and they reject the legitimacy of any organization that arrogates power over the individuals composing it. In works such as George Orwell's *1984*, we find dystopic visions of the most insane sort of institutional reification, wherein the institution becomes an organism capable of obliterating the rights and totally ignoring the needs and desires of those for whom it was originally erected. A single charismatic psychopath can turn an institution teeming with unreflective bureaucrats concerned with doing their job, that is, with following the orders of their superiors, into a moral monster of the Orwellian sort. Witness Nazi Germany.

This problem arises because, qua administrator, one's first and foremost obligation is to maintain the institution. But things comprise all and only their properties. Modifications of policies constitute modifications of the very identity of an institution. In other words, every proposed change constitutes, in some sense, an assault upon the institution, and so will be opposed by individual administrators and their subordinate bureaucrats, whose vocational duty it is to defend the structure as it stands.

The ultimate anarchist argument may be that if a given policy is good, then the people will themselves assent to it uncoerced. Any policy to which they will not assent should not be a policy to which they are obliged to adhere. After all, our governments are *our* governments. We create them, and we should be able to disband them when they fail to serve the purpose for which they were fashioned. When a government or, more generally, an institution begins to take on its own properties, to espouse its own self-serving agenda, which serves to perpetuate the selfish interests of the administration, then it has lost touch with its raison d'être. We find this phenomenon, of bureaucracies run rampant, throughout our society, even though the Declaration of Independence of the United States of America clearly states:

> We hold these Truths to be self-evident, that all Men are created equal, that they are endowed by their Creator with certain unalienable Rights, that among these are Life, Liberty, and the Pursuit of Happiness—That to secure these Rights, Governments are instituted among Men, deriving their just Powers from the consent of the Governed, that whenever any Form of Government becomes destructive of these Ends, it is the Right of the People to alter or to abolish it, and to institute new Government, laying its Foundation on such Principles, and organizing its Powers in such Form, as to them shall seem most likely to effect their Safety and Happiness.

The problem with an exhortation to group loyalty is entirely analogous to that encountered in defending the "right to life" of a thoroughly corrupt institution. If a given policy or principle is advocated by a group, then, according to those who believe in the value of loyalty, each individual should agree to it *in the name of the group,* even if it conflicts with the individual's personal values. But, as the anarchist correctly recognizes, the group's favoring a policy or principle is not a *moral* reason for adopting it. Either sound reasons for its adoption exist, or they do not. That others accept it is not, in and of itself, a sufficient reason for accepting it.

When should we dissent from the policies of our groups? Precisely and only when they conflict with our deepest convictions and values. If a policy is sound, then we should support it. If it is not, then we should not support it. The extra value supposedly imparted to a policy due to the majority of one's group having accepted it is illusory. That value should *not* be added to the supposed value of a bad policy, because a bad policy should not be supported at all. When invoked, loyalty supports good policies when they are already good, and bad policies when they are bad.

Arguably, more atrocities have been committed throughout human history in the name of morality than for any other reason. To condone practices and policies merely because they are supported by one's group is equally absurd. For if one's group advocates immoral or bad policies, then something is wrong with the group, and one should seek above all to free oneself from its influence. A group is not good simply because it is a group. Some groups are bound by principles that we deem legitimate; others are not (for example, the Ku Klux Klan, the Nazis). When the interests and values of a group, once thought to be consonant with one's own, metamorphose radically, then the individual must either metamorphose radically or abandon the group.[6] To conform to the changes wrought within a group by the more powerful members is to capitulate to their wills. To permit oneself to be assimilated into a homogeneous mass of compromising chameleons is to renounce one's individuality, which consists of those very values that gave rise to the idea that loyalty is a good thing. In other words, such capitulation amounts to a practical contradiction of sorts. Loyalty becomes no more and no less than a religious tenet. And although religions may appease the human need for security, they become irrational when they begin to erode people's fundamental values.

A CLOSER LOOK AT RELATIVISM AND PRUDENCE

I claimed early on that my criticisms of loyalty would not rely on the specific moral character of any particular group. To substantiate this claim, I now explain in greater detail how a valorization of loyalty is irrational for the moral relativist. Needless to say, a relativist would not find the "wager argument" very persuasive. Nonetheless, and strikingly, perhaps our most persuasive data regarding the inadequacy of group loyalty to a tenable and rational outlook is found in relativistic systems of organized crime. In such systems one minor betrayal, one act of treachery by a member of a group whose paramount value is loyalty and which therefore demands its members' loyalty, causes the inevitable disintegration of the system, due to something like a ricocheting effect. The bullet of treachery ricochets back and forth against the walls, from ceiling to floor, until everyone in the room is either wounded or dead. And when the wounded recover, they wreak destructive and terminal vengeance on the traitors.

Some may think that the problem with the organized crime "families" really has to do with the content of their "moral" principles. But the problem is deeper than that: a prioritization of loyalty is untenable regardless of the content of the moral principles held by the members of a group. I have argued that a commitment to a value of loyalty is fundamentally irrational for anyone who leaves open the possibility of genuine moral fallibility. Because it provides the most illuminating example of the problem of loyalty for the relativist, let us examine more closely the phenomenon of organized crime, the systems of which inevitably come to ruin, sooner or later. The problem with loyalty diagnosed earlier, that it leads to a contentless reification of the group as an institution, is graphically evident in organized crime, where time and again betrayal ultimately leads to the collapse of the entire system. The persons who conducted their lives ostensibly in allegiance to the group, holding loyalty sacred while condoning and committing cold-blooded murder, find themselves all alone in the end, their comrades having been killed or incarcerated.

The agents deploy an idiom replete with allusions to honor and loyalty, describe what law-abiding citizens regard as abominable actions in moral terms, and redraw the lines between murder and self-defense, on the one hand, and murder and just execution, on the other. In spite of the rhetoric of honor and respect found in crime families, in the end such cases betray a fundamental Hobbesian drive to band together for egocentric ends. Ultimately, a concern to better their mundane conditions and those of their nuclear families drives men to become involved in organized crime. Mafiosi, hit men, and other lackeys share the American fascination with wealth and success (Arlacchi 1987; Forman 1993). They choose organized crime as the simplest route to financial success and community respect, the latter arising in a capitalist society as a natural concomitant of the former. By sheltering themselves from outsiders and distancing themselves from their victims and their victims' families, the participants in organized crime come to view themselves as businessmen who have developed clever means by which to acquire everything they want without ever having to pay, so long as they do not betray the other members of their group.[7]

The seeming inevitability of betrayal is best understood as an expression of the structural conflict between any individual and any group to which the individual belongs. In crime families, sooner or later an individual allows his greed, jealousy, or quest for power to win out against the supreme dictates of the group. Then the destruction of the entire system ensues in short order as the group divides into subgroups, each of whose members have stronger attachments to fellow members of the subgroup than to the larger group that subsumes all the subgroups. Such fragmentation is inevitable because these men get involved in the system to begin with only to further their own selfish interests. If they can further their own interests better by banding together with some small subset of the larger group, then, as rational agents, they will do so. Once the disintegration begins, the internecine destruction continues to the point of obliteration.

The subset of a group with the strongest sense of loyalty is always the unit individual. Therefore, when finally faced with the looming threat of life imprisonment or execution, the apprehended criminal will naturally opt for betraying the entire system. It would be irrational to remain loyal to a system that has failed him, as evidenced by his having been apprehended and therefore no longer being able to obtain the objects of his desire without paying for any of them. When one of the complices is called upon to pay for the crimes of all of the rest, the bond to them magically dissolves. The apprehended criminal may well face death whether or not he betrays his former colleagues, because they will fear him as a mortal enemy even in prison so long as he has information about their crimes, in other words, so long as he is alive and his mental faculties remain intact. Accordingly, in the interest of self-preservation, some apprehended criminals enter witness protection programs, adopt new identities, and vow to renounce their former criminal ways in return for being granted immunity from the law for having surrendered the information necessary to incriminate and convict the other members of their former groups. The chimerical solidarity of the group, referred to in ostensibly virtuous terms, especially "loyalty" and "honor," reveals itself to have been no more than an elaborately constructed facade of simple egoism.

Whenever one believes that all members of one's group are committed to the group in order to further their own selfish aims, then that individual must, rationally speaking, recognize that his bond to the others is strongest when all group members' interests are being better served than they would be were the members to leave the group. Given the original motivation of any individual to enter a relativistic group arrangement, it is imprudent and even quixotic to suppose that anyone will remain loyal to the group when it ceases to further his own interests better than he can do himself as an unattached individual. This condition leads us to the previous conclusion, through yet another route, and even if we assume relativism: When one's values, interests, and opinions collide with those of the majority of one's group, one commits an error of reasoning in capitulating to the will of the group. The relativist is convinced that the other members of his group belong to the group only to further their own selfish ends. In other words, when he defers to the group, he sacrifices his values for theirs. But he has no rational grounds for doing so. He is rather like a person who has erected a temple to a God that he claims does not exist.

Advocates of cooperative enterprises will insist that, in reality, the nature of human commerce necessitates that we sometimes compromise in order to achieve our more important goals. But in truth the relativist never has any reason to believe that even his highest priorities will be supported by the other members of his group. Perhaps they will be, perhaps they will not. And when the acquisition of material wealth *and* the maintenance of power structures constitute a group's predominant concerns, the inherent tension among the members will lead, sooner or later, to the demise of the group. Assuming that resources are finite, the maximization of one's own mundane interests entails, of necessity, a failure to maximize the interests of others.

The tendency of mercenarily motivated groups to disintegrate will also favor the formation of progressively smaller and smaller groups, for the expulsion of members from a group bound by a commitment to the acquisition of wealth will always increase the benefits to those remaining. The group will tend to become smaller and smaller until it reaches the point at which further diminution would impede satisfaction of the aims of the individual members of the group. To take a simple example, it is difficult for one person to rob a bank successfully. But there is some number, greater than one and less than, say, ten, that maximizes the expected profits of each of the complices. A degree of commitment to the goals of the group is required of each of the members of the group, but the moment one of them senses that the weighted probability of his getting caught exceeds the weighted probability of his not getting caught, he will abandon the group in order to secure his own survival, that is, out of self-defense.

These dynamics explain why, when capital offenders are apprehended and convicted, it is often due to their having been in complicity with other persons or having committed the blunder of telling others about their crimes (Kurland 1994). The success of crimes of complicity depends crucially upon the group members' loyalty to one another, but that loyalty is never outweighed by perceived threats to the individual's perceived safety. The members of the group must also depend on the simple prudence of the others. One slip-up by just one member of the group may implicate all the others. Consider, for example, the case of the Tate-LaBianca murders committed by the Manson family in 1969. After the murders, Susan Atkins was arrested on independent charges. Had she not vaunted the murders to her cell mate, the mystery of the murders might have gone unsolved.

Self-reliance is important for criminals and noncriminals, relativists and non-relativists alike. Ultimately, the group is only as good as its members. Indeed, groups often prove worse than the sum of their members, owing to the unsavory tendency of human beings to fall to the level of the lowest common denominator and act upon normally suppressed or sublimated impulses to violence and destruction.

"YOU HAVE TO DO IT! FOR *US*!"

Sociological and historical phenomena such as the group behavior of men in gang rapes, the Inquisition, and complex cover-ups of government corruption all tell against the allegedly superior perspective of "the group." In reality, groups often foster and reward what is most common, superficial, and base in human beings. The tendency of people to conform to the status quo and to the fads of their time could be documented virtually ad infinitum. We naturally form groups as a means of achieving not only mundane ends but also the psychological benefits of acceptance and comradeship. Such benefits often lead people to develop attitudes of complacency with regard to what outsiders allege to be problems of the society in which they live. That complacency rewards homogeneity, conformity, and silence and concomitantly discourages heterogeneity, dissent, and dialogue.

Anyone who does not believe that he has achieved the absolute truth about morality and the ways of the world must continue to entertain new perspectives from which his own errors might be illuminated. But when one prioritizes loyalty to one's group, then the best course of action is to express no dissent, meekly to accept whatever the opinion of the majority happens to be, no matter how haphazard their "method" of arriving at it may have been and no matter how outrageous their policies may seem.

Obviously, we are all products of our past experiences and environments. Accordingly, from the perspective of a moral skeptic, one has no more reason to believe that our current groups have arrived at the truth than the German people had to believe that they had arrived at the truth when they enthusiastically agreed to slaughter the Jews. Put simply, temporal subsequence is not obviously epistemically relevant, and if it is, it must be demonstrated to be so (Calhoun 1997a). Still, even the Germans did not promulgate any view so radical as that it was morally permissible to *murder* the Jews. Rather, the Germans interpreted their heinous deeds along the lines of good people confronting nocent pests. Denying that the Jews were moral persons, the Germans thought that the Jews could not be murdered. Murder is a moral concept that, as such, applies only to moral things (Calhoun 1997b).

One may object that surely nothing we are doing right now has the character of what the Germans did under the Nazi regime. And it is indeed true that, under our own interpretations of our actions, nothing we are doing now could possibly come close to what the Germans did to the Jews. Still, future generations may reinterpret as immoral what the Americans did to the Iraqis in 1991, to cite only one of many possible examples. In fact, it did not take long for some of the staunchest supporters of the Vietnam War (for example, Robert McNamara) to confess that in their nationalistic fervor they had made egregious errors that cost humanity millions of lives. Nationalistic fervor and its most pernicious expressions arise out of an erroneous valorization of group loyalty.

We are no more immune to moral error than any other people throughout history. But unless we are willing to keep our eyes open for new ways of looking at our actions and those of our fellows, then we risk spiraling into yet another dark tunnel of evil while vainly attempting to exculpate ourselves along the way by claiming that we are only doing our duty, "supporting our group."

We naturally associate with others in groups not only for obviously prudential reasons but also, somewhat ironically, as an apparent means of escaping from our egocentric outlooks. We feel better about ourselves when we can interpret our actions in terms of something beyond us, some supposedly greater cause in our group. It is merely an appearance of objectivity and morality that leads people to attach such great importance to and to view in a favorable light the notion of loyalty.

Besides arguing that a commitment to loyalty is irrational, I have considered two concrete cases: that of the Germans under Hitler's regime and that of organized crime. Both illustrate how a commitment to loyalty can lead one astray, whether or not one is an absolutist about morality. Without presupposing any single true moral theory, we have found that the prioritization of loyalty over one's fundamental convictions and values is, at best, irrational and self-delusive and, at worst, dangerous. To describe a human being as "loyal" is not to pay him a compliment.

NOTES

1 The correct interpretation of the Holocaust is of course open to debate, but certain glaring examples support my interpretation, for example, the case of Adolf Eichmann, who, until the bitter end, claimed that he had merely done his duty.

2 Fallacious appeals to authority, *argumenta ad verecundiam*, involve invoking the opinions of persons on matters outside their domain of expertise. I am assuming that the charlatans at issue do not distinguish what they practice from what they preach. Still, even if they do and are flagrantly hypocritical (which television evangelists in particular may be), my criticism is not an instance of *argumentum ad hominem*, because in regard to moral matters, one's moral conduct is relevant to one's suitability to offer moral advice.

3 Later I discuss the regrettable tendency of groups to descend to the lowest common denominator. In group behavior, more minds lead not to a greater probability of truth but rather to a greater probability of agreement with the most persistent member(s) of the group.

4 I am aware of the utilitarian counterintuitive analysis of such a case. To offer one hyperbolic example, die-hard utilitarians would insist that if a drunk driver accidentally hit a car, killing an occupant who was on the way to bomb a public gathering, which would have killed hundreds of people, then the drunk driver's action would be morally permissible, which is to say, right, which is to say, obligatory (because, for utilitarians, maximization of social utility is not only permissible but obligatory), and any other action would have been impermissible.

5 In the sort of utilitarian case cited in the previous footnote, advice one way or another is irrelevant to the agent in question, who is not at all *intent* upon acting one way or another. Accordingly, ascribing moral blame or credit in the case seems rather like ascribing moral properties to a bolt of lightening or a hurricane.

6 In many cases of apostasy, an individual's own view of the group and its values, interests, and principles has changed, leading him to believe that he was mistaken to have allied himself with that group.

7 For an excellent depiction of this form of life, see the film *Goodfellas* (1992, directed by Martin Scorsese), which is based on the true story of Henry Hill. Although they are works of fiction, Francis Ford Coppola's *Godfather* (1972) and *Godfather Part II* (1974) also portray realistically the sorts of group dynamics that operate in modern systems of organized crime.

REFERENCES

Arlacchi, Pino. 1987. *Mafia Business: The Mafia Ethic and the Spirit of Capitalism*. London: Verso.

Botwinick, Rita Steinhardt, ed. 1998. *A Holocaust Reader: From Ideology to Annihilation*. Upper Saddle River, N.J.: Prentice Hall.

Calhoun, Laurie. 1994. Institutions and Deviance: Art and Psychiatry. *Critical Review* 8, no. 3: 393–409.

———. 1997a. *Philosophy Unmasked: A Skeptic's Critique*. Lawrence: University Press of Kansas.

———. 1997b. The Strange Case of Pluto and the Power of Persuasive Interpretation. *Ethica* 9, no 2: 118–26.

Forman, Laura, ed. 1993. *True Crime: Mafia*. New York: Time-Life Books.

Harman, Gilbert. 1975. Moral Relativism Defended. *Philosophical Review* 94:3–22.

———. *The Nature of Morality*. 1977. New York: Oxford University Press.

———. 1984. Is There a Single True Morality? In *Morality, Reason and Truth: New Essays on the Foundations of Ethics*, edited by D. Copp and D. Zimmerman, 27–48. Totowa, N.J.: Rowman and Littlefield.

Hobbes, Thomas. [1651] 1962. *Leviathan*, edited by Michael Oakeshott. New York: Collier.

Kurland, Michael. 1994. *A Gallery of Rogues: Portraits in True Crime*. New York: Prentice Hall.

Acknowledgments: Reprinted from *The Independent Review*, 3, no. 1 (Summer 1998), pp. 5–19. Copyright © 1998. An earlier version of this chapter was presented as a colloquium talk at Ohio University. I would like to thank those in attendance and an anonymous referee for *The Independent Review* for their helpful criticisms. I would also like to thank John Cooper for the title of the final section.

16

The Therapeutic State
The Tyranny of Pharmacracy
Thomas S. Szasz

One of the symbols of sovereign states is the postage stamp. Traditionally, U.S. stamps have depicted a famous American or an important historical scene. In 1893, to increase revenues, the U.S. Post Office began to issue commemorative stamps. The first stamps with health-related themes—for example, a stamp depicting children playing and smiling, commemorating the centennial of the American Dental Association—appeared in 1959. In 1999, the Postal Service unveiled two stamps emblematic of the escalation of America's wars on diseases. On one, the inscription recommended, "Prostate Cancer Awareness: Annual Checkups and Tests"; on the other, it exhorted, "Breast Cancer: Fund the Fight. Find a Cure" (Woloshin and Schwartz 1999).

THE MEDICALIZATION OF POLITICS

Webster's Third New International Dictionary defines the state as "The political organization that has supreme civil authority and political power and serves as the basis of government." Instead of offering definitions of the state, political scientists prefer to identify its characteristic features, such as the possession of "organized police powers, defined spatial boundaries, or a formal judiciary" [and] "a deep and abiding association between the state as a form of social organization and warfare as a political and economic policy" (Fried 1968, 143, 149). I regard monopoly of the legitimate use of force as the quintessential characteristic of the modern state. In this chapter, I focus on the beliefs and values that justify the possession of such force and the aims it serves.

The need to justify the use of force seems instinctive. For the child, the parents' power to coerce—by word or deed, intimidation or punishment—appears justified by their superior wisdom and by the child's innate lawlessness and socially imposed duty to become domesticated. The combination of the natural authority of the superiors, the natural nonconformity of the subordinates and their need to learn the rules of the game and to adhere to them, and the supreme importance of the welfare of the group (family, society, nation), which rests on conformity to social convention, form the template for religious, political, and medical justifications of coercive domination.

Three familiar ideologies of legitimation result: theocracy (God's will), democracy (consent of the governed), and socialism (economic equality, "social justice"). In 1963, in *Law, Liberty, and Psychiatry,* I suggested that modern Western societies, especially the United States, are developing a fourth ideology of legitimation: "Although we may not know it, we have, in our day, witnessed the birth of the Therapeutic State" (212). Since then, in articles and books, I have described and documented the characteristic features of this polity: medical symbols playing the role formerly played by patriotic symbols and the rule of medical discretion and "therapy" replacing the rule of law and punishment (see Szasz 1965, [1970] 1977, 1980, 1982, 1984, 1994a, 1994b, 1995, 1996).

It is undeniable that the state is primarily an apparatus of coercion with a monopoly of the legitimate use of violence. "Government," warned George Washington, "is not reason; it is not eloquence. It is force. Like fire it is a dangerous servant and a fearful master" (qtd. in *Cato Newsletter,* June 1, 2000, 1). Hence, as the reach of the legitimate influence of this "fearful master" expands, the sphere of personal liberties contracts. What, then, ought to belong to the state, and what to the individual? The history of the West may be viewed in part as the history of the growth of freedom, characterized by a lively debate about where to draw the line between the state's duty to safeguard the interests of the community and its obligation to protect individual liberty. Accustomed to hearing phrases such as "freedom of religion," "freedom of speech," and "the free market," we recognize that each refers to a set of activities free from interference by the coercive apparatus of the state. Should we similarly possess "freedom to be sick," "freedom to make ourselves sick," "freedom to treat ourselves," "freedom to obtain medical care," and so forth?

Informed debate about where to draw the line between the welfare of the community and the health of the individual requires that we be clear about the legal distinction between public health and private health. Edward P. Richards and Katharine C. Rathbun—a law professor and a public-health physician, respectively—explain: "Public health is not about making individuals healthy; it is about keeping society healthy by preventing individuals from doing things that endanger others" (1999, 356). Hence, preserving and promoting public health often require coercion, whereas preserving and promoting private health require liberty and responsibility. "Persuading people to wear seatbelts, treat their hypertension, eat a healthy diet, and stop smoking," Richards and Rathbun continue, "is personal health protection. Stopping drunk drivers, treating tuberculosis, condemning bad meat, and making people stop smoking where others are exposed to their smoke is public health.... *Public health should be narrowly defined* in terms of controlling the spread of communicable diseases in society" (1999, 356, emphasis added). Instead of confronting the differences and conflicts between public health and private health, politicians, physicians, and lay people debate slogans, such as the right to health, a patient's bill of rights, patient autonomy, war on drugs, and war on cancer.

Medical Ideology and the Total State

In the nineteenth century, when scientific medicine was in its infancy, disease was defined by pathologists; effective remedies were virtually nonexistent; the term *treatment* meant medical care sought and paid for by the patient; and the state showed little interest in the concept of therapy.

Today, when scientific medicine is a robust adult, physicians routinely effect near-miraculous cures; politicians and their lackeys, led by Surgeons General, define disease; the state shows intense interest in the concept of disease; and the term *treatment* is often used in lieu of the term *coercion*.

Fifty years ago, few Americans others than politicians and physicians knew there was a bureaucrat in America called the Surgeon General. Today, he is America's Physician General, preaching ceaselessly from the bully pulpit—a symbol and symptom of pharmacracy and of the growing power of the therapeutic state. Dan E. Beauchamp, an emeritus professor at the State University of New York at Albany, hails the sudden prominence of the Surgeon General as a sign of the "democratization" of health policy. He writes: "The role that democratic discussion now plays in health policy is perhaps best illustrated by the radical redefinition of the role of the U.S. Surgeon General from head of a rather obscure commissioned officer corps of the Public Health Service to our leading national spokesman on public health issues" (1988, 136).

Rudolf Virchow (1821–1902), the father of modern pathology, longed for a future in which the physician qua Platonic philosopher would serve as a guide to the politician-king. "What other science," he asked rhetorically, "is better suited *to propose laws* as the basis of social structure, in order to make effective those which are inherent in man himself?" ([1849] 1958, 66, emphasis added). He suggested that "once medicine is established as anthropology ... the physiologist and the practitioner will be counted among the elder statesmen who *support the social structure*" (66, emphasis added). Virchow was politically naive: he thought the future doctor would be a solid scientist and a wise leader instead of, as is the case, a bureaucratic toady ignorant of scientific medicine. Furthermore, if the physician's task is to support the social structure, his actual job may be to harm, not help, the person called the "patient."

We know that the proposition that *medical practice* is a science cannot be true (see Szasz 2001, chaps. 3 and 5). Nevertheless, the idea is superficially attractive, even plausible. To resolve human problems, all we need to do is define them as the symptoms of diseases and, presto, they become maladies remediable by medical measures.

Medicine and the Metaphor of War

The illnesses first understood and conquered by scientific medicine were the infectious diseases. Because the response of the immune system to pathogenic microorganisms is readily analogized to a nation resisting an invading army, the military or war metaphor has become congenial in thinking about illness and treatment. When we speak about microbes "attacking" the body, antibiotics as magic "bullets," doctors as "fighting" against diseases, and so forth, we use metaphors to convey the idea that the doctor is like the soldier who *protects the homeland from foreign invaders.* However, when we speak about the war on drugs or the war on mental illness, we use metaphors to convey the idea that the state is like a doctor when it uses doctors as soldiers to *protect people from themselves.* In one case, we speak about doctors helping patients to overcome *diseases*, in the other about doctors preventing citizens from *doing what they want to do.*

In the case of infectious diseases—the microbe as alien pathogen threatening the host (the patient's body)—the war metaphor helps us understand the mechanism of the disease and justifies the coercive segregation (quarantine) of contagious persons, animals, or materials. In the case of psychiatric diseases—the war metaphor casting the mental patient in the role of alien pathogen threatening the host (society)—the metaphor prevents us from understanding the problem misidentified as a disease: it convinces the patient's family, society, and sometimes the patient himself that the mental patient *is* (like) a pathogen, justifying the coercive segregation of the subject as "dangerous to himself or others." Failure to understand the abuses of the military metaphor in medicine and psychiatry precludes perceiving medical coercion as a problem.

Viewing the state as primarily an apparatus of coercion with a monopoly of the legitimate use of force does not commit one to denying that the state can do good as well as evil. Probably no individual or institution is exclusively inclined to do evil. Moreover, doing evil to some often benefits others. The paradigmatic organ of the state is the army, which Robert Heinlein aptly characterized as "a permanent organization for the destruction of life and property" (qtd. in Porter 1994, xiii). The fact that armies are deployed to rescue people and help guard property after natural disasters does not alter their primary role.

It took centuries of terrible wars before people began to recognize that because the *state is*, par excellence, an instrument of violence, whereas the *church ought to be*, par excellence, an instrument of nonviolence, the two should get a divorce or at least a legal separation. Medicine and the state also ought to get a divorce, with primary custody of the citizens (as potential patients) granted to themselves and institutionalized medicine given only visitation rights. However, we do not view the relationship between medicine and the state the same way we view the relationship between church and state. The reason may be that the physical illness of the individual, unlike his spiritual illness, can *directly* affect the physical health of the group. That relationship has justified certain public-health measures as legitimate instruments of state coercion. However, this reasoning does not justify state coercion as a morally legitimate instrument for protecting people from themselves. What should be the role of the state with respect to protecting the individual from diseases that do not by themselves pose a threat to others?

- Should protecting one's health be the responsibility of the individual, just as it is his responsibility to feed and house himself and provide for his spiritual health?
- Should the state assume responsibility for providing "health care," as it used to assume responsibility for providing "religious care" (a responsibility it still assumes in many parts of the world, even in some societies where church and state are in principle separated—for example, Germany and Switzerland)?
- Should the state assume responsibility for protecting the individual from himself if in the opinion of medical (psychiatric) experts he poses a danger to his own health and well-being?

In my view, the coercive apparatus of the state ought to be as separate from the professional treatment of medical illness as it is from professional treatment of spiritual illness. Such a separation of medicine and the state is necessary for the protection and promotion of individual liberty, responsibility, and dignity.

Because the state has a monopoly of the legitimate use of force, it is the only institution legally empowered to wage war (and punish crime). Although the Constitution reserves to Congress the ultimate authority to engage the nation in war, that restraint is no longer operative. Since the end of World War II, American governments have waged wars, abroad and at home, on the basis of bureaucratic regulations and executive orders. Some of these wars have been justified on essentially medical grounds, for example, the invasion of Panama. Illustrative of how far the blending of the concept of disease with the concept of war has gone is the declaration by the president and the secretary of state in June 2000 that AIDS in Africa poses a problem to America's *national security* (both are qtd. in Buckley 2000, 62–63).

Regardless of why the government sends military personnel to foreign countries and of whether those in command call the operation "peacekeeping" or a "war on narcoterrorism," the deployment of such force is an act of war. The enemy may be literal, an invading soldier, or metaphorical, a crop or chemical. The Germans and the Japanese in World War II were literal enemies. The people who cause unrest in Haiti or Somalia, the peasants who grow coca in Colombia, the "drug lords" in Mexico, and the substances the government bans are metaphorical enemies. We sow metaphors of war and reap literal violence. The fight against polio, let us remember, was called the March of Dimes, not a "war against polio," and it entailed no participation, assuredly no use of force, by the government. We ought to view America's unending wars on diseases and drugs against this background.

To understand our present dilemma, we must understand the growth of the American state, especially since the Roosevelt years (see Flynn [1948] 1998). The United States has become a complex, bureaucratic, regulatory, welfare state—a condition brought about by means of the time-honored political tactic of declaring a national emergency and requiring that all of the state's "human resources" be mobilized. "Every collective revolution," warned Herbert Hoover (1874–1964), "rides in on a Trojan horse of 'Emergency.' It was the tactic of Lenin, Hitler, and Mussolini.... This technique of creating emergency is the greatest achievement that demagoguery attains"(qtd. in Higgs 1987, 159). The infamous George Jacques Danton (1759–94) declared: "Everything belongs to the fatherland when the fatherland is in danger" (*Bartlett's Familiar Quotations*, 16th ed., 364). Two years later, the fatherland repossessed his head. To the executioner about to guillotine him, he said: "Show my head to the people" (*Encyclopedia Britannica* 7:64).

In *Crisis and Leviathan* (1987), Robert Higgs expands on this theme. "Knowing how the government has grown," he observes, "requires an examination of what, exactly, the government does: the growth of government has resulted not so much from doing more to accomplish traditional governmental functions; rather, it has resulted largely from the government's taking on new functions, activities, and programs—some of them completely novel, others previously the responsibility of the private citizen"(x). Higgs's thesis is that government expansion has been nurtured by a succession of "crises" that the government proceeds to "fix." After a crisis subsides, the new government functions remain, heaping bureaucracies upon bureaucracies. Although Higgs does not include health emergencies among the crises he discusses, they belong on top of the list.

Despite the evidence I have presented, well-respected social analysts maintain that the power and scope of the state are dwindling. In *The Rise and Decline of the State*, Martin van Creveld, a professor of history at Hebrew University in Jerusalem, writes: "The state, which since the middle of the seventeenth century has been the most important and most characteristic of all modern institutions, is in decline" (1999, vii). How does Creveld arrive at this conclusion? By emphasizing growing popular resistance to the cost of socialist-inspired welfare-state measures and by ignoring the growing popularity of a medically rationalized therapeutic state. Although Creveld's book runs to 438 pages, he does not mention the war on drugs or the pervasive influence of psychiatric-social controls. Others celebrate the "retreat of the state" (for example, Lawson 2000, Strange 1996, and Swann 1998—each book titled *The Retreat of the State*). I agree with economist Robert J. Samuelson's observation that the government is "getting bigger because, paradoxically, we think it's getting smaller" (2000, 33). That curious outcome is just one of the results of the politicization of medicine and of the medicalization of politics.

PHARMACRACY IN AMERICA

From 1776 until 1914, when the first antinarcotic legislation was enacted, the federal government played no role in civilian medicine. Medical licensure and the funding and management of state mental hospitals were functions of the state governments. After World War II, the situation changed rapidly and radically: the establishment of the National Institutes of Health, the enactment of Medicare and Medicaid legislation, and the war on drugs soon made medical expenditures the largest component of the national budget, eclipsing defense. The following statistics illustrate the explosive growth of the therapeutic state since the end of World War II and especially since the early 1960s.

· In 1950, funding for the National Institute of Mental Health was less than $1 million; ten years later, it was $87 million; in 1992, it reached $1 billion ("1993 Appropriations" 1992, A-27). In 1965, when Medicare and Medicaid were enacted, their cost was $65 billion; in 1993, it was nearly $939 billion (Sharkey 1994, 240). Between 1969 and 1994, the national mental health budget increased from about $3 billion to $80 billion (Sharkey 1999). Between 1968 and 1983, the number of clinical psychologists tripled, from 12,000 to more than 40,000; the number of clinical social workers grew from 25,000 in 1970 to 80,000 in 1990; and membership in the American Psychological Association grew from fewer than 3,000 in 1970 to more than 120,000 in 1993 (Nolan 1998, 7–8; see also Hogan 1995).

· Between 1960 and 1996, the total "national health expenditures" share of national product rose about two and a half times, from 5.1 percent of the gross domestic product (GDP) to 13.6 percent, and the share of "federal government expenditures" on health rose more than six times, from 3.3 percent of the GDP to 20.7 percent. In 1995, total health expenditure, as a percentage of the GDP, was 13.6 percent in the United States, 10.4 percent in Germany, 8.6 percent in Australia, and 6.9 percent in the United Kingdom. In health expenditures per capita that year, the United States led all other countries by even bigger margins. The figures were $3,633 for the United States, $2,134 for Germany, $1,741 for Australia, and $1,246 for the United Kingdom (U.S. Department of Health and Human Services 1998, 341–42).

· Perhaps the most striking statistic is that between 1960 (before Medicare and Medicaid) and 1998, public expenditure on health care per capita increased more than one hundred times, from $35 to $3,633 (ibid., 345).

The growth of the state is dramatically and unequivocally illustrated by its cost to the taxpayer, that is, by the federal budget. The following figures are in nominal dollars. In fiscal year 1941, before the United States entered World War II, the budget was $13.6 billion; today, the war on drugs alone costs $19 billion. In 1942, the budget more than doubled, to $35.1 billion; then in 1943, it was $78.5 billion, but it did not reach $100 billion until 1962. In the next thirty-six years, the budget increased about sixteen times, to $1.65 trillion in 1998 (*World Almanac*, 108–9). According to James M. Buchanan, "In the seven decades from 1900 to 1970, total government spending in real terms increased forty times over, attaining a share of one-third in national product" (1975, 162).

The explosive expansion of the government after the 1960s is attributable largely to adding civilian medical care to the functions of the state. This transformation of medicine has utterly distorted the relationship between the private and public realms in general, especially the relationship between private health and public health. What makes the explosive expansion of the therapeutic state especially alarming is the widespread belief that the government is niggardly with respect to health care, especially mental health care—a myth largely fueled by the fact that the number of persons housed in buildings called "state mental hospitals" has decreased since the 1960s. I have documented elsewhere that although it is true that fewer people now reside in state hospitals than did thirty years ago, it is an illusion to think that the scope and power of psychiatry have diminished. The number of persons cared for in one way or another by the mental health system has steadily increased since the end of World War II, as have mental health expenditures (Szasz [1994] 1998, esp. 150–86). Despite these facts, the author of a "special report" in the *American Bar Association Journal* declares, "No one disputes that government support for the treatment of mental illness has dropped to dangerously low levels" (Gibeaut 2000).

The Anatomy of Pharmacracy: Secret Censorship as Health Care

The United States is the only country explicitly founded on the principle that in the inevitable contest between the private and public realms, the scope of the former should be wider than that of the latter. That principle is what made America the "land of the free," especially in the nineteenth century. "There is a balance of power," writes Bruce D. Porter, "between the state and civil society. This internal balance of power demarcates the line between the public and the private—*if a thing is public, it is subject to state authority; if it is private, it is not*" (1994, 9, emphasis added). Pharmacrats want to abolish the private realm altogether. "It is the private sphere that is problematic for public health," declares Dan E. Beauchamp (1999a, 59), seemingly not realizing that the private sphere is none of the business of public health.

It is a truism that people have more liberty in proportion as more aspects of their lives are private. The American people invited the state to take over the management of their health, and now they are surprised that they have less control not only over the health care they receive but also over other aspects of their lives. Nor is that loss of control the end of the mischief. The more tax monies are spent on health care, the more firmly entrenched becomes the idea in nearly everyone's mind that caring for people's health requires not individual self-control, but political control—that is, control by deception, seduction, and coercion. The state commands vast resources of misinformation (propaganda) and seduction (money and other economic rewards) and has a monopoly of legitimate force (the law and the police).

Censorship of information has long been a tool of totalitarian states, both religious and secular. Such states need not and do not justify the practice by claiming that it serves the best interests of individuals. However, the First Amendment, which guarantees freedom of the press, prohibits the U.S. government from indulging in the despot's passion to deceive people in their own best interest. Not only has the U.S. government violated this prohibition, it has done so secretly and, after the practice was exposed, defended the violation as a valuable weapon in the war on drugs.

Thanks to the sleuthing of the Internet magazine *Salon*, in January 2000 we learned that for the past three years the government had secretly censored many of the major television shows. What made the practice possible was a law requiring broadcast networks "to match the amount of 'anti-drug' advertising bought by the federal government with an equal amount of 'anti-drug' public-service announcements," plus the policy that if the "drug-czar's office approves a TV program's anti-drug content, the show itself can be credited against the requirement, allowing the network to then substitute full-price advertising for public-service announcements" (Streisand 2000, 26). The arrangement created a temptation for TV executives to augment their revenues by cooperating with the offers of the antidrug censors. "Under the sway of the office of President Clinton's drug czar, Gen. Barry R. McCaffrey, many of the most popular shows have filled their episodes with anti-drug pitches.... McCaffrey never let on that his office had been turned into a full-blown script-review board" (Forbes 2000; see also Frankel 2000). After the scheme was exposed, McCaffrey offered no apologies: "We plead guilty to using every lawful means to save America's children," declared his spokesman (Streisand 2000, 26). President Clinton was equally self-righteous: "I think this guy [McCaffrey] is intense and passionate and committed and we've got way too many kids using drugs, still" (Morgan 2000). Richard D. Bonnette, president and chief executive of Partnership for a Drug-Free America, lauded the censors: "The major television networks should be applauded for working with the Office of National, Drug Control policy to include anti-drug story-lines in television shows" (Bonnette 2000, A26).

The Vatican's *Index of Prohibited Books* was a public document that proudly proclaimed the Roman Catholic Church's struggle against values it considered subversive. In contrast, the clandestine nature of the White House Office of National Drug Control Policy's tampering with TV scripts is evidence that those responsible for it knew full well that they were subverting America's values and perhaps its laws as well.

Private Health versus Public Health: Protecting People from Themselves

In the case of illness, drawing the line between the private and public realms requires careful consideration of many issues. As a first approximation, we may say that we have a "right to be sick"—an aspect of the right to be let alone—provided our illness does not *directly* harm others. We have a "right" to be sick with hay fever because it does not endanger others, but we do not have a right to be sick with infectious tuberculosis because it does endanger others.

Yet even such a seemingly uncontroversial example as hay fever oversimplifies the matter. To alleviate symptoms, the person suffering from hay fever may ingest antihistamines that, in turn, may render him just as impaired to drive an automobile as would intoxication with alcohol. In fact, simply being a young adult or an old adult makes the person, statistically, a dangerous driver. What constitutes a danger to the public depends in part on what people perceive as a risk—a perception shaped by subjective judgment rather than by statistical probability—and in part on whether people perceive a particular risk as under their own control. Regardless of the statistical risk, people do not worry much about risks they believe they can control.

To complicate matters, the sickness of persons and the sickness of populations represent very different problems for patients, physicians, and politicians. Private-health measures that benefit the individual may help or harm the community. Public-health measures that benefit the community may help or harm the individual. The potential conflict between private health and public health is an integral part of the tension between civil society and the state. In his article "Sick Individuals and Sick Populations," epidemiologist Geoffrey Rose notes that "a preventive measure which brings much benefit to the population offers little to each participating individual. This has been the history of public health—immunization, the wearing of seatbelts, and now the attempt to change various lifestyle characteristics. Of enormous potential importance to the population as a whole, these measures offer very little—particularly in the short term—to each individual" ([1985] 1999, 36–37).

Dealing with health care as a public good raises certain questions, such as: Can we create an insurance system that makes every treatment deemed useful or necessary by a physician also affordable by and available to every member of the community? How can we calculate the cost of health insurance if medical science and technology create and people clamor for ever more expensive treatments? If people take good care of their health and live longer, what cost do they impose on those who pay their pensions or other old-age benefits? If the community pays for the treatment of those who fall ill, doesn't it inevitably acquire a claim on its members to try as hard as they can not to fall ill? Doesn't the community also acquire an interest in identifying and penalizing those who frivolously neglect their health or deliberately make themselves ill?

If we assume that people truly value their health, why don't we expect them to be willing to spend at least as much on medical care as they do on drinking, smoking, gambling, entertainment, and veterinary care for their pets? If some people do not value their own health, then it is a folly twice over for the taxpayer to pay for their health insurance. In other words, why don't we subject health-care coverage funded by tax monies to a means test? And why don't we model health insurance on private casualty insurance with a substantial deductibility clause—the insured being responsible for his own health care up to, say, 10 percent of taxable income, before becoming eligible for reimbursement? Indeed, shouldn't we try to return to the situation in which medical care was available mainly to those who were able and willing to pay for it, with care for those who could not pay being distributed on some other basis?

These are difficult questions that most people and all politicians prefer to avoid. Instead, politicians pander to the public with slogans that promise health-care benefits without health-care responsibilities, and people like that pandering. However, with the increasing cost of health insurance and the mounting dissatisfaction of both patients and doctors with mandated "insurance" schemes for health-care coverage, we ought to confront rather than shirk these questions. The truth is that before the federal government went into the business of health care, poor people received free medical services, often of very good quality, at municipal and teaching hospitals. It is doubtful that they receive better care now, but those who can pay often receive worse care than they did formerly. (The terms *better* and *worse* refer here to the human, not the technical, quality of the service.) Moreover, physicians are far less proud of or satisfied with being physicians than they were fifty years ago.

The advocates of pharmacratic politics threaten liberty because they obscure or even deny the differences between the kinds of risks posed by a public water supply contaminated with cholera bacilli and the risks posed by a private lifestyle that includes the recreational use of a prohibited psychoactive drug. Individuals cannot *by an act of will* provide themselves with a safe public water supply, but they can *by an act of will* protect themselves from the hazards of smoking marijuana. What makes coercive health measures justified is not so much that they protect everyone equally, but that they do so by means not available to the individual. By the same token, what makes coercive health measures unjustified is not only that they do not protect everyone equally but that they replace personally assumed self-protection by self-control with legal sanctions difficult or impossible to enforce. The rhetoric of categorizing certain groups—typically children or the residents of neglected neighborhoods—as "at risk" needs to be mentioned here. The term implies that the persons in question lack self-control and hence need the help of the government to protect them from certain kinds of temptations. Health statists on both the left and the right agree.

Gerald Dworkin, for example, believes that "a man may know the facts [about the dangers of smoking], wish to stop, but not have the requisite willpower.... In [such a case] there is no theoretical problem. We are not imposing a good on someone who rejects it. *We are simply using coercion to enable people to carry out their own goals*" ([1972] 1999, 127–28). This notion is coercive paternalism in pure culture. I maintain that the only means we possess for ascertaining that a man wants to stop smoking more than he wants to enjoy smoking is by observing whether he stops or continues to smoke. Moreover, it is irresponsible for moral theorists to ignore that coercive sanctions aimed at protecting people from themselves are not only unenforceable but create black markets and horrifying legal abuses.

The idea that the state has a duty to protect people from themselves is an integral part of the authoritarian, religious-paternalistic outlook on life—now favored by many atheists as well. Once people agree that they have identified the one true God, or Good, it follows that they must guard members of the group, and nonmembers as well, from the temptation to worship false gods or goods. The post-Enlightenment version of this view arose from a secularization of God and the medicalization of good. Once people agree that they have identified the one true reason, it follows that they must guard against the temptation to worship unreason—that is, madness.

Confronted with the problem of "madness," Western individualism was ill prepared to defend the rights of the individual: modern man has no more right to be a madman than medieval man had a right to be a heretic. In the seventeenth century, when madness appeared in its modern guise, the problem it presented resembled not only the problem of heresy but also the problem of disease, especially of the brain. Madness was perceived as an illness of the mind, caused by a hypothesized disease of the brain, an image that invited the conflation of risk to the public with risk to the self—hence the view of the insane person as "dangerous to himself or others." For centuries, this verbal formula has justified involuntary mental hospitalization. There is a large literature on this subject, to which I have contributed my share, and I shall say no more about it here. Instead, I shall limit the discussion to a few remarks about medical-legal coercion whose avowed aim is to protect *mentally healthy* people from themselves.

Aside from suicide, whose legal-political status is obscured by its being authoritatively attributed to mental illness, a classic contemporary example of potentially self-injurious behavior is riding a motorcycle without a helmet (Germer 2000). (That riding a motorcycle *with* a helmet is also dangerous is beside the point here.) How do courts interpret the constitutionality of prohibiting people from riding a motorcycle without a helmet? Can helmet laws be justified by invoking the police power inherent in the sovereignty of states, enabling the legislatures "to act for the protection of the public health, safety, morals, and general welfare" (Stone 1969, 112), even though such laws are silent about protecting people from themselves? Some authorities say yes, some say no; the answer depends on whether the observer regards the subject's behavior as a private matter that affects only him or as a public matter that affects others as well. One court "held the statute to be an unconstitutional exercise of the police power," citing the following legal maxims: "The individual is not accountable for his actions, insofar as these concern the interest of no person but himself" and "So use your own that you do not harm that of another" (Stone 1969, 113–14). Another court held that the state has an interest in having robust, healthy citizens and, therefore, "the statute forcing an individual to protect himself falls within the scope of the police power" (114).

The issue comes down to *whether the individual is viewed as a private person or as public property*: the former has no obligation to the community to be or stay healthy; the latter does. In proportion as medical care is provided by the state, doctors and patients alike cease to be private persons and forfeit their "rights" against the opposing interests of the state. Declares Alan I. Leshner, head of the National Institute on Drug Abuse (NIDA): "My belief is that today, in 1998, you [the physician] should be put in jail if you refuse to prescribe S.S.R.I.s [Selective Serotonin Reuptake Inhibitors, a type of so-called antidepressant medication] for depression. I also believe that five years from now you should be put in jail if you don't give crack addicts the medication we're working on now" (qtd. in Samuels 1998, 48–49). In plain English, Leshner dreams of *coercing physicians to drug patients forcibly*.

History teaches us that we ought to be cautious about embracing professional protectors as our guardians: they often demean, coerce, and injure their beneficiaries and do their best to render them abjectly dependent on their tormentors. Transforming the United States from a constitutional republic into a therapeutic state has shifted the internal balance of power in favor of the government and against the individual. Ironically, this shift has been accompanied by widespread complaints by the cognoscenti about a surfeit of autonomy plaguing Americans (Gaylin and Jennings 1996). They mistake for autonomy what is in fact selfishness engendered by the growth of pharmacratic regulations and the therapeutic state. (I use the term *pharmacratic regulations* to refer to controls exercised by bureaucratic health-care regulations and enforced by health-care personnel, such as alcohol treatment and other addiction programs, school psychology, suicide prevention, and the mandatory reporting of personal [mis]behavior as part of the duties of pediatricians, internists, psychiatrists, and other health-care personnel.)

COERCION AS TREATMENT: JUSTIFYING PHARMACRACY

Coercion masquerading as medical treatment is the bedrock of political medicine. Long before the Nazis rose to power, physician-eugenicists advocated killing certain ill or disabled persons as a form of treatment for both patient and society. What transforms coercion into therapy? Physicians *diagnosing* the subject's condition a "disease," *declaring* the intervention they impose on the victim a "treatment," and legislators and judges *ratifying these categorizations* as "diseases" and "treatments." Simply put, the pharmacrat's stock-in-trade is denying the differences between the medical care that patients seek and the "treatments" imposed on them against their will—in short, defining violence as beneficence.

The normal applications of the criminal law tell us that the difference between depriving a person of his liberty and depriving him of his life is a matter of degree, not kind. The history of religious persecution teaches the same lesson more dramatically. Medical ethicists and psychiatrists ignore this evidence: they embrace medicalized deprivation of liberty, provided it is called "hospitalization," "outpatient commitment," "drug treatment," and so forth. Many of them approve even deprivations of life, provided it is called "physician-assisted suicide" or "euthanasia." Let me restate the elements necessary to qualify a medical *intervention* as a medical *treatment*. From a scientific point of view, an intervention counts as treatment only if its aim is to remedy a true disease; the identity of the person doing the remedying does not matter: self-medication with an analgesic for pain or with an antihistamine for hay fever counts as treatment. From a legal point of view, an intervention counts as treatment only if it is performed by a physician licensed to practice medicine, with the consent of the subject or his guardian; disease, diagnosis, and medical benefit are irrelevant. Consensual treatment is treatment only if the patient has a true disease, regardless of whether that treatment is effective or does more harm than good. Nonconsensual "treatment" is assault, even if it cures the patient of his disease.

The Perversion of Medicine: Disease as "Treatability"

"When meditating over a disease," wrote Louis Pasteur, "I never think of finding a remedy for it" (qtd. in Dubos 1950, 307). When the pharmacrat meditates over disease, he thinks of nothing but how to remedy it, and because he views benevolent coercion as treatment, he discovers diseases where his patient/victim sees only behaviors that the pharmacrat wants to change or punish.

The idea of defining disease in terms of treatability is not new. The prescientific physician and his clients often perceived illness that way. The principal difference between the old-fashioned quackery of, say, Mesmer, and the newfangled quackery of, say, our Surgeons General, is that Mesmeric "treatments" were never imposed on persons against their will, whereas the "treatments" endorsed by the Surgeons General often are.

Nazi pharmacracy was based on the premise that the Jew was a cancer on the body politic of the Reich; it had to be removed at any cost. American pharmacracy is based on the premise that the individual with a dangerous disease, epitomized by the drug abuser, is a threat to the well-being of the nation; he has to be cured at any cost. In a brief article in the *Journal of the American Medical Association* (*JAMA*), A. I. Leshner repeats this theme three times: "There are now extensive data showing that addiction is eminently treatable"; "addiction is a treatable disease"; and "overall, treatment of addiction is as successful as treatment of other chronic diseases, such as diabetes, hypertension, and asthma" (1999, 1314–16). Leshner studiously refrains from acknowledging that "treatment" for "addiction" is typically imposed on the subject by force.

Sally Satel, a psychiatrist at Yale University, is more forthright. "As a psychiatrist who treats addicts," she writes in a 1998 op-ed essay in the *Wall Street Journal*, "I have learned that legal sanctions—either imposed or threatened—may provide the leverage needed to keep them alive by keeping them in treatment. Voluntary help is often not enough" (6). The essay is titled "For Addicts, Force Is the Best Medicine." It does not bode well for liberty that even the editors of the *Wall Street Journal* apparently agree.

The proposition that the use of illegal drugs is a brain disease poses problems of its own. Brain diseases cannot be treated without the patient's consent. How, then, do Leshner, Satel, and others justify using force to treat *this* brain disease but not others? Satel declares, "Addicts would be better off if more of them were arrested and forced to enroll in treatment programs.... [This is] the essence of humane therapy" (1998, 6). The truth is that persons with real brain diseases need not be coerced into treatment because they can be persuaded to accept it. Is it any surprise that coercion is necessary to treat nondiseases?

In June 2000, Judith S. Kaye, chief judge of the state of New York, announced that "[New York] State courts will start using their 'coercive' powers immediately to get nonviolent drug offenders into treatment programs" (Finkelstein 2000). Although defendants are under duress to accept "treatment," the therapists maintain that "accepting treatment is ultimately *voluntary*. ... To be eligible, offenders will have to be ... *willing to plead guilty*. ... Even if a defendant chooses to stand trial, the judges and district attorneys will still have the discretion to refer them to drug treatment until trial. *If they are found not guilty, in all likelihood treatment will be continued*, said a court spokesman. ... If they relapse, they will go to jail, most likely receiving stiffer sentences than normally given now" ("Plan for Nonviolent Addicts Coming" 2000, emphasis added). This example shows what happens to the concepts of disease, treatment, and voluntariness when politicians define illness and treatment.

Judge Kaye is proud of what she calls her "hands-on court" that promotes "problem solving." The problem she has in mind is how to get people to stop doing what they like to do—in this case, using illegal drugs. What makes Judge Kaye think that the drug-treatment sentences she imposes solve drug problems? "We know," she writes, "that a defendant in a court-ordered drug treatment is twice as likely to complete the program as someone who gets help voluntarily" (1999, 13). The fact that drug prisoners complete court-ordered "programs" proves that they want to be free of meddling judges, not that they are free of the desire to take drugs. Moreover, completing a "drug-treatment program" means simply being present at required meetings; it does not entail acquiring new knowledge or skills, as does completing an academic program. The result of Judge Kaye's sentence is exactly the opposite of what happens in a genuine educational program: it is unlikely that a person participating in such a program against his will would complete it, but it is likely a person who participates voluntarily (and pays for it) would do so.

Stories of judges practicing therapeutic jurisprudence abound in the media (see "Fat Man Is Told" 1995, "Internet-Addicted Mom" 1998). In Dade County, Florida, persons "caught using or purchasing drugs are considered 'clients' or 'members' rather than 'offenders' or 'defendants.' ... [I]nstead of trying to prosecute the defendant, the district attorney becomes part of the Drug Court team trying to help the defendant toward recovery" (Nolan 1998, 99, 97). A judge in Florida uses the phrase "'therapeutic jurisprudence' to describe the court's role as a facilitator of the healing process. ... 'This is a helping court ... which *defendants enter voluntarily*'" ("MH Courts" 1999, 10, emphasis added; see also Christian 1999, A13). Sadly, we have no Swifts, Menckens, or Orwells warning people against Gulliverian tales of court-coerced habit retraining portrayed as "voluntary treatment" or of courtrooms characterized as places that "defendants enter voluntarily."

Leading physicians fuel the propaganda for therapeutic coercions as remedies for social problems. In 1992, Surgeon General C. Everett Koop and *JAMA* editor-in-chief George D. Lundberg declared, "One million US inhabitants die prematurely each year as a result of intentional homicide or suicide.... We believe violence in America to be a public health emergency" (Koop and Lundberg 1992, 3076). Being murdered and dying voluntarily are here treated as similar phenomena, and both are categorized as preventable diseases posing a "public health emergency." Articles about smoking, violence, and war are staples in the pages of *JAMA*. Some typical titles: "Tobacco Dependence Curriculum in US Undergraduate Medical Education" (Ferry, Grissino, and Runfola 1999); "The Medical Costs of Gunshot Injuries in the United States" (Cook et al. 1999); "The Future of Firearm Violence Prevention" (Wintemute 1999); "War and Health: From Solferino to Kosovo" (Iacopino and Waldman 1999); and "What Can We Do about Violence?" (Cole and Flanagin 1999).

In Great Britain, too, the medical establishment is solidifying its marriage to the state. In July 1999, the British Medical Association proposed that in order to increase "the number of donated organs, everyone should be assumed to be a donor unless they opted out" (Phillips 1999). With body ownership vested in the state, it is reasonable that the state should decide what counts as disease and treatment. In July 1999, a three-judge Court of Appeals in Britain ruled that the National Health Service (NHS) "wrongly regarded transsexualism as a state of mind that did not warrant medical treatment rather than as an illness.... [The judges ordered the NHS to] provide sex-change operations for transsexuals because they suffer from a *legitimate illness....* About 1,000 transsexuals ... will be entitled to the $13,000 sex-change surgery free of charge" (qtd. in "Notable & Quotable" 1999, A14). According to the judges, sex-change operation is "*the proper treatment of a recognized illness*" (qtd. in MacCarthy 1999, 19, emphasis added). Recognized by whom? The bureaucrats of the therapeutic state.

In September 1999, the *Sunday Times* (London) reported that "the government is considering proposals to appoint secular 'vicars,' paid for by the state, to give pastoral care to families ... offering pastoral advice and urging parents who do not attend church to put their children through a 'civil naming ceremony'" (Bevan and Prescott 1998). Evidently in vain did Daniel Defoe (1660–1731) warn, "Of all plagues with which mankind are cursd, / Ecclesiastic tyranny's the worst" (*The Oxford Dictionary of Quotations*, 234). Secularism may protect us from the dangers of theological tyranny, but it does not protect us from the dangers of therapeutic tyranny. Electing a national leader by a majority of the people's votes may protect us from being ruled by an aristocracy, but it does not protect us from being ruled by a pharmacracy.

MEDICAL IDEOLOGY, PUBLIC HEALTH, AND SOCIALISM

Before considering the connections between medicine and the state in National Socialist Germany, it may be instructive to review briefly the connections among antipoverty policies, public-health measures, and the state.

Health, Poverty, and the State

For centuries, the relief of both poverty and illness, especially illness affecting the poor, was the responsibility of the church. "It is interesting to notice," wrote socialist dreamers Sidney and Beatrice Webb in 1910, "that the Public Health medical service and the Poor Law medical service sprang historically from the same source, namely the prevalence of disease among the pauper class, and the economy of diminishing it" (Webb and Webb 1910, 1). In the modern world, the state assumes both functions. Since World War II, the relief of illness has increasingly been perceived as a duty the state owes all its citizens.

The state's subvention of medical care creates many problems, as we have seen already. Becoming ill and recovering from illness have a great deal to do with motivation, personal habits, and self-discipline. The Webbs, though ardent lovers of Leviathan, recognized this fact and warned against it, anticipating the criticisms of Ludwig von Mises, the ardent enemy of Leviathan. "The very humanity and professional excellence of the Poor Law infirmary," the Webbs explained, "*constitute elements in the breaking down of personal character and integrity, and may even be said actually to subsidize licentiousness, feeble-mindedness, and disease*" (1910, 238, emphasis added). To prevent the cure from being worse than the disease, the Webbs proposed that "the curative treatment of individual patients by the Public Health Service ... [be accompanied by] a *constant stream of moral suasion, and when necessary, disciplinary supervision*, to promote physical self-restraint and the due care of offspring" (239, emphasis added).

In the Soviet Union, the socialization of the economy led to widespread economic dissatisfaction. In Western democracies, the socialization of medicine is now leading to a similar widespread dissatisfaction with medicine, among patients and physicians alike. Because the interests of the state as producer of goods or provider of medical services are not the same as the interests of people as consumers or patients, this result is hardly surprisingly.

Health and the National Socialist State

Hitler recognized that the direct takeover of private property provokes powerful emotional and political resistance. One of the secrets of his rise to power was that he managed to portray the National Socialist movement as opposed to such a measure, indeed as opposed to communism itself. As Robert Proctor notes, Hitler understood that there was no need to "nationalize industry when you can nationalize the people" (1999, 74). I want to emphasize here that I regard "right-wing" Nazism and "left-wing" communism not as two antagonistic political systems, but as two similar types of socialism (statism)—one brown or national, the other red or international. Both kinds of statists were very successful in their efforts to undermine autonomy and to destroy morality.

The therapeutic state as a type of total state with a sacred and therefore unopposable mission is not a new historical phenomenon. The theological state, the Soviet state, and the Nazi state may be viewed as former incarnations of it (see Szasz [1970] 1997 and 1984, esp. 213–38; and Bloch and Reddaway 1977). To illustrate and underscore the problems intrinsic to the alliance between modern medicine and the modern state, I shall briefly review the anatomy of National Socialist Germany as a type of therapeutic state.

From the beginning of his political career, Hitler couched his struggle against "enemies of the state" in medical rhetoric. In 1934, addressing the Reichstag, he boasted, "I gave the order ... to burn out down to the raw flesh the ulcers of our internal well-poisoning" (qtd. in Kershaw 1999, 494). National Socialist politicians and the entire German nation learned to speak and think in such terms. Werner Best, Reinhard Heydrich's deputy, declared that the task of the police was "to root out all symptoms of disease and germs of destruction that threatened the political health of the nation.... [In addition to Jews,] most [of the germs] were weak, unpopular and marginalized groups, such as gypsies, homosexuals, beggars, 'antisocials,' 'work-shy,' and 'habitual criminals'" (qtd. in ibid., 541).

None of this was a Nazi invention. The use of medical metaphors to justify the exclusion and destruction of unwanted persons and groups both antedates Hitler's rise to power and flourishes today. In 1895, a member of the Reichstag called Jews "cholera bacilli" (Gilman 1993, 435). In 1967, Susan Sontag, the celebrated feminist-liberal writer, declared, "The truth is that Mozart, Pascal, Boolean algebra, Shakespeare, parliamentary government, baroque churches, Newton, the emancipation of women, Kant, Marx, Balanchine ballets, *et al.*, don't redeem what this particular civilization has wrought upon the world. *The white race is the cancer of human history*; it is the white race and it alone—its ideologies and inventions—which eradicates autonomous civilizations wherever it spreads, which has upset the ecological balance of the planet, which now threatens the very existence of life itself" (57–58).

Despite all the evidence, the political implications of the therapeutic character of Nazism and of the use of medical metaphors in modern democracies remain underappreciated or, more often, ignored. It is a touchy subject not because the story makes psychiatrists in Nazi Germany look bad. That practice has been dismissed as an "abuse of psychiatry." Rather, it is a touchy subject because it highlights the dramatic similarities between pharmacratic controls in Germany under National Socialism and those in the United States under what is euphemistically called the "free market."

Nazi Pharmacracy: I. Socialist Health Care

The definitive work on pharmacracy in Nazi Germany is *Health, Race, and German Politics between National Unification and Nazism, 1870–1945* by Paul Weindling, a scholar at the Wellcome Institute for the History of Medicine in London. Unlike many students of the Holocaust, Weindling does not shy away from noting the similarities between the medicalization of politics and the politicization of health both in Nazi Germany and in the West. Many of Weindling's observations and comments about Nazi Germany as a therapeutic state (a term he does not use) sound as if they made reference to conditions in the United States today. He writes:

> Scientifically-educated experts acquired a directing role as prescribers of social policies and personal lifestyle ... science and medicine provided an alternative to party politics, by forming a basis for collective social policies to remedy social ills. (1989, 1)

> The sense of responsibility of the doctor to sick individuals weakened as awareness dawned of the economic costs of poverty and disease.... Medicine was transformed from a free profession ... to the doctor carrying out duties of state officials in the interests not of the individual patient but of society and of future generations.... Doctors became a part of a growing state apparatus. (2, 6)

Weindling retraces the political-economic history of modern medicine, reminding us that "In 1868 medicine was proclaimed a 'free trade,' open to all to practice....without legal penalties against quackery.... Leaders of the profession such as Rudolf Virchow were convinced that scientific excellence guaranteed the future of the profession" (14). *That* was a free market in medicine. Today, in contrast, the state stringently regulates trade in medical goods and services.

Long before Hitler rose to power, observes Weindling, physicians "sought to colonize new areas for medicine, such as sexuality, mental illness, and deviant social behaviour. What had been private or moral spheres were subjugated to a hereditarian social pathology.... As the medical categories invaded the terrain of social categories, the greater became the potential for creating a society corresponding to a total institution" (7, 19). Deception and self-deception by medical rhetoric were popular as far back as 1914, when German military service was glorified "as healthier than urban life. The fresh air and exercise of the front meant that it could be a vast open air sanatorium. Another indicator of health was the fall in the number of mental patients and a decrease of suicides" (283). Indeed, war is the political health of the state and the mental health of the individual.

Bedazzled by the myth of mental illness and seduced by psychiatry's usefulness for disposing of unwanted persons, the modern mind recoils from confronting the irreconcilable conflict between the political ideals of a free society and the coercive practices of psychiatry. Let us keep in mind that psychiatry began as a statist enterprise: the insane asylum was a public institution, supported by the state and operated by employees of the state. The main impetus for converting private health into public health came and continues to come from psychiatrists.

In 1933, the year Hitler assumed power, a law was passed against "compulsive criminality ... enabling preventive detention and castration .... [for] schizophrenia, manic-depression, [etc.].... The medical profession and especially psychiatrists benefited greatly from the drive for sterilization" (Weindling 1989, 525). Reich Health Leader (*Reichgesundheistführer*) Leonardo Conti (1900–1945) stated that "no one had the right to regard health as a personal private matter, which could be disposed of according to individualistic preference. Therapy had to be administered in the interests of the race and society rather than of the sick individual" (518).

In 1939, medical killing in Germany went into high gear. "Reliable helpers were recruited from the ranks of psychiatrists," who defined lying for the state as a higher form of morality: "Each euthanasia institution had a registry office to issue the false [death] certificates" (Weindling 1989, 544, 549). In the case of tuberculosis, modern diagnostic technology was employed as a tool for determining who qualified for therapeutic killing: "In occupied Poland and the Soviet Union, SS X-ray units sought out the tubercular, who were then shot. It is estimated that 100,000 died in this way" (550).

The more power physicians exercised, the more intoxicated with power they became. "The doctor was to be a Führer of the *Volk* to better personal and racial health.... Terms like 'euthanasia' and 'the incurable' were a euphemistic medicalized camouflage with connotations of relief of the individual suffering of the terminally ill" (Weindling 1989, 576–77, 542–43). Amidst all the carnage, the Nazis remained obsessed with health: "A plantation for herbal medicines was established at the Dachau concentration camp" (537).

Nazi Pharmacracy: II. Waging War for Health

In *The Nazi War on Cancer*, Robert N. Proctor, professor of history at Pennsylvania State University, remarks on the similarities between pharmacratic controls in Nazi Germany and those in the United States today, only to dismiss those similarities as irrelevant. "My intention," writes Proctor, "is not to argue that today's antitobacco efforts have fascist roots, or that public health measures are in principle totalitarian—as some libertarians seem to want us to believe" (1999, 277). Proctor's systematic labeling of Nazi health measures as "fascist" is as misleading as it is politically correct. Hitler was not a fascist, and National Socialism was not a fascist movement. It was a socialist movement wrapped in the flag of nationalism. The terms *fascist* and *fascism* belong to Mussolini and his movement and to Franco and his movement, neither of which exhibited the kind of interest in health or genocide exhibited by Hitler and the Nazis.

Proctor steers clear of discussing psychiatric practices in Nazi Germany, such as the following typical episode, even though they closely resemble psychiatric practices in the United States today. A father, a retired philologist, complains about the sudden death of his physically healthy schizophrenic son, Hans. He writes to the head of the institution where Hans had been confined, complaining that the explanation for his death was "contrary to the truth" and that "this affair appears to be rather murky." The psychiatrist replies: "The content of your letter … forces me to consider psychiatric measures against you …. should you continue to harass us with further communications, I shall be forced to have you examined by public health physician" (qtd. in Friedlander 1995, 180–81). Although Proctor's apologetics for pharmacracy in America diminishes the intellectual significance of his work, it does not impair the value of his documentation.

As Proctor himself shows, it was principally psychiatry that provided the "scientific" justification and personnel for medical mass murder in Nazi Germany. Nevertheless, he declares, "I should reassure the reader that I have no desire to efface the brute and simple facts—the complicity in crime or the sinister stupidities of Nazi ideology" (1999, 252). To call Nazi ideology "stupid" is like calling a distasteful religious belief "stupid." It is a self-righteous refusal to understand the Other's ideology on its own terms, as if understanding it were tantamount to approving it. The truth is that the Nazi health ideology closely resembles the

American health ideology. Each rests on the same premises—that the individual is incompetent to protect himself from himself and needs the protection of the paternalistic state, thus turning private health into public health. Proctor is too eager to efface the method in the madness of the Nazis' *furor therapeuticus politicus*, perhaps because it is so alarmingly relevant to our version of it.

"Nazism itself," he writes, "I will be treating as ... a vast hygienic experiment designed to bring about an exclusionist sanitary utopia. That sanitary utopia was a vision not unconnected with *fascism's* [*sic*] more familiar genocidal aspects" (Proctor 1999, 11, emphasis added). It was not fascism, which was not genocidal, but medical puritanism that motivated the Nazis to wage therapeutic wars against cancer and Jews. This is a crucial point. Once we begin to worship health as an all-pervasive good—a moral value that trumps all others, especially liberty—it becomes sanctified as a kind of secular holiness.

With respect to the relationship between health and the state, Hitler's basic goal was the same as Plato's, Aristotle's, and the modern public-health zealots'— namely, abolishing the boundary between private and public health. Here are some striking examples, all of which Proctor misleadingly interprets as manifestations of "fascism":

- Your body belongs to the nation! Your body belongs to the Führer! You have the duty to be healthy! Food is not a private matter! (National Socialist slogans) (1999, 120)
- We have the duty, if necessary, to die for the Fatherland; why should we not also have the duty to be healthy? Has the Führer not explicitly demanded this? (Antitobacco activist, 1939) (58)
- Nicotine damages not just the individual but the population as a whole. (Antitobacco activist, 1940) (26)

Hitler and his entourage were health fanatics obsessed with cleanliness and with killing "bugs," the latter category including unwanted people, especially Jews, Gypsies, homosexuals, and mental patients. Hitler neither drank nor smoked and was a vegetarian. Preoccupied with the fear of illness and the welfare of animals, he could not "tolerate the idea of animals' being killed for human consumption" (Proctor 1999, 136). After Hitler became chancellor, Reichsmarshall Hermann Goring announced an end to the "unbearable torture and suffering in animal experiments." The medical mass murder of mental patients went hand in hand with the prohibition of vivisection, which was declared a capital offense (129; see also Borkin [1978] 1997, 58). The fact that the Nazi public-health ethic demanded not only respect for the health of the greatest numbers (of Aryans) but also for the health of animals (except "bugs") illustrates the connections between the love of pharmacracy and animal rights, on one hand, and the loathing of human rights and the lives of imperfect persons, on the other hand. (The work of bioethicist Peter Singer (1994) also illustrates these connections; see also "Dangerous Words" 2000 and Szasz 1999, 89, 96–97.)

Instead of viewing the Nazi experience with medicalized politics as a cautionary tale illuminating the dangers lurking in the alliance between medicine and the state, Proctor uses it to speculate about what the Nazi war on cancer "tells us about the nature of *fascism*" (1999, 249). He arrives at the comforting conclusion that "the Nazi analogy is pretty marginal to contemporary discussions about euthanasia and criticizes "pro-tobacco activists"—as if opposing antitobacco legislation made one automatically a "pro-tobacco activist"—who "play the Nazi card" (271). Our future liberty, and health as well, may depend on whether we dismiss the analogy between pharmacracy in Nazi Germany and pharmacracy in contemporary America as "pretty marginal," as Proctor believes we should, or whether, as I suggest, we view it as terrifyingly relevant and treat it with utmost seriousness.

MEDICALIZING "PSYCHOLOGICAL TRAUMA"

To future students of U.S. history, 1999 may seem to have been a peaceful year. But the medicalizers of life did not see it that way. "The world as we approach the millennium," intones a physician in *JAMA*, "is full of horrific events, in addition to warfare, that can lead to post-traumatic stress disorder (PTSD). Survivors of natural disasters and life-threatening violence, including recent attacks at schools, religious centers, and other venues not normally associated with bloodshed in the United States, may develop PTSD, *particularly if they do not receive immediate mental health care*" (Jefferson 1999).

Because the diagnosis of PTSD rests on the concept of trauma, we must be clear about what we mean when we use that term. *Webster's* primary definition of *trauma* is "an injury or wound to a living *body* caused by the application of *external force or violence*" (emphasis added). The diagnosis of PTSD, like that of mental illness itself, thus rests on metaphorizing the word "trauma," changing its meaning from physical injury to the body to psychological injury to the mind. Making the diagnosis does not require that the subject suffer an actual injury. Having *witnessed* a "traumatic situation" is enough. Every such witness is presumed to suffer from or to be a candidate for PTSD unless he receives prompt mental health care *to prevent it*.

PTSD is now routinely *imputed* to people, especially to children helpless to reject the label. A child is murdered or kills himself. Instantly, his classmates—perhaps all of the children in the school—become patient fodder for "grief counselors," who are forcibly imposed on them by the health-care commissars of the therapeutic state (Labi 1999; Seligman 2000; Toolis 1999). Adults, too, are treated as if they could not manage their own grief unassisted by helpers they do not seek. A plane crashes. Relatives and friends of the victims are met by "grief counselors." What in the past Americans would have considered ugly meddling, they now accept as medically sound mental health care.

Madison was right when he warned his fellow Americans that of all the enemies to public liberty, war is "the most to be dreaded, because it ... is the parent of armies." However, perhaps because he was so secure in being an adult, he ignored the infantilism that often clings to people throughout life, manifested by their love of soldiering and their adoration of military heroes. Socialist leaders love soldiers, and the socialist masses love soldiering for those leaders: "The Nazi state declared civil servants to be 'administrative soldiers,' school teachers 'soldiers of education,' doctors 'soldiers of medicine'" (Porter 1994, 200). Soviet propaganda employed similar images. The American therapeutic state also loves soldiers—waging wars against diseases, drugs, and other "social problems," such as teenage pregnancy, suicide, violence, and war itself. Literal soldiers, sent abroad by the government, are "peacekeepers" where there is no peace and "liberators" where the term *liberty* means the opportunity to persecute and kill your adversary. Metaphorical soldiers, often led by arrogant and ignorant First Ladies, are people whose mantra W. H. Auden aptly satirized: "We are all here on earth to help others; what on earth the others are here for, I don't know" ([1962] 1968, 14).

In the United States today, the passion to judge, condemn, stigmatize, and denounce others often masquerades as "helping." From elementary school onward, children are indoctrinated to report the "misbehavior" of siblings and parents at home and fellow students at school. This indoctrination, presented as health education, never ceases; for adults, it is peddled as suicide prevention, drug-abuse prevention, and the promotion of mental health—the emblems of good citizenship in the therapeutic state. The view that certain disapproved or disliked behaviors are not necessarily "problems" and might not be the business of others is considered heresy. The individual as informant—"helping" others with their "health problems"—has become our ideal of the "responsible" person and model citizen. The fact that many such persons are unwilling or unable to assume responsibility for their own behavior only enhances the model citizen's image.

It takes a lot of helpless people to keep all the helpers happy, and the helpers, thanks to their diligence and army of informants, are never at a loss to find people who are in dire need of their help. In such circumstances, the medicalization of everyday life becomes useful. Most people have come to accept that bad deeds are attributable to diseases and hence the doer is blameless, whereas good deeds spring from free will and hence the doer deserves credit for them.

Post-traumatic Stress Disorder

The *Diagnostic and Statistical Manual of Mental Disorders (DSM-IV)* defines PTSD as a set of distressing feelings that follow "witnessing an event that involves death, injury, or other threat to the physical integrity of another person, or learning about unexpected or violent death, serious harm, or threat of death or injury by a family member or other close associate" (424). By this definition, the entire population of Europe between 1939 and 1945 was the victim of undiagnosed and untreated PTSD.

James M. Turnbull, a professor of family medicine at East Tennessee State University, warns physicians to be on the alert for PTSD among "battered women and men, adult children of alcoholics, police officers and firefighters, medical personnel who deal directly with trauma victims, noncombatants in war-torn areas such as—to choose just two recent ones—Kosovo and East Timor, and occasionally even spouses and children of persons with PTSD" (qtd. in Jefferson 1999). The mere act of living with someone with PTSD is here construed as a risk for contracting it. For good measure, Turnbull reembraces the traditional religious view of suicide as murder: "Grief following the suicide of a friend or relative presents a special case of emotional trauma . . . A survivor's reaction during this time almost always includes . . . anger at the dead person, who is not only the victim but also the *killer* of the survivor's loved one" (emphasis added).

To the psychiatrically enlightened, anything connected with death is now a symptom of mental illness: thinking about death is "suicidal ideation"; wanting to die is "being a suicidal risk"; witnessing death is "PTSD." Because death is an integral part of life, the medicalization of death goes a long way toward creating an endless supply of patients in need of help. In the past, attending a funeral was a somber social custom, honoring the deceased and his relatives. Today, especially if the deceased is displayed in an open casket, it is "witnessing an event that involves death," hence a pathogen causing PTSD. A movie reviewer remarks: "In past ages, Joan [of Arc] has been seen as a mystic, a saint, a national hero. Now, in keeping with the times, she is a victim of post-traumatic stress disorder" (Acocella 1999, 98).

Because mental patients often kill themselves, psychiatric residents are especially prone to become victims of PTSD: twenty percent report symptoms of it after patient suicide. "My first reaction," says [Cindy] Grief [*sic*], after one of her patients killed herself, "was to tell myself that she had a disease like cancer and that it was her illness that caused her death." Although that notion is part of the psychiatric catechism she was taught, it did not help: soon she was named in a lawsuit brought by the family ("Residents Need" 1999, 24). Psychiatric residents are upset after a patient's suicide because they are not taught that killing oneself is a basic human right and incarcerating people in mental hospitals is a grave moral wrong and that, although the suicide is not their fault (because it is not in their power to prevent it), when a mental patient kills himself, his "loved ones" and the lawyers they hire are likely to interpret the act as prima facie evidence of the psychiatrist's having committed medical malpractice (Szasz 1999).

HEALTH ÜBER ALLES

Clearly, many Americans believe that the coercive medical control of most (bad) behaviors is justified and proper because those behaviors are diseases or are caused by diseases or are the causes of diseases. Barry R. Bloom, dean of the Harvard School of Public Health, states: "The real culprits behind heart disease, cancer, stroke, and injuries are *the underlying causes* of these conditions—tobacco use (leading to 19 percent of all deaths), unhealthy diet and inactivity (14 percent), alcohol (5 percent), infectious disease (5 percent), firearms (about 2 percent), and accidents (1 percent)" (1999, 92, emphasis added). What, one wonders, will people die of after all the preventable causes of diseases have been prevented?

When Health Trumps Liberty

When health is equated with freedom, liberty as a political concept vanishes. We understand and accept the person who prefers security over liberty, but we do not understand or accept the person who prefers disease over health, death over life.

In 1999, at the Eleventh World Congress of the World Psychiatric Association, Benedetto Saraceno, M.D., director of the World Health Organization's Department of Mental Health, urged psychiatrists "to embrace a conceptual shift that expands on the traditional boundaries of psychiatry ... [and] serve people affected by violent conflicts, civil wars, and disasters ... and displaced people, many of whom will suffer from anxiety disorders, depression, and substance abuse" ("Psychiatry in 21st Century" 1999, 25). (I am not aware of a psychiatric leader ever urging his colleagues to narrow the scope of psychiatry.) The pharmacrats' agenda, based on the new *coercive-therapeutic concept of disease*, differs radically from the medical scientist's agenda, based on the old *noncoercive-pathological concept of disease*. To advance their agenda, the pharmacrats shift the focus—their own and the public's—from phenomenon to tactic, from objectively demonstrable *disease* to dramatically advertised *prevention and treatment*.

The medical doctor treats cancer of the lung. The political doctor treats smoking, preventable by legislation, litigation, and taxation, and curable with nicotine administered by any route other than inhalation. Sanctimony and hypocrisy replace honesty and self-discipline. The Renaissance popes preached celibacy and fornicated. Political doctors preach zero tolerance for tobacco and smoke. At the Fifty-second World Health Assembly, Surgeon General David Satcher publicly whined: "I was personally concerned to see delegates from many countries smoking ... allowing harmful exposure of UN employees, visitors, and delegates to environmental tobacco smoke, a known carcinogen" (Satcher 1999, 424). Satcher did not engage in a more meaningful protest at the convention, such as walking out of smoke-filled rooms, nor did he propose a more meaningful protest in the pages of the *JAMA*.

Suicide prevention is another, perhaps the most dramatic, example of coercion masquerading as care. In September 1999, Surgeon General Satcher declared "suicide a serious public health threat" and proposed "educating the public to recognize when someone seems 'at risk' for suicide and how to better help that person get help. That includes doctors and nurses, but also the clergy and others who interact with people and hear about their problems. *We want coaches, we want schoolteachers, we want hairdressers* [to be informants]" ("Surgeon General Seeks" 1999, emphasis added). Satcher's spokesman explained, "It's simple, it's understandable, and there's *near universal agreement* that these 15 steps can prevent suicide" (ibid., emphasis added). Recognizing that the term *suicide prevention* is a euphemism for psychiatric coercion is taboo; rejecting the premise that all suicide ought to be prevented is unthinkable. Satcher's antisuicide proposals, like the wars on drugs and smoking, reek of hypocrisy. He must know that the suicide rate among physicians is two to three times that among the general public.

THE STATIST-SOCIALIST BIAS IN HEALTH-CARE THINKING

The way we think about medical care and the language we use to talk about it are themselves problematic and deserving of attention. Health-care planners think in terms of *other people's needs*, as determined by physicians or politicians. Patients think in term of their *own wants*, which they themselves determine. People buy health care *not because they want health care, but because they do not want to be sick.* This negative motivation creates a more intense consumer dependence on authority for health care than for other goods and services. On whose authority can or should the consumer depend? The physician's? The medical profession's? The government's? For the greater part of the twentieth century, it was not enough that the practicing physician be well trained. He also had to be *licensed by the state.* Medical licensure *by the states* was supposed to guarantee the public a high level of physician competence and therefore of medical care. By the end of the twentieth century, most Americans concluded, probably without giving the matter much thought, that this assurance was not enough, that the time had come to place their trust for the provision of reliable medical care in the *federal government.*

We have come to take our dependence on the federal government for *health protection* so much for granted that we no longer notice how it has infected the way we speak and think about *prohibitions* imposed on us by the state. On December 28, 1999, President Clinton proposed "a new initiative to *protect consumers from the illegal sale* of pharmaceuticals over the Internet." The proposed regulation, designed to protect "unsuspecting consumers [who] may fall prey to fly-by-night Internet pharmacies ... , [will] identify, investigate, and *prosecute websites selling such items as: prescription drugs without a valid prescription*" (Office of the Press Secretary 1999, emphasis added). This is typical pharmacratic newspeak. The consumers Clinton offered to "protect" cannot be *unsuspecting* if they know how to use a computer and the Internet, nor can they be *prey* to unscrupulous vendors if their aim is to free themselves of the constraints of our prescription-drug laws. Depriving people of the opportunity to evade our draconian drug laws is here portrayed as an act of liberation-protection from health fraud. Pharmacratic controls may yet prove to be the Achilles' heel of the unregulated Internet.

Loving Leviathan: Deifying and Medicalizing the State

The belief that providing health care to people is a function of the state is a part of the view of the state as a secular God. A few examples of the deification of the state, foreign and American, should suffice here (more generally, see Bovard 1999).

In 1928, Grigori Pyatakov, a Soviet leader, declared: "According to Lenin, the Communist Party is based on the principle of coercion which doesn't recognize any limitations or inhibitions ... moral, political, or even physical. Such a Party is capable of achieving miracles" (qtd. in Bovard 1999, 15). In 1997, a French communist official justified the Soviet Union's murder of millions of its own citizens as follows: "Agreed, both Nazis and communists killed. But while Nazis killed from hatred of humanity, the communists killed from love" (qtd. in Bovard 1999, 15).

The deification of the state was and is as popular in the United States as it was and is in Europe. In 1916, John Dewey declared, "The question of the limits of individual powers, or liberties, or rights, is finally a question of the most efficient use of means for ends .... [some] forms of *liberty may be obstructive*" (qtd. in Bovard 1999, 55, emphasis added). Alexander Meiklejohn—a less well-known but perhaps more influential political philosopher—abjured personal liberty more subtly but perhaps even more deeply. In 1935, he wrote that "Life, Liberty, and Property ... may even be taken away [by the government] provided that the action by which this is done is justly and properly performed" (qtd. in Bovard 1999, 55). And in 1960, he declared, "Political freedom does not mean freedom from control. It means self-control" (Meiklejohn 1960, 13). Tito put it more simply: "The more powerful the State, the more freedom" (qtd. in Bovard 1999, 51). The pharmacratic version of this maxim becomes "The more powerful Medicine, the more health, and the more health, the more freedom."

The socialization of health care in the United States is, for all practical purposes, a fait accompli. However, that reality has been obscured by the absence of a directly nationalized ("socialized") system of health care, as well as by the American system being decked out with the vocabulary of choice, market competition, and patient autonomy. The result is deeply ironic: the more thoroughly socialized our health-care system becomes, the more physicians and patients alike complain that its shortcomings lie in its capitalistic excesses.

Health-policy expert Dan E. Beauchamp writes: "When I came to New York in 1988, my view of health care reform was captured in the image of the 'big wave' that would *transform everything, not only altering health care from a private to a social good but permanently reshaping the body politic, enlarging the communal sphere*" (1996, 113, emphasis added). Like a good Jacobin, Beauchamp dreamed of "universal health care ... to change people and politics" (38). He acknowledges that he is not interested in improving anyone's *private health*. "I began this task [formulating health-care policy]," he writes, "seeking to translate the public health viewpoint into the language of social justice and equality, suggesting that 'public health,' not 'health care' should be the primary or basic good" (1988, ix). Beauchamp is not interested in improving the health of any particular person as that person might want to improve it. To the contrary, he is interested in depriving individuals of their freedom to use their own funds to purchase medical care. "Republican equality would limit the power of money ... over health policy ... [and would limit] liberty to protect the health and safety of citizens as a body, the *public health—a central goal of all republican schemes of government*" (1988, 3 and 8, emphasis added).

By redefining freedom as the protection of the collective from disease, Beauchamp denies that he wants to abridge liberty: "The idea of liberty should mean, above all else, the liberation of society from the injustices of preventable disability and early death .... extending life and health to all persons will require some diminution of personal choices.... [S]uch restrictions are not only fair and do not constitute abridgment of fundamental liberties, they are a basic sign and imprint of a just society and a guarantee of the most basic of all freedom—protection against man's most ancient foe" (1999b, 109). According to Beauchamp, the market is a "prison [that] diminishes justice.... The truth of the market rests on a private and *interested* view. The truth of the political sphere rests on a more general and *disinterested* view" (1988, 51, 150). He concludes: "Giving everyone roughly the same level of care based on their need makes everyone aware that they are equals" (1988, 40). This statement is a proposal to use health-care policy to justify political coercion in the service of a dystopian goal that has no relation whatever to health as a medical concept. Finally, taking the New Deal as his model for social engineering, Beauchamp prescribes for us our state religion: "Our myth for the next American republic should be that *we do things together in order to live together.* This new myth would build on the New Deal and its ideal of national community" (1988, 155, emphasis in original). What we need, in short, is a New Leviathan led by a medical führer—"a new leader who battles on behalf of the people and launches the last big wave of reform, putting in place a powerful new institution that secures our health-care future and much else besides" (1988, 156).

In a similar vein, Howard Waitzkin, professor of medicine at the University of New Mexico, advocates reforming America's medical services along explicitly socialist lines. In his book *The Second Sickness* (2000), he explains: "Under capitalism, illness is exploited for a variety of purposes by a number of groups, including profit-making corporations, health care professionals, and medical centers" (7). Waitzkin's excuse for alcoholism illustrates the meshing of the psychiatric and socialist perspectives on drug abuse. "Alcoholism [according to Engels] was rooted finally in social structure; the attribution of responsibility to the individual worker was misguided" (67–68). Americans have accepted this viewpoint without any recognition of its Marxist, pseudoscientific roots.

Like Beauchamp, Waitzkin is more interested in creating "state power" and eliminating private medicine than in letting individuals choose the kind of health care they prefer. Physicians, Waitzkin declares, "hold class interests that often impede progress toward a more egalitarian distribution of goods and services. Doctors, like bankers and corporate managers, possess economic advantages and customary life styles that they do not willingly sacrifice on behalf of the poor" (2000, 211). Waitzkin evidently believes that degrading the rich would elevate the poor. The Soviet experience, one would have thought, has decisively disproved this fantasy, but not in Waitzkin's socialist construction of reality: "The Soviet Union eliminated its chronic problems of epidemics and cut its infant mortality rate by more than half in one generation" (224). The Soviet Union also succeeded in increasing its adult mortality rate, reducing the life expectancy of its citizens by some two decades below that of people in the West or in Japan.

Most academic physicians now champion statist medicine as the embodiment of a higher, altruistic morality. Leon Eisenberg, a professor of psychiatry at Harvard, calls Milton Friedman "the high priest of laissez-faire capitalism," as if capitalism were self-evidently sinful, and concludes his plea for socialist medicine with this self-flattering outcry: "Will we try to save our skins by delivering minimally adequate care on the cheap or will we stand up and be counted in the fight for universal health insurance?" (1999, 2256).

The right-thinking physician is now an advocate of merging medicine and the state. He does not call this merger "socialized medicine," a taboo phrase. He calls it the "single-payer" system or "universal health-care coverage." Speaking at a meeting in January 2000, Arnold Relman, the former editor-in-chief of the *New England Journal of Medicine*, endorsed "three examples of single payers: Britain, Canada, and U.S. Medicare. One advantage, he stated, was physician autonomy: British and Canadian doctors are 'free to do what they want with the resources provided.' U.S. Medicare, which [according to Relman] 'is not socialized at all, exerts virtually no control over the practice of medicine'" ("Payer Failure" 2000, 1). Marcia Angell, editor-in-chief of the *New England Journal of Medicine*, declares: "In a 1993 editorial ... I called for a universal, single-payer system and suggested that we could attain that goal by extending Medicare to all Americans.... Medicare is far more efficient than the market-based part of our health care system" (2000, 1664). Herbert Pardes, president of New York–Presbyterian Healthcare System, complains: "Academic medicine has been turned over to the marketplace and treated like a product. We need universal health care coverage to help both *indigent people and the institutions that serve them*" (2000, emphasis added). Relman's views sound like nothing so much as the enthusiastic reports of liberals returning from their visits to the Soviet Union in the 1930s. The "single-payer" system, which Angell calls "market based," has, of course, not the remotest similarity to what classical liberals call a "free market." Finally, Pardes recommends that we return to the health-care system of the 1940s, with this difference: *every patient* should be in the same position of economic-existential dependence on the system in which the charity patient used to be.

CONCLUSIONS

The collectivization of American medicine, like the collectivization of much else in America, began during the presidency of Franklin D. Roosevelt. In 1940, in a speech delivered at the dedication of the newly established National Institutes of Health, Roosevelt declared: "The defense this nation seeks involves a great deal more than building airplanes, ships, guns, and bombs. We cannot be a strong nation unless we are a healthy nation" (qtd. in Fallows 1999, 68). With equal justification, Roosevelt might have said: "We cannot be a strong nation unless we are a prosperous nation."

We have become a prosperous nation by separating the economy and the state, not by making the state the source of employment, as have the communists, with the disastrous results now known to all. We can become a healthy nation only by separating medicine and the state, not by making the state the source of health care, as have the communists, with similarly disastrous results.

Long before the reign of modern totalitarianisms, English economist and statesman Richard Cobden (1804–65) warned: "They who propose to influence by force the traffic of the world, forget that affairs of trade, like matters of conscience, change their very nature if touched by the hand of violence; for as faith, if forced, would no longer be religion, but hypocrisy, so commerce becomes robbery if coerced by war-like armaments" (qtd. in *Ideas on Liberty* [February 2000], back cover). The same principle applies to medicine. As "affairs of trade ... change their very nature if touched by the hand of violence," so affairs of medicine also change their very nature if touched by the hand of violence and, if forced, cease to be forms of treatment, instead becoming forms of tyranny.

Americans' love affair with pharmacracy now transcends traditional distinctions between left and right, liberal and conservative, Democrat and Republican (Szasz [1976] 1985). Even libertarians are often indifferent to the dangers posed by Leviathan, provided it has an M.D. degree and prescribes drugs (see, for example, McCloskey 1999). Physicians, who ought to know better but for the most part don't, are perhaps the most naive and at the same time the most zealous advocates of medical interventions for all manner of human problems. Writing in *JAMA*, two physicians plead for a "comprehensive public health surveillance of firearm injuries." Why? Because "firearm injuries are a leading cause of death and disability in the United States" (Hayes and LeBrun 1999, 429). We are building a society based on the false premise that if x is a "leading cause" of death, then x is a disease and a public-health problem whose prevention and treatment justify massive infringements on personal freedom.

Clearly, the leading cause of death is being alive. The therapeutic state thus swallows up everything human on the seemingly rational ground that nothing falls outside the province of health and medicine, just as the theological state had swallowed up everything human on the perfectly rational ground that nothing falls outside the province of God and religion. Lest it seem that I exaggerate the parallels between these two total states and the religious nature of the therapeutic state, consider Vice President Al Gore's by no means atypical remarks, offered in an address at Emory University on June 1, 2000. Pledging to wage the war on cancer with renewed vigor, he declared: "Within ten years, no one in America should have to die from colon cancer, breast cancer, or prostate cancer.... The power to fight cancer comes from the heart and from the human spirit. But most of all, it comes from being able to imagine a day when you are cancer-free." His Web site carried his message under the banner headline, "Gore Sets Goal for a Cancer Free-America" (Gore 2000; see also Dalrymple 2000). Thus do Christian Science and the wars on diseases blend into political vapidity and pharmacratic tyranny.

Because much of the work of the pharmacrats entails legislation, regulation, and coercion, the need for lawyers expands even more rapidly than does the need for doctors. The steady increase in the number of lawyers compared to the number of physicians is consistent both with the expansion of pharmacratic tyranny and with the underlying conflict between health and freedom that so many people sense. In 1956, approximately 7,500 law degrees and 6,000 medical degrees were awarded in the United States, for a ratio of 1.2 law degrees for every medical degree. In 1996, 40,000 law degrees and 15,000 medical degrees were awarded, for a ratio of 2.6 to 1 (Brimelow 1999, 150).

America's drift toward pharmacracy has not escaped the attention of perceptive social commentators. "Our politicians," observes Andrew Ferguson, "are transcending politics.... How is it ... that politicians who for years promised to keep government out of our bedrooms now see fit to invite their way into our souls? They have cast themselves as empaths; soul-fixing is their job.... Their bet is that America today wants a Therapist in Chief" (1999, 52). Indeed, the medical metaphors regularly used by our leaders—and by their wives and cabinet members—have made them seem such.

Actually, I believe, Americans want a therapist-in-chief who is both physician and priest—an authority that will protect them from having to assume responsibility not only for their own health care but also for their behaviors that make them ill, literally or figuratively. Pandering to this passion, politicians assure them they have a "right to health" and that their maladies are "no-fault diseases"; promise them a "patient's bill of rights" and an America "free of cancer" and "free of drugs"; and stupefy them with an inexhaustible torrent of mind-altering prescription drugs and mind-numbing antidisease and antidrug propaganda—as if anyone could be *for* illness or drug abuse.

Formerly, people rushed to embrace totalitarian states. Now they rush to embrace the therapeutic state. By the time they discover that the therapeutic state is about tyranny, not therapy, it will be too late.

REFERENCES

Acocella, J. 1999. Burned Again. *New Yorker* (November 15): 98.

Angell, Marcia. 2000. Patients' Rights Bills and Other Futile Gestures. Editorial. *New England Journal of Medicine* 342 (June 1): 1663–64.

Auden, W. H. [1962] 1968. *The Dyer's Hand, and Other Essays*. New York: Vintage.

Beauchamp, Dan E. 1988. *The Health of the Republic: Epidemics, Medicine, and Moralism as Challenges to Democracy*. Philadelphia: Temple University Press.

———. 1996. *Health Care Reform and the Battle for the Body Politic*. Philadelphia: Temple University Press.

———. 1999a. Community: The Neglected Tradition of Public Health. In *New Ethics for the Public's Health*, edited by D. E. Beauchamp and B. Steinbock. New York: Oxford University Press.

———. 1999b. Public Health as Social Justice. In *New Ethics for the Public's Health*, edited by D. E. Beauchamp and B. Steinbock. New York: Oxford University Press.

Bevan, S., and M. Prescott. 1998. Blair Launches Personal Carers to Save Family. *Sunday Times* (London), September 27, Internet edition.

Bloch, S., and P. Reddaway. 1977. *Psychiatric Terror: How Soviet Psychiatry Is Used to Suppress Dissent*. New York: Basic Books.

Bloom, B. R. 1999. The Wrong Rights: We Need Rights to Prevention, Not Just Treatment. Newsweek, October 11, 92.

Bonnette, R. D. 2000. Anti-drug TV Scripts. *New York Times*, January 18, A26.

Borkin, J. [1978] 1997. *The Crime and Punishment of I. G. Farben*. New York: Barnes and Noble.

Bovard, James. 1999. *Freedom in Chains: The Rise of the State and the Demise of the Citizen*. New York: St. Martin's.

Brimelow, Peter. 1999. The Lawyer Spigot. *Forbes* (September 20): 150.

Buchanan, James M. 1975. *The Limits of Liberty: Between Anarchy and Leviathan*. Chicago: University of Chicago Press.

Buckley, William F., Jr. 2000. The Pursuit of AIDS in Africa. *National Review* (June 5): 62–63.

Christian, S. E. 1999. Special Court for Mentally Ill in Talking Stage. *Chicago Tribune*, November 7, A13.

Cole, T. B., and A. Flanagin. 1999. What Can We Do about Violence? *Journal of the American Medical Association* 282 (August 4): 481–82.

Cook, P. J., et al. 1999. The Medical Costs of Gunshot Injuries in the United States. *Journal of the American Medical Association* 282 (August 4): 447–54.

Creveld, Martin van. 1999. *The Rise and Decline of the State*. Cambridge: Cambridge University Press.

Dalrymple, T. 2000. War against Cancer Won't Be Won Soon. *Wall Street Journal*, June 11, A30.

Dangerous Words. 2000. *Princeton Alumni Weekly*, January 26, 18–19.

Dubos, Rene J. 1950. *Louis Pasteur: Free Lance of Science*. Boston: Little, Brown.

Dworkin, Gerald. [1972] 1999. Paternalism. In *New Ethics for the Public's Health*, edited by D. E. Beauchamp and B. Steinbock. New York: Oxford University Press.

Eisenberg, Leon. 1999. Whatever Happened to the Faculty on the Way to the Agora? *Archives of Internal Medicine* 159 (October 25): 2251–56.

Fallows, James. 1999. The Political Scientist: Harold Varmus Has Ambitious Plans for the Future of Medicine. *New Yorker* (June 7): 66–75.

Fat Man Is Told: To Jail or Shape Up. 1995. *New York Times*, August 27, 12.

Ferguson, A. 1999. What Politicians Can't Do. *Time*, May 3, 52.

Ferry, L. H., L. M. Grissino, and P. S. Runfola. 1999. Tobacco Dependence Curriculum in US Undergraduate Medical Education. *Journal of the American Medical Association* 282 (September 1): 825–28.

Finkelstein, K. E. 2000. New York to Offer Most Addicts Treatment Instead of Jail Terms. *New York Times*, June 23, Internet edition.

Flynn, John T. [1948] 1998. *The Roosevelt Myth*. San Francisco: Fox and Wilkes.

Forbes, D. 2000. Washington Script Doctors: How the Government Rewrote an Episode of the WB's "Smart Guy." *Salon* (Internet magazine), January 13.

Frankel, M. 2000. Plots for Hire: Media Mercenaries Join the War on Drugs. *New York Times Magazine*, February 6, 32–33.

Fried, Morton H. 1968. State: The Institution. In *International Encyclopedia of the Social Sciences*, edited by D. L. Sills. New York: Macmillan and Free Press, 15:143–50.

Friedlander, H. 1995. *The Origins of Nazi Genocide: From Euthanasia to the Final Solution*. Chapel Hill: University of North Carolina Press.

Gaylin, W., and B. Jennings. 1996. *The Perversion of Autonomy: The Proper Uses of Coercion and Constraints in a Liberal Society*. New York: Free Press.

Germer, F. 2000. The Helmet Issue—Again. *U.S. News & World Report* (June 19): 30.

Gibeaut, J. 2000. Who Knows Best? It's an Ongoing Debate: Should the Government Force Treatment on the Mentally Ill? *American Bar Association Journal* (January). http://www.abanet.org/journal.

Gilman, S. L. 1993. The Image of the Hysteric. In *Hysteria beyond Freud*, edited by S. L. Gilman, H. King, R. Porter, G. S. Rousseau, and E. Showalter. Berkeley and Los Angeles: UC Press.

Gore, Al. 2000. Gore Sets Goal for a Cancer-Free America. www.algore2000.com/briefingroom/releases/pr_06t01_GA_1.html.

Hayes, R., and E. LeBrun. 1999. Public Health Surveillance for Firearm Injuries. *Journal of the American Medical Association* 282 (August 4): 429–30.

Higgs, Robert. 1987. *Crisis and Leviathan: Critical Episodes in the Growth of American Government*. New York: Oxford University Press.

Hogan, J. D. 1995. International Psychology in the Next Century: Comment and Speculation from a U.S. Perspective. *World Psychology* 1 (January): 9–25.

Iacopino, V., and R. J. Waldman. 1999. War and Health: From Solferino to Kosovo—The Revolving Role of the Physician. *Journal of the American Medical Association* 282 (August 4): 475–78.

Internet-Addicted Mom Loses Custody of Kids. 1998. *Syracuse Herald-Journal*, March 22.

Jefferson, T. 1999. Primary Care Physicians and Posttraumatic Stress Disorder. *Journal of the American Medical Association* 282 (November 10), Internet edition.

Kaye, J. S. 1999. My Turn: Making the Case for Hands-on Courts. *Newsweek* (October 11): 13.

Kershaw, I. 1999. *Hitler: 1889–1936*. New York: W. W. Norton.

Koop, C. E., and G. D. Lundberg. 1992. Violence in America: A Public Health Emergency. Editorial. *Journal of the American Medical Association* 267 (June 10): 3076.

Labi, N. 1999. The Grief Brigade. *Time* (May 17): 69.

Lawson, N. 2000. *The Retreat of the State*. Norwich, U.K.: Canterbury.

Leshner, A. I. 1999. Science-based Views of Drug Addiction and Its Treatment. *Journal of the American Medical Association* 282 (October 13): 1314–16.

MacCarthy, F. 1999. Skin Deep. *New York Review of Books* (October 7): 19–20.

McCloskey, Dierdre. 1999. *Crossing: A Memoir*. Chicago: University of Chicago Press.

Meiklejohn, A. 1960. *Political Freedom: The Constitutional Powers of the People*. New York: Harper and Brothers.

MH Courts Said to Keep Mentally Ill out of Jail. 1999. *Psychiatric News* 34 (November 5): 10.

Morgan, F. 2000. Is the White House Involved in Prime-Time Propaganda? *Salon* (Internet magazine), January 15.

1993 Appropriations for National Institutes of Health. 1992. *Chronicle of Higher Education* (October 14): A-27.

Nolan, James L., Jr. 1998. *The Therapeutic State: Justifying Government at Century's End*. New York: New York University Press.

Notable & Quotable. 1999. *Wall Street Journal*, July 30, A14.

Office of the Press Secretary, the White House. 1999. The Clinton Administration Unveils Initiative to Protect Consumers Buying Prescription Drug Products over the Internet. December 28. http://www.whitehouse.gov/library/thisweek.

Pardes, Herbert. 2000. Academic Medicine: Perilous Condition. Letter. *New York Times*, June 24, Internet edition.

Payer Failure. 2000. *Association of American Physicians and Surgeons News* 56 (March): 1.

Phillips, M. 1999. Tyranny of the New Body Snatchers. *Sunday Times* (London), July 11, 1/17.

Plan for Nonviolent Addicts Coming. 2000. *New York Times*, June 23, Internet edition.

Porter, Bruce D. 1994. *War and the Rise of the State: The Military Foundations of Modern Politics*. New York: Free Press.

Proctor, Robert N. 1999. *The Nazi War on Cancer*. Princeton, N.J.: Princeton University Press.

Psychiatry in 21st Century Requires Shift in Public Health Model. 1999. *Psychiatric News* 34 (October 1): 25, 43.

Residents Need Support after Patient Suicide. 1999. *Psychiatric News* 34 (November 5): 24.

Richards, E. P., and K. C. Rathbun. 1999. The Role of the Police Power in 21st Century Public Health. *Sexually Transmitted Diseases* 26 (July): 350–57.

Rose, G. [1985] 1999. Sick Individuals and Sick Populations. *International Journal of Epidemiology* 14: 32–38. Reprinted in *New Ethics for the Public's Health*, edited by D. E. Beauchamp and B. Steinbock. New York: Oxford University Press.

Samuels, D. 1998. Saying Yes to Drugs. *New Yorker* (March 23): 48–55.

Samuelson, R. J. 2000. Who Governs? *Newsweek* (February 21): 33.

Satcher, D. 1999. The Framework Convention on Tobacco Control: A Report from the 52nd World Health Assembly. *Journal of the American Medical Association* 282 (August 4): 424.

Satel, Sally. 1998. For Addicts, Force Is the Best Medicine. *Wall Street Journal*, January 7, 6.

Seligman, D. 2000. Good Grief! The Counselors Are Everywhere! *Forbes* (March 20): 122–24.

Sharkey, J. 1994. *Bedlam: Greed, Profiteering, and Fraud in a Mental Health System Gone Crazy*. New York: St. Martin's.

———. 1999. Mental Illness Hits the Money Trail. *New York Times*, June 6. Internet edition.

Singer, Peter. 1994. *Rethinking Life and Death: The Collapse of Our Traditional Ethics*. New York: St. Martin's.

Sontag, Susan. 1967. America. *Partisan Review* (Winter): 51–58.

Strange, S. 1996. *The Retreat of the State: The Diffusion of Power in the World Economy*. Cambridge: Cambridge University Press.

Streisand, B. 2000. Network Noodling: Who Controls Content? *U.S. News & World Report* (January 24): 26.

Stone, W. F., Jr. 1969. State's Power to Require an Individual to Protect Himself. *Washington and Lee Law Review* 26: 112–19.

Surgeon General Seeks Effort to Halt Epidemic of Suicide. 1999. *Washington Times*, September 29. Internet edition.

Swann, D. 1998. *The Retreat of the State: Deregulation and Privation in the UK and US*. Ann Arbor: University of Michigan Press.

Szasz, Thomas S. [1963] 1989. *Law, Liberty, and Psychiatry: An Inquiry Into the Social Uses of Mental Health Practices.* Syracuse, N.Y.: Syracuse University Press.

———. 1965. Toward the Therapeutic State. *New Republic,* December 11, 26–29.

———. [1970] 1977. Justice in the Therapeutic State. In *The Theology of Medicine: The Political-Philosophical Foundations of Medical Ethics.* Syracuse, N.Y.: Syracuse University Press.

———. [1970] 1997. *The Manufacture of Madness: A Comparative Study of the Inquisition and the Mental Health Movement.* With a new preface. Syracuse, N.Y.: Syracuse University Press.

———. [1976] 1985. *Ceremonial Chemistry: The Ritual Persecution of Drugs, Addicts, and Pushers.* Rev. ed. Holmes Beach, Fla.: Learning.

———. 1980. Therapeutic Tyranny. *Omni* (March): 43.

———. 1982. Building the Therapeutic State. *Contemporary Psychology* 27 (April): 27.

———. 1984. *The Therapeutic State: Psychiatry in the Mirror of Current Events.* Buffalo, N.Y.: Prometheus.

———. 1994a. Diagnosis in the Therapeutic State. *Liberty* 7 (September): 25–28.

———. 1994b. The Therapeutic State Is a Modern Leviathan. *Wall Street Journal* (European ed.), January 11, 9.

———. [1994] 1998. *Cruel Compassion: The Psychiatric Control of Society's Unwanted.* Syracuse, N.Y.: Syracuse University Press.

———. 1995. Idleness and Lawlessness in the Therapeutic State. *Society* 32 (May–June): 30–35.

———. 1996. Routine Neonatal Circumcision: Symbol of the Birth of the Therapeutic State. *Journal of Medicine and Philosophy* 21: 137–48.

———. 1999. *Fatal Freedom: The Ethics and Politics of Suicide.* Westport, Conn.: Praeger.

———. 2001. *Pharmacracy: Medicine and Politics in America.* New York: Greenwood.

Toolis, K. 1999. Shock Tactics. *Guardian Weekend* (UK), November 13, 27–35.

U.S. Department of Health and Human Services. 1998. *Health, United States, 1998.* Washington, D.C.: Department of Health and Human Services Publication Number (PHS) 98-1232.

Virchow, Rudolf. [1849] 1958. Scientific Method and Therapeutic Standpoints. In *Disease, Life, and Man: Selected Essays by Rudolf Virchow,* edited by L. J. Rather. Stanford, Calif.: Stanford University Press.

Waitzkin, Howard. 2000. *The Second Sickness: Contradictions of Capitalist Health Care.* Rev. ed. Lanham, Md.: Rowman and Littlefield.

Webb, Sidney, and Beatrice Webb. 1910. *The State and the Doctor.* London: Longmans, Green.

Weindling, Paul. 1989. *Health, Race, and German Politics between National Unification and Nazism, 1870–1945.* Cambridge: Cambridge University Press.

Wintemute, G. J. 1999. The Future of Firearm Violence Prevention. *Journal of the American Medical Association* 282 (August 4): 475–78.

Woloshin, S., and L. M. Schwartz. 1999. The U.S. Postal Service and Cancer Screening—Stamps of Approval? *New England Journal of Medicine* 340 (March 18): 884–87.

Acknowledgments: Reprinted from *The Independent Review,* 5, no. 4 (Spring 2001), pp. 485–521. Copyright © 2001. This chapter is a revised version of chapter 7 of my book *Pharmacracy: Medicine and Politics in America* (Westport, Conn.: Praeger, 2001), used by permission of the Greenwood Publishing Group.

PART V

Classical Liberals
Respond to Their Critics

17

What Is Living and What Is Dead in Classical Liberalism

Charles K. Rowley

The momentous upheaval in Eastern Europe in 1989, followed by the complete disintegration of the USSR, did not usher in the "end of history" as claimed by overly enthusiastic Western commentators such as Fukuyama (1992) in the first wave of euphoria over the collapse of Marxist-Leninist dogma. How-ever, as James M. Buchanan (1991) noted, it did end a vision of socioeconomic political reality based on collectivist-socialist ideas. It is now possible to analyze the complexities of social interaction among individuals without regard to the collectivist-socialist shadow that has been cast over such discussions for the better part of the twentieth century.

Especially important, in such circumstances, is that those who place a high value on individual freedom do not become complacent about their cause. On the one hand, the collapse of the Soviet Empire has provided unequivocal evidence that socialism cannot create wealth and cannot tolerate liberty. If the proposition is accepted that ideas have consequences, then the failure of the socialist idea should open up opportunities for halting and reversing the drift toward collectiv-ization in advanced Western democracies. On the other hand, false complacency among pro-market scholars and advocates, based on unfounded notions that the philosophic and economic debate has ended in a decisive victory, may lower the vigilance that is continuously necessary to protect liberty against the forces of mercantilism.

As Buchanan (1991) has observed, the demise of socialism has discredited, perhaps forever, the appeal of "politics in the large" in the sense of the centrally planned and controlled economy in which individuals must seek their own real-ization as integral components of a socialist community. However, the demise of socialism does not seem to have discredited the appeal of "politics in the small" in the sense of piece-by-piece interference with market processes. The electorate in its majority has not come to any robust acceptance of the notion that if politicization does not work when applied over all markets, then it will not work in the case of particular markets, taken one at a time.

In large part, this hesitancy is explained by pressures of public choice. In not inconsiderable measure, however, it is reinforced by a failure of conviction or of continuing resolve among classical liberal scholars, including those who once were the intellectual giants of the classical liberal movement.

IN RETREAT FROM UTOPIA

In 1974, Robert Nozick challenged the most commonly held political and social positions of that time—liberal democrat, socialist, and conservative—by reasserting that individuals have rights and that there are things no person or group may do to them without violating their rights. So strong and far-reaching are these rights that they raise the question of what, if anything, the state and its officials may do.

Nozick's main conclusions were that a minimal state, limited to the narrow functions of protection against force, theft, and fraud, and concerned with the enforcement of contracts, is justified; that a more extensive state must violate individuals' rights to do certain things, and is unjustified; and that the minimal state is inspiring as well as right. Two implications are that the state may not use its coercive apparatus to (1) require some citizens to aid others or (2) prohibit individuals from certain activities for their own good or protection.

In 1989, Nozick categorically repudiated this concept of utopia, denied the relevance of philosophy for matters of substantive policy, and opted for the "zigzag of politics" rather than for the principled position of his earlier political philosophy. This retreat from classical liberalism was driven by a judgment that any focus on individual rights detracts from communitarian impulses and fails to embrace humane considerations and joint cooperative activities: "There are some things we choose to do together through government in solemn marking of our human solidarity, served by the fact that we do them together in this official fashion and often also by the content of the action itself" (287).

In this view, democracy is a mechanism through which individuals seek symbolic self-expression as a means of intensifying the reality of social solidarity and humane concern for others. In contrast, the libertarian view, by looking exclusively at the purpose of government, fails to take account of the meaning of government.

More than this, joint political action does not merely express our ties of concern; it constitutes a relational tie itself. So important are these relational ties that individuals who are not included in such ties should be required to pay taxes to support the programs that such ties involve. If a democratic majority desires jointly and symbolically to express its most solemn ties of concern and solidarity, the minority who prefers differently will have to participate sufficiently to be spoken for.

Such bonds of concern, according to Nozick, may imply limitations on liberty concerning particular kinds of human action, for example, justification of antidiscrimination laws in employment, public accommodations rental, or sale of dwelling units, and so on. They may lead even to justified limits on the freedom of speech and assembly. No general principle draws the line on such limitations on liberty. All decisions depend on the extent and range of the general population's actual feelings of solidarity and concern, and their need to give these feelings symbolic political expression.

Let us suppose there are multiple competing values that can be fostered, encouraged, and realized in the political realm. Further suppose it impossible to include all such goals in some consistent manner. Despite this conflict, argues Nozick, many goals that cannot be pursued together at the same time can be reconciled over time by pursuing one for some years, then another some years later. This explains why the electorate zigzags between political parties over time. Given a choice between permanently institutionalizing the particular content of any group of political principles thus far articulated and the zigzag process of democratic politics, Nozick is clear which direction he will take: "I'll vote for the zigzag every time" (1989, 296).

IN THE BUNKERS OF CIVIL SOCIETY

John Gray's early writings on the philosophies of John Stuart Mill, F. A. Hayek, and Isaiah Berlin placed him forthrightly in the camp of classical liberal political philosophy. Surely, his writings never embraced the concept of the minimal or nightwatchman state in the sense of Robert Nozick (1974). Yet throughout the period of 1976 to 1988, he embraced the notion that individual liberty represents a worthwhile ethical goal and that classical liberalism can be justified by reference to extant political philosophy.

In his 1976 paper on John Stuart Mill, Gray acknowledges that "if there is a consensus on the value of Mill's political writings, it is that we may turn to them for the sort of moral uplift that sustains the liberal hope" (1989a, 1). He continues by noting that "Mill's writings contain an argument for an open society which has not yet been decisively refuted, and of which every generation needs reminding" (1). He endorses the central argument of Mill's *On Liberty*, "the claim that a liberal society is the only kind of society in which men confident of their own manifold possibilities but critical of their own powers and of each other, men who aspire to the status of autonomous agents and who cherish their own individuality, will consent to live" (2).

Following a detailed review of Mill's utilitarian-driven political philosophy, Gray concludes that "though we must not expect from Mill's writings a blueprint for the achievement of a liberal society in a world in many ways very different from Mill's— radicals will be unreasonable if they neglect Mill's thought on some of the principal dilemmas that perplex us today" (1989a, 8).

In his 1980 paper on negative and positive liberty, Gray extols the analysis of Isaiah Berlin, whose paper "Two Concepts of Liberty" (1968) argues that the concept of negative freedom (the absence of coercion of one individual by another) is to be favored over all other concepts of freedom. Gray endorses Berlin's doctrine of value pluralism and his preference for a liberal society in which a wide diversity of ends is promoted.

In his 1981 essay on F. A. Hayek, Gray criticizes Hayek for blurring the boundaries of individual freedom and for assimilating it to other goods such as the rule of law and social stability. For this reason, Gray contends, "Hayek's account of law and liberty runs the risk of losing the peculiar importance of individual freedom conceived as a virtue of political order" (1989a, 97). Gray concludes that a conception of individual rights can be defended only as abstraction from political experience.

Yet, in 1989, Gray pronounced that his twelve-year project to define classical liberalism and to give it a foundation had been a failure, and he condemned classical liberal ideology as an impossibility. The various projects of grounding liberalism as a set of universal principles in a comprehensive moral theory— rights-based, utilitarian, contractarian, or otherwise—had all turned out to be inadequate and essentially incoherent.

This failure was not to be lamented, he argued, "since liberal political philosophy expresses a conception of the task and limits of theorizing that is hubristic and defective" (Gray 1989a, vii). He also described the ruin of classical liberal political philosophy as "only the most spectacular instance of the debacle of the received tradition, modern as much as classical, of philosophy as a discipline" (vii).

In his 1993 book *Post-liberalism*, Gray pokes around among the rubble of classical liberal philosophy to determine what, if anything, is left. He concludes that none of the four constitutive elements of doctrinal liberalism—universalism, individualism, egalitarianism, and meliorism (or human flourishing)—can survive the ordeal by value pluralism, and that liberalism, as a political philosophy, therefore is dead. What is living in liberalism, he maintains, is the historic inheritance of a civil society whose institutions protect liberty and permit civil peace. He reasons that such a civil society is the best one for all contemporary cultures, because they harbor a diversity of incommensurable conceptions of the good.

If civil society is all that is left—the living kernel—of classical liberalism, what then is its nature? Gray's response to this question is expansive. If there is an ultimate diversity of forms of human flourishing, embodied in ways of life only some of which can be accommodated within a classical regime, then classical liberal orders have no general superiority over orders that are not classically liberal. In short, value pluralism dictates pluralism in political regimes and undermines the claim that only classically liberal regimes are fully legitimate.

A civil society, for John Gray, is one tolerant of the diversity of views, religious and political, that it contains, one in which the state does not seek to impose on all any comprehensive doctrine. Thus, Calvin's Geneva was not a civil society, and none of the twentieth-century species of totalitarianism encompassed civil societies.

A second feature of civil society is that both government and its subjects are restrained in their conduct by a rule of law. A state in which the will of the ruler is the law, and for whom, therefore, all things are permissible, cannot contain or shelter a civil society. One implication of this construct is that civil society presupposes a government that is limited, not omnipotent.

A third feature of civil society is the institution of private or several property. Societies in which property is vested in tribes, or in which most assets are owned or controlled by governments, cannot be civil societies.

In Gray's view, civil societies thus defined need not have the political and economic institutions of liberal democracy; in historical terms, most do not. Nor need they contain the moral culture of individualism. In his view, czarist Russia was a civil society for the last fifty years of its existence, as was Bismarckian Prussia. According to this model, the authoritarian societies of modern East Asia—South Korea, Taiwan, and Hong Kong—are also all civil societies.

Nor, for John Gray, is civil society to be identified with market capitalism. Several or private property may come in a variety of forms, each of them artifacts of law. The institution of the capitalist corporation is only one species of the private or several property institution on which a civil society rests.

Considered in light of these ideas, Russia will go badly astray if it seeks to replicate the Western form of capitalism. What is needed in post-1991 Russia is a radical deconcentration of economic activity to municipal, village, and cooperative levels in which the Russian tradition of cooperation can be revived. In Japan, also, Westernization would only involve injury to valuable social systems, with few, if any, corresponding advantages.

Evidently, civil societies come in many varieties. They may be democratic or authoritarian, capitalist or noncapitalist, individualist or nonindividualist in nature. What they have in common is the practice of liberty—as evidenced in the rule of law and private, or several, property—and the civil liberties of voluntary association, conscience, travel, and expression. They need not shelter democratic freedom.

This broad tent is put forward as the living kernel of classical liberalism—all that remains from several centuries of classical liberal philosophy. In my view, it is not a living kernel but an empty shell. In the remainder of this chapter, I search for an explanation of what has prompted leading scholars to abandon classical liberal philosophy, and I attempt to set the record straight by outlining a consistent and coherent Lockean justification for the minimal state.

ANARCHY VERSUS ORDER: THE POLITICAL PHILOSOPHY OF THOMAS HOBBES

Two great dichotomies dominate the political thought of all times: oppression versus freedom, and anarchy versus order (Bobbio 1993, 29). Thomas Hobbes (1588–1679) belongs in the company of those whose political thought has been inspired by the latter dichotomy: the ideal he defends is not liberty against oppression, but order against anarchy. Hobbes is obsessed with the idea of the dissolution of authority, the disorder that results from the freedom to disagree about what is just and what is unjust, and with the disintegration of the unity of power, which he views as inevitable once individuals begin to contend that power must be limited. The ultimate goal that motivates individuals in his moral philosophy is pursuit of peace and not of liberty.

Hobbes's fundamental obsession is the threat of anarchy, which he considers to be the return of mankind to the state of nature. The evil he fears most is not oppression, which derives from the excess of power, but insecurity, which derives from the lack of power. Hobbes feels called upon to erect a philosophical system as "the supreme and insuperable defense against insecurity" (Bobbio 1993, 29)—insecurity, first of all, about one's life; second, about material goods; and last, about that small or great liberty an individual may enjoy while living in society.

Hobbes's three main political works, *The Elements of Law Natural and Politic* (1650), *De Cive* (1651), and *Leviathan* (1651), provide descriptions of the state of nature that substantively are identical and meant to play the same role. The principal objective condition is that human beings, de facto, are equal. Being equal by nature, they are capable of inflicting the greatest of evils on one another: death. To this he adds the second objective condition, scarcity of goods, which causes individuals each to desire the same thing. This combination of equality and relative scarcity generates a permanent state of reciprocal lack of trust, which induces all to prepare for war, and to make war if necessary, rather than to seek peace.

One of the objective conditions emphasized in *Elements* and *De Cive* is the *ius de omnia*, the right to all things nature gives to anyone living outside civil society. De facto equality, together with the scarcity of resources and the right to all things, inevitably generates a situation of merciless competition, which always threatens to turn into a violent struggle. This situation is made worse by the fact that nature has placed in this predicament individuals dominated by passions that incline them to unsociability.

Hobbes does not have a flattering opinion of his fellow human beings. While discussing freedom and necessity with Bishop Bramhall, Hobbes asserts that "human beings resist truth because they covet riches and privilege; they crave sensual pleasures, they cannot bear to mediate, and they mindlessly embrace erroneous principles" (Bobbio 1993, 40). In *Leviathan*, he divides human beings into those devoted to covetousness and those devoted to sloth, then comments that these "two sorts of man take up the greatest part of mankind" (Hobbes 1946, chap. 30, para. 224). Furthermore, a description of the state of nature in Elements stresses vainglory as the passion "which deriveth from the imagination of our own power above the power of him that contendeth with us" (Hobbes 1928, I,9,1,28).

In Leviathan, Hobbes links together three causes of conflict: competition, which makes individuals fight for gain; diffidence, which makes them fight for security; and vainglory, which makes them fight for reputation. These conflicts give rise to the problem of power, the fundamental problem of political science, which Hobbes clarifies in two lines: "So that in the first place, I put forward a general inclination of all mankind, a perpetual and restless desire for power after power, that ceaseth only in death" (1946, chap. 11, para. 24). The state of nature is terrifying because the desire for power generates a state of war. This is an intolerable condition, one that individuals sooner or later must abandon if they wish to save what is most precious to them: their lives.

Right reason suggests to human beings a set of rules in the form of laws of nature that aim at ensuring peaceful cohabitation. These rules are subordinated to a primary rule that prescribes the seeking of peace. Individuals have no interest in observing a rule if they are not certain that others will do the same. There is but one way to make the laws of nature effective and to make human beings act according to their reason and not their passions: the institution of the irresistible power of the state. To exit the state of nature and to establish civil society, reasoning individuals must enter into a universal and permanent "covenant of union."

Because the state of nature is insecure, the principal aim of the agreement is to eliminate the causes of insecurity, greatest of which is the lack of a shared power.

The aim of the contract that founds the state is to constitute a shared power. The only way to do so is for all individuals to consent to give up their own power and transfer it to one person, be it natural or artificial; for example, an assembly. This entity will have as much power as is necessary to prevent all individuals from harming others by the exercise of their own power.

Individuals acquire a fundamental obligation as a consequence of this *pactum subjectionis* (pact of subjection), namely, the obligation to obey all commands of the holder of shared power. Within this covenant of union, an agreement in which all parties agree to subject themselves to a third party who does not participate in the contract, the third party's power combines the supreme economic power (*dominium*) and the supreme coercive power (*imperium*). "There is no power on earth," says the verse from the Book of Job that describes the sea monster Leviathan, "which is equal to it" (Job 41:24).

By holding that the sovereign power is irrevocable, Hobbes opposes the theory of trust on which Locke later rests his social contract. By holding that the sovereign power is absolute, in the sense of *legibus salutus* (not bound by laws), he denies the various theories that favor limiting the power of the state. Since individuals give up the right to all things in the covenant in order to preserve their lives, they retain only the right to their own lives. Thus, human beings must consider themselves released from the obligation to obedience only if the sovereign endangers their lives.

Hobbes's justification of absolutism runs counter to a long-held principle of English constitutional doctrine, according to Bracton's classical formulation: "The king must not be under man, but under God and under the law, because law makes the king" (Bracton 1968, 33). Hobbes easily rejects the thesis according to which the sovereign is subject to civil law (thesis in the terminology of Hayek), with the argument that no one can oblige oneself. Since civil laws are issued by sovereigns, the sovereigns would impose an obligation on themselves, were they subject to obligations.

But a more serious question must be answered: how is this unlimited sovereign power to be reconciled with other laws, namely, the common law (*nomos* in the terminology of Hayek) and natural law? Not surprisingly, Hobbes is a declared enemy of common-law supporters, most notably hostile to Sir Edward Coke, the great protagonist of the common law. "Custom of itself maketh no law," Hobbes states in *Leviathan* (1946, chap. 26, para. 176).

As a proponent of natural law, Hobbes repeatedly affirms that the sovereign is subject to the laws of nature and of God. However, in his view, the laws of nature are rules of prudence, or technical norms, compliance with which depends on one's judgment about the feasibility of pursuing one's objectives in given circumstances. Only sovereigns can make this judgment in their relations with their subjects, toward whom they are not bound by any covenant; they have no external obligation to anyone to comply with the dictates of right reason.

Since the laws of nature oblige only in conscience, the dictates of right reason do not limit the sovereign's power. Once the state has been instituted, there exist for the subjects no criteria of just or unjust other than the civil laws. This view makes Hobbes's moral theory one of the most extreme expressions of ethical legalism: what is right is what the sovereign commands. For example, Hobbes insists in *De Cive* that "though the law of nature forbids theft, adultery, etc. yet if the civil law commands us to invade anything, that invasion is not theft, adultery, etc.," and "[n]o civil law whatsoever, which tends not to a reproach of the Deity—can possibly be against the law of nature" (1845, chap. 10, para. 190–91).

In this perspective, there can be no theory of the abuse of power, since abuse consists of going beyond established limits. On the contrary, what may prompt subjects to consider themselves released from the duty of obedience is not abuse, but defect of power. Sovereigns who prove incapable of preventing their subjects from relapsing into the state of nature do not perform their task. Subjects then, and only then, have the right to look for another protector.

Interpreted along these lines, Hobbes's political philosophy conforms to only one version of modern natural-law theory: that natural law constitutes the foundation of validity of the positive legal order, taken as a whole (Bobbio 1993, 157). This version of natural-law theory serves his purpose of founding rationally the ideology of the absolute state. The distinct feature of this version of natural-law theory is its acknowledgment that once the state has been instituted, only one law of nature survives, namely, the law that imposes on human beings the obligation to obey civil laws.

Thus, if a conflict were possible between civil law and natural law, "the citizen who obeyed the latter rather than the former would violate the general law of nature which prescribes obedience to civil laws" (Bobbio 1993, 165). Civil law is based on the law of nature, but once civil law has been established, the norms of the system derive their validity from the authority of the sovereign and not from the particular laws of nature. Hobbes admits only two exceptions to this duty of obedience: (1) when sovereigns command subjects to offend God; (2) when sovereigns command subjects to honor them as if the sovereigns were God. In this way, Hobbes deploys the most sophisticated ingredients of natural law—the state of nature, individual rights, and the social contract—to develop a logically consistent theory of obedience to the state.

I shall attempt to demonstrate in this essay that classical liberal scholars who seek to justify limited government by reference to Hobbesian arguments logically must fail to do so and, almost inevitably, end up at some point on the anarchy-order spectrum with their original classical liberal principles in disarray.

OPPRESSION VERSUS FREEDOM:
THE POLITICAL PHILOSOPHY OF JOHN LOCKE

To understand the political philosophy of John Locke (1632–1704) and to distinguish it from that of Hobbes, it is essential to return to the concept of the state of nature, which is the starting point in Locke's genetic account of the rise of civil societies. For Locke's concept of the state of nature differs fundamentally from that of Hobbes in moral as well as in strictly positive characteristics.

Hobbes's social characterization of the state of nature in *Leviathan* is unambiguous. Life is portrayed as "solitary, poor, nasty, brutish, and short," a condition of war with "every man against every man," in which there is no industry, no culture, and no real society (1946, chap. 13, para. 8–9). The moral condition of individuals in that state is less clear, although it is evident that they have no moral rights or obligations at all in the ordinary sense—"the notions of right and wrong, justice and injustice, have there no place" (chap. 13, para. 13).

Locke's social characterization of the state of nature is much less bleak than that of Hobbes. In *Two Treatises of Government*, first published in 1690, he asserts that "want of a common judge with authority, puts all persons in the state of nature" (bk. II, para. 19) and "men living together according to reason, without a common superior on earth, with authority to judge between them, is properly the state of nature." Locke consistently claims that wherever no one is entitled to settle controversies between two persons, wherever there is no authorized referee to judge between them, those persons are in the state of nature. It is important to note that he considers this a sufficient and not a necessary condition.

Within this characterization, the presence or absence of effective government is not at issue. According to Locke, individuals may be living under effective, highly organized government and still be in the state of nature, if the government is illegitimate with respect to these individuals. At the very least, it is necessary to build into the definition the absence of legitimate government. To deal with this concept, one must to take account of Locke's moral characterization of the state of nature, which also differs sharply from that of Hobbes.

Locke's definition of the state of nature clearly incorporates moral elements, making use of such notions as legitimacy and voluntary agreement. Individuals are endowed with full-blown moral rights and obligations defined by the eternal and immutable law of nature (bk. II, para. 135). Although the particulars of the law of nature are not defined in any detail, their general form is clear. They consist of duties to preserve oneself and others by not harming persons in their lives, liberties, and properties. In the state of nature, persons enjoy their full complement of "natural rights," which correlate with the natural duties of others to respect those rights.

Each individual, Locke affirms, is born to inherit this set of rights and duties and receives them fully on reaching maturity (bk. II, para. 55, 59). Natural rights are a "grant or gift from God" (bk. I, para. 116), which individuals possess intact until they consent to enter a legitimate civil society, surrendering some of these rights in the process. However, private contracts between individuals are fully consistent with the state of nature. Such contracts may alter the existing structure of rights and duties among mature individuals, save only those rights and duties that in principle are inalienable. In this sense, consent "carves the boundaries of natural law" (Simmons 1993, 25).

What is the social characterization of the state of nature? Locke sets forth two contrasting situations. At one extreme, he describes the state of nature as "a state of peace, good will, mutual assistance and preservation" (bk. II, para. 19). At the other extreme, he describes it as "a state of enmity, malice, violence and mutual destruction" (bk. II, para. 19). Both descriptions are of possible states of nature, but neither is of the state of nature (Simmons 1993, 28). Where individuals almost always abide by the laws of nature, the state of nature will be one of peace, goodwill, and the like; where individuals typically disregard the law, the state of nature will be one of enmity, malice, and the like.

Since individual behavior almost always falls between these two extremes, the social characterization of the state of nature in the *Two Treatises* is a mixed account, or as Locke puts it, "one of mediocrity" (journal entry, March 20, 1678). It is a state of limited safety and considerable uncertainty, of significant but not desperate inconveniences, and in which only certain limited forms of political society will be preferable. Locke, in contrast with Hobbes, focuses more on the moral than on the social characterization of the state of nature. For Locke, the only intelligible choice is between some limited form of government and anarchy. Along these lines, the absolute government favored by Hobbes is clearly worse than the worst consequences of anarchy.

In one respect, both Hobbes and Locke share the same view. They are fundamentally opposed to political naturalism, which holds that the natural condition of humans is a political condition; that individuals naturally are subject to political authority; that there can be no understanding of morality or social understanding except within the context of some form of political organization. Contemporary political naturalists take their inspiration from Aristotle or Hegel. Locke was more concerned with defenders of the divine right of kings, like Filmer (1680), whose patriarchal theories of authority defended the autocracy of the House of Stuart.

The Lockean assertion that each individual is born free in the state of nature correctly recognizes that we are not born into political communities, even if we are born into the territories of such communities. We are not naturally citizens and must do something to become citizens. The claim that our natural moral condition is nonpolitical "is a refusal to accept mere accidents of birth as the source of substantial moral differences among persons" (Simmons 1993, 38). It is from this strong foundation that Lockean political volunteerism begins and develops and from which Nozick's (1989) retreat into communitarianism can be seen to be philosophically flawed.

Locke clearly depicts the state of nature as a state of "perfect freedom to order their Actions, and dispose of their Possessions, and Persons as they think fit, within the bounds of the law of Nature, without asking leave, or depending upon the Will of any other Man" (bk. II, para 4). In this sense, his political philosophy clearly runs on the freedom-versus-oppression and not on the anarchy-versus-order spectrum. Locke's state of liberty, however, is not a state of license. The state of nature has a law of nature to govern it, which obliges every individual: no individual "ought to harm another in his Life, Health, Liberty, or Possessions" (bk. II, para. 6).

The law of nature essentially reflects the moral claim of each individual to negative freedom and the duty of each individual to uphold the negative freedom of all others. To this end, each individual has an executive power to punish the transgressors of the law of nature "to such a Degree as may hinder its Violation" (bk. II, para. 7). Indeed, those who transgress the law of nature to a sufficient degree may forfeit their own rights to life, liberty, and property. The constant danger of the state of nature degenerating into a state of war is the chief reason advanced by Locke for preferring a limited government (civil society) to the state of nature.

Locke was fully aware of the inconveniences of the state of nature, which he deemed "must certainly be great" because men may be judges of their own case. Yet he considered this a much better situation than that in which individuals are bound to submit to the unjust will of others. At least, in the state of nature, if individuals judge wrongly in their own or any other case, they are answerable to the rest of mankind. By agreeing to leave the state of nature and to enter into civil society, individuals necessarily sacrifice their right to judge and to punish the breaches of natural law by others. This is no mean sacrifice, and it will not be countenanced unless the civil society is strictly limited with respect to the authority that it subsumes.

Civil societies and governments do not possess rights naturally; only individuals have that capacity. For Locke, there is only one possible process by which such political rights can be secured. Only voluntary alienation by the right holder—consent, contract, trust—can give another person or body political power over the right holder. "Men being—by nature, all free, equal, and independent, no one can be put out of his estate, and subjected to the political power of another, without his own consent" (bk. II, para. 95). "No government," he adds, "can have a right to obedience from a people who have not freely consented to it" (bk. II, para. 192).

Locke's wording makes it clear that by "consent" he means the actual personal consent of each individual. Hypothetical contractarianism plays no role in his political philosophy. Once actual consent is abandoned as the ground on which civil society is made to rest, we also abandon much of what is most compelling about classical consent theory—namely, the clear, uncontroversial ground of obligation on which it relies, and the high value of self-government with which it remains consistent (Simmons 1993, 78). Societies that refuse to permit or fail to facilitate free choice of political allegiance are simply illegitimate; however, many such societies might actually exist.

Locke's emphasis on personal consent does not imply any special commitment to democratic government. Consent, for Locke, is the source of a just government authority and its citizens' obligations. It does not determine the form that the government will take. Democracies may be legitimized by consent, but so may oligarchies and monarchies, hereditary or elected. Individuals consent to membership in the society. The majority then determines the form of government to be entrusted with that society's political power. However, a separate, special consent (bk. II, para. 138-40) is always required to resolve the issue of taxation under any form of government.

That all individuals possess certain natural, inalienable rights, a thesis closely associated with Locke, is seen as strictly limiting the proper sphere of government. The concept of inalienability should, however, receive close examination. One view, closely associated with resisting oppression, is that an inalienable right is a right that no person can take away. A different, and more extensive, view is that it is a right that cannot be lost in any way, whether voluntarily or involuntarily.

According to Simmons (1993, 103), neither of these interpretations of inalienability is true to the seventeenth- and eighteenth-century employments of the concept. Revolutionary authors typically viewed inalienable rights as rights that no citizen could be understood to have given away. This view conforms with Locke's rule that "nobody can give more power [rights] than he has himself" (bk. II, para 23). We can alienate only rights not connected with the preservation of ourselves or others.

From this perspective, governments cannot have the power to take our lives (unless we commit an appropriate crime), to deprive us of property at will, to rule by arbitrary decrees, or to tax us without our consent, because all these actions amount to the exercise of arbitrary powers that might endanger our lives if exercised maliciously. Each such transfer of power would be contrary to the natural law of preservation, "which stands as an eternal rule to all men, legislators as well as others" (bk. II, para 135). In this sense, Locke's limits on government power imply that we cannot transfer to government rights that we ourselves lack. Only in this sense does Locke construe the moral limits on government to be limits set by the citizens' inalienable rights.

Precisely because Locke's philosophy is focused on the freedom-versus-oppression spectrum, the *Two Treatises* may be viewed as a work designed "to assert a right of resistance to unjust authority, a right, in the last resort, of revolution" (Dunn 1969, 28). It is Locke's attempt to evaluate the moral consequences of governmental transgressions of its limited authority. Locke's use of strong-rights claims allows the revolutionary a moral high ground to stand on in resisting government (Simmons 1993, 152). When Locke's citizen defends his rights, those who oppose him also wrong him by breaching their duties to respect his rights. Crucial to this judgment is Locke's argument that rights can only be alienated by those who possess them and that certain rights are inalienable in the sense just defined.

Locke employs two distinct lines of argument in justifying a popular right of resistance to oppressive government. In his first line of argument, he justifies such resistance on the ground that, under certain conditions, a state of war exists between the people and their government. Here Locke focuses, naturally, on the case of tyrannical executive power (James II). In such cases, the oppressors forfeit all rights under the law of nature and may themselves be lawfully killed or used at will by any other person.

In his second line of argument, Locke notes that when governments act contrary to the terms of trust "by this breach of trust they forfeit the power the people" have "put into their hands" (bk. II, para. 222). Such a breach of trust need not involve either a basic breach of natural law or the forfeiture of all natural rights. Governors who breach their trust reduce themselves to the status of ordinary persons without authority (bk. II, para. 235).

Being thus deprived of their referee, the common judge over them all, the people might seem to be returned to the state of nature as a consequence of the misconduct of their government. Locke, perhaps incorrectly, rejects this inference: "The usual and almost only way" political societies themselves are dissolved "is the inroad of foreign force making a conquest upon them" (bk. II, para. 211). Otherwise, political societies remain and the governments actually "dissolve themselves," leaving the people morally free to seek new avenues for securing their rights (Simmons 1993, 163).

THE SHIFT TO THE ANARCHY-VERSUS-ORDER SPECTRUM

Having presented the foundations of the two political spectrums, I will now explain the apparent retreat from classical liberal philosophy evident in the writings of Robert Nozick and John Gray in the very year (1989) that witnessed the final collapse of classical liberalism's archenemy, Marxist-Leninist philosophy. I shall attempt to explain that this inexplicable change of course occurred not as a retreat but as a shift of focus from the freedom-versus-oppression to the anarchy-versus-order dichotomy. It is entirely possible that this shift of focus occurred unconsciously rather than explicitly on the part of Nozick and of Gray. The consequences, in any event, are profound.

Robert Nozick

In 1974, starting with a strong assumption of value pluralism, Robert Nozick concluded that there was indeed a utopia, one best society for everyone to live in, even though there would not be one kind of community existing and one kind of life led in utopia. He conceived of this utopia as a framework for utopias: "a place where people are at liberty to join together voluntarily to attempt to realize their own vision of the good life" (309). Utopia in this sense is a society governed by the Lockean minimal state. This morally favored state, "the only morally legitimate state, the only morally tolerable one" (333), is the one that best realizes the utopian aspirations of untold dreamers and visionaries:

> The minimal state treats us as inviolate individuals, who may not be used in certain ways by others as means or tools or instruments or resources; it treats us as persons having individual rights with the dignity this consti-tutes—How dare any state or group of individuals do more. Or less. (334)

In 1989, this vision of utopia was denied by Nozick as "a book of political philosophy that marked out a distinctive view, one that now seems seriously in-adequate to me" (17). A careful reading of *The Examined Life* suggests that in the act of denying his early scholarship, Nozick has shifted focus from the freedom-versus-oppression to the anarchy-versus-order dichotomy.

First, in his discussion of different stances, Nozick suggests that the very question, How can I be free? is rooted in excessive egoism. He suggests that the relative stance, in contrast, asks how one can be related to external reality and can prize determination of action. What would be regrettable, from the point of view of this stance, would be a determinism that was only partial, one that was not complete enough (Nozick 1989, 161). Second, in his discussion of authority, Nozick (1989, 175) notes that authority has legitimacy to the extent that those commanded feel obligated to obey. A leader functions to resolve the competition of goals. Only under special conditions can society avoid the need for leadership of some sort. Third, in his discussion of Plato's degree of reality theory, Nozick (1989, 199) emphasizes such criteria as being invariant under certain transformations, being more permanent, specifying a goal toward which things move. In all these observations, a yearning for unity or order is apparent.

This yearning for unity takes shape fully in Nozick's retreat from the minimal state with all the disorder that laissez-faire seems to imply. Democratic institutions now are viewed as vehicles through which we express the values that bind us together, the solemn marking of our human solidarity (Nozick 1989, 287). The zigzag of politics, that sorry Nozickean retreat from the inspiring vision of the moral minimal state, is the only alternative to Leviathan for a scholar who has abandoned freedom for order and unity as the supreme goal of mankind.

John Gray

In a sequence of papers published over the period from 1976 to 1988, John Gray pursued the ambitious project of defining classical liberalism and giving it a foundation. Although he always reviewed the writings of the great classical liberal scholars—John Stuart Mill, Isaiah Berlin, F. A. Hayek, Herbert Spencer, and James M. Buchanan—in an appropriately critical manner, Gray culled from their contributions ideas that clearly provided the moral foundations for the limited, if not for the minimal, state. There was no real hint in these papers that his project would end in 1989 with a condemnation of classical liberal ideology as an inevitable failure: "Our circumstance, then, is the paradoxical one of post-moderns, whose self-understanding is shaped by the liberal form of life, but without its legitimizing myths, which philosophic inquiry has dispelled" (Gray 1989a, 240).

A careful reading of Gray's scholarship, in both his 1989 volume, *Liberalisms*, and his 1993 *Post-liberalism*, suggests that Gray also has shifted from the freedom-versus-oppression to the anarchy-versus-order dichotomy in his denial of his early scholarship. This shift of focus apparently has been driven by the influence of

Thomas Hobbes and Michael Oakeshott and by a misunderstanding of the writings of James M. Buchanan.

In his paper on Hobbes (Gray 1989b), Gray comments that "there is an arresting contemporaneity about many of Hobbes's insights that we can well profit from," and in his 1993 volume he states that "far from being an anachronistic irrelevance, Hobbes's thought is supremely relevant to us, who live at the end of the modern era whose ills he sought to diagnose" (3). In Gray's view, "The modern state has failed in its task of delivering us from a condition of universal predation or war of all against all into the peace of civil society" (1993, 3). In its weakness, the modern state has re-created in a political form that very state of nature from which it is the task of the state to deliver us: "In this political state of nature, modern democratic states are driven by a legal and political war of all against all and the institutions of civil society are progressively enfeebled" (Gray 1993, 3).

According to Gray, the paradox of the Hobbesian state is that whereas its authority is unlimited, its duty, the maintenance of civil peace, is minimal. Civil peace encompasses that framework of civil institutions whereby men coexist in peace with one another, notwithstanding the diversity of their beliefs and enterprises and the scarcity of the means whereby these are promoted. In this Hobbesian perspective, the liberties of the subjects of a civil society "are not absolute or inalienable rights, since they may be circumscribed by the requirements of a civil peace in the absence of which they are altogether extinguished" (Gray 1993, 10). Liberties (such as they are) are intimated by the spirit of civil society itself, which is held together only by recognition of the sovereign. The Hobbesian state, according to Gray, is the classical solution of the prisoner's dilemma "in that the Hobbesian contract, by providing for agreed-upon coercion to obey known rules, releases its covenanters from destructive conflict into the peace of civil life" (13).

In his 1992 paper on Michael Oakeshott, Gray notes approvingly that Oakeshott rejected, as a prime example of rationalism in politics, the attempts by Locke, Kant, and Mill to fix, once and for all, the proper scope and limits of the authority of government. This rejection is based on the belief that the proper tasks and limits of government cannot be determined by reasoning from first principles.

In Oakeshott's view, political discourse is not an argument, but a conversation. Gray (1993) is especially enamored of Oakeshott's "pluralist affirmation of the diversity of modes of discourse and experience, of moralities as vernacular languages whose nature it is to be many and divergent, and of the miscellaneity of practice, which no theory can hope to capture, that embodies his most distinctive contribution to philosophy" (46).

Gray captures the spirit of Oakeshott's thought in a single phrase: "critique of purposefulness." The image of human life that Oakeshott conveys to him is not that of a problem to solve or a situation to master. It is, instead, our image of being lost in a world in which our vocation is to play earnestly and to be earnest playfully, living without thought of any final distinction. That image does contain freedom, but not the kind of freedom that requires eternal vigilance as characterized in classical scholarship. Rather, it is the freedom of the boat without the compass.

Gray is not content, however, to end his philosophical journey in some Oakeshottian skepticism of human action, viewing philosophical discourse as so much flotsam and jetsam, tossed here and there on the tides of political events. Gray instead seeks out an anchor, in the wake of classical liberal philosophy, in the form of civil society. He anchors the concept of civil society, at least in part, in the scholarship of Buchanan, who, paradoxically, he recognizes as focusing a "profound moral concern for the fate of free man and free peoples" in his reconstitution of classical political economy (Gray 1993, 47).

Gray is particularly attracted to Buchanan's indirect, proceduralist contractarianism based on methodological individualism but presupposing the cultural inheritance of Western individualism, with its roots in Christianity and Stoicism. In Gray's view, it is this cultural context that enables Buchanan to make the hazardous passage from Hobbesian despair to Humean hope, from the Leviathan of unconstrained majoritarian democracy to the limited government of constitutional democracy.

In his 1990 paper, Gray places at the crux of his inquiry the question, What is the place of liberty in Buchanan's contractarian approach? He notes that Buchanan does not privilege liberty from the outset, that his approach does not issue in a determinate list of basic liberties that are fixed and unalterable. This is not surprising, given the Hobbesian pedigree of Buchanan's political philosophy (Buchanan 1975).

Buchanan is also clear, argues Gray, that in any plausible real-world situation, contractarian choice will not yield a Lockean, Nozickean, or Spencerian minimal state, nor will it necessarily issue in unencumbered Lockean rights. Indeed, limited government, according to Buchanan, would surely have some redistributional functions. According to Gray (1993), in Buchanan's system "liberty is not given the apodictive priority it has been in Kantian-inspired contractarianism, nor is it the case that the role of the state is defined by the protection of Lockean rights" (60).

Nevertheless, suggests Gray, Buchanan's contractarianism is bound to bring about, in most real-world contexts, the enhancement and protection of individual liberty. It does so by virtue of its exploitation of the classical insight that voluntary exchange is mutually beneficial. It does so again because it defends the market economy in terms of its contribution to human autonomy rather than of any abstract conception of general well-being or collective welfare. And it does so finally in virtue of its insight that, provided there is a suitable framework of law, the undesigned coordination of the market is superior to any that can be generated by command or coercion.

Buchanan's contractarianism, Gray concludes, cannot give universal protection to the personal or civil liberties central to the Western individualist tradition. Gray finds this limitation to be both inevitable and even desirable: "It is far from self-evident, and sometimes plainly false, that the institutions and civil liberties of even limited democratic government are always and everywhere appropriate and defensible" (1993, 61). In Gray's judgment, if liberty has a future, it will have been fortified by Buchanan's work. For the final message of Buchanan's thought, as he interprets it, is that if we wish to preserve the precious heritage of Western individualism, we are bound to engage in the project of theorizing the world as it is, without illusion or groundless hope.

CONCLUSION

In my view, the retreat from classical liberalism on the part of both Nozick and Gray is completely explained by their shift, in a troubled world, from a preoccupation with the goal of preserving liberty to that of preserving order, that is, from a commitment to the philosophy of Locke to that of Hobbes. In both cases, reliance is now placed on some broad-tent notion of civil society as a basis for preserving the political legacy of classical liberal philosophy from the ravages of totalitarian pressures.

I am far from optimistic about this pragmatic judgment for a number of reasons, some of which Buchanan (1975) himself shares. First, if Gray is truly correct about the Hobbesian nature of man, there really is no prospect of a social contract short of that which creates Leviathan. All potential parties to a Hobbesian contract, except for a contract in which they hand over all authority to a superior being, must surely anticipate that the parchment of that contract will be shredded by amoral individuals in the postcontractual environment. Civil society, in such circumstances, swiftly must collapse into Jasay's (1985) plantation state, whatever the status of the constitutional agreement.

In this respect, Gray simply misunderstands Buchanan's insight in *The Limits of Liberty* (1975). Surely, Buchanan employs the Hobbesian model when he rationalizes contractual consent for limited government as an alternative to anarchy.

Like Locke, however, Buchanan employs Hobbes as the pessimistic scenario of the state of nature, the threat that leads free individuals into civil society. This does not imply that Buchanan believes Hobbesian man to be the norm. Far from it. All his scholarship on constitutional political economy is predicated on the notion that humans possess Lockean characteristics, search for release from the prisoner's dilemma of unlimited democracy, and wish to force themselves to be free. This grievous misunderstanding leaves Gray with a concept of civil society that has little resemblance to the strictly limited state of Buchanan.

Second, Gray, far more than Buchanan, is willing to countenance redistributionist transfers as a legitimate function of civil society. In so doing, he denies the Lockean notion of the right to property that prevents the minimal state from being mutilated as a commons in which the rent-seeking dilemma leads to a war of each against all.

Third, once attention is diverted from the priority of preserving liberty to the priority of preserving order, the dike is opened for those who would invade individual rights to do so under the guise of avoiding anarchy. One has only to review the reactions in all branches of government to the tragedy of Oklahoma City to see how quickly opportunities to trample on liberties are seized upon by those who perceive economic or political gain.

Finally, and almost inevitably, those who embrace Hobbesian philosophy tend to focus either exclusively on analyzing what is or what conditionally might be (avoiding entirely all moral discourse) or to ignore Hume's naturalistic fallacy and seek to create an ought from an is. Ultimately, of course, such an endeavor is doomed to failure.

In this vale of tears, if one believes in a moral philosophy, one had better articulate it clearly and pursue it with a heart that pumps more than blood. In my view, classical liberal philosophy is far from dead. Indeed, it is alive and well and worthy of the most serious consideration in the postcommunist world order.

REFERENCES

Berlin, I. 1968. *Four Essays on Liberty*. Oxford: Oxford University Press.

Bobbio, N. 1993. *Thomas Hobbes and the Natural Law Tradition*. Chicago: University of Chicago Press.

Bracton, H. 1968. *On the Laws and Customs of England*. Cambridge: Cambridge University Press.

Buchanan, J. M. 1975. *The Limits of Liberty: Between Anarchy and Leviathan*. Chicago: University of Chicago Press.

———. 1991. *Analysis, Ideology and the Events of 1989*. Chicago: University of Chicago Press.

Dunn, J. 1969. *The Political Thought of John Locke*. London: Cambridge University Press.

Filmer, R. 1947. Patriarcha. In J. Locke, *Two Treatises of Government*. Edited by T. Cook. New York: Hafner.

Fukuyama, F. C. 1992. *The End of History and the Last Man*. New York: Free Press.

Gray, J. 1976. John Stuart Mill and the Future of Liberalism. *Contemporary Review* 220 (September).

———. 1980. On Negative and Positive Liberty. *Political Studies* 28.

———. 1981. Hayek on Liberty, Rights and Justice. *Ethics* 92, no. 1.

———. 1989a. *Liberalisms: Essays in Political Philosophy*. London: Routledge.

———. 1989b. Hobbes and the Modern State. In *The World and I*. Washington, D.C.

———. 1990. Buchanan on Liberty. *Constitutional Political Economy* 1, no. 2.

———. 1992. Oakeshott as a Liberal. *Salisbury Review* (January).

———. 1993. *Post-liberalism: Studies in Political Thought*. London: Routledge.

Hobbes, T. 1928. *The Elements of Law Natural and Politic*. Edited by F. Tonnies. Cambridge: Cambridge University Press.

———. 1845. *De Cive (Philosophical Rudiments Concerning Government and Society)*. Vol. 2 of *English Works*. Edited by W. Molesworth. London: J. Bohn.

———. 1946. *Leviathan*. Edited by M. Oakeshott. Oxford: Basil Blackwell.

Jasay, A. de. 1985. *The State*. Oxford: Basil Blackwell.

Locke, J. 1963. *Two Treatises of Government*. Edited by P. Laslett. Cambridge: Cambridge University Press.

Nozick, R. 1974. *Anarchy, State, and Utopia*. New York: Basic Books.

———. 1989. *The Examined Life: Philosophical Meditations*. New York: Simon and Schuster.

Simmons, A. J. 1993. *On the Edge of Anarchy: Locke, Consent and the Limits of Society*. Princeton, N.J.: Princeton University Press.

Acknowledgments: Reprinted from *The Independent Review*, 1, no. 1 (Spring 1996), pp. 9–28. Copyright © 1996. This chapter is a revised version of the introductory chapter in *The Political Economy of the Minimal State*, edited by Charles K. Rowley and published by Edward Elgar Publishing (1996). Permission to republish is gratefully acknowledged. I wish to express deep appreciation to the Lynde and Harry Bradley Foundation for financial support for this project. I am also grateful to Robert Higgs for sound editorial advice.

18

The Ways of John Gray
A Libertarian Commentary
Daniel B. Klein

      In writing about classical liberal ideas and libertarian reforms, John Gray uses various terms. Besides "classical liberalism" and "libertarianism," he uses "neo-liberalism," "market liberalism," "paleo-liberal," "the New Right," "the market," "free market ideology," and, most broadly, "the Enlightenment Project." To understand why a libertarian such as myself might feel an urge to comment on Gray's writings, consider the following statements in which Gray disparages libertarianism:

> The argument of *Beyond the New Right* [Gray 1993a] ... suggested that the historic inheritance of liberal institutions and practice was endangered, not as hitherto by left-liberal policy and ideology, but by the market fundamentalism sponsored by the New Right. (1995a, vii)

> The libertarian condemnation of the state and celebration of the free market is a recipe for social breakdown and political instability. (1997, 133)

> The celebration of consumer choice, as the only undisputed value in market societies, devalues commitment and stability in personal relationships and encourages the view of marriage and the family as vehicles of self-realization. The dynamism of market processes dissolves social hierarchies and overturns established expectations. Status is ephemeral, trust frail, and contract sovereign. This dissolution of communities promoted by market-driven labour mobility weakens, where it does not entirely destroy, the informal social monitoring of behaviour which is the most effective preventive measure against crime. (1995a, 99)

> The tendency of market liberal policy is significantly to reinforce subjec-

tivist and even antinomian tendencies which are already very powerful in modernist societies and thereby to render surviving enclaves and remnants of traditional life powerless before them. (1995a, 99)

The desolation of settled communities and the ruin of established expectations will not be mourned and may well be welcomed by fundamentalist market liberals. For them, nothing much of any value is threatened by the unfettered operation of market institutions. Communities and ways of life which cannot renew themselves through the exercise of consumer choice deserve to perish. The protection from market forces of valuable cultural forms is a form of unacceptable paternalism. And so the familiar and tedious litany goes on. (1995a, 100)

In this paleo-liberal or libertarian view, the erosion of distinctive cultures by market processes is, if anything, to be welcomed as a sign of progress toward a universal rational civilization. Here paleo-liberalism shows its affinities not with European conservatism but with the Old Left project of doing away with, or marginalizing politically, the human inheritance of cultural difference.... This perspective is a hallucinatory and utopian one. (1995a, 102)

Market liberal ideologists will argue that the stability of a market society is only a matter of enforcing its laws. This thoroughly foolish reply need not detain us. (1995a, 102)

Communities need shelter from the gale of market competition, else they will be scattered to the winds. (1995a, 112)

At present, the principal obstacle we face in the struggle to renew our inheritance of liberal practice is the burden on thought and policy of market liberal dogma. (1995a, 113)

It is in social policy, however, that the errors of unrestrained neo-liberalism are most egregious. (1993a, 53)

Conservative government has the responsibility of protecting and renewing the public environment without which the lifestyle of market individualism is squalid and impoverished. Conservative individualists, unlike their liberal and libertarian counterparts, recognise that the capacity for unfettered choice has little value when it must be exercised in a public space that—like many American cities—is filthy, desolate, and dangerous. (1993a, 60)

Liberal ideologues, in the nescience of their rationalist conceit, suppose that they can answer the question posed by the greatest twentieth-century Tory poet: what are days for? These ideologues have still to learn that, when local knowledge is squandered in incessant self-criticism, people realise that

> solving that question
> Brings the priest and the doctor
> In their long coats
> Running over the fields
> (Gray 1993a, 53 [quoting Philip Larkin's poetry])

Gray's vituperation is especially remarkable because Gray was once a classical liberal. Although he did not begin as a classical liberal, he apparently moved in that direction during his thirties. For years, he contributed to the intellectual refinement and social cause of classical liberalism. He wrote books on John Stuart Mill, on F. A. Hayek, and on the history of liberalism. The back cover of his *Beyond the New Right* (1993a) contains the statement that "for over a decade [Gray] has been associated with the ideas and think-tanks of the New Right." In the United States he worked with libertarian or classical liberal organizations, including the Institute for Humane Studies, the Cato Institute, the Liberty Fund, and the Social Philosophy and Policy Center. In Britain he worked with the Institute of Economic Affairs, which in 1989 published his classical liberal booklet *Limited Government: A Positive Agenda*. But early on, Gray's work had shown a definite discomfort with classical liberal ideology, and that discomfort evolved into harsh denunciation.

I came to read Gray's books in the course of researching a project on ideological migration. Gray is significant because he migrated far and especially because, subsequent to his more classical liberal phase, he migrated in an uncommon direction—from belief in small government to belief in not-so-small government. In researching Gray for the ideological migration project, I found that he habitually argued in certain ways. Once I had discerned his characteristic ways, reading his work became much easier.

I present here a memorandum on the ways of John Gray, which takes the form of a broadside against his writings. Although I set myself up as Gray's opponent,

I do so with significant misgivings. I share what is perhaps most fundamental in this thought—an agonistic attitude, as he aptly puts it, about political philosophy and about liberalism in particular (Gray 1993b, chap. 6; 1995a, chap. 6; 1996, chap. 6). Also, I admire his wide learning, his daring, and his industriousness. Yet I feel that he has been intellectually irresponsible in ways that damage the cause of good policy reform. My aim is to expose and counteract certain regrettable themes and rhetorical tactics in his work. The ways of Gray that I will treat are as follows:

· Gray habitually sets up a straw man and then knocks it down. He often neglects to specify whom or what he is attacking.

· Gray often attributes an extreme brittleness to his opponent's ideas, insisting that as soon as any ambiguity or incompleteness is identified, the entire body of ideas shatters. Yet Gray does not hold his own ideas to the same extreme standard for definitiveness and completeness.

· In many cases when Gray does identify the opposition, he flagrantly misrepresents it. He presents citations and truncated quotations to signify ideas that are quite at variance with what the sources are really saying. (I will consider in particular his misrepresentation of Hayek.)

· Gray often casts the opposition in hyperbolic terms, turning his opponent into an apocalyptic bugaboo.

Two themes in Gray's writings to which I call special attention are Gray's hostile view of the United States and his elitism.

THE LIBERTY MAXIM AND ITS LIMITATIONS

Gray has always opposed the foundationalist and rationalist strains in classical liberal thought. Finding the same antipathy in Hayek's writings, he praised Hayek in 1984 as follows:

> We find in Hayek a restatement of classical liberalism in which it is purified of errors—specifically, the errors of abstract individualism and uncritical rationalism—which inform the work of even the greatest of the classical liberals and which Hayek has been able to correct by absorbing some of the deepest insights of conservative philosophy. (1984, viii)

As Gray began his turn away from classical liberalism, he began using charges of rationalism, foundationalism, and fundamentalism to flog classical liberalism. This maneuver, which he has employed regularly since 1989, depends on constructing a straw man and on attributing a false brittleness to the victim. Before considering examples, let us explore the significance and relevance of foundationalism and rationalism in libertarian and classical liberal thought.

The central idea of libertarianism is liberty—the maxim of private property and freedom of consent and contract. But the maxim has limitations of several kinds.

First, it is sometimes ambiguous. The terms of consent and the rights inhering in property are sometimes unclear and indeterminate. Consider the following gray areas: the unsightliness of a neighbor's house; unpleasant noises; the basis of consent by the young, the senile, and the mentally retarded; issues relating to the unborn fetus; the tacit terms of ongoing relationships, including employment and marriage; the continuum that spans private voluntary agreement and coercive local government. The maxim also is ambiguous about whether the taxation to finance a minimal state ought to be deemed coercive and in violation of liberty. Ambiguities abound.

Second, the maxim is incomplete. It stipulates no rules to govern the use of government resources; it is silent on ten thousand issues of public administration. Given that the government imposes taxes and raises revenue, the maxim of liberty, by itself, does not say whether that revenue may be used for welfare benefits. Where we believe that government resources should be privatized, it fails to tell us how and how fast to privatize. It does not instruct us about meting out punishment and enforcing restitution. Incompleteness abounds.

Third, in some cases, abiding by the maxim is undesirable. A policy maker with the power to rush toward liberty may be unwise to do so. Piecemeal steps in the direction of liberty, such as the deregulation of the U.S. savings-and-loan industry in the 1980s, may be unwise. Should all governments do nothing to control air pollution in Los Angeles today? Should the government not grant eminent-domain powers in the construction of a particular highway today? Should all levels of government allow a free market in machine guns and bombs? Instances of undesirability abound.

Fourth, libertarians think the desirability of liberty is much more frequent and much more decisive than current policy admits, and they oppose high taxes and the welfare state. But no body of argument provides an authoritative justification, or "rational foundation," for libertarian reform; no body of argument represents fundamental truths from which the validity of one's libertarian position can be derived.

Gray reminds us again and again that libertarianism has these four limitations. What are objectionable are his claims, first, that all libertarian theorists deny these limitations and, second, that the limitations make libertarianism meaningless and absurd.

GRAY SETS UP A STRAW MAN

The following statements exemplify Gray's claims that classical liberalism or libertarianism denies the limitations just identified:

> The classical liberal idea that our liberties, negative and positive, can be specified, once and for all in a highly determinate fashion, is a mere illusion. (1993a, 82)

> This species of political rationalism ... represents political reasoning as an application of first principles of justice or rights.... It supposes that the functions and limits of state activity can be specified, once and for all, by a theory, instead of varying with the history, traditions, and circumstances that peoples and their governments inherit. It demands of political discourse a determinacy in its outcomes and a certainty in its foundations that it does not and never can possess. (1993a, xii)

> Traditional varieties of liberalism are all exemplars of conceptions of rational choice. They are also all exemplars of a universalist anthropology for which cultural difference is not an essential but only an incidental and transitional attribute of human beings. (1995a, 66)

> In all of its varieties, traditional liberalism is a universalist political theory. Its content is a set of principles which prescribe the best regime, the ideally best institutions, for all mankind. (1995a, 64)

> Classical liberalism, or what I have termed market fundamentalism, is, like Marxism, a variation on the Enlightenment project, which is the project of transcending the contingencies of history and cultural difference and founding a universal civilization that is qualitatively different from any that has ever before existed. (1995a, 100)

> The kinship of market fundamentalism with classical Marxism is evident.... Both are forms of *economism* in that their model of humankind is that of *Homo economicus* and they theorize cultural and political life in the reductionist terms of economic determinism. (1995a, 101)

> My focus here has been on the specious claims of paleo-liberal ideology, in which individual choice is elevated to the supreme value and at the same time emptied of all moral significance. (1995a, 118)

The danger of the neo-liberalism that has lately come to dominate conservative thinking is the danger of utopianism—the belief or hope that
the predicament in which people find themselves, in which goods are not
always combinable and sometimes depend upon evils, and in which the
elimination of one evil often discloses another, can somehow be tran-
scended. This was the danger inherent in the domination of conservative
thought by the ideology of the New Right—the dangerous delusion that
contemporary problems could be conjured away, in their entirety and presumably forever, by the resurrection of the theorisings of the Manchester
School of *laissez-faire* liberalism. (1993a, 65)

Young Randians—adolescent boys and girls searching for a simple salvation— may discover libertarianism and neglect, or even deny, its limitations. But
Gray's assault is not aimed at seventeen-year-olds. Among the condemned are
leading libertarian thinkers—indeed, all thinkers and classical liberal thinkers,
including not only Ayn Rand, Murray Rothbard, and Robert Nozick but also
Adam Smith, William Graham Sumner, Ludwig von Mises, Milton Friedman,
and F. A. Hayek.

Many classical liberals have shunned precepts of "natural law" and "natural
rights" and have in no way pretended to possess, or even hoped for, an authoritative "rational foundation" for their views. Hayek warned against the pitfalls of
rationalism and foundationalism, shunned simple maxims such as laissez-faire,
called attention to ambiguities, incompleteness, and undesirabilities, and argued
against a narrow conception of the individual as a unified utility maximizer.

GRAY'S BRITTLENESS PLOY

The four limitations of libertarianism are not philosophically damaging because
the same limitations—ambiguity, incompleteness, undesirability, and lack of
foundation— mark all rival political philosophies as well. A political philosophy—an agenda for government reform and a supporting body of argument—is
bound to fall short of the qualities that seventeen-year-olds seek. Yet Gray pretends that classical liberal thought depends on being a brittle system of that sort.
He supposes that ambiguity, incompleteness, undesirability, and lack of foundation are sufficient to shatter classical liberal thought. He argues as though, so long
as there is a twilight, there is no meaningful distinction between day and night.
Gray recognizes that the same limitations mark his own thought. Why then don't
they undermine his own arguments as well?

The following statements exemplify Gray's false attribution of brittleness to classical liberal or libertarian thought:

> The objection to negative liberty, taken in and of itself, is that its content is radically indeterminate. (1993a, 78)

> This indeterminacy in the very notion of negative liberty spells ruin for the classical liberal project of stating a principle—Spencer's principle of Greatest Equal Freedom, say, or J. S. Mill's "one very simple principle" about not restraining liberty save where harm to others is at issue—which can authoritatively guide thought and policy on the restraint of liberty. Because we cannot identify "the greatest liberty," principles which speak of maximising it are empty. To talk, as classical liberals still do, of minimising coercion by maximising negative liberty, is merely to traffic in illusions. (1993a, 78)

> Classical liberal conceptions of the role of the state that are spelt out in terms of a principle of *laissez-faire* suffer from the disability that that principle is itself practically vacuous.... The ideal of *laissez-faire* is only a mirage. (1993a, 6)

> Theories of the minimum state, therefore, are worse than uninformative; they are virtually empty of content. (1993a, 6)

> In truth, because their content is open-ended and their very definition uncertain, the negative rights in terms of which the minimum state is theorised confer upon [the minimum state] all of the indeterminacy which characterises my own account of the proper functions of government. (1993a, 6)

The brittleness ploy shows at least a lack of graciousness on Gray's part. Even when an opponent's case has weaknesses, they do not subvert strengths that stand independently. Consider the use of the term *rights* in David Boaz's book *Libertarianism: A Primer* (1997). Boaz writes:

> The corollary of the libertarian principle that "every person has the right to live his life as he chooses, so long as he does not interfere with the equal rights of others" is this: *No one has the right to initiate aggression against the person or property of anyone else.* This is what libertarians call the nonaggression axiom, and it is a central principle of libertarianism. (74)

I agree with Gray that it is misleading to speak in terms of axioms and corollaries and that, in referring to abstract maxims about what should be, it is not useful to speak in terms of rights (which Boaz elsewhere identifies as "natural rights"). I might fault Boaz for not paying more attention to the ambiguities, incompletenesses, and hard cases of his maxim. But such criticism would not detract greatly from his book. Most of the book is argumentation about the relative robustness of the libertarian maxim. The argumentation speaks of the role of property, consent, and contract, not only in achieving economic prosperity but also in affirming people's dignity, encouraging toleration of diverse lifestyles, generating trust in social relations, and vivifying civil society. Boaz's weak handling of the twilight does not destroy the value of his distinction between day and night, nor does it invalidate his argumentation in favor of one over the other. (And it is doubtful that a primer should dwell on the twilight.) Gray pretends that the whole of libertarian thought is a brittle doctrine critically dependent on the absence of twilight. Yet most of libertarian thought—including the writings of Thomas Paine, Thomas Jefferson, Lysander Spooner, Herbert Spencer, Albert Jay Nock, Rothbard, and other utopian liberal rationalist Enlightenment dogmatists—consists of day-versus-night discussions that weather Gray's unrelenting objection, "But there is a twilight!"

Chandran Kukathas comments on Gray's brittleness ploy:

> According to Gray, the content of negative liberty is "*radically* indeterminate." Now if by this he means that we cannot, from a principle enjoining respect for negative liberty, derive a definitive set of entitlements and prohibitions on individual and institutional conduct, he is perfectly correct. But I fail to see why this is a serious objection. Political theory does not end with the assertion of a set of principles; political argument and moral reasoning must still continue; principles have to be interpreted and interpretations have to be defended. Social theory generally is "indeterminate." We should indeed accept Aristotle's wise suggestion that we not look for more precision than a subject will allow. (1992, 105, emphasis in original)

GRAY'S MISREPRESENTATION OF ADAM SMITH

Gray's writings are flawed both in their citation of supporting authorities and in their criticism of opposing authorities. Consider Gray's use of Adam Smith as a supporting authority.

Gray has always paid attention to the effects of commerce and market forces on manners and morals. As early as 1984, he began using Smith's authority in the following way: "In both Adam Smith and the neoconservatives it is suggested that the unregulated market or commercial society tends to produce a sort of mindless hedonism which renders it defenceless against more vital tyrannies" (1984, 131).

Gray's own attitude about the moral consequences of commercial society have flip-flopped. He has written, for example, that "the prejudice that markets promote egoism, while collective procedures facilitate altruism, is, if anything, the reverse of the truth" (1993a, 79). Since 1992, however, his portrayal of market processes as ravagers of cultural bonds and norms of decency has escalated, as shown by quotations already provided. "The market," he insists, scatters communities to the winds, makes "trust frail," "overturns established expectations," and unleashes crime. Gray seeks to protect communities from the "ravages" of the market (1995a, 181).

To support the ravages view, Gray has repeatedly called on Smith's authority (1984, 131; 1995a, 55, 98; 1997, 5). He does so most fully when he quotes *Lectures on Jurisprudence*, in which Smith describes the disadvantages of commercial society. After quoting Smith at length, Gray concludes with the following:

> Most of Smith's latter-day epigones seem nevertheless not to have taken to heart his wise summary and conclusion: "These are the disadvantages of a commercial spirit. The minds of men are contracted and rendered incapable of elevation, education is despised or at least neglected, and heroic spirit is almost utterly extinguished. To remedy these defects would be an object worthy of serious attention." These moral and cultural shortcomings of a commercial society, so vividly captured by one of its seminal theorists, figure less prominently, if at all, in the banal discourse of free market ideology. (1995a, 98)

One cannot deny that libertarian-liberal scholarship has paid insufficient attention to issues of conduct and community in commercial society. But one may fault Gray for his one-sided use of Smith's writings. Smith's discussion of "the influence of commerce on manners"—from which Gray amply quotes—begins as follows: "Whenever commerce is introduced into any country, probity and punctuality always accompany it" (Smith 1978, 538). Smith provides a lengthy account of how frequent dealings and reputation encourage good conduct in commercial society. He rounds out the discussion by declaring:

> Whenever dealings are frequent, a man does not expect to gain so much by

any one contract as by probity and punctuality in the whole, and a prudent dealer, who is sensible of his real interest, would rather chuse to lose what he has a right to than give any ground for suspicion. Every thing of this kind is [as] odious as it is rare. When the greater part of people are merchants they always bring probity and punctuality into fashion, and these therefore are the principal virtues of a commercial nation. (1978, 539)

Only after expressing such optimism does Smith turn to the pessimistic elements, which he prefaces by stating, "There are some inconveniences, however, arising from a commercial spirit." Gray's account begins where Smith's optimism ends. Nowhere does Gray let on that Smith warmly praised commerce for promoting trust and good conduct. (For a discussion of Smith's views on morals and commercial society, see Shearmur and Klein 1999.)

GRAY'S TREATMENT OF HAYEK

As noted, Gray apparently moved toward classical liberalism while in his thirties. But he has always exhibited chameleon-like qualities. Jeremy Shearmur (1997) writes that "some of [Gray's] more recent work contains a fair bit of posturing and playing to the gallery." In his treatment of Hayek, Gray played up conservatism for the *Salisbury Review* in 1983 (reprinted in Gray 1993b). He was more enthusiastic about Hayek's liberalism and antistatism when visiting the Institute for Humane Studies to write his book on Hayek (1984) and when sketching policy agendas for the Institute of Economic Affairs in 1989 and 1992 (reprinted in Gray 1993a). As political opinion shifted away from the market vanguard, and as Gray's prominence as an opinion maker increased, Gray—whether writing for the conservative Centre for Policy Studies or, in recent years, for Green and Labour auditors—anxiously denounced Hayek. Gray now portrays Hayek as a "neo-liberal ideologue" (1995a, 53) and a single-minded exponent of "the impersonal nexus of market exchange" (1993a, 52).

My View of Hayek

Hayek was candid about the ambiguities and incompleteness of his philosophy. He neither pretended to possess nor hoped to find an authoritative body of reasoning that one could claim to be a "rational foundation" for classical liberal positions. He was at ease with the twilight regions and the infinite regress of justification (and of the self; see citations to Hayek in Klein 1999b). What he attempted in *The Constitution of Liberty* was not to give the desirable in law and government policy a definitive characterization, but to give it a fuller, more comprehensive, and more palatable characterization than others with similar sensibilities about the desirable had given it.

Yet, one feature of Hayek's approach does expose him to charges of rationalism: his concept of liberty always accords with his sensibilities about the desirable (desirable, that is, in a society that he imagines to be entertaining his proposals). Maintaining that the desirable always accords with liberty led him into convolutions about liberty being dependent on the absence of coercion by arbitrary acts, which is dependent on the rule of law, which is dependent on a standard of abstractness for rules and principles (see Hayek 1960, esp. 11, 142–44). The result was an arcane, abstract, and often unintelligible notion of liberty.

I prefer to use *liberty* in its Rothbardian sense (see Rothbard 1982)—property, consent, and contract—but I regard liberty merely as a maxim that exhibits the limitations set out earlier. Hayek admitted limitations with respect to ambiguity, incompleteness, and lack of foundation, but he resisted the idea that the desirable sometimes conflicts with liberty. Rothbard also held that the desirable always accords with liberty, but he molded the desirable to fit his idea of liberty, whereas Hayek molded liberty to fit his sensibilities about the desirable. My own approach is Rothbardian in its notion of liberty but Hayekian in its sensibility of desirable reform. Restrictions on the ownership of bazookas, for example, by my and Rothbard's lights, violate liberty, but in given circumstances may, by my but not Rothbard's lights, be desirable. Hayek would perhaps agree on the desirability, but also might see such restrictions as compatible with his notion of liberty.

The flaw in Hayek's *Constitution of Liberty*, however, is not fatal. At bottom, the issues on which Rothbardian and Hayekian judgments about the desirable might disagree, such as the bazooka issue, are not especially important. Rothbard and Hayek basically agree on desirable reform—they are both libertarians—and Hayek's book nicely advances the case for the common agenda.

Hayek's approach was, perhaps, appropriate to his circumstances. Had he taken up the more concrete, Rothbardian maxim of liberty, Hayek's deep anti-statism, acquired from von Mises, would have become more obvious and would have driven away many readers who were indeed moved by Hayek's arguments. Any way of conceptualizing a political philosophy will have similar problems—my preferred conceptualization, which readily admits the identified limitations, not excepted.

In his portrayal of Hayek's thought, Gray has flip-flopped in at least three respects: whether Hayek is a rationalist (Gray said no, then yes), whether Hayek is more a conservative or a libertarian-liberal (Gray has varied, depending on his audience), and whether Hayek's thinking is laudable (Gray said yes, then no).

Hayek a Rationalist?

When we speak of rationalism, we mean the conviction, aspiration, or intention to definitively characterize the desirable, or to give a final (metacultural) "rational" foundation for the desirability of whatever it is that one holds to be desirable. Rationalism is the denial or undue neglect of the limitations I have identified.

In 1981, Gray's article "Hayek on Liberty, Rights and Justice" was published in the academic journal *Ethics* (reprinted in Gray 1989). The article concentrates on the problem already raised, that Hayek set up "liberty" to fit the desirable. In Gray's characterization, Hayek's theory of liberty is "underdetermined": "The conceptual connections which hold between liberty and justice [or, the desirable] thus become, in Hayek's doctrine, relations between mutually constitutive concepts" (1989, 97; see also 91–92). The aligning of liberty with the desirable leads Gray to claim that Hayek's thinking had an element of rationalism: "The main interest of Hayek's work in social and political philosophy lies in his attempt to marry ... the rationalist and the sceptical" (89). Gray notes that Hayek pretends neither to give rational foundation to his characterization of the desirable (90), nor that his vision of the desirable is appropriate (or takes the same forms) for all people (Gray 1989, 94). On the whole, Gray's article is academic and, compared to his other writings, reserved. It shows that Gray has always been preoccupied with points of philosophical form, rather than substance. His article does not deal with Hayek's vast body of rich argumentation for smaller government. It considers only Hayek's characterization of liberty and justice.

In 1983, Gray's article "Hayek as a Conservative" was published in the *Salisbury Review* (reprinted in Gray 1993b). There the portrayal of Hayek is more decisively that of an antirationalist:

> Most distinctive in Hayek's sceptical and Kantian theory of knowledge, however, is his insight that all our theoretical, propositional or explicit knowledge presupposes a vast background of tacit, practical and inarticulate knowledge. Hayek's insight here parallels those of Oakeshott, Ryle, Heidegger, and Polanyi; like them he perceives that the kind of knowledge that can be embodied in theories is not only distinct from, but also at every point dependent upon, another sort of knowledge, embodied in habits and dispositions to act. (Gray 1993b, 34)

We can never know our own minds sufficiently to be able to govern them, since our explicit knowledge is only the visible surface of a vast fund of tacit knowing. Hence the rationalist ideal of the government of the mind by itself is delusive. How much more of a mirage, then, is the ideal of a society of minds that governs itself by the light of conscious reason. The myriad projects of modern rationalism—constructivist rationalism, as Hayek calls it—founder on the awkward fact that conscious reason is not the mother of order in the life of the mind, but rather its humble stepchild. All of the modern radical movements—liberalism after the younger Mill as much as Marxism—are, for Hayek, attempts to achieve the impossible. (Gray 1993b, 35)

Hayek's criticism echoes a distinguished line of antirationalist thinkers. (Gray 1993b, 36)

[Hayek's] chief importance, I think, is that he has freed classical liberalism from the burden of an hubristic rationalism. (Gray 1993a, p. 37)

In Gray's 1984 book on Hayek, the antirationalism is still uppermost (as the quotation from the preface, provided earlier, indicates). Gray does find in Hayek's thought "a conflict between its rationalist and its sceptical aspects" (1984, 139), but he concludes:

None of these revisions compromises the central insights of Hayek's research programme—that social institutions emerge as the unintended consequence of human actions, and are fruitfully to be conceived as vehicles or bearers of tacit social knowledge.... Hayek liberates contemporary inquiry from the dead weight of the superseded intellectual tradition of constructivist rationalism. (Gray 1984, 140; see also 114, 130)

In Gray's later writings, in which Hayek is repudiated, Hayek is suddenly transformed into a rationalist, with no explanation of Gray's change of mind. Gray claims that the liberalism of Hayek (and others) "turns on a conception of rational choice" (1996, 8; see also 1995a, 66). Hayek's treatment of the idea of social justice, earlier praised by Gray as "devastating" (1993a, 36; 1993b, 33), becomes a "rationalistic critique" (1995a, 187 n. 20), but Gray does not elaborate or provide any page reference directing us to the rationalist element in Hayek's writing. As Shearmur has noted, Gray's attitude toward Hayek's social-justice critique "shifts from earlier fulsome praise to condemnation ... without discussion of the respects in which he now thinks Hayek was incorrect." In his 1997 collection, Gray writes of the "crassly rationalistic terms" of "Hayekian theory" (37) and denounces the New Right for being influenced by "classical liberal rationalism, as that has been revised in our time by such thinkers as Popper and Hayek" (6).

HAYEK: CONSERVATIVE, LIBERAL, OR BOTH?

In his 1981 article in *Ethics*, Gray did not dwell on Hayek's ideological affinities; he did declare that "Hayek's writings compose one of the most ambitious efforts at a liberal ideology made this century" (1989, 89), and he characterized Hayek as a liberal (100), not a conservative.

In "Hayek as a Conservative" (*Salisbury Review*, 1983), Gray wrote that Hayek's thought "embodies the best elements of classical liberalism" (1993b, 32; see also 33, 38), but "at the same time it derives from some of the most profound insights of conservative philosophy, and puts them in an original and uncompromising fashion" (1993b, 32).

In his 1984 book on Hayek, Gray again portrayed Hayek as a mixture, but, in this case, he emphasized the classical liberalism. Gray concluded that Hayek "returns thought about man and society to the great tradition of the Scottish Enlightenment, and opens up to us the abandoned road to genuine knowledge of man and of the conditions of his freedom and welfare first laid down by the thinkers of classical liberalism" (1984, 140; see also viii, 114, 130, 139).

Subsequently, Gray's writings became steadily more statist. In "The Moral Foundations of Market Institutions," first published with critical commentaries in 1992 by the Institute of Economic Affairs, Gray cited Hayek approvingly while developing a rather activist policy agenda. At one point Gray suggested the goal of "reduction of state expenditures to around a quarter of national product, as advocated by Hayek" (reprinted in Gray 1993a, 121). Did Hayek actually advocate that government spend a quarter of national product? Gray refers to a page on which Hayek discusses taxation in these words:

> What is needed is a principle that will limit the maximum rate of direct taxation in some relation to the total burden of taxation. The most reasonable rule of the kind would seem to be one that fixed the maximum admissible (marginal) rate of direct taxation at that percentage of the total national income which the government takes in taxation. This would mean that if the government took 25 per cent of the national income, 25 per cent would also be the maximum rate of direct taxation of any part of individual incomes. (Hayek 1960, 323)

Clearly, Hayek was merely illustrating his point about the relationship between marginal and average tax rates with a numerical example, not advocating 25 percent as a desirable rate. Gray misrepresented Hayek, perhaps in an attempt to smooth the transition from his former enthusiasm for Hayekian ideas to his more statist positions.

Soon, however, Gray began to repudiate Hayek's thinking. In the introduction to his 1993 collection *Beyond the New Right*, he wrote that "[in questioning the] dogmas of modernism ... the conservative thinker will find most sustenance in the thought not of Hayek or Popper but of Oakeshott and Polanyi" (1993a, xv; see also xiii). Not long afterward, Gray wrote that "neither of them [Hayek and Popper] belonged to a recognizable tradition of British or European *conservative* thought" (1997, 187 n. 3; Gray's italics). Gray began to refer to "the free market libertarianism of Herbert Spencer and F. A. Hayek" (1997, 74) and "neo-liberal ideologues such as Hayek" (1995a, 55).

Gray charges Hayek with "technological hubris" (1993a, 144) and a devotion to ideas of progress:

The idea of progress reinforces the restless discontent that is one of the diseases of modernity, a disease symptomatically expressed in Hayek's nihilistic and characteristically candid statement that "Progress is movement for movement's sake." No view of human life could be further from either Green thought or genuine conservative philosophy. (Gray 1993a, 139)

"Progress is movement for movement's sake"—a nihilistic remark, we are told without further discussion. (Gray even fails to provide the page reference for the quotation.) Here, from Hayek, is the full context of those six words:

It is knowing what we have not known before that makes us wiser men.

But often it also makes us sadder men. Though progress consists in part in achieving things we have been striving for, this does not mean that we shall like all its results or that all will be gainers. And since our wishes and aims are also subject to change in the course of the process, it is questionable whether the statement has a clear meaning that the new state of affairs that progress creates is a better one. Progress in the sense of the cumulative growth of knowledge and power over nature is a term that says little about whether the new state will give us more satisfaction than the old. The pleasure may be solely in achieving what we have been striving for, and the assured possession may give us little satisfaction. The question whether, if

we had to stop at our present stage of development, we would in any significant sense be better off or happier than if we had stopped a hundred or
a thousand years ago is probably unanswerable.

The answer, however, does not matter. What matters is the successful striving for what at each moment seems attainable. It is not the fruits of past
success but the living in and for the future in which human intelligence
proves itself. Progress is movement for movement's sake, for it is in progress
of learning, and in the effects of having learned something new, that man
enjoys the gift of his intelligence. (Hayek 1960, 41)

Could anyone honestly read this passage as a profession of idealistic faith
in progress? Does Hayek express a nihilistic will to advance progress, even if it
means scattering communities to the winds? (And by the way, in what sense is the
remark quoted by Gray "characteristically candid" of Hayek?)

For his statement that Hayek "seems to subscribe to a doctrine of historical
progress which ... cannot be endorsed by any twentieth-century conservative"
(1993b, 38), Gray provides no documentation. He claims that Hayek "generalizes
from the English experience to put forward a grandiose theory of the spontaneous
emergence of market institutions that is reminiscent in its unhistorical generality
of Herbert Spencer and Karl Marx at their most incautious" (1995a, 40; see also
1998a, 8). One expects a scholar to support such a grand claim with references,
but Gray provides merely a footnote that refers to Hayek's *Fatal Conceit* without
a page reference. He adds that "Hayek's treatment of the emergence of market
institutions in England as paradigmatic is evidenced in many of his earlier works"
(1995a, 186 n. 8), again without providing any reference. Gray would be hard-
pressed to make good on the assertion.

Is Hayekian Thinking Laudable?

In his earlier works, Gray clearly praised and favored Hayek's thought (especially
1984, the reprint in 1993b, and the two IEA publications reprinted in 1993a). But,
as already noted, Gray later repudiated Hayekian thinking. Hayek becomes, in
Gray's prose, emblematic of nasty market forces and the turmoil they generate.
Gray refers to the "Hayekian" privatization in Russia that has yielded "a sort of
anarcho-capitalism of competing mafias" (1995a, 57). He refers to "the wager on
indefinite economic growth and unfettered market forces" as "Hayek's wager"
(1995a, 88). He speaks of the "view of society, explicit in Hayek and before him in

Herbert Spencer, in which it is nothing but a nexus of market exchanges" (1995a, 101). "A society held together solely by the impersonal nexus of market exchanges, as envisaged by Hayek," declares Gray, "is at best a mirage, at worst a prescription for a return to the state of nature" (1993a, 52).

Does Gray attempt to support his new view of Hayek's thought? The only elaboration is a footnote (attached to this last quotation) in which he merely quotes the following words from Hayek: "The only ties which hold together the whole of a Great Society are purely 'economic' " (quoted in Gray 1993a, 180 n. 6). Again we must go to the source, in this case Hayek's *Mirage of Social Justice* (vol. 2 of *Law, Legislation and Liberty*):

> It is the great advantage of the spontaneous order of the market that it is merely means-connected and that, therefore, it makes agreement on ends unnecessary and a reconciliation of divergent purposes possible. What are commonly called economic relations are indeed relations determined by the fact that the use of all means is affected by the striving for those many different purposes. It is in this wide sense of the term "economic" that the interdependence or coherence of the parts of the Great Society is purely economic.

> The suggestion that in this wide sense the only ties which hold the whole of a Great Society together are purely "economic" (more precisely "catallactic") arouse[s] great emotional resistance.... It is of course true that within the overall framework of the Great Society there exist numerous networks of other relations that are in no sense economic. (Hayek 1976, 112)

Hayek was saying that the whole of a great society represents the pursuit of many different purposes. As any Hayek scholar knows, Hayek took pains to prevent the very misrepresentation that Gray perpetrates. Hayek's use of quotation marks around "economic" and his repeated mention of the "wide sense" with which he is using the term speak for themselves. Hayek often pointed out, as in the passage just provided, that all manner of nonmarket social organizations—families, churches, communities, clubs, friendships—coexist and thrive in a great society (see, for example, Hayek 1944, 42; 1948, 23; 1973, 46; 1960, 37; 1988, 37).

Final Remarks about Gray on Hayek

Although he tries to dissociate himself from Hayek, Gray continues to use insights he gained from Hayek. Even as he denounces Hayek, Gray tells us how "theories, at their best, can only remind us how little we know" (1993a, 65). He might have quoted Hayek: "The most important task of science might be to discover ... [the] limits to our knowledge or reason" (Hayek 1988, 62). In announcing that "liberalism is to be regarded as a form of moral and political practice, a species of partisanship" (1989, 100), Gray might again have quoted Hayek: Liberalism's "aim, indeed, is to persuade the majority to observe certain principles" (Hayek 1960, 103-04). Articulating and endorsing Isaiah Berlin's view of man as "inherently unfinished and incomplete, as essentially self-transforming and only partly determinate" (Gray 1996, 9), Gray could have quoted Hayek's statement that "human decisions must always appear as the result of the whole of a human personality ... [that] we cannot reduce to something else" (Hayek 1952, 193). Arguing against "[the construction of] a critical morality, rationally binding on all human beings, and, as a corollary, the creation of a universal civilization" (1995a, 123), Gray could have quoted Hayek:

> Whether a new norm fits into an existing system of norms will not be a problem solely of logic, but will usually be a problem of whether, in the existing factual circumstances, the new norm will lead to an order of compatible actions.... A new norm that logically may seem to be wholly consistent with the already recognized ones may yet prove to be in conflict with them if in some set of circumstances it allows actions which will clash with others permitted by the existing norms. This is the reason why the Cartesian or "geometric" treatment of law as a pure "science of norms," where all rules of law are deduced from explicit premises, is so misleading. (Hayek 1973, 105–6)

If Hayek could comment on Gray, he might echo something Karl Kraus once wrote: "X said disparagingly that nothing would remain of me but a few good jokes. That, at least, would be something, but unfortunately not even that will remain, for the few good jokes were stolen long ago—by X" (Kraus 1990, 45).

PROPHECY AND APOCALYPSE

Gray writes about current affairs with alarm. In the introduction to *Beyond the New Right* (1993a, xv), he states: "By returning to the homely truths of traditional conservatism ... the ever-present prospect of disaster is staved off for another day." In *Endgames* (1997, 140), he writes that our "everyday freedoms to walk the streets without fear as well as democratic freedoms to challenge the increasingly anonymous institutions that rule our lives ... are everywhere at risk." In *False Dawn*, "we stand on the brink [of] a tragic epoch, in which anarchic market forces and shrinking natural resources drag sovereign states into ever more dangerous rivalries" (1998a, 207).

But the peril would be even greater were we to adopt the policies of the "New Right," "the market," and so forth: "Western liberal projects as GATT," for example, "aim to subject all human cultures and communities to the hegemony of unfettered technology and of global market institutions." Such processes "cannot avoid desolating the earth's human settlements and its non-human environments" (1995a, 181). Attempting to construct "a market liberal utopia ... has as its only sure outcome the spawning of atavistic movements that wreak havoc on the historic inheritance of liberal institutions" (1995a, 104). Policies such as open immigration undercut the common culture and must be rejected—"or else Beirut will be the likely fate" (1993a, 59).

Like Schumpeter, Gray believes that market liberalism plants the seeds of its own destruction: "Neo-liberalism itself can now be seen as a self-undermining political project. Its political success depended upon cultural traditions, and constellations of interests, that neo-liberal policy was bound to dissipate" (1995a, 87). In particular, "the political legitimacy of Western capitalist market institutions depends upon incessant economic growth; it is endangered whenever growth falters" (1993a, 152). Don't support the libertarian wing, Gray warns, because it is headed for a crash.

But doomsaying is somewhat self-limiting. To alarm people, one must make *specific* prophecies, and such prophecies are accountable to time. Gray has made some prophecies that he may well hope no one remembers:

> Any prospect of cultural recovery from the nihilism that the Enlightenment has spawned may lie with non-Occidental peoples, whose task will then be in part that of protecting themselves from the debris cast up by Western shipwreck. (1995a, 184)

> The likely result of the GATT agreements, if they are ever implemented, is not only ruin for Third World agriculture, with a billion or more peasants being displaced from the land in the space of a generation or less, but also—as Sir James Goldsmith has warned—class war in the advanced countries as wages fall and the return of offshore capital rises. (1995a, 114)

> In Britain, the Internet culture seems likely to remain as marginal, and perhaps as ephemeral, as that which grew up around manned spaceflight. Already the sites of space missions evoke less interest than those of the Pyr-

amids. Similarly, in much less than a generation, the Internet will provoke stifled yawns rather than passionate controversy. For all its aura of futuristic novelty, the Internet worldview harks back to a culture of technological optimism that—at least in Britain—is irretrievably dated. (1997, 139–40)

The United States, through the initiative of a Congress dominated by the free-market and religious Right, is now engaged in an experiment which is indeed unparalleled in any other country—that of withdrawing government from any responsibility for the welfare of society or the protection of communities and confining its functions to a repressive core having to do with the maintenance of law and order and the inculcation of certain supposedly basic national values. (1997, 111)

Gray claims the United States has "epidemic crime" (1997, 100; 1995a, 97). He writes, "American cities have ceased to be enduring human settlements and are approaching the condition of states of nature" (1997, 112). Meanwhile, the U.S. Bureau of Justice reports that the rate of serious violent crime (rape, robbery, aggravated assault, and homicide) has declined significantly since 1993 and is the lowest it has been in at least twenty-five years.

On the heels of the stock-market crash of the summer of 1998, Gray cranked up his prophecies and his long-practiced ploy of identifying processes that deeply involve state institutions—such as central banks, the International Monetary Fund, and governmental bodies that insure, guarantee, and restrict private lending and investment—as "the free market" or "capitalism":

It is beginning to be accepted that global capitalism is in serious trouble. That has not always been so. When my book *False Dawn* was published this past spring, I expected it to be attacked. I was not disappointed. Most reviewers were incredulous. Some dismissed the claim that the global market was heading for a breakdown as an apocalyptic fantasy. Less than six months after *False Dawn* was published, that claim has been largely vindicated. The regime that a seemingly unshakable consensus took to be permanent has begun to fall apart. Soon, I have no doubt, it will be an irrecoverable memory.

A year or so from now, it will be difficult to find a single person who admits ever having believed that a global free market is a sensible way of running a world economy. (Gray 1998b)

Less than three months after Gray's article appeared, the Dow Jones industrial index had recovered fully and was achieving new highs.

GRAY'S DENIGRATION OF THE UNITED STATES

The United States looms large in Gray's work as the dystopia that Britain and Europe must avoid. He refers to

> a divergence between the United States and Europe—in their economies, their forms of social life and their public cultures—which is deep, growing and very probably irreversible.... Their differences were masked for a generation or more by the common interest they had in defeating Nazism and responding to the perceived danger of Soviet expansionism. In the post-communist period these differences are likely to be increasingly profound. (1997, 110)

"What is needed in Britain," he writes, is "a clear perception of the distinctively European values which we do not share with the Americans" (111). It is common for academics and intellectuals, including those in the United States, to disparage American culture. But Gray seems intent on inciting in Britain a truly invidious attitude toward America:

> The spectacle of American decline, and of America's slow, faltering but inexorable disengagement from Europe, should embolden opinion in all parties in Britain to make the choice it has always so far steadfastly avoided—that between our being an outpost of a fictitious Atlantic civilization and our real destiny as a European nation. (1997, 113)

Robert Skidelsky comments: "Gray's hatred of American capitalism is visceral" (1998, 12).

> Gray's denunciations of the United States may strike one as an effort to foster an inferiority anxiety and a need to proclaim a distinctive British identity. I suspect that Gray has miscalculated the popular effect of his tactic. I suspect that British citizens on the whole do not find their selfhood in distinguishing a national character, to be called theirs, from the supposed national characters of other countries. I suspect that since World War II, and especially since the end of the cold war, the trend in the West has

been away from just that source of selfhood. I think the trend is healthy and something for all liberals to celebrate. Other institutions can serve much better than national identity in creating for people a rich, humane, and becoming sense of self. Westerners increasingly find their selfhood in their relationships with friends, families, lovers, colleagues, clients, and customers, personal rivals and competitors, church communities, chess and bridge and poker partners, softball and bowling mates, e-mail correspondents, and in their work, hobbies, and interests—literature, film, music, television, sports, and so on.

Gray, obviously, is uncomfortable with the trend. He expresses his discomfort this way: "For us, in Britain today, individualism and pluralism are an historical fate. We may reasonably hope to temper this fate, and thereby to make the best of the opportunities it offers us; we cannot hope to escape it" (1995a, 111).

According to Gray, individualism and pluralism are rampant in the United States, eviscerating whatever merit exists in the culture:

The ongoing implosion of the United States, its wild oscillations between cultural introversion and messianic intervention, and its likely slide in coming decades into a kind of Brazilianization, are significant for Europeans, if at all, as evidences of the decline of the American model of unfettered individualism. (1997, 112)

The result [in the United States] has been further social division, including what amounts to a low-intensity civil war between the races. As things stand, the likelihood in the United States is of a slow slide into ungovernability, as the remaining patrimony of a common cultural inheritance is frittered away by the fragmenting forces of multiculturalism. (1995a, 24)

It is hard to guess what Gray means by "individualism." It would not make sense to interpret the term to mean, specifically, libertarian policy. Gray often notes that America has high rates of crime and incarceration (1995a, 97; 1997, 112, 140–43; 1998a, 2, 113, 116–17). But these problems are to a large extent the result of highly unlibertarian policies that define victimless crimes, as Gray has acknowledged (1993a, 53). At present, approximately 20 percent of the state prison population and 60 percent of the federal inmates are incarcerated for drug violations, and drug prohibition generates a significant portion of all violent crime. Many of America's problems, including crime, bad schools, poor housing, and disorder in public places are no doubt caused in part by highly unlibertarian policies.

Misleading claims about the United States abound in Gray's work. Some claims— that over the past two decades the incomes of 80 percent of Americans "have stagnated or fallen" (1998a, 114), that free-market policies prevail in America (1998a, chap. 5), or that an "ideal of minimum government ... animates the Washington consensus" (1998a, 200)—are so preposterous that to refute them would be to rehearse evidence well known to anyone commenting on the issues (for refutation of the poor-getting-poorer claim, see Cox and Alm 1999). Attempting to correct all of Gray's misleading claims about America would require a separate chapter.

I do wish to note, however, in relation to three of Gray's statements, the significance of church participation in the United States. First, Gray portrays America as a place poor in meaningful community institutions, a country careening toward "Brazilianization." (What must Brazilians think about this expression?) Yet church participation is much higher in the United States than in virtually every European country (Iannaccone, Finke, and Stark 1997, 352; Iannaccone 1998, 1487). Gray (1998a, 126–27) acknowledges the vibrancy of America's churches, but cites it only as further evidence of atavistic American fundamentalism. Second, Gray declares that "individualism" and "the market competition" scatter communities to the winds, dissolve social bonds, and so on, but it has been argued that the chief cause of the success of U.S. churches is the complete lack of government intervention or subsidization (Iannaccone, Finke, and Stark 1997; Iannaccone 1998, 1489). Third, Gray disparages American "legalism" and trust in constitutional guarantees (Gray 1997, 21), citing the U.S. Constitution itself as a failed attempt to constrain government (Gray 1993a, 8), yet one robust explanation for the absence of government involvement in American churches is the First Amendment, which mandates a laissez-faire policy for religion (Iannaccone 1998, 1488).

GRAY'S ELITISM

As mentioned previously, Gray maintains that a market-liberal society is self-undermining. The greatest danger, he writes, is allowing policy "to be formed on the tacit supposition that the cultural preconditions of the market can safely be left to look after themselves" (1993a, 64). To sustain individual freedom and civil society, it is not enough that the state affirm and uphold libertarian principles of property, consent, and tort (1993a, 64). Political stability and legitimacy depend on a broad appeal to the polity, a concordance with conceptions of fairness, cultural norms, and established expectations (1995a, 102). Here, as elsewhere, in criticizing libertarian policy, Gray shifts between claiming that it would be undesirable and claiming that it is not politically realistic.[1]

Gray writes about British society as if it were a club with its own peculiar rules: "Entry into civil society in Britain presupposes subscription to its norms.... This common culture may be reinforced by laws and policies which resist pluralism when pluralism threatens the norms of civil society itself" (1993a, 59).

Every club, of course, has its officers and directors. Sustaining the club depends on a class of "guardians of continuity in national life" (1995a, 87). They appreciate the club's multiple values and delicately tend its common culture. Club directors must preserve "our institutional inheritance—that precious and irreplaceable patrimony of mediating structures and autonomous professions" (1995a, 87).

Gray's vision of the club and its guardians leads him to reject pragmatic libertarian policy. He opposes free international trade because the global market "has destroyed the idea of a career or a vocation on which our inherited culture of work was founded" (1997, 123). Regarding drug prohibition, Gray writes: "The siren voices now calling for drug legalization should be resisted by all who seek to preserve what still remains of Britain's inheritance of social cohesion and civilized government" (1997, 133). Regarding transportation policy: "The impact of the car on cities is to destroy them as human settlements in which generations of people live and work together"; hence the need for "the drastic curtailment within cities of the motor car" (1993a, 160). In many areas of public policy, Gray condemns libertarian policies because they upset traditional patterns of the club. In the unfettered market, "status is ephemeral" (1995a, 99).

Although Gray often notes the importance of voluntary mediating institutions, in the end he views the club as the nation and the club directors as government officials. His depiction of the nation-state as "the preeminent political form" (1996, 115) is most fully developed in his characterization of Isaiah Berlin's view of nationalism. Because that characterization conforms with the broad patterns of Gray's thought, and because Gray does not criticize what he conceives to be Berlin's view on the matter, I take Gray's words to represent his own views:

> The essential human unit in which man's nature is fully realized is not the individual, or a voluntary association which can be dissolved or altered or abandoned at will, but the nation; ... it is to the creation and maintenance of the nation that the lives of subordinate units, the family, the tribe, the clan, the province, must be due, for their nature and purpose, what is often called their meaning, are derived from its nature and its purpose; and ... these are revealed not by rational analysis, but by a special awareness, which need not be fully conscious, of the unique relationship that binds individual human beings into the indissoluble and unanalysable organ-

ic whole which Burke identified with society, Rousseau with the people, Hegel with the state, but which for nationalists is, and can only be, the nation, whatever its social structure or form of government. (1996, 105–6)

The book on Berlin is not the only place where Gray affirms politics and government. Elsewhere he writes of "[restoring] the primacy of the political" (1995a, 130), of the British state as "on balance a civilizing institution" (1997, 133), of "[enfranchising] all people as active citizens in a polity to which everyone can profess allegiance" (1993a, 59).

For a pragmatic libertarian such as myself, there are two interpretations of Gray's embrace of government as guardian and shepherd of the national club. One interpretation is that Gray simply does not see the reason to believe the following claims. First, as a basis for community or club identity, the state is severely flawed and inferior to voluntary and local institutions. Second, libertarian principles can be shared and sustained even when—especially when—government remains small (indeed, Gray [1993a, 35] says as much). Third, the need for trust in a large, mobile society is best met by voluntary institutions functioning within a libertarian legal framework (Klein 1997b, 1999a). Fourth, the basis for community and a fabric of life in a large, mobile society is best met by voluntary institutions functioning within a libertarian legal framework. Fifth, from where we stand, the principal reforms needed to advance individual dignity and individual responsibility are libertarian reforms (Klein 1997a). Sixth, neither in Britain nor in the United States is society coming apart at the seams.

Gray should admit these claims, or at least some of them. Because he does not, we are led to suspect that what troubles him is that he sees a world undergoing change, a world that has less and less use for the likes of John Gray. His agenda, at the core, seems to be to preserve the status of an elite governing class, in which he yearns to be a well-regarded and influential member. I take this view because it fits the patterns in Gray's work.

Why, for example, does Gray need to portray the United States in false and exaggerated terms? Because, as he rightly states, "The United States no longer possesses any recognizable common culture or a political class that could speak for such a culture" (1997, 112). Although public policy in America is not becoming more libertarian, the government is floundering badly as the leader of any national club or common culture. (Gray [1998b] writes amusingly of recent events: "The political class in the United States is currently preoccupied with whether serial fellatio constitutes a sexual relationship.") Every day, America becomes less and less a club.

But that development hardly foretells the social collapse that Gray luridly conjures. Gray needs to see an America in moral decay and disarray in order to maintain that society needs a governing class of traditional elites.

JOHN GRAY, IDEOLOGICAL MIGRANT

In his writings since *Beyond the New Right*, save the book on Berlin, Gray has demonstrated a heightened propensity to speak out of both corners of his mouth. At one point he condemns a policy or its supporters, but elsewhere those who oppose the policy. Discerning Gray's position becomes an exercise in weighing abuses. Shearmur (1997) has commented: "One of the strange features of Gray's writings is that he frequently offers us criticisms of various positions which he himself seems to have held until fairly recently, but which are then characterized in the most pejorative of terms, and as if only a fool or a knave could hold them." In a review of *False Dawn*, Skidelsky remarks on Gray's migration patterns:

> Gray's intellectual gyrations have become legendary. I am told he was a socialist in the 1970s. He was a Thatcherite in the 1980s. (The Iron Lady once said to me: "What ever happened to John Gray? He used to be one of us.") Then he adopted the fashionable communitarianism. Judging from his latest book, he is what Marx would have called a "Reactionist"—with hope extinguished, but with a lively apprehension of disaster. He plays each role with passion and panache. But with so much here today, gone tomorrow, it is hard to know how seriously to take his arguments. (1998, 11)

Gray is one of the more notable instances of an intellectual who has migrated away from classical liberalism. There is a certain notoriety in ideological migration. The back cover of *Beyond the New Right* (1993a) notes that Gray had been closely associated with the "New Right" but now he offers "a criticism of the ideological excesses of the New Right ideology and a radical critique of the New Right itself." The back cover of *Enlightenment's Wake* (1995a) says the book "stakes out the elements of John Gray's new position." The back cover of the second edition (1995b) of *Liberalism* notes that since the first edition (1986) "the author's views have changed significantly." The dust jacket of False Dawn (1998a) declares, "John Gray, a former supporter of the New Right, believes...."

Ideological migrants are special and important cases. The intellectual shifts found in the work of ideological migrants can offer special insights into contending perspectives in public philosophy. To profitably examine an individual instance of ideological migration, it is important to gain an appreciation of the overall character of the person and his thought.

LIBERTARIANISM DOUBLY CURSED

Libertarianism does not stipulate that the levers of positive government power should be used in this way or that. Basically, it maintains that the levers shouldn't exist. Meanwhile, power influences public discourse by virtue of its being power. Governments control broadcast licenses and run schools, universities, radio programs, and the postal system. Government officials speak to journalists, who rely on their cooperation for news. Government makes news. It employs tens of millions in the United States and spends about 40 percent of national income. It taxes and regulates all, and, to varying extents, it subsidizes everyone. Anyone aspiring to eminence in polite society knows he had better not laugh out loud at conventional ideas about government. Anyone seeking invitations to sit and talk with power ought to avoid libertarian associations and rid himself of any cause for suspicion.

Libertarianism is a reform agenda cursed also by its own strength. The extent to which sensible libertarians regard the liberty maxim as well defined, widely applicable, and widely desirable is much greater than the extent to which those in other ideological camps regard their leading maxims as well defined, widely applicable, and widely desirable. In a sense, it is a curse to be the most in anything, because it arouses accusations of being entire. The cogency of the liberty maxim in the libertarian's mind often leads others to think that he regards it as an axiom that is always clearly defined, everywhere applicable, and always desirable. Critics such as Gray condemn libertarianism for pretending to possess airtight definitions, absolutes, and foundations, and therefore they attempt to dispose of libertarianism on formalistic grounds rather than engaging the substantive arguments offered for the reform agenda.

Libertarians might deter slights and hectoring by emphasizing the limitations of the liberty maxim and expressing its virtues in comparative terms.

NOTE

1 For instances, see Gray 1993a, 6, 10, 25, 51, 63, 115. Chandran Kukathas (1992, 113) comments: "One of the reasons for [Gray's] rejection of classical liberalism, I suspect, is that he sees such a philosophy as having no capacity to play a practical role in the real world of politics."

REFERENCES

Boaz, David. 1997. *Libertarianism: A Primer.* New York: Free Press.
Cox, W. Michael, and Richard G. Alm. 1999. *The Myth of Rich and Poor.* New York: Basic Books.
Gray, John. 1983. *Mill on Liberty: A Defence.* London: Routledge and Kegan Paul.
———. 1984. *Hayek on Liberty.* Oxford: Blackwell.

———. 1989. *Liberalisms: Essays in Political Philosophy.* London: Routledge.

———. 1993a. *Beyond the New Right: Markets, Government and the Common Environment.* London: Routledge.

———. 1993b. *Post-liberalism: Studies in Political Thought.* London: Routledge.

———. 1995a. Enlightenment's Wake: Politics and Culture at the Close of the Modern Age. London: Routledge.

———. 1995b. *Liberalism.* 2d ed. Minneapolis: University of Minnesota Press.

———. 1996. *Isaiah Berlin.* Princeton, N.J.: Princeton University Press.

———. 1997. *Endgames: Questions in Late Modern Political Thought.* Cambridge: Polity Press.

———. 1998a. *False Dawn: The Delusions of Global Capitalism.* London: Granta.

———. 1998b. Not for the First Time, World Sours on Free Markets. *Nation,* October 19.

Hayek, Friedrich A. 1944. *The Road to Serfdom.* Chicago: University of Chicago Press.

———. 1948. *Individualism and Economic Order.* Chicago: University of Chicago Press.

———. 1952. *The Sensory Order: An Inquiry into the Foundations of Theoretical Psychology.* Chicago: University of Chicago Press.

———. 1960. *The Constitution of Liberty.* Chicago: University of Chicago Press.

———. 1973. *Law, Legislation and Liberty.* Vol. 1, *Rules and Order.* Chicago: University of Chicago Press.

———. 1976. *Law, Legislation and Liberty.* Vol. 2, *The Mirage of Social Justice.* Chicago: University of Chicago Press.

———. 1988. *The Fatal Conceit: The Errors of Socialism.* Chicago: University of Chicago Press.

Iannaccone, Laurence R. 1998. Introduction to the Economics of Religion. *Journal of Economic Literature* 36 (September): 1465–96.

Iannaccone, Laurence R., Roger Finke, and Rodney Stark. 1997. Deregulating Religion: The Economics of Church and State. *Economic Inquiry* 35 (April): 350–64.

Klein, Daniel B. 1997a. Liberty, Dignity, and Responsibility: The Moral Triad of a Good Society. *The Independent Review* 1 (Winter): 325–51.

———, ed. 1997b. *Reputation: Studies in the Voluntary Elicitation of Good Conduct.* Ann Arbor: University of Michigan Press.

———. 1999a. *Assurance and Trust in a Great Society.* FEE Occasional Paper no. 2. Irvington, N.Y.: Foundation for Economic Education.

———. 1999b. Discovery and the Deepself. *Review of Austrian Economics* 11:47–76.

Kraus, Karl. 1990. *Half-Truths and One-and-a-Half Truths.* Edited by Harry Zohn. Chicago: University of Chicago Press.

Kukathas, Chandran. 1992. Freedom versus Autonomy. A commentary on (and printed with) *The Moral Foundations of Market Institutions,* by John Gray. London: Institute of Economic Affairs.

Rothbard, Murray N. 1982. *The Ethics of Liberty.* Atlantic Highlands, N.J.: Humanities Press.

Shearmur, Jeremy. 1997. Gray's Progress. Manuscript, Department of Political Science, Australian National University.

Shearmur, Jeremy, and Daniel B. Klein. 1999. Good Conduct in a Great Society: Adam Smith and the Role of Reputation. Reprinted in Klein, Daniel B. 1999. *Assurance and Trust in a Great Society.* FEE Occasional Paper no. 2. Irvington, N.Y.: Foundation for Economic Education.

Skidelsky, Robert. 1998. What's Wrong with Global Capitalism? *Times Literary Supplement* no. 4956 (March 27): 11–12.

Smith, Adam. 1978. *Lectures on Jurisprudence.* Edited by R. L. Meek, D. D. Raphael, and P. G. Stein. New York: Oxford University Press.

Acknowledgments: Reprinted from *The Independent Review,* 4, no. 1 (Summer 1999), pp. 63–89. Copyright © 1999.

19

An Original Omission?
Property in Rawls's Political Thought
Quentin P. Taylor

John Rawls has been hailed recently as "the most distinguished political philosopher" of the twentieth century (Nussbaum 1999, 424). In large part, this accolade is based on the Harvard philosopher's *originality* as a political thinker. Rawls's *Theory of Justice* ([1971] 1999) single-handedly revived the tradition of "grand theory" at a time when political philosophy as a constructive, creative enterprise was widely viewed as "dead in the water." Moreover, Rawls provided a sophisticated and novel account of *justice* that captured the imagination of an entire generation of scholars and students. Indeed, no single work has had a wider impact or greater influence on formal political thinking over the past thirty years than *A Theory of Justice*. As a result, Rawls's leading tenets—"justice as fairness," "the difference principle," "fair equality of opportunity," "equal basic liberties," "the original position," "the veil of ignorance"—have become permanent fixtures in the lexicon of academic political discourse. Like many of his famous predecessors in the field of political speculation, Rawls owes his notoriety as much to his critics as to his admirers. On sheer volume alone, the critical responses to *A Theory of Justice* suggest that its author had something important, provocative, and original to say. An inventory of these responses confirms this suspicion because no thinker of common metal could have generated the heated, voluminous, and sustained outpouring of debate that has surrounded Rawls's chief work. Agree or disagree with its teaching, *A Theory of Justice* has attained the status of a political classic, an honor that rests in large part on the originality of its author's philosophical achievement.

Although studies of Rawls continue apace, the leading tenets of *Theory* have received serious, sustained, and comprehensive examination. I am not claiming that nothing remains to be said, for by definition a classic provides an inexhaustible supply of grist for the mill. On the whole, however, it is questionable that another critique of the "original position," the "difference principle," and so forth will yield much of scholarly interest or value. In fact, the better-known and more original of Rawls's doctrines have been scrutinized ad nauseam, and further inquiry along conventional lines runs the risk of irrelevance and redundancy.

One original feature of *Theory*, however, has escaped the notice of readers for the most part—namely, that Rawls's theory of justice "leaves open the question whether its principles are best realized by some form of property-owning democracy or by a liberal socialist regime" ([1971] 1999, xv). "Justice as fairness" theory does not entail the determination of specific economic arrangements or even take up the matter of ownership of the means of production (242).

At first glance, this omission may appear unimportant. Why should the status of property relations necessarily be part of a theory of justice? Is it not possible—indeed, reasonable—to assume that justice is compatible with either a capitalist economy or a socialist economy? This position, which Rawls takes, deserves more scrutiny than it has received. Perhaps he is perfectly justified in excluding property relations from his account of "justice as fairness," but given the importance of property in the history of political philosophy, the exclusion cries out for an explanation. At the least, it would seem apposite to provide a rationale for leaving this important question open-ended. We may then consider whether this rationale is internally consistent with Rawls's principles of justice. Finally, we may ask if a theory of justice that fails to deal with the vital issue of property relations qualifies as a political philosophy in the comprehensive sense.

RAWLS'S BASIC VIEW OF PROPERTY RELATIONS

In the first chapter of *Theory*, Rawls asserts that the topic of his book "is ... social justice." He then provides a summary of that subject:

> For us the primary subject of justice is the basic structure of society, or more exactly, the way in which the major social institutions distribute fundamental rights and duties and determine the division of advantages from social cooperation. By major institutions I understand the political constitution and the principal economic and social arrangements. Thus the legal protection of freedom of thought and liberty of conscience, competitive markets, private property in the means of production, and the monogamous family are examples of major social institutions. Taken together as one scheme, the major institutions define men's rights and duties and influence their life prospects.... The basic structure is the primary subject of justice because its effects are so profound and present from the start. ([1971] 1999, 6–7)

From Rawls's summary we learn that "justice" involves political *as well as* economic arrangements and that "private property in the means of production" exemplifies a major social institution. We learn also that economic arrangements are part of the "basic structure" of society and fall under the subject of justice owing to their "profound" impact on people's lives. The notion that "[t]he primary subject of the principles of justice is the basic structure of society" (47) is repeated throughout *Theory*, therefore creating the impression that the determination of economic arrangements (including property relations) constitutes a vital and necessary component of justice. This impression is strengthened by the fact that Rawls invariably links "the arrangement of major social institutions" to the basic structure, or the "primary subject of justice." "Our concern," he writes, "is solely with the basic structure of society and its major institutions and therefore with the standard cases of social justice" (50).

Such statements appear to indicate clearly that "justice as fairness" will include, at the very least, a consideration of the merits of basic economic arrangements. Insofar as the principles of justice will "regulate the choice of a political constitution *and* the main elements of the economic and social system" (7, emphasis added), we may reasonably expect Rawls to specify the relation between justice and the "main elements" (that is, the property relations) of economic arrangements. The expectation is piqued by the first formulation of Rawls's "two principles of justice." The first principle states that "each person is to have an equal right to the most extensive scheme of equal basic liberties compatible with a similar scheme of liberties for others" (53). Among the basic liberties, Rawls includes "the right to hold personal property," a right he justifies on the basis of individual autonomy and integrity. The second principle pertains to economic issues more directly: "social and economic inequalities are to be arranged so that they are both (a) reasonably expected to be to everyone's advantage, and (b) attached to positions and offices open to all" (53). Implicit in this principle is the toleration of economic *inequality*, the condition in which some persons possess more wealth and income than others. As long as such inequalities are mutually advantageous and do not involve exclusion from any remunerative position, they are consistent with "justice as fairness."

At this point in the argument, one may suspect that Rawls is providing a rationale for the inequalities that exist in capitalist democracies. His critics on the left often read him in this way. The reader need only turn the page, however, to discover that Rawls, though unequivocally committed to democracy, is by no means committed to capitalism. As noted earlier, he includes "the right to hold personal property" under the basic liberties but excludes "the right to own certain kinds of property (e.g., means of production) and freedom of contract as understood by the doctrine of laissez-faire" (54). For Rawls, such rights "are not basic; and so they are not protected by the priority of the first principle [of justice]" (54). The exclusion of property rights beyond personal items from the list of basic liberties raises a number of important questions. If such rights are not basic to liberty, what *is* their relation to liberty, if any? Is there *any* right to property beyond personal holdings? If so, what is the basis of this right, and how may it be justified? If no such right exists, does this lack imply that justice requires public ownership of the means of production? If so, how far may the right of *personal* ownership extend before it encroaches on the right of *public* ownership? Furthermore, on what basis does the "right" of public ownership stand? Rawls does provide something like answers to these questions in the form of the "difference principle" (the second principle of justice), but for the moment let us defer consideration of this controversial aspect of his thought.

PROPERTY RELATIONS AND ECONOMIC EQUALITY

The assertion that private ownership beyond personal property is not a basic liberty is a red flag for readers who suspect Rawls is "privileging" capitalism. Indeed, any hopes (or fears) that Rawls aims to defend private ownership *tout court* are immediately dashed by his "general conception of justice," which states that "[a]ll social values," including "income and wealth," "are to be distributed equally," but he completes the sentence with a caveat: "unless an unequal distribution ... is to everyone's advantage" (54). As we shall see, this qualification is a crucial (perhaps *the* crucial) element in his theory of justice. Significant in the present context, however, is that the initial presumption rests on the side of an *equal* distribution of wealth and income. Only the *in*equality thereof (however slight) requires justification, a position that places Rawls firmly in the *socialist* camp of political thinkers. This characterization is confirmed later in *Theory*, where he argues that an equal distribution of "primary goods" (including wealth and income) is not only "reasonable," but self-evident: "Since it is not reasonable for him [the hypothetical person or an unbiased person] to expect more than an equal share in the division of social primary goods, and since it is not rational for him to agree to less, the sensible thing is to acknowledge as the first step a principle of justice requiring an equal distribution. Indeed, this principle is so obvious given the symmetry of the parties that it would occur to everyone immediately" (130).

Here Rawls is describing the reasoning process that takes place in the "original position," a hypothetical scenario in which the parties aim to reach a consensus on the first principles of justice. To ensure that the choice of principles is not influenced by bias or morally irrelevant factors, persons in the "initial situation" have no knowledge of their social circumstances, natural endowments, or life chances. Rawls argues that it would be *rational* for the parties operating behind this "veil of ignorance" to agree to an equal distribution of everything of basic value, including material goods. Such a distribution presumably would constitute justice par excellence, for the veil of ignorance eliminates all those "factors which are so arbitrary from a moral point of view" (63) and permits the parties to choose those (egalitarian) principles most consistent with the principle of fairness. Why, then, does Rawls reject this solution to the problem of distributive justice? What could possibly justify a deviation from an unbiased, rational, and unanimous decision to divide shares equally?

As noted earlier, Rawls states that inequalities of wealth and income are defensible only when they are to everyone's advantage. This condition is the famous "difference principle" that has attracted so much attention among students of *Theory.* The difference principle is based on three basic assumptions. First, the leading principle of justice (equal basic liberties) is prior in that it is never justifiable to sacrifice basic liberties in exchange for greater economic advantages. Second, parties in the original position "normally prefer more primary social goods rather than less," and "it is rational" to do so (123). Finally, the difference principle assumes that everyone (including the least fortunate) will be better off if economic institutions are arranged on the basis of "efficiency" (57), including "a division of a labor" (244). With these assumptions in place, Rawls can abandon the economic equality that seems so "reasonable" to parties in the original position because it is presumably *more* reasonable to procure additional social goods even when those goods are divided unequally. The special conditions attached to economic inequality make the difference principle even more "attractive" to the least fortunate because inequalities are justified only when they are "to everyone's advantage" and where no formal barriers obstruct positions of monetary gain ("fair equality of opportunity"). Given these assumptions and safeguards, Rawls argues that parties in the original position would opt unanimously for the difference principle as a pillar of justice.

Whatever the merit of this argument, Rawls makes clear that the integrity of the difference principle does not depend on specific economic arrangements or property relations. He does assume, however, "that the economy is roughly a free market system, although the means of production may or may not be privately owned" (57). Although the notion that a "free market system" is equally compatible with either capitalist or socialist property relations may sound odd, it presents no real difficulty for Rawls. In fact, he takes far greater pains to defend against egalitarian attacks on the difference principle than to justify his glib neutrality with respect to the issue of private versus public ownership. After outlining the difference principle, Rawls observes that although his "liberal conception seems clearly preferable to the system of natural liberty, intuitively it still appears defective" (63–64) because "it still permits the distribution of wealth and income to be determined by the natural distribution of abilities and talents.... [D]istributive shares are decided by the outcome of the natural lottery; and this outcome is arbitrary from a moral perspective" (64).

The idea that injustice exists if persons of greater abilities and talents procure a greater share of wealth and income will appear peculiar to many. May we accurately or reasonably characterize this state of affairs as "arbitrary from a moral perspective," even with the difference principle in place? Strictly speaking, according to Rawls we may, for "[t]here is no more reason to permit the distribution of income and wealth to be settled by the distribution of natural assets than by historical and social fortune" (64). Unfortunately, it is impossible to secure equal chances for the acquisition of equal goods, "at least as long as some form of the family exists." In lieu of perfect "fair equality of opportunity," Rawls looks to the difference principle as the "best choice" among the alternatives he considers. In this sense, the difference principle represents a "second-best" solution to the problem of justice (247), an imperfect approximation of the ideal, similar in spirit to Plato's "second-best" state in *The Laws*. And just as Plato clung to the ideal of the *Republic*, Rawls remains attached to the justice of economic equality because "unless there is a distribution that makes both persons [i.e., the less and more fortunate] better off ... an equal distribution is to be preferred" (65–66).

The foregoing discussion suggests that economic equality has a *moral priority* for Rawls. He never attempts to defend it, but he assumes that on the whole it is more just to distribute wealth and income equally than to permit inequalities that do not benefit the least advantaged. As we have seen, Rawls goes to notable lengths to defend inequality—one might fairly describe his efforts as an apologia. Still, for him, inequality is regrettable and unfair insofar as it results from life's "natural lottery." By implication, then, *nature itself* is unfair because it distributes talents and abilities unevenly, thus giving some persons an undue advantage that is totally "undeserved" (86). Even so, Rawls hopes to show how inequality can be made legitimate, much in the manner that Jean-Jacques Rousseau believed he could show the legitimacy of man's social "chains." Yet not even Rousseau (or for that matter any of the classical political philosophers) believed that doing so required overturning "the arbitrariness found in nature" (88).

CAPITALIST VERSUS SOCIALIST PROPERTY RELATIONS

For the first half of *Theory*, Rawls ignores almost completely the question of property relations. He does assume the presence of a free market or "competitive economy" (137), but he expresses no concern as to whether the ownership of the means of production is public or private. Only near the middle of *Theory* does he consider this question in a sustained manner. At the beginning of the chapter titled "Distributive Shares," Rawls reiterates that "the choice between a private-property owning economy and socialism is left open; from the standpoint of justice alone, various basic structures would appear to satisfy its principles" (228). In itself, Rawls's neutrality on economic systems seems consistent with his difference principle. Difficulties would arise, however, if one system can produce greater economic advantages than another for all persons. Moreover, what if inequalities in the more prosperous society are not to everyone's benefit, but the least fortunate are still better off than in the society where the difference principle prevails? Rawls considers neither question directly, but his theory of distributive justice would seem to require an answer. Instead, he simply leaves the determination of economic arrangements to individual circumstances; it is a matter "best left to the course of events to decide" (230).

Those committed to a market or a socialist or a mixed economy will find Rawls's lack of interest in this question alarming. If "justice as fairness" establishes equal basic liberties once and for all, regardless of social or cultural conditions, should it not establish something more definitive about the economic institutions that have such a "profound" impact on people's lives? Rawls repeatedly observes that economic arrangements are part of the basic structure, which is the "primary subject of justice" (82). Why then should the decision be left to "circumstances, institutions, and historical traditions" (248)? Might not the same be said with regard to *political* rights and liberties? Why, for example, are political rights non-contingent and absolute, on the one hand, but property relations contingent and relative, on the other?

Rawls appears to have a fourfold response. First, he claims *agnosticism*: "There is presumably no answer to this question" of private versus public ownership of the economy (242). Second, he pleads *ignorance*: "The theory of justice does not include these matters" (242). Third, he invokes *historicism*: the choice of economic arrangements "depends in large part upon the traditions, institutions, and social forces of each country, and its particular historical circumstances" (242). Finally, Rawls argues that a socialist economy is *consistent* with free-market principles and is potentially as productive as a capitalist system. As for the last of these points, the philosopher-cum-economist assures his readers that "there is no essential tie between the use of free markets and private ownership of the instruments of production" (239); on the contrary, he maintains, there is a basic "consistency of market arrangements with socialist institutions" (241). Moreover, inasmuch as "socialist systems normally allow for the free choice of occupation and of one's place of work" (239), they do not violate the first principles of justice. Indeed, "it is clear that, in theory anyway, a liberal socialist regime can also answer to the two principles of justice. We have only to suppose that the means of production are publicly owned and that firms are managed by workers' councils say, or by agents appointed by them" (248). (Just how worker-managed firms meet the requirements of equal basic liberties and the difference principle is unclear, however.) Accordingly, because a socialist regime can embody "justice as fairness" as well as a capitalist system, "[t]he theory of justice does not by itself favor either form of regime" (248). The question of private, public, or mixed ownership of land, farms, businesses, industry, and natural resources is not one of principle, but one of practice. It is a matter for "political judgment," a question of "which variation is most likely to work out best in practice" (242).

On the surface, Rawls's "response" to the proponents of market, socialist, or mixed economic systems appears reasonable and complete. As long as the two principles of justice are satisfied, each society should be free to work out its economic destiny in accordance with its particular circumstances. Considerations of justice will play a "necessary part" in the process, but "justice as fairness" does not provide a "sufficient" basis for selecting any particular set of economic arrangements (242). Of course, Rawls can define justice or limit its scope in any manner he chooses. Still, in taking the question of economic arrangements off the table, does he not truncate his conception of justice, which takes the "basic structure" (including economic arrangements) as the "primary subject of justice"? His answer to this objection is that economic policy (including property relations) is a second-order question left to the determination of the "constitutional" or "legislative" stages of social formation. Here (and not at the initial stage of deliberation) is where persons "ascertain how the principles of justice apply" to economic arrangements (229). Yet by Rawls's own account, such principles will be largely *relative* insofar as they depend on the "traditions, institutions, and social forces of each country" (242). And what if these traditions do not honor the difference principle, or if the existing institutions exhibit pervasive inequalities yet enjoy widespread support, or if existing social forces oppose Rawlsian policies of economic justice? Is a society then simply "unjust" in spite of itself? One further caveat: If in the "original position" Rawls is willing to settle the matter of distributive justice (equal shares), why should he be unwilling to do so once the "veil of ignorance" is removed? He is not necessarily required to give a *definitive* answer to the question of public, private, or mixed ownership, of course, but ignoring it altogether leaves a curious gap in his political philosophy.

That Rawls himself was not entirely satisfied with this lacuna is suggested in the preface he added to *Theory* in 1999, where he observes that in hindsight he would have "distinguish[ed] more sharply the idea of a property-owning democracy ... from the idea of a welfare state" (xiv). The need to underscore this distinction presumably stems from the common (mis)conception that Rawls was advancing an argument for the modern welfare state. Given his call for a "social minimum," progressive taxation, reallocation of resources, and other features commonly associated with welfarism, it is not difficult to see how readers arrived at this conclusion. Yet Rawls insists that the model he advanced in *Theory* was not the welfare state, which permits unjustifiable inequalities in exchange for a social minimum, but an "ideal property-owning system" (242), which satisfies the two principles of justice. A careful reading of sections 41–43 makes this distinction apparent if not entirely clear (hence the proposed "revision" mentioned in the preface). First, Rawls eschews the phrase "welfare economics" because of its association with utilitarianism (228–29), which he explicitly rejects as a philosophical framework for working out his theory of justice. Next, he argues that neither a capitalist nor a socialist system is, ceteris paribus, more consistent with the principles of justice than the other. (He does go to great lengths, however, to prove that, "theoretically at least, a socialist regime can avail itself of the advantages of this [free-market] system" [240].) Finally, he provides a sketch of an "ideal scheme" of economic arrangements for a "property-owning democracy" (242). Again, lest it be thought that he is "privileging" capitalism in selecting this model, he hastens to add that his choice of schemes springs simply from the fact that "this case is likely to be better known": it is not, however, "intended to prejudge the choice of regimes in particular cases" (242).

Although this disclaimer would appear sufficient, Rawls seeks to distance himself further from capitalist societies and their "grave injustices." Just because we can imagine "an ideal property-owning system that would be just does not imply that historical forms are just, or even tolerable" (242). Rawls admits that "the same is true of socialism" (242), but he is far more concerned (here and elsewhere) with disavowing any preference for capitalism than with distancing himself from socialism. As we have seen, Rawls provides a spirited defense of socialism as a viable economic system. In his originalist defense of "equal shares," his a priori belief that political liberty is fully consistent with public ownership of the means of production, and his implicit attack on the "grave injustices" of capitalist societies, he seems to express a tacit preference for socialism, "in theory anyway."

RAWLS'S "IDEAL" ECONOMIC DEMOCRACY

The principal difference between a welfare state and a property-owning democracy is that the latter ensures "the widespread ownership of productive assets and human capital (educated abilities and trained skills)" (xv). More specifically,

> basic institutions must from the outset put in the hands of citizens generally, and not only of a few, the productive means to be fully cooperating members of a society. The emphasis falls on the steady dispersal over time of the ownership of capital and resources by the laws of inheritance and bequest, on fair equality of opportunity secured by provisions for education and training, and the like, as well as on institutions that support the fair value of the political liberties.... [The purpose of such arrangements is to] put all citizens in a position to manage their own affairs and to take part in social cooperation on a footing of mutual respect and under appropriately equal conditions. (xv)

Whatever else may be said of Rawls's "ideal" democracy, he is certainly correct in distinguishing it from the welfare state. In *Theory,* Rawls provides a few details regarding property rights, the regulation of business, taxation, education, and welfare. Here, too, the aims are to "prevent concentrations of power" and to "encourage the wide dispersal of property" (245). Indeed, only by "gradually and continually ... correct[ing] the distribution of wealth" is it possible to ensure "the fair value of political liberty and fair equality of opportunity" (245). I have yet to discuss these terms, but they are central to Rawls's theory of justice and contribute substantially to its novelty. By adding *fair* to these familiar concepts, Rawls aims to give political liberty and equality of opportunity a greater substantive (as opposed to a merely formal) value. Although he is characteristically short on specifics, by fair he means something more than the mere absence of legal discrimination or arbitrary barriers to positions and offices. Just what this condition would mean in practice, however, is unclear.

What is clear is that Rawls believes that "fairness" is not possible in a society that fails to institute the widespread (re)distribution of wealth and income. He might well have specified (if only approximately) how wide the "dispersal" of capital and resources must be in order to qualify as *fair* or *just*. His failure to do so raises an important question. Would considerations of efficiency limit the degree of economic decentralization, or would "fairness" considerations trump efficiency? The same might be asked with regard to taxation-cum-redistribution policies. In any event, Rawls clearly suggests that the concentration of economic power would be a perennial problem *even under ideal arrangements*. As noted earlier, policy makers would be required "gradually and *continually* to correct the distribution of wealth and to prevent concentrations of power" (245, emphasis added). The implication is that the concentration of wealth is "natural" in a capitalist economy, even when the means of production are widely dispersed. A further implication is that the widespread dispersal of the means of production would be notably inefficient. If so, would it be necessary for the Rawlsian state to subsidize inefficient or noncompetitive firms in the interest of maintaining economic pluralism and the "fairness" it serves?

Just how the economic arrangements of Rawls's "ideal" democracy would affect the principles of efficiency, productivity, innovation, and incentive is not immediately clear, but one need not be an economist to suspect a negative result for each. More important, Rawls shows no signs of recognizing this prospect, which perhaps is not surprising in light of his faith in the efficacy of market socialism. Perhaps he simply is willing to sacrifice efficiency, productivity, and so forth in the interest of his "strongly egalitarian" (65) conception of justice. This reading would be consistent with Rawls's belief that in choosing between economic systems, "[c]onsiderations of efficiency are but one basis of decision and often relatively minor at that" (229). Because the decision "involves some view of the human good," it "must ... be made on moral and political as well as on economic grounds" (229). This position is certainly reasonable and fully consistent with his view that justice has a priority over efficiency, just as liberties have a privilege above economic advantages. Nevertheless, it is reasonable to ask: To what degree should efficiency be sacrificed in the name of justice? Is there not a point at which a disregard for efficiency in the name of fairness encroaches on justice itself? Rawls does not consider this possibility, but it is curious that although minimizing the importance of efficiency when raising the question of choice of economic systems, he proceeds to defend the market system on the basis of its "efficiency" (240).

The reader concerned about the status of property rights in *Theory* may presume that in Rawls's "property-owning democracy"—where "private ownership of capital and natural resources" is admitted (243)—individual property rights are secure. Such, however, does not appear to be the case. In discussing the "allocation branch" (one of five proposed governmental "background institutions"—the others are the "stabilization," "transfer," "distribution," and "exchange" branches), Rawls notes that one of its chief functions is to effect "changes in the definition of property rights" (244). Ironically, the purpose of such changes (along with affecting "reasonably full employment," the task of the "stabilization" branch) is "to maintain the efficiency of the market economy generally" (244). Similarly, Rawls proposes "necessary adjustments in the rights of property" in order to "preserve an approximate justice in distributive shares" (245), the task of the "distribution" branch. (The "transfer" branch is charged with maintaining a "social minimum," and the "exchange" branch considers measures outside the scope of justice.)

Even in Rawls's "property-owning democracy," then, private-property rights (outside of "personal property") clearly are *not* secure. The heavy tax rates Rawls proposes on inheritance and income apparently suffice to ensure a distribution of wealth consistent with the "fair value" of liberty and opportunity demanded by "justice" (246–47). Property itself is made subject to redistribution whenever its accumulation is perceived to violate the canons of "fairness," but Rawls (conveniently) leaves unstated precisely how such a determination would be made. More to the point, the prospect that property rights in the means of production will be subject to continual "adjustments" strongly suggests that they are not "rights" at all—at least not in the conventional sense. Furthermore, the practical consequences of this conception of property appear disturbing at best and disastrous at worst. A government authorized to "redefine" and "readjust" property relations in the ways Rawls suggests (for example, through redistribution of privately owned capital and natural resources) is ill-suited to gain the confidence of those whose fortunes are tied to private enterprise (owners *and* workers), much less to encourage an entrepreneurial spirit. The insecurity of property rights and the shadowy nature of property relations under Rawls's scheme would more likely create a climate of uncertainty, distrust, and complacency. In lieu of clearly defined property rights and stable relations in property, individuals would have little incentive to behave in a manner consistent with the principles of efficiency, productivity, and innovation. Unless Rawls envisages a relatively stagnant economy in which productive capacities are held in check by heavy taxes and the threat of expropriation, his provisions for a "*property-owning* democracy" are likely to be self-defeating. Indeed, given these provisions, is he not misleading readers in calling his scheme a property-owning democracy? Insofar as Rawls's model aspires to a condition of economic equality through the "steady dispersal" of collective assets over time, should it not be more accurately characterized as a species of *socialism?*

A COMPLETE POLITICAL THEORY?

Having surveyed Rawls's remarks on property and economic systems, we are now in a position to consider whether the teaching in *Theory* constitutes a political philosophy in the comprehensive sense. Before doing so, however, it may be advisable to consult Rawls's other major treatise, *Political Liberalism* (1993). Because this book restricts itself to a "political conception of justice" (as opposed to the comprehensive moral doctrine articulated in *Theory*), we might expect that property relations (and economic arrangements generally) will receive more substantial and definitive treatment there. This expectation is disappointed, however. We find only a restatement of the position taken in *Theory*: that private ownership beyond "personal property" is not a "basic right" (1993, 338); that "the question of private property in the means of production or their social ownership … [is] not settled at the level of the first principles of justice, but depend[s] upon the traditions and social institutions of a country and its particular problems and historical circumstances" (338); and that the determination of property relations is left to the "legislative stage" of social formation (339). Rawls's rationale for taking this position is based on the limits of "[p]hilosophical argument" to persuade others of the "correct" view of ownership of the means of production (338, 339). (He does not consider, however, the notion that empirical considerations might be relevant to the question.) He does add that the two principles of justice provide "a possible common court of appeal for settling the question of property" (339), but (as in *Theory*) the relation between the imperative of "justice as fairness" and the reality of historical contingency remains unexplored. In fine, the question of "private-property democracy versus liberal socialism" is left "on all fours" (416).

Inasmuch as *Political Liberalism* (or the subsequent *Justice as Fairness: A Restatement* [2001]) adds nothing new to Rawls's view of property relations, we may proceed to our final query. To rephrase the question: Does "justice as fairness" qualify as a complete political theory even though it fails to specify the nature of property relations or economic arrangements? More specifically, can Rawls's theory qualify as comprehensive when it remains totally *agnostic* on matters widely acknowledged as central to considerations of prudence, efficiency, and justice? Given the mass of available evidence from the work of economists and economic historians, is it acceptable for a political philosophy that aspires to completeness to express *no preference whatsoever* for a particular economic system or to abjure a consideration of the *merits* of various economic systems? Is it sufficient simply to stipulate, as Rawls does in *Theory*, that "justice as fairness includes no natural right of private property in the means of production … nor a natural right to worker-owned and -managed firms" ([1971] 1999, xvi) and leave the matter there?

The answer to these questions hinges on two considerations. First, property relations are arguably as vital a concern to citizens and as critical to the well being of a society as political rights and civil liberties. As Rousseau wrote in his *Discourse on Political Economy*, "The right to property is the most sacred of all the citizens' rights, and more important in certain respects than liberty itself.… [P]roperty is the true foundation of civil society and the true guarantee of the citizens' commitments" (qtd. in Cress 1987, 127). Like Rawls, Rousseau denied a "natural right" to private property and grounds its legitimacy in convention and positive title. Yet Rousseau (who was no less an egalitarian than Rawls) clearly recognized that property rights are *foundational* in a sense that Rawls apparently fails to appreciate. By this statement, I mean that the right of ownership is not something simply to be juxtaposed with liberty (as Rawls does); it lies at the very heart of liberty. This observation is hardly new; political philosophers and philosophical economists have voiced it for centuries. The belief that private ownership is central to liberty per se does not imply, however, that it is a "natural" right or justify a right to unlimited accumulation. It does create, nonetheless, a presumption that property constitutes a *species* of liberty and should not be sequestered from political rights as Rawls has done.

Reference to the history of political thought provides a second standard for assessing the status of Rawls's political philosophy. Those familiar with the canon of political classics (and with the history of political theory generally) know that questions of property relations have figured importantly (and sometimes prominently) in the works of nearly all the major political philosophers. Plato, Aristotle, Cicero, Aquinas, Machiavelli, Hobbes, Locke, Montesquieu, Hume, Rousseau, Publius, Kant, Burke, Hegel, Marx, and Mill had something significant (and often something definite) to say about property in one form or another. As Howard Williams, a Kant scholar, writes: "That the concept of property has been a central concern of political philosophy from classical times onward is not surprising in view of the fact that the way in which wealth and goods are held determines a great deal of the structure and make-up of a community. Property relations go to the root of any social system" (1983, 77).

The main point is that no major political thinker (nor a host of lesser figures) believed that the determination of basic property relations lies beyond the fundamental concerns of political speculation. To leave such a profound question—whether a society is to be capitalist or socialist—"on all fours" would have struck most of them as a fatal omission. Similarly, to say that considerations of justice alone can tell us *nothing* about the desirability of radically different economic systems would have elicited perplexity, and perhaps disdain. That Rawls does provide a characterization of society that includes a discussion of economic arrangements (his "property-owning democracy") might mitigate such responses, yet, as we have seen, his ideal makes no claim to priority or privilege over a "liberal socialist regime." If either system is privileged, it is *socialism*, for the reasons given earlier. This position creates an interesting (and largely unobserved) tension in Rawls's political thought. It also speaks to what is perhaps the greatest frustration surrounding his philosophy: his sphinx-like silence on the relation of his theory of justice to existing societies and on the matter of his political commitments. On the basis of the foregoing analysis, one is tempted to implore: "Professor Rawls, come out of your ivory closet, check your fancy philosophy at the door, and confirm that you are, indeed, a 'bourgeois socialist'" (Bayer 1990, 574)! Such a revelation would be the first step in elevating Rawls's status as the creator of a comprehensive political philosophy. It would not only comport with the principles outlined in *Theory* but also free Rawls to commit himself on the matter of property. In doing so, he then might justifiably claim his place among the titans of political thought. Short of this confession, however, John Rawls must remain in the second tier of political authors who, notwithstanding their fame and influence, articulate only a partial philosophy of politics.

Of course, we might read Rawls's "original omission" on the subject of property in other ways. It is possible to represent the exclusion of property relations as an *advance* in political speculation that, on one hand, serves to direct the focus of political philosophy toward (formal) questions of justice "transcending" specific economic arrangements and that, on the other hand, subordinates economics to the requirements of justice, thus providing a rational-cum-moral basis for assessing a whole range of economic arrangements. Although justice *tout court* cannot settle the matter of property relations, we might argue that it can "set out in a schematic way the outlines of a just economic system that admits of several variations" (Rawls [1971] 1999, 242).

Whether Rawls's (admittedly "limited") construction of justice constitutes an advance over the tradition of political philosophy (or merely a valid alternative) must be left ultimately to each observer. Yet even if we grant the legitimacy of Rawls's "omission," there remains the matter of his "ideal" scheme, which entails widespread distribution of (nonpersonal) property, progressive rates of taxation, marked restrictions of the right of bequest, ongoing "adjustments" in property rights, and the redistribution of income, capital, and natural resources. As suggested earlier, this scheme—along with other facets of his theory of justice—suggests that his putative neutrality on economic systems actually veils a discernable preference for principles, policies, and outcomes closely associated with the socialist tradition. He even defends his adoption of free-market principles (in part) on the basis of its consistency with *public* ownership of the means of production. In fine, Rawls's *capitalist* model of democracy looks suspiciously like a species of *socialism* insofar as it truncates property rights, widely redistributes wealth and income, and aims to place the means of production in the hands of "the people." If his "property-owning democracy" represents capitalism under "justice as fairness," one can only conclude that his "liberal socialist regime" would impose further restrictions on property rights and intensify redistributivist policies. In light of these considerations, we may conclude that perhaps Rawls has not omitted the question of property after all and that "justice as fairness" naturally leads to a society of a distinctively socialist caste, "theoretically at least."

REFERENCES

Bayer, Richard C. 1990. On John Rawls' *A Theory of Justice*: Empirical Application of Justice Theories: A Test Case. *International Social Science Journal* 126: 568–78.

Cress, Donald A., ed. 1987. *Jean-Jacques Rousseau: The Basic Political Writings*. Indianapolis, Ind.: Hackett.

Nussbaum, Martha C. 1999. Conversing with the Tradition: John Rawls and the History of Ethics. *Ethics* 109: 424–30.

Rawls, John. 1993. *Political Liberalism*. New York: Columbia University Press.

———. [1971] 1999. *A Theory of Justice*. Rev. ed. Cambridge, Mass.: Harvard University Press.

———. 2001. *Justice as Fairness: A Restatement*. Cambridge, Mass.: Harvard University Press.

Williams, Howard. 1983. *Kant's Political Philosophy*. New York: Macmillan.

Acknowledgments: Reprinted from *The Independent Review*, 8, no. 3 (Winter 2004), pp. 387–400. Copyright © 2004.

20

Has John Roemer Resurrected Market Socialism?
Michael Wohlgemuth

John E. Roemer, a leading socialist economist, in 1994 proclaimed a "future for socialism" (Roemer 1994). His book was advertised as being "measured, highly accessible, and most of all compelling." I have come to the opposite conclusions. Roemer's most provocative assertion is his claim to have found "ways of reformulating the concept of market socialism in response to the Hayekian critique" (2). In his attempt to convince central planners as well as communitarians in the socialist camp of the virtues of the market, Roemer indeed goes a long way in accepting the objections that F. A. Hayek and others put forward during the calculation debate of the 1930s. It is helpful to recall the debate on socialist economics from the early warnings of Ludwig von Mises and Hayek to the later analyses of Yugoslav and Hungarian market socialism by Svetozar Pejovich or János Kornai. These critiques form the background of what Roemer calls the "fifth generation" of market-socialist proposals, which he claims lack the defects of those associated with former generations.

Whether this assertion can be substantiated is the central question of this chapter. First, we must reconstruct Roemer's model of market socialism. Because Roemer leaves important elements of this system unexplained or unconnected, my account can only mirror his eclecticism, but I shall try to avoid unfriendly misreadings. Next I shall describe Roemer's own normative scheme of reference, finding his concept of "equal opportunities" highly ambiguous. Furthermore, whatever the interpretation of equal opportunities, it is hardly reconcilable with the effects that Roemer's proposals for institutional reform must be expected to have. I analyze these effects in the following sections. They all involve substantial obstructions of market competition in different dimensions and can be summarized as evidence of a fundamental conclusion: spontaneous market competition and egalitarian market socialism are as incompatible as Hayek and other critics always believed them to be.

FOUR GENERATIONS OF SOCIALIST MISCARRIAGES: THE DEBATES IN RETROSPECT

According to Roemer (1994, chap. 4), the market-socialism debate has now entered its fifth stage. My recapitulation of the preceding four generations of market-socialist ideas and refutations serves a twofold purpose: (1) to show that the debate was a catalyst in the development of Austrian ideas of the market process and (2) to show the defects of former market-socialist ideas that Roemer now claims to have avoided.

The Calculation Debate

The theoretical deliberations on the economics of socialism began with "the belief that socialism will dispense entirely with calculation in terms of value and will replace it with some sort of calculation *in natura* based on some units of energy or some other physical magnitude" (Hayek [1940] 1994, 235). This view, traditionally held by European Marxists such as Friedrich Engels or Karl Kautsky, was first challenged by Mises ([1920] 1994). Mises provoked socialist economists to enter the debate with his "impossibility theorem," usually summarized as follows: there is no basis for rational calculations of value if there are no market prices, and there are no market prices without the voluntary exchange of private property rights. Hence, if socialists want to allocate of resources "rationally"—sacrificing a less valued opportunity in favor of a more highly valued one in view of consumers' preferences and producers' capabilities—they cannot at the same time dispense with production goods as objects of market exchange. Only full-fledged capital markets reveal monetary values of production goods and thus provide information and incentives necessary for a rational use of the means of production. One decisive qualification Mises probably considered unnecessary to dwell on at length. Its due consideration by his critics, however, would have avoided many misunderstandings:

> The static state can dispense with economic calculation. For here the same
> events in economic life are ever recurring.... But ... our economic data are
> ever changing, so that the static nature of economic activity is only a theo-
> retical assumption corresponding to no real state of affairs.... Thus, in the
> socialist commonwealth every economic change becomes an undertaking
> whose success can be neither appraised in advance nor later retrospectively
> determined. There is only groping in the dark. (Mises [1920] 1994, 16)

In addition, appreciating the knowledge problem arising from "the uncertainty of future conditions, which is an inevitable concomitant of the dynamic nature of economic life" (17), Mises clearly foresaw the incentive problems of expropriated socialist actors. Not only the signaling function of market prices but also their controlling and motivating qualities depend on free markets for the exchange of private property. Mises understood that "the exclusion of free initiative and individual responsibility ... constitutes the most serious menace to the socialist economic organization" (20).

Perceiving Mises's twofold argument in this way instead of just picking his bluntly stated conclusions—"Where there is no free market, there is no pricing mechanism, without a pricing mechanism, there is no economic calculation" (17)—one is compelled to conclude that the replies of socialist economists badly missed the point. They hardly ever considered the incentive problems of planners and producers. Their "possibility theorems" rested on static economic theories in which all circumstances relevant for economic calculation are assumed to be constant and "given." Hence they referred to a utopian state for which even Mises denied a serious calculation problem. Contrary to the declarations of critics and reviewers throughout the subsequent generations, we must conclude that Mises's criticism was not actually refuted. Still, the discussion led to the "realization by socialists that prices must be used for economic calculation under socialism" (Roemer 1994, 28), as expressed by Oscar Lange in his gibing praise: "Socialists have certainly reason to be grateful to Professor Mises, the great *advocatus diaboli* of their cause. For it was his powerful challenge that forced socialists to recognize the importance of an adequate system of economic accounting to guide the allocation of resources in a socialist economy" (Lange [1936] 1994b, 252).

This recognition led to a second stage of socialist economics "characterized by the view that it would be possible to calculate the prices at which general equilibrium would be reached in a socialist economy by solving a complicated system of simultaneous equations—and so socialism need only await the invention of powerful computers" (Roemer 1994, 28).[1] The equations of general equilibrium as depicted by Leon Walras, Vilfredo Pareto, and Enrico Barone were presented as proof of the possibility of rational socialist calculation. To prove that abstract equations have an equally abstract solution in terms of equilibrium values that ought to guide central planning agencies was not, however, to prove that they could in practice be of any use in the absence of a market for the exchange of property rights. The debate remained as open as ever. Hayek ([1935] 1948b, 153ff.) stressed the inadequacy of the metaphor of the Walrasian auctioneer as a description of market processes and as a prescription for planning purposes. Later he summarized his view as follows:

The problem is thus in no way solved if we can show that all the facts, if they were known to a single mind (as we hypothetically assume them to be given to the observing economist), would uniquely determine the solution; instead we must show how a solution is produced by the interactions of people each of whom possesses only partial knowledge. To assume all the knowledge to be given to us as the explaining economists is to assume the problem away and to disregard everything that is important and significant in the real world. (Hayek 1945, 530)

Hayek's insistence on recognizing the practical problems of centralizing the knowledge necessary to mimic the workings of competitive capitalism induced Lange to open the third stage of the debate by making some "practical" proposals. Only then did the term *market socialism* attain some institutional context as a result of "the realization ... that actual markets would indeed be required to find the socialist equilibrium—and this because the central planning bureau could not possibly have the information necessary to make the calculation" (Roemer 1994, 28ff.). Prices for consumer goods would be set in actual markets; even wages would be determined by decentralized bargaining in real labor markets. "But there is no market for capital goods and productive resources outside of labour" (Lange [1936] 1994b, 260). Here the Central Planning Board (CPB) would replace market transactions, conducting a procedure of trial and error analogous to the tâtonnement of the Walrasian auctioneer (259ff.).

It would start by decreeing randomly chosen prices for the collectively owned producer goods. All managers ("assumed to be public officials" [260]) are instructed to set output so that price equals marginal cost, taking the prices of inputs and of their products as given; hence firms are mandated to act as if they were suppliers under perfect competition. The CPB now checks whether any shortages or surpluses of factors and goods exist and corrects its errors by new trials, altering prices until it finds the market-clearing ones. Thus, Lange argues:

The Central Planning Board performs the functions of the market. It establishes the rules for combining factors of production and choosing the scale of output of a plant, for determining the output of an industry, for the allocation of resources, and for the parametric use of prices in accounting. Finally, it fixes the prices so as to balance the quantity supplied and demanded of each commodity. It follows that a substitution of planning for the functions of the market is quite possible and workable. ([1936] 1994b, 263)

Hayek ([1940] 1994) challenged this conclusion,[2] contrasting the practicability and performance of Lange's system of centralized information and decreed prices with a market system "where the required changes are brought about by the spontaneous action of the persons immediately concerned" (240). All his objections pertain to fundamental shortcomings of the neoclassical paradigm or to an "excessive preoccupation with problems of the pure theory of stationary equilibrium" (240).

First, because of "the daily changing conditions in different places and different industries" (240), Lange's bureaucratic tâtonnement will not converge. At each phase of the cumbersome procedure, the specific circumstances to which rational calculation ought to adapt will already have changed again. While decentralized market procedures elicit rapid and differentiated adjustments, centralized trial and error can react only with delays and undue generalizations.

Second, undue generalizations must occur because of the heterogeneous character of production goods. Economically, each machine of a different age or in different combinations has its individual value. The CPB can hardly even know of their overall existence; even less can it fix particular values in terms of the shadow prices of each of the different production goods. Furthermore, the tâtonnement procedure is inapplicable to nonstandardized commodities, which form a great part of the socialized production goods (for example, machinery, buildings, and ships produced only on special contract). For such goods, the CPB has no market-clearing prices to decree in advance; hence it would have to take "all the functions of the entrepreneur on itself" (241).

Third, the managers, even if loyal and capable, cannot be expected to find the lowest-cost production methods. Because the CPB is confined to establishing uniform prices for goods of economically different value, "the managers of production will have no inducement, and even no real possibility, to make use of special opportunities, special bargains, and all the little advantages offered by their special local conditions" (244). This nonresponsiveness also reflects their obligation to treat prices as "given." As pure quantity adjusters with price competition outlawed, managers have no reason to "incur extra costs to remedy a sudden scarcity, since a local or temporary scarcity could not affect prices until the official machinery has acted" (244). In an evolutionary and complex environment, forced marginal-cost calculations based on artificially sticky and uniform prices must lead to a misallocation of resources. Fourth, for the same reason, there is no room for entry and innovation. Decreed prices destroy

> the opportunity for anybody who knows a cheaper method to come in at
> his own risk and attract customers by underbidding the other producers

... Since the man with the new idea will have no possibility of establishing himself by undercutting, the new idea cannot be proved by experiment until he has convinced [the CPB] that his way of producing the thing is cheaper. (247)

Indeed, just as innovation cannot be depicted in Walrasian equilibrium formulas, it cannot be managed in Lange's price-fixing procedures. Because the new good or technique has no established market, the CPB has no price to fix in advance. For the same reason, technical knowledge is usually assumed to be "given" in the neoclassical model of the market. To assume every producer's know-how to be equally available to the CPB, however, turns an assumption of a static environment into a pretense of knowledge.[3]

As Hayek switched from considering problems of theoretical possibility to considering those of practical workability concerning market socialism, he discovered theoretical inadequacies of the neoclassical paradigm concerning core questions of economics. The ensuing reactions of the scientific community can be interpreted as exemplary vindications of Kuhnian themes: the neoclassical camp failed to perceive the focus and rigor of the critique and remained confident that Lange's claims had not been seriously damaged.[4] The Austrians, in turn, gradually realized that they had reformulated the economic problem in a fundamental way.[5] A growing awareness of paradigmatic incompatibilities led them to develop their own research program based on such notions as "competition as a discovery procedure" (Hayek [1968] 1978a), "competition and entrepreneurship" (Kirzner 1973), and "the market as an economic process" (Lachmann 1986).[6]

Modern Variants of Market Socialism

Roemer (1994, 32) assigns the fourth stage to the first real-life attempts to establish forms of market socialism in Yugoslavia (1950), Hungary (1968), China (1978), and Poland (1980s). In all cases, Soviet-type central planning was partly replaced by other systems of reluctantly decentralized decision-making. These experiments yielded the first empirical evidence on the performance of market socialism, thus allowing the debate to turn from the practical relevance of theories to theoretical explanations of reality.[7] The first stages of the debate on market socialism fostered the formulation of Austrian theories of the market process, but empirical examination, especially of the Yugoslav and Hungarian experiments, contributed to the development of property-rights theories and comparative institutional analysis.

Furubotn and Pejovich (1972, 1973) analyzed Yugoslav worker-managed firms and compared them to capitalist corporations. They emphasized the interconnectedness of property rights, transaction costs, incentives, and economic behavior. In terms of property rights, the Yugoslav system can be described as follows: (1) the workers' collective has the right to produce, buy, or sell most capital goods; and (2) it owns the residual net profits, which it allocates between the wage fund and retained earnings for reinvestment; but (3) "the employees can neither sell the rights specified above nor continue to enjoy them when they leave the employ of the firm" (Pejovich [1976] 1979, 152).

The incentives in this arrangement give rise to certain behavioral patterns of self-interested actors: neglect of reinvestments in favor of consumption via the wage fund, massive debt-financed expenditures instead of self-financed investments, and a particular reluctance to hire new workers who would share the wage fund. The economic results of such incentive schemes can be observed and explained: "inflation, unemployment, the liquidity crisis, low level of self-financed investment and the virtually complete dependence of business firms on the banks—can be traced to the incentive patterns generated by the prevailing property relations and the absence of capital markets" (161).

Similarly, the Hungarian experiment, which relied on a combination of limited central planning and limited market coordination (both restricted in favor of increased indirect regulation and bargaining), permitted a fruitful analysis of the effects of rules on individual behavior and social outcomes. The property rights of both the regulating bureaucracy and the managers in highly monopolized industries were insufficiently specified and distinguished. Decisions on prices, taxes, subsidies, credits and investment projects arose mostly from bargaining as Hungary's "third way" around the discipline of both the market and direct central planning. János Kornai (for example, 1992) made the most influential theoretical assessment. His analysis, which also helps to explain failures of corporatistic rent-seeking in capitalist welfare states, centers on the political economy of the "soft budget constraint" (Kornai 1986): semi-independent firms and political agencies both escape individual responsibility for inefficiencies, losses, and mistakes as competition in capital and goods markets is corporatistically administered and politically cushioned.

According to Roemer (1994, 33), the debate on market socialism has now entered its fifth stage. Market socialists of the fifth generation are described as having inherited from their ancestors not much more than a set of egalitarian ends; in terms of means, they claim to have cut the umbilical cord from earlier socialists such as Lange, with Hayek and Kornai being the foremost obstetricians:

Not only have the proponents of market socialism retracted Lange's insistence that industrial prices be set by the planners instead of the market, but they have also dispensed with public ownership (in the sense of exclusive state control) of firms.... Kornai's and Hayek's point has been accepted, that as long as the government cannot credibly commit itself to noninterference in the competitive process, managers will not be profit-maximizers and economic inefficiency will result. (Roemer 1994, 34f.)

Today we find various models, most of them relying on "real" markets and competition within a wide spectrum of different combinations of management, labor- or state-run firms. They are owned or financed by shareholders with differently restricted rights to dispose of their assets, by more or less state-owned banks and other firms, by the workers themselves, or by the state.[8] They all share a commitment to egalitarian values, but differ in their specific contents and policy implications.[9] The youngest generation of market socialists is large and fragmented; the family ties are too loose to justify discussion of the whole family as one. Therefore, I have selected one proponent for a more substantiated presentation and critique. I chose the work of Roemer (1994) because this author claims that his model is particularly immune against failures of former market socialist models.

ROEMER'S MARKET SOCIALISM: COMPROMISING ON MARKET COMPETITION AND EQUAL OPPORTUNITIES

It is extremely difficult to extract a consistent line of reasoning from Roemer's mixture of anticapitalist and promarket rhetoric as well as his vindications and accusations of real-life socialism. It is equally difficult to identify a coherent and comprehensive specification of his own system of market socialism. However, the reader gets at least some clear statements about what Roemer's market socialism is not: "direct control of firms by the state is not necessary for socialist goals" (4), and labor-managed firms are also rejected as inefficient substitutes for markets (122f.). In both instances, Roemer attributes the failures mainly to inappropriate incentives to work efficiently, to make use of decentralized knowledge, and to seek innovation—the characteristic effects of the "soft budget constraint," unsolved principal-agent problems, and insufficient competition. In Roemer's model, therefore, neither central planners nor workers' committees are supposed to "own" firms in the sense of deciding how to produce, invest, and share the surplus.

One is impelled to ask: Socialism, where is thy sting? Where are the systemic differences between this form and capitalist systems? Once more, the clearest answer is a negative one: "Under market socialism, the poor are precluded from liquidating their shares" (73).

Indeed, this condition remains the only continuous feature of Roemer's system of market socialism: coupons are substituted for transferable shares. This idea, however, appears in three different, even contradictory presentations. Proceeding through the three stages of Roemer's approach, one finds that the significance of the coupon system, but also of market coordination, gives way more and more to traditional forms of socialist state intervention.

Coupon-Market Socialism: A First Approach

In a first formal presentation of a neoclassical model depicting a "market-socialist politico-economic equilibrium" (chap. 8), the existence of coupons instead of transferable shares is the only institutional assumption that sets the system apart from capitalism: "The coupon economy is equivalent to the capitalist economy except for one missing market: one cannot trade coupons for the good" (73). In Roemer's model of an economy with one good (representing the national product), every adult citizen receives a fixed amount of coupons, which cannot be sold in exchange for money. Coupons, like capitalist stock, are entitlements to firms' profits that can be invested in firms of the individuals' choice, but unlike capitalist stock they cannot be sold or bequeathed. In terms of property rights, coupons lack the attribute of transferability. "All else," Roemer states, "is the same as in the description of the C[apitalist] P[olitical] E[conomic] E[quilibrium]" (67). We must infer that in this model, firms are actually financed by coupon holders and private banks and that speculation on coupon dividends is assumed to create the same incentives for investors to incur information costs and for entrepreneurs to act in the interests of principals and consumers as under capitalism. We must also infer that savings and investments are coordinated through an interest-rate mechanism just as in a capitalist economy and that labor markets also are no different from those in market economies.

Most of these hidden ceteris paribus assumptions (in the sense of "all else remains equal to capitalist economies") are either withdrawn by Roemer himself in the following paragraphs or must be doubted by a critical reader right from the beginning. Nevertheless, from this simplistic model, Roemer draws far-reaching conclusions: "public bads" would be drastically reduced in coupon-market socialism, thus increasing "total utility in the population" (71). The logic is as follows:

in capitalism, a few "rich" own the firms; in a coupon system, the many "poor will be the controlling group in most firms, as they own the majority of coupons in society. Thus, the firms will choose their levels of investments in the interests of the poor" (68). Because the "poor" are assumed to amount to a vast majority (95 percent) of the population (73)[10] and everyone's coupon holdings are the same, there is much less concentration of stock ownership. The latter, in turn, is made responsible for people's views on "the optimal level of the public bad" (65): the larger the fraction an individual asset-holder owns in the stock of firms, the higher the level of public bads he or she would permit, as private profits would be concentrated in a few owners, whereas the concomitant public bads would be widely dispersed. Roemer's concepts of "public bads,"[11] typical interests of "the rich" and of "the poor," and firm management as "a perfect agent of the firm's controlling group" (75) are dubious. To add to the confusion, Roemer assumes that "the level of the public bad is the outcome of the political process"; hence firms (socialist or capitalist) are assumed to treat the level of public bads as "given" (66f.), even though they "produce" them.

Coupons and the Banking System: A Second Approach

Some of the open questions about crucial elements of Roemer's market socialism are answered in the following paragraphs, which may move away from formal modeling to the consideration of real institutions. These answers, however, partly contradict the ceteris paribus assumptions (all else remains equal to ordinary capitalist economies) referred to earlier. Now (chap. 9) we are told that firms cannot use the coupon stock market for raising capital (76).[12] Therefore, a banking system has to be introduced. According to Roemer,

> firms in the coupon economy would be organized around a fairly small number of main banks, as in the Japanese keiretsu. A main bank would be primarily responsible for putting together loan consortia to finance the operations of the firms in its group; it would, correlatively, be responsible for monitoring these firms. (76)

Roemer gives no further specifications concerning those formal and informal institutions of a Japanese *keiretsu* that he wants to imitate. We can infer only that "the universe of public firms is partitioned into groups" and that the firms in each group "are associated with a main bank" (49). The ownership of banks is not further discussed; it is only casually assumed "that they are publicly owned in the sense that their profits go in large part directly to the state treasury" (156, n. 3). Hence, we find here a different type of public ownership without being given an explanation of why the alleged virtues of the coupon system should not apply to the ownership of banks as well. Indeed, after this introduction of the banking system, it becomes extremely difficult to discern the remaining significance of the coupon system. Because in Roemer's second representation of market socialism, the coupon market cannot be used to raise capital, its influence on firms' decisions must be negligible. All it might do to affect resource allocation would be to inform the loan-giving banks about the current bets of coupon holders. Roemer, however, does not seem to give much credit even to this informational role of his own system. Eventually, he is led to "recommend safeguards that enabled banks to monitor firms independently of what the stock market is saying" (82).

The Banking System and Central Investment Planning: A Third Approach

The relevance of the coupon system having been superseded by that of the banking system, Roemer (in chaps. 11 and 12) introduces the state as a new player. This shift further reduces the role of the coupon market and brings into question the independence of banking system. Now, we learn that the state would be "engaging in investment planning, both by providing incentives for firms to invest in particular sectors or regions and by direct government investment" (90). As we shall see later, interest rates are manipulated in order to encourage particular investments against the signals of the market. More and more, the meaning of market socialism loses its connection to markets and returns to its traditional focus: state intervention.

In addition, Roemer's arguments lose coherence. The role attributed to central investment planning now supersedes the "provisions that grant the banks considerable independence from state control" (76).[13] Roemer asks the right question: "But why should the bank, which is itself a publicly owned institution, perform its monitoring job well? ... The principal question is whether the banks would operate with sufficient independence of the state, making decisions about firms using economic and not political criteria" (76). The principal answer given, however, is not that firms and independent banks should be primarily responsible for investment decisions (the coupon holder having long since been dispensed with). Now, government agencies using political rather than economic criteria make investment decisions! All this adds up to an enormous confusion for the reader, who can never be quite sure just who is really in charge of financing and investment decisions.

To summarize, all we know for sure is that Roemer's market socialism has no stock market for trading transferable ownership titles. Coupons represent entitlements to firms' profits but they, at least in later versions of the model, can neither be emitted by firms in order to raise capital nor be bought and sold by citizens in order to accumulate or liquidate assets. Although coupons are first (chap. 8) described as the central property of market socialism, yielding massive welfare gains, it becomes clear later that neither firms' managers nor loan-giving banks should take the coupon market seriously. This revision brings to the fore a banking system that should now do the monitoring and financing of firms (chap. 9) using purely economic criteria. Soon, however, we are confronted with a second revision calling for governmental investment planning (chap. 12), which supersedes the banking system that, in turn, dominates the coupon system.

What Roemer Wants Socialists to Want

Roemer's model of market socialism ought to be judged by the ends he himself proclaims. His normative frame of reference remains, however, as ambiguous as his institutional proposals. Roemer describes the socialist creed as follows: "I believe socialists want equality of opportunity for: (1) self-realization and welfare, (2) political influence, and (3) social status" (11).

Stressing equality of opportunity rather than social outcomes, the classical liberal might agree with Roemer, while clarifying the concept by emphasizing the need for rules to protect equal rights to pursue individual ends ("self-realization and welfare") in market transactions and to allow competitive market entry of outsiders. Adoption of such rules would be possible if the unequal opportunity of exercising "political influence" in rent-seeking societies were discouraged by a strict rule of law. A constitution of equal rights would restrict preferential treatment of powerful groups, defending equal opportunity in markets against the cementing of a given "social status."

Roemer, of course, defines equal opportunity not in terms of individual rights against interference from the state or from fellow citizens but in terms of social claims on support from the state (that is, claims on the money of other citizens). Equal access to equal rights is disparagingly said to "only touch the surface of a much larger task. Equality of opportunity requires special compensation or subsidy for those denied access to privilege. Most generally, equality of opportunity requires that people be compensated for handicaps induced by factors over which they have no control" (12).

Roemer neglects the legal and politico-economic consequences of his egalitarian precepts, consequences that were at the heart of Hayek's critique of socialism following the calculation debate (beginning with his *Road to Serfdom* [1944], extensively discussed in his *Mirage of Social Justice* [1976], and ending with his *Fatal Conceit* [1988]). Briefly put, the Hayekian objection would be that equality under the law is not associated with Roemer's notion of equality of opportunity; rather, pursuit of the latter must seriously damage the former. The general rule of law cannot serve as a "surface" to legally enforced special compensations on grounds of redistributive justice. It would be increasingly destroyed by privileges granted to powerful interests who call for compensation of market outcomes that are, indeed, induced by factors over which no one has control. If the political system is given unspecified (and hence unrestricted) control over market results, there would be "a future for socialism," even in its totalitarian variants. In the same measure, however, there would be no future for the rule of law and its economic counterpart: dynamic market competition.

To be sure, I do not accuse Roemer of paving the "road to serfdom." There can be, and there actually are, at least viable compromises between equal individual liberty under the rule of law and equalized social status under the will of government. However, the compromises of conflicting values should be described as such. Unspecified rights to government compensation for alleged handicaps of special groups cannot be simply brushed under a "surface" of rights against state interference. My argument is not about the superiority of values as such; it is about the opportunity costs of pursuing clouded objectives such as distributive justice in view of their institutional consequences. These arise primarily on a constitutional level, describing the relationship between government and the individual, and critically affect the workings of a competitive order.

Paternalistically Forced Savings and Equal Nonopportunities

Roemer's socialist state distributes an equal amount of coupons or stock vouchers to every adult citizen. The government's "gift" represents a claim on national wealth,[14] but its disposition is seriously constrained. Individual coupon holders cannot dispose of their assets as freely as capitalist stockholders can. They cannot reduce their coupon holdings in favor of what they believe to be more profitable investments (in foreign stock, bonds, human capital, own business ventures) or more urgent needs (a honeymoon, a house, a car, a conference on market socialism). Socialist "investors" cannot liquidate, transfer, or bequeath their claims in accordance with their individual propensity to consume, risk preference, and time preference. For the sake of "equal opportunities," in the sense of an equal distribution of dividends, Roemer's "rich" as well as his (95 percent) "poor" are deprived of the opportunity to pursue their own individual ends by freely disposing of their coupon budget.

For Roemer (73f.), starting with an equal distribution of transferable shares would not do; one has "to prevent the poor from selling prematurely to the rich ... this phenomenon could happen ... if the poor had poorer information than the rich." This view not only brings to light a blatant paternalism. It also contradicts the assertion that a coupon economy would make use of the same quality of actors' knowledge and skill as does a capitalist stock market. What can we expect of a "market" composed of actors who are forced to take part, who are described as having inferior information, and who are not even trusted to make mature decisions?

In Roemer's coupon economy, all have to invest their fixed coupons' share whether or not they are informed, interested, and skilled in such affairs. Such involuntary "market participation" cannot match the spontaneous division of labor, knowledge, risks, and skills that follows from a voluntary participation of those who have a specific interest and experience in speculating on the future performance of firms. A real stock market "makes possible, whether in the form of 'take-over bids' or otherwise, the transfer of the control of material resources from pessimists to optimists, i.e. to those who believe they can make better use of them than others can" (Lachmann [1969] 1977, 162). A coupon lacks these properties. Because exit from and additional entry into the coupon market is outlawed, those with "poor" information or willingness to speculate must stay put along with those who want to bear risks and incur information costs. In this publicly organized "stock-exchange game" the stakes are paid by "the state" and can be neither lowered nor increased by the players. With no chance to win or lose much more than the average from the allocation of given coupons, no one has a great incentive to invest in information and monitoring. Abolishing the opportunity to accumulate and transfer capital also obstructs the accumulation of knowledge and diversification of risk (Alchian [1965] 1977, 140ff.).

From the firms' perspective, a coupon "market" bears almost no resemblance to a capital market, simply because there is no capital to be raised. No supply-and-demand relationship connects firms and coupon holders. Unlike managers in capitalist systems, Roemer's managers face no pecuniary external effects if citizens change their portfolio, nor are they confronted with the risk of take-over. Consequently, one is at a loss to understand why "the coupon stock market should provide the same discipline over firm management as a capitalist stock market" (50). The revisions of the concept that Roemer adds later in his book indicate that he himself envisages the coupon economy as not much more than a coercive transfer mechanism with some gambling properties for the receivers. In considering the "efficiency of firms under market socialism" (chap. 9), we must, as Roemer does, concentrate on the workings of the banking system.

Cartelizing the Economy: The Banking System

Whereas the coupon system is characterized by an excessively high dispersion of involuntary "market" participation (for the sake of equalized profit distribution), the other basic functions of a capital market (financing and monitoring) are assigned to a banking system with excessive concentration. Roemer's reliance on "a fairly small number of main banks" (76) entails a concentration of capital supply and monitoring capacity that exceeds by far that of any capitalist stock market and is exceeded only by the workings of a CPB. In capitalist systems that rely on a combination of financing via asset markets and competing private banks, we can expect the number and competitiveness of sources for risky investment funds to be higher. The same is true for the sources of independent information acquisition. In Roemer's market socialism, capital can be raised only via bargaining with the one main bank in charge of a given group of firms. Under this regime, competition on capital markets and on product markets is likely to give way to a producers' cartel organized around its leading bank. If firms form a group financed by one and the same bank, the bank has the incentive not only to monitor but also to coordinate the operations of the firms in its group. It would be ill-advised to have the investments of one of its clients threatened by competitive attacks from others. This incentive to collude holds against competition from the members within the group as well as from newcomers and foreigners. These often criticized tendencies of the Japanese keiretsu (for example, Lawrence 1991) become systematic features of Roemer's market socialism.

Obstructing Competition I: New Firms

How does "the man with the new idea" enter the socialist market? Is there an equal "opportunity for anybody who knows a cheaper method to come at his own risk and attract customers by underbidding the other producers" (Hayek ([1940] 1994, 247)? We must expect that in Roemer's coupon and banking system, innovative entry to markets confronts problems similar to those arising in Lange's model of a price-fixing CPB. Any new firm must eventually be integrated into the coupon system and into the keiretsu-like financing group; it cannot rely on the raising of private capital by issuing shares; it cannot at the same time be owned by profit-sharing associates and be integrated into the coupon system. Indeed, why should an entrepreneur start a risky venture at all if losses fall back on him privately whereas profits are "owned" publicly?

Roemer recognizes that eventually he must allow a private sector in order to "provide almost the same incentives that exist in capitalism for those who form new firms in order to bring innovations to market" (78f.). But the existence of even "almost" equal opportunities and incentives for innovators must be seriously doubted. In his proposal, "It is envisaged that many growing firms would eventually be bought by large firms in the 'public' sector" (78).[15] If this acquisition does not occur voluntarily, "the government might auction the private firm to firms in the public (coupon) sector" (78). Even if "the proceeds [are] going to the erstwhile owner" (78), however, entrepreneurial pioneers are treated badly: as soon as they become successful and competitive, they are forced out of the market. Is it far fetched to expect that "the man with the new idea," with entrepreneurial spirit and pride, would try his luck abroad, in real capitalist countries that offer him an equal opportunity to exploit his knowledge without being forced to accept a "golden handshake" from incumbent competitors?

Roemer's public sector is deliberately designed to frustrate the emergence of private ventures right from the beginning: "Perhaps joining the public sector would be a prerequisite to receiving loans from the main banks or loans at preferential interest rates. There would be a statute requiring nationalization of private firms that reach a given size" (78).

Obviously, "the man with the new idea will have no possibility of establishing himself by undercutting" (Hayek [1940] 1994, 247). Whereas in Lange's system "every calculation by an outsider who believes that he can do better will have to be examined and approved by the authority" (247), in Roemer's system every request for loans by an outsider has to be addressed to banking consortia that either discourage or absorb new competitors who threaten the insiders (for example, in their ability to repay loans). We must conclude that Roemer's praise of market competition is muted as soon as it encounters the hard necessities of his market socialism. There is a protective belt around the socialist market cartel; there cannot be equal opportunity for new ventures and incumbent firms.

Obstructing Competition II: International Capital Flows

Referring to international capital flows, Roemer asks: "Would domestic firms attempt to set up foreign subsidiaries to escape high wages at home?" (82). Of course they would like to invest abroad—and for many more reasons than high wages at home. One possible reason would be to escape socialist markets designed by Roemer to frustrate successful private profit-seekers. In addition, firms prevented from taking full advantage of the international division of labor, capital, and knowledge could hardly succeed in modern global markets. Such impediments, however, do characterize Roemer's market socialism: "This is an important sense in which the firms of the market-socialist economy would remain socially controlled: they would not necessarily have the right freely to export capital" (82).[16] Roemer welcomes some foreign investment in domestic firms at least within the boundaries "circumscribed by law." Foreign private capital, however, cannot be integrated into the coupon system, as it would bring in real money. Hence, "the possibility arises that citizens might use foreign firms as their agents to invest their capital in domestic firms. This would have to be outlawed" (82). Thus, the government interferes with international capital flows in a way that discriminates against individuals kept within their market-socialist system. There must be a protective belt around the market-socialist economy; there cannot be equal opportunity for domestic and foreign market participants.

Obstructing Competition III: Investment Planning

The case against equal opportunities (and risks) for market participants to enter and exit the market according to general rules of the game is further strengthened by Roemer in his digressions on state intervention and investment planning (chaps. 11, 12). Here one can most directly observe a "pretense of knowledge" (Hayek [1975] 1978b) flowing from an attitude with deep roots in mainstream economics. According to Roemer, "The essential element that causes investment to be often inefficient in market economies [is] the fact that it takes time in an uncertain world" (91).

I shall not consider here the interesting methodological question of how to characterize states of (in)efficiency while at the same time taking into account that investment takes place in an ever-changing, complex, and inherently uncertain world.[17] Instead, I ask: How are nonmarket arrangements supposed to cope better with an uncertain world? Roemer presents two mechanisms aimed at socializing entrepreneurial risks through government intervention.

The first proposal (chap. 11) is that the government should promise (ex ante) to subsidize (ex post) those investments that fail because of "bad shocks for which the firm is clearly not responsible, such as a recession of the economy" (92). This procedure should increase the propensity to invest, regardless of the individual "firms' pessimistic estimates concerning the future" (93). Such promises are usually not provided by private insurance agencies, because "significant 'moral hazard,' the possibility that the insured will take fewer precautions against a bad because he is insured, may be involved" (92). The same, of course, is true for the kind of contingent public subsidizing advocated by Roemer. The government, however, is trusted to be able to distinguish clearly between a firm's bad management and its "bad luck." Like Lange's CPB, Roemer's central investment-subsidizing bureau would have to imitate entrepreneurial calculi "on much the same scale as if it were actually running the enterprise" (Hayek [1940] 1994, 251).[19] By its very assignment, however, the bureau must honor political judgments about where resources should go, and hence it must encourage investments at times and in areas that private agents would avoid. Subsidizing investments contrary to individuals' independent "estimates concerning the future" is a very costly procedure. It opens the gates for all aspects of rent seeking, using taxpayers' money to encourage firms to act in opposition to market signals. Although entrepreneurs' risks are alleviated, they become concentrated on the political level, where we expect to find highly unequal opportunities to soften one's budget constraint. Kornai's warnings do not seem to have impressed Roemer deeply.

Similar deficiencies beset Roemer's second proposal for investment planning (chap. 12). To make things worse, it takes the form of a relapse into fallacies of third-generation market socialism. Once again we are presented a "Lange equilibrium" as the market-socialist counterpart of a capitalist "Walrasian equilibrium." Both rely on assumptions of perfect information and foresight of maximizing individuals and a static state of perfect competition (97f., 100f.). Neither therefore accommodates the fact that investment takes time in an uncertain world.[19] Nevertheless, far-reaching conclusions are drawn. Roemer distinguishes the Lange equilibrium from the capitalist one by a more equal distribution of profits (attained through the coupon market) and a centrally "proposed level and pattern of investment for the economy" (99f.). The desired regional or sectoral patterns of investment are to result from "a democratic process that elects a party that is empowered to implement its economic program" (99). The instruments of investment planning are "discounts and surcharges on the market interest rate" (100). As all investments are financed by loans, interest-rate manipulations are a powerful instrument for guiding investments. Prices for loans are now varied according to political considerations, regardless of the amount of voluntary savings in the economy.

The whole process of structural change—the innovation-spurring entry of firms into old and new markets as well as the exit of firms that no longer meet the market test—is now subject to political guidance. Loans are granted according to political considerations (picking the winners, protecting the losers), deliberately ignoring the market signals of competitive markets. At the same time, interest rates no longer serve as meaningful signals of the opportunity costs of consumers (time preferences and risk preferences) but rather as indicators of the political opportunities for rent seeking. Once more, "competition as a discovery procedure" (Hayek [1968] 1978a) is replaced by intervention as a discriminatory procedure. Therefore, one cannot believe that "Kornai's and Hayek's point has been accepted, that as long as the government cannot credibly commit itself to noninterference in the competitive process, managers will not be profit-maximizers and economic inefficiency will result" (34).[20] There is an interventionist core in the market-socialist economy; there cannot be equal opportunity for organized and unorganized market participants.

CONCLUSION

What is to be gained from continuing an intellectual debate on socialist economics that has now grown older than most socialist economies? Considering Roemer's lines of reasoning, one is inclined to say: "Very little." However, taking up the intellectual challenge of market socialists remains of considerable value for the adequate analysis of capitalist systems for at least one reason: the meanings and, perhaps, the virtues of certain capitalist institutions might well be clarified. Mises ([1949] 1966, 703) made a similar assessment of the old calculation debate, arguing that "such examination offers a good opportunity to bring into relief fundamental features both of the market economy and of the imaginary construction of a nonmarket society." Indeed, we best appreciate what we have when we imagine it lost. Ultimately, Roemer's book is very helpful in substantiating an old Austrian view

> that it is hardly an exaggeration to say that without a Stock Exchange there can be no market economy. What really distinguishes the latter from a socialist economy is not the size of the "private sector of the economy," but the ability of the individual freely to buy and sell shares in the material resources of production. Their inability to exercise their ingenuity in this respect is perhaps the most important disability suffered by the citizens of socialist societies. (Lachmann [1969] 1977, 161)

NOTES

1 See, for example, Taylor 1929 or Dickinson 1933. Computopia fallacies remained fashionable in later works of Lange ([1965] 1994a). Even Kenneth Arrow (1974) once adhered to this nirvana: "Indeed, with the development of mathematical programming and high-speed computers, the centralized alternative no longer seems preposterous. After all, it would appear that one could mimic the workings of a decentralized system by an appropriately chosen centralized algorithm" (5).

2 It should be noted that Mises did not leave the debate at the first stage (Roemer does not mention Mises's contribution at all!). Even though his reactions to market socialism were not as prominent as Hayek's prompt and detailed rebuttal of Lange, they were equally substantive. Mises ([1949] 1966, chap. 26) now stressed the lack of capital markets, which alone can generate reliable asset prices and interest rates as the basis of factor evaluations in changing environments. The relevant aspect of human action is speculation and investment. Mises argued that "one cannot play speculation and investment. The speculators and investors expose their own wealth, their own destiny. This fact makes them responsible to the consumers" (709). In the Austrian camp, a fierce debate has recently occurred about whether Mises or Hayek gave the "right" and "final" answer to socialist planning (see the *Review of Austrian Economics* in recent years). This is not the place to contribute to the internal Austrian debate; agree with Kirzner (1996) that the view of two conflicting Austrian paradigms is based on grave exaggerations and misunderstandings sometimes even leading to lamentable "verbal terrorism" (148). It may be more rewarding to return to the debate with socialist proposals that should not remain unnoticed.

3 This point was made earlier by Hayek ([1935] 1948b, 155). Here, he also anticipated some of Polanyi's (1967) ideas on the tacit dimension of subjective knowledge: "much of the knowledge that is actually utilized is by no means 'in existence' in this ready-made form. Most of it consists in a technique of thought which enables an individual engineer to find new solutions rapidly as soon as he is confronted with new constellations of circumstances" (155). There is no justification "to assume that the concentration of knowledge at the central authority would also include a capacity to discover any improvement of this sort" (155).

4 The view that the socialists had "won" the debate can be found in most retrospectives at least until the 1980s. See the critical survey of Lavoie (1985, 10ff.).

5 See also Kirzner 1988, Vaughn 1994, chap. 3, or Keizer 1994.

6 For an overview, see Streit 1993 or Vaughn 1994. Meanwhile, in his famous *Road to Serfdom*, Hayek (1944) added a political warning of creeping totalitarianism, stressing his early prediction that partial attempts to plan "will necessitate further and further measures of control until all economic activity is brought under one central authority" ([1935] 1994, 134).

7 The blueprints of Lange, Lerner, or Taylor were hardly influential in designing the reforms. A theory of the labor-managed firm did not exist at the time it was tried out in Yugoslavia. It was delivered later, by such individuals as Ward (1958) and Vanek (1970).

8 For an overview, see Roemer 1994, chap. 6. The variety of "fifth-generation" models of market socialism is further increased when one takes references in the essays collected in Roosevelt and Belkin 1995, Bardhan and Roemer 1993, and Le Grand and Estrin 1989 or in the approaches of Pierson 1995, Arnold 1994, Miller 1994, Yunker 1992, 1993, Nove 1991, and Brus and Laski 1989.

9 See, for example, Miller 1993, Arneson 1993, or Plant 1989.

10 This assumption is upheld in the capitalist as well as the market-socialist environment! The labor market is not integrated in Roemer's model. All the egalitarian thrust is on the stock market due to Roemer's "skepticism concerning the existence of alternatives to a competitive labor market for allocating labor in an efficient manner" (120).

11 I could find no sound, coherent theoretical reasoning on these matters. The traditional concept of public bads is made virtually inoperative by including all sorts of things anathema to socialists, including unemployment, pollution, imperialistic wars, apartheid, noxious advertising, fast assembly-line speeds, and low taxes on profits.

12 Note that the assertion that under a regime of coupons "the poor will be the controlling group in most firms" (68) becomes totally incredible under the specifications given now. If coupon holders neither give nor withdraw any means relevant for firms, how do they control? Why should firms "choose their levels of investments in the interest of the poor" (68) if the "poor" only take their share of profits but cannot give their share of investment?

13 His proposals once more contradict themselves: there should be "constitutional ... guarantees that bank management be evaluated on economic criteria only," while at the same time bank management "should be elected by citizens in the bank's district" (76ff.)!

14 This may be illustrated by imagining the transition from a capitalist to a coupon system: all former owners, shareholders, and partners must be expropriated or paid off.

15 Roemer adds: "as happens under capitalism." We are puzzled to find that the alleged empirical tendencies toward "monopoly capitalism" (Sweezy 1966) that used to be at the heart of Marxist critiques of the market now serve as a normative recipe for market socialism. Is this considered "shortening the labor pains of a coming communism"? We don't believe this is what Roemer intends; but we conclude that competition is not perceived as a procedure of eminent importance.

16 See also 113: "With public bank directors popularly elected and legal provisions limiting the freedom of firms to export capital, the 'structural power of capital' over society as a whole would be broken. Those who control capital would not be able to hold society hostage by threatening to take the means of production (and the jobs that go with it) overseas." The opportunity costs (and the jobs that go with it) that arise if firms cannot seek the best uses of resources outside a reservation-like market socialism are totally ignored.

17 This problem has often been raised by Hayek (see, for example, [1968] 1978a): "If we do not know the facts we hope to discover by the means of competition, we can never ascertain how effective it has been in discovering those facts that might be discovered" (180).

18 The controlling problems resemble those of Lange's CPB also in the following aspects: "From the point of view of the manager it will be much more important that he should always be able to prove that in the light of the knowledge which he possessed the decision actually taken was the right one than that he should prove to be right in the end. If this will not lead to the worst forms of bureaucracy, I do not know what will" (Hayek [1940] 1994, 248).

19 Roemer argues: "Just as one assumes that the market finds the Walrasian equilibrium in a capitalist economy, so we assume that the market will find, after the Government's announcement, this Lange equilibrium in the market-socialist economy. One assumption is as robust as the other" (102f.). However, comparing one nirvana with another is of no help either for identifying real-life problems of investments under genuine uncertainty or for comparing the properties of real-life institutions for coping with such problems.

20 Hayek's point against central (investment) planning is probably more adequately stated along the following lines: "If we can agree that the economic problem of society is mainly one of rapid adaptation to changes in the particular circumstances of time and place, it would seem to follow that the ultimate decisions must be left to the people who are familiar with these circumstances, who know directly of the relevant changes and of the resources immediately available to them" (Hayek 1945, 524). See also Streit (1995) for a Hayekian critique of modern industrial policy.

REFERENCES

Alchian, Armen A. [1965] 1977. Some Economics of Property Rights. In *Economic Forces at Work: Selected Works*, by Armen A. Alchian. Indianapolis, Ind.: Liberty Press.

Arneson, Richard J. 1993. Market Socialism and Egalitarian Ethics. In *Market Socialism: The Current Debate*, edited by P. K. Bardhan and J. E. Roemer. New York and Oxford: Oxford University Press.

Arnold, Scott N. 1994. *The Philosophy and Economics of Market Socialism: A Critical Study*. New York and Oxford: Oxford University Press.

Arrow, Kenneth J. 1974. Limited Knowledge and Economic Analysis. *American Economic Review* 64 (1): 1–10.

Bardhan, Pranab K., and John E. Roemer, eds. 1993. *Market Socialism: The Current Debate*. New York and Oxford: Oxford University Press.

Brus, W., and K. Laski. 1989. *From Marx to Market: Socialism in Search of an Economic System*. Oxford: Oxford University Press.

Dickinson, H. D. 1933. Price Formation in a Socialist Community. *Economic Journal* 43: 237–50.

Furubotn, Eirik, and Svetozar Pejovich. 1972. Property Rights and Economic Theory. *Journal of Economic Literature* 10:1137–62.

———. 1973. Property Rights, Economic Decentralization, and the Evolution of the Yugoslav Firm, 1965–1972. Journal of Law and Economics 16:275–302.

Hayek, Friedrich A. 1944. *The Road to Serfdom*. Chicago: University of Chicago Press.

———. 1945. The Use of Knowledge in Society. *American Economic Review* 35:519–30.

———. [1935] 1948a. Socialist Calculation I: The Nature and History of the Problem. In *Individualism and Economic Order*. Chicago: University of Chicago Press.

———. [1935] 1948b. Socialist Calculation II: The State of the Debate. In *Individualism and Economic Order*. Chicago: University of Chicago Press.

———. 1976. *Law, Legislation and Liberty*. Vol. 2, *The Mirage of Social Justice*. Chicago: University of Chicago Press.

———. [1968] 1978a. Competition as a Discovery Procedure. In *New Studies in Philosophy, Politics, Economics and the History of Ideas*. London: Routledge and Kegan Paul.

———. [1975] 1978b. The Pretense of Knowledge. In *New Studies in Philosophy, Politics, Economics and the History of Ideas*. London: Routledge and Kegan Paul.

———. 1988. *The Fatal Conceit: The Errors of Socialism*. London: Routledge.

———. [1940] 1994. Socialist Calculation III: The Competitive "Solution." In *Classics in Austrian Economics: A Sampling in the History of a Tradition*. Vol. 3, *The Age of Mises and Hayek*, edited by I. M. Kirzner. London: William Pickering.

Keizer, Willem. 1994. Hayek's Critique of Socialism. In *Hayek, Co-ordination and Evolution: His Legacy in Philosophy, Politics, Economics and the History of Ideas*, edited by J. Birner and R. van Zijp. London: Routledge.

Kirzner, Israel M. 1973. *Competition and Entrepreneurship*. Chicago: University of Chicago Press.

———. 1988. The Economic Calculation Debate: Lessons for Austrians. *Review of Austrian Economics* 2:1–18.

———. 1996. Reflections on the Misesian Legacy in Economics. *Review of Austrian Economics* 9:140–55.

Kornai, János. 1986. The Soft Budget Constraint. *Kyklos* 39 (1): 3–30.

———. 1992. *The Socialist System: The Political Economy of Communism*. Oxford: Clarendon.

Lachmann, Ludwig M. [1969] 1977. Methodological Individualism and the Market Economy. In *Capital, Expectations, and the Market Process: Essays on the Theory of the Market Economy*, by Ludwig M. Lachmann. Kansas City, Kans.: Sheed Andrews and McNeel.

———. 1986. *The Market as an Economic Process*. Oxford: Basil Blackwell.

Lange, Oskar. [1965] 1994a. The Computer and the Market. Reprinted in *Economic Theory and Market Socialism: Selected Essays of Oskar Lange*, edited by T. Kowalik. Aldershot, U.K.: Edward Elgar.

———. [1936] 1994b. On the Economic Theory of Socialism, Part I and II. Reprinted in *Economic Theory and Market Socialism: Selected Essays of Oskar Lange*, edited by T. Kowalik. Aldershot, U.K.: Edward Elgar.

Lavoie, Don. 1985. *Rivalry and Central Planning: The Socialist Calculation Debate Reconsidered*. Cambridge: Cambridge University Press.

Lawrence, Robert Z. 1991. Efficient or Exclusionist? The Import Behavior of Japanese Corporate Groups. *Brookings Papers on Economic Activity*, 311–30.

Le Grand, Julian, and Saul Estrin, eds. 1989. *Market Socialism*. Oxford: Clarendon.

Miller, David. 1993. Equality and Market Socialism. In *Market Socialism: The Current Debate*, edited by P. K. Bardhan and J. E. Roemer. New York and Oxford: Oxford University Press.

———. 1994. *Market, State, and Community: Theoretical Foundations of Market Socialism*. Oxford: Clarendon.

Mises, Ludwig von. 1944. *Bureaucracy*. New Haven, Conn.: Yale University Press.

———. [1949] 1966. *Human Action: A Treatise on Economics*, 3d rev. ed. Chicago: Henry Regnery.

———. [1920] 1994. Economic Calculation in the Socialist Commonwealth. In *Classics in Austrian Economics: A Sampling in the History of a Tradition*. Vol. 3, *The Age of Mises and Hayek*, edited by I. M. Kirzner. London: William Pickering.

Nove, Alec. 1991. *The Economics of Feasible Socialism Revisited*. 2d ed. London: HarperCollins.

Pejovich, Svetozar. [1976] 1979. The Capitalist Corporation and the Socialist Firm: A Study of Comparative Efficiency. In *Economics & Social Institutions: Insights from the Conferences on Analysis & Ideology*, edited by K. Brunner. Boston: Nijhoff.

Pierson, Christopher. 1995. *Socialism after Communism: The New Market Socialism*. University Park: Pennsylvania State University Press.

Plant, Raymond. 1989. Socialism, Markets, and End States. In *Market Socialism*, edited by J. Le Grand and S. Estrin. Oxford: Clarendon.

Polanyi, Michael. 1967. *The Tacit Dimension*. New York: Doubleday.

Roemer, John E. 1994. *A Future for Socialism*. Cambridge, Mass.: Harvard University Press.

Roosevelt, Frank, and David Belkin, eds. 1995. *Why Market Socialism? Voices from "Dissent."* Armonk, N.Y., and London: M. E. Sharpe.

Streit, Manfred E. 1993. Cognition, Competition, and Catallaxy—In Memory of Friedrich August von Hayek. *Constitutional Political Economy* 4(2): 223–62.

———. 1995. Constitutional Ignorance, Spontaneous Order and Rule-Orientation: Hayekian Paradigms from a Policy Perspective. In *Hayek: Economist and Social Philosopher: A Critical Retrospect*, edited by S. F. Frowen. London: Macmillan.

Sweezy, Paul M. 1966. *Monopoly Capital*. New York and London: Monthly Review.

Taylor, Fred M. 1929. The Guidance of Production in a Socialist State. *American Economic Review* 19:1–8.

Vanek, Jaroslav. 1970. *The General Theory of Labor-Managed Economies*. Ithaca, N.Y.: Cornell University.

Vaughn, Karen E. 1994. *Austrian Economics in America: The Migration of a Tradition*. Cambridge: Cambridge University Press.

Ward, Benjamin. 1958. The Firm in Illyria: Market Syndicalism. *American Economic Review* 48:566–89.

Yunker, James A. 1992. *Socialism Revised and Modernized: The Case for Pragmatic Market Socialism*. Westport and London: Greenwood, Praeger.

———. 1993. *Capitalism versus Pragmatic Market Socialism: A General Equilibrium Evaluation*. Boston and Dordrecht: Kluwer.

Acknowledgments: Reprinted from *The Independent Review*, 2, no. 2 (Fall 1997), pp. 201–224. Copyright © 1997. I wish to thank Annette Jung, Daniel Kiwit, Wolfgang Kasper, Antje Mangels, Uwe Mummert, Werner Mussler, Axel D. Schulz, Stefan Voigt, Oliver Volckart, and Tobias Winkler for criticisms and suggestions. I am also grateful for the insightful comments of three anonymous referees. I owe particular thanks to Manfred E. Streit, who went through two versions of this essay.

About the Authors

ROBERT HIGGS is Senior Fellow in Political Economy at The Independent Institute and Editor of the Institute's quarterly journal, *The Independent Review: A Journal of Political Economy*. He received his Ph.D. in economics from the Johns Hopkins University, and he has taught at the University of Washington, Lafayette College, and Seattle University. He has been a visiting scholar at Oxford University and Stanford University.

Dr. Higgs is the author of *Depression, War, and Cold War* (2006), *Resurgence of the Warfare State: The Crisis Since 9/11* (2005), *Against Leviathan: Government Power and a Free Society* (2004), *Crisis and Leviathan: Critical Episodes in the Growth of American Government* (1987), *Competition and Coercion: Blacks in the American Economy, 1865–1914* (1977), and *The Transformation of the American Economy, 1865–1914: An Essay in Interpretation* (1971). He is also the co-editor of *Re-Thinking Green: Alternatives to Environmental Bureaucracy* (2005) and editor of *Hazardous to Our Health? FDA Regulation of Health Care Products* (1995), *Arms, Politics, and the Economy: Historical and Contemporary Perspectives* (1990), and *Emergence of the Modern Political Economy* (1985). A contributor to numerous scholarly volumes, he is the author of more than 100 articles and reviews in academic journals of economics, demography, history, and public policy.

His popular articles have appeared in the *Wall Street Journal, Los Angeles Times, Providence Journal, Chicago Tribune, San Francisco Examiner, San Francisco Chronicle, Society, Reason, AlterNet*, and many other newspapers, magazines, and Web sites, and he has appeared on NPR, NBC, ABC, C-SPAN, CBN, CNBC, PBS, America's Talking Television, Radio America Network, Radio Free Europe, Talk Radio Network, Voice of America, Newstalk TV, the Organization of American Historians' public radio program, and scores of local radio and television stations. He has also been interviewed for articles in the *New York Times, Washington Post, Al-Ahram Weekly, Terra Libera, Investor's*

Business Daily, UPI, *Congressional Quarterly*, *Orlando Sentinel*, *Seattle Times*, *Chicago Tribune*, *National Journal*, *Reason*, *Washington Times*, WorldNetDaily, *Folha de São Paulo*, Newsmax, *Financial Times*, Creators Syndicate, *Insight*, *Christian Science Monitor*, and many other news media.

Dr. Higgs has spoken at more than 100 colleges and universities and to such professional organizations as the Economic History Association, Western Economic Association, Population Association of America, Southern Economic Association, International Economic History Congress, Public Choice Society, International Studies Association, Cliometric Society, Allied Social Sciences Association, American Political Science Association, American Historical Association, and many others.

CARL P. CLOSE is Academic Affairs Director of the Independent Institute and Assistant Editor of *The Independent Review*. He is co-editor (with Robert Higgs) of *Re-Thinking Green: Alternatives to Environmental Bureaucracy* (2005). His research interests include environmental policy, the history of economic and political thought, and the political economy of propaganda. He received his masters degree in economics from the University of California, Santa Barbara.

About the Contributors

JAMES M. BUCHANAN is the advisory-general director of the Center for Study of Public Choice, George Mason University, and 1986 recipient of the Alfred Nobel Memorial Prize in Economic Sciences. Among the many influential books he has written are *The Calculus of Consent: Logical Foundations of Constitutional Democracy* (coauthored by Gordon Tullock), *Cost and Choice*, *The Limits of Liberty*, and *Liberty, Market, and State*.

LAURIE CALHOUN is the managing editor of *Du Bois Review: Social Science Research on Race*. She is the author of *Philosophy Unmasked: A Skeptic's Critique* and the forthcoming Independent Institute book, *War and Delusion*.

JAMES A. DORN is vice president for academic affairs at the Cato Institute and a professor of economics at Towson University in Maryland. He is the author of numerous scholarly articles on reform in China and editor of *The Cato Journal*.

STEVEN HORWITZ is an associate professor in the Department of Economics at St. Lawrence University, Canton, New York. He is the author of *Microfoundations and Macroeconomics: An Austrian Perspective* and *Monetary Evolution, Free Banking, and Economic Order*.

JEFFREY ROGERS HUMMEL is an assistant professor in the Department of Economics at San Jose State University. He is the author of *Emancipating Slaves, Enslaving Free Men: A History of the American Civil War*.

ANTHONY DE JASAY is an independent scholar and author living in Paluel, France. He is author of *The State*, *Against Politics: On Government, Anarchy, and Order*, and *Justice and Its Surroundings*.

DANIEL B. KLEIN is a professor of economics in the Department of Economics at George Mason University. He is the coauthor of *Curb Rights: A Foundation for*

Free Enterprise in Urban Transit and editor of *Reputation: Studies in the Voluntary Elicitation of Good Conduct.*

DWIGHT R. LEE is the Ramsey Professor of Economics at the University of Georgia. A prolific author, his scholarly articles have appeared in such publications as *Public Choice*, the *Journal of Political Economy*, and the *American Economic Review.*

JAMES R. OTTESON is a professor of philosophy at the University of Alabama. His book *Adam Smith's Marketplace of Life* was named an Outstanding Academic Title of 2003 by the American Library Association.

LINDA C. RAEDER is an assistant professor of humanities at Palm Beach Atlantic University. She is the author of *John Stuart Mill and the Religion of Humanity.*

SURI RATNAPALA is a professor of law at the T. C. Beirne School of Law, University of Queensland; director of the Center for Legal and Economic Study of Institutions; and a fellow of the International Center for Economic Research, Turin, Italy. He is the author of *Jurisprudence of Liberty* and coauthor of *Evolutionary Jurisprudence.*

CHARLES K. ROWLEY is a professor of economics at George Mason University and General Director of the Locke Institute. He has edited more than two dozen books and more than 125 articles on such subjects as classical liberalism and public choice.

HANS SHERRER is an author living in Auburn, Washington.

THOMAS S. SZASZ is Professor of Psychiatry Emeritus at the State University of New York Upstate Medical University in Syracuse, New York. He is the author of *The Myth of Mental Illness, The Manufacture of Madness, Our Right to Drugs: The Case for a Free Market*, and numerous other books.

QUENTIN P. TAYLOR is an assistant professor of history and political science at Rogers State University, Bartlesville, Oklahoma. He has written books on Nietzsche, Machiavelli, and the Federalist Papers.

MICHAEL WOHLGEMUTH is managing research associate at the Walter Eucken Institut in Freiburg, Germany. He has authored numerous articles on political economy for German-language publications.

Index

A

absolute liberty, 73
absolutism, 310
abstract conditions, concrete patterns versus, 126–28, 133–35
abstract legal framework, 129–31, 132, 134, 137n5
abstract value, common good as, 127–28
accountability. *See* individual responsibility
Act for Establishing Religious Freedom in the State of Virginia (Jefferson), 229n10
actions
    collective, 11
    differential advantage of group action, 232
    of finding and keeping, 57–58
    market prices as guide to, 126–27
    as product of beliefs, 218
    See also human action
addiction as treatable disease, 276–77, 292
admissible actions, 53–54
Agricultural Revolution, 183–85, 186–87, 195n2
AIDS in Africa as problem for national security in U.S., 266
Alchian, Armen, 167
Alkidamas, xi
altruism, 25–26
American Bar Association Journal, 269
American liberalism, 41
American Psychological Association, 268
amoral flexibility of bureaucrats, 210–11
Amoral Politics (Scharfstein), 206
anarchocapitalist society, 192–96, 195n1, 196n19
anarchy
    equilibrium condition of ordered, 46, 52–53
    and liberal agenda, 46
    orderliness of international, 241–42
    political philosophy of order versus, 308–12
    potential to spread, 194
    public good from, 194
    -versus-order spectrum, 317–21
Angell, Marcia, 293
antiliberalism of new communitarians, 121–22
antirationalism, 337–38
apartheid and rule of law, 145, 146
Arendt, Hannah, 200–201
Areopagitica (Milton), 219
aristocracy, bureaucrats as, 208
Aristotle, 59, 61, 97, 102, 121, 122
Arrow, Kenneth, 390n1
assembly-line methods of bureaucracies, 204
atomistic, defining, 33
Auden, W. H., 286
Australian aborigines, 156–58
Australian Constitution, 152
authority, ethics of, 247–49, 259n2
authority, obedience to, 201–3, 318
autonomy, rejection of in bureaucratic systems, 203–4
Ayau, Manuel, 18–19

B

banking system in market socialism, 380–82, 383–89, 391n13–16
Bastiat, Frederic, 167, 168
Bauer, Peter, 116, 155, 162, 168
Bauman, Zygmunt, 201, 202, 212n2
Beauchamp, Dan E., 263, 269, 291–92
Becker, Gary, 173
Before Resorting to Politics (Jasay), 61–62

INDEPENDENT STUDIES IN POLITICAL ECONOMY

For further information and a catalog of publications, please contact:

THE INDEPENDENT INSTITUTE
100 Swan Way, Oakland, California 94621-1428, U.S.A.
510-632-1366 · Fax 510-568-6040 · info@independent.org · www.independent.org